Thomas Benedikter

100 Years of Modern Territorial Autonomy
Autonomy around the World

Autonomie und Politik
Autonomy and Politics

Band/Volume 2

LIT

Thomas Benedikter

100 Years of Modern Territorial Autonomy
Autonomy around the World

Background, Assessments, Experiences

This work is dedicated to my father, Alfons Benedikter (1918–2010), who most of his life gave his all for autonomy and self-determination in South Tyrol.

This publication has been edited in collaboration with POLITiS (South Tyrol's Center for Political Studies and Civic Education).

This publication has received a funding by the Südtiroler Sparkasse Foundation.

This book is printed on acid-free paper.

Bibliographic information published by the Deutsche Nationalbibliothek
The Deutsche Nationalbibliothek lists this publication in the Deutsche Nationalbibliografie; detailed bibliographic data are available in the Internet at http://dnb.dnb.de.

ISBN 978-3-643-91401-9 (pb)
ISBN 978-3-643-96401-4 (PDF)

A catalogue record for this book is available from the British Library.

© LIT VERLAG GmbH & Co. KG Wien,
Zweigniederlassung Zürich 2021
Flössergasse 10
CH-8001 Zürich
Tel. +41 (0) 76-632 84 35
E-Mail: zuerich@lit-verlag.ch   https://www.lit-verlag.ch
Distribution:
In the UK: Global Book Marketing, e-mail: mo@centralbooks.com
In North America: Independent Publishers Group, e-mail: orders@ipgbook.com
In Germany: LIT Verlag Fresnostr. 2, D-48159 Münster
Tel. +49 (0) 2 51-620 32 22, Fax +49 (0) 2 51-922 60 99, e-mail: vertrieb@lit-verlag.de

Content

	Foreword *Oskar Peterlini, Senator (ret.), Free University of Bozen-Bolzano*	8
	Introduction 2021: 100 years of modern territorial autonomy	11
1	**What actually is territorial autonomy? A clarification**	15
	The regions of the world with territorial autonomy	23
2	**Fake autonomy: when the label is deceptive**	27
3	**From Åland to Bangsamoro: a brief history of autonomy**	31
	Timeline of territorial autonomy 1920-2020	38
	From Memelland to the Crimea: Failed Autonomies	41
4	**The first modern territorial autonomy: the Åland Islands**	45
5	**Rescuing a language through autonomy: the Basque Country**	53
	A conversation with Prof. Eduardo Ruiz Vieytez, University of Deusto, Bilbao	61
6	**Italy's rocky road to more regional autonomy**	71
	An interview with Prof. Robert Louvin, former President of the Autonomous Region of Aosta Valley	80
7	**A much-vaunted but incomplete autonomy: South Tyrol**	87
	A conversation with Luis Durnwalder, former governor of South Tyrol	97
	Autonomy or reservation? Ethnic autonomy versus territorial autonomy	104
8	**Conflict resolution through autonomy: Northern Ireland**	109
9	**On the road to autonomy: Corsica**	119
	An interview with Jean-Guy Talamoni, President of the Regional Assembly of Corsica	129
10	**Hungarians struggle for autonomy: the Szeklerland in Romania**	137
	A conversation with Balász Izsák, President of the Szekler National Council	146
11	**The German-speaking Community of East Belgium: „The happiest Belgians"**	157
	An interview with Karl-Heinz Lambertz, President of the Parliament of East Belgium	165
	Autonomy in Oceania: Bougainville and New Caledonia	173
12	**A state offers autonomy: Morocco and Western Sahara**	179

13	Autonomy in name only: Xinjiang/East Turkestan and the autonomous entities of China	187
	A conversation with Dolkun Isa, President of the World Uyghur Congress	195
	Hong Kong: "One Country - Two Systems"?	202
14	Doing justice to ethnic diversity: autonomy in India	207
	A conversation with P.K. Hazoari, former General Secretary of the Bodoland Autonomous Region (Assam, India)	218
15	Autonomy in crisis: the Caribbean Coast of Nicaragua and Indian Kashmir	221
16	Between autonomy and independence: the Kurds in Iraq and Syria	231
	An interview with Khaled Davrisch, Representation of the Federation of Northern and Eastern Syria	242
17	The dream of autonomy: Turkish Kurdistan	247
	Autonomy for the Yezidi of Sinjar?	254
	Referendums on the status of sub-state territories 1994 - 2020	256
18	When autonomy is no longer enough: Catalonia and Scotland	259
19	Open domestic conflicts: territorial autonomy as a viable option	273
	A conversation with Loránt Vincze, President of the Federal Union of European Nationalities FUEN and Member of the European Parliament	285
	A binding right to autonomy?	292
20	An interim balance sheet and outlook on the future of territorial autonomy	294
	References and further readings	302
	The author	312

Tables
1. Forms of power sharing in modern states
2. Forms of vertical division of power
3. Regions of the world with territorial autonomy
4. The scope of autonomous powers - Three examples
5. Timeline territorial autonomy 1920-2020
6. The Autonomous Districts of India
7. Referendums on the political status of sub-state entities 1994-2020

Abbreviations
ADC Autonomous District Council
ABSU All Bodo Students Union
BIA Bureau of Indian Affairs
BTC Bodoland Territorial Council
CCP Chinese Communist Party
CiU Convergencia i Unió (Catalonia)
DG Deutschsprachige Gemeinschaft (German speaking Community)
DUP Democratic Unionist Party
DTK Democratic Congress of the Society (Kurdish people of Turkey)
ETA Euskadi ta Askatasuna (Basque Country)
EVTZ European Grouping of Territorial Cooperation
EZLN Ejercito Zapatista de Liberación Nacional
FSLN Frente Sandinista de Liberación Nacional
HDP Halklarin Demokratik Partisi (Democatic Party of the Peoples)
IRA Irish Republican Army
LRNA Law on Regional National Autonomy (China)
MPP Hungarian Citizens' Party
OSCE Organization for Security and Cooperation in Europe
PKK Partiya Karkeren Kurdistane (Kurdish Workers' Party)
PNV Partido Nacionalista Vasco
RMDSZ Democratic Alliance of the Hungarians of Romania
SDF Syrian Democratic Forces
SDLP Social Democratic and Labour Party
SNP Scottish National Party
SVP Südtiroler Volkspartei
UPC Unione di u Populu Corsu
UUP Ulster Unionist Party
SNC Szekler National Council
XUAR Xinjiang Uyghur Autonomous Region

Photo credits
Cover photo: Demonstration for the autonomy of Szeklerland (Romania) by the Hungarian Szeklers in Marosvásárhely 2018: Toró Attila. Page 11 - motto „Åland 100" on ferry: Åland Provincial Government/Åland 100. Page 47 - The Parliament of Åland in Mariehamn: norden.org. Author: Magne Kneseth. Page 97 - Luis Durnwalder: Flickr/WIKIPEDIA. Attribution 2.0 Generic (CC BY 2.0). Page 106 - Navajo Parliament: Author: William Nakai https://www.flickr.com/photos/nihihiro/ (shihiro & nihihiro) - CC BY-SA 3.0. Page 143 - Demonstration Day of Szekler Freedom, page 146 - Balász Izsák at demonstration and page 155 - Human chain for autonomy in Szeklerland 2013: Toró Attila. Page 195 - Dolkun Isa: World Uyghur Congress. Page 57 - Basque Government: Mikel Arrazola, CC attribution 3.0, source: argazki.irekia.euskadi.net. Page 269 - Parliament of Catalonia (2006), author: 1997, GNU Free Documentation Licence. Page 113 - Stormont: flickr.com/photos, author: Robert Paul Young, Licence CC-BY-SA 3.0 Generic.
All other photos: Thomas Benedikter

Foreword

Imagine an ideal map of the world in which the borders between all states run exactly along the dividing lines of the settlement areas of peoples and tribes, and all peoples are free to determine their own destiny. Even small peoples have their own land. There is peace. There are no oppressed minorities, no attempts to break away or to be annexed to another country, at least not on ethnic grounds. The international community recognizes these „natural borders", international law protects them, and aggressors are repelled to their borders.

Such ideal borders were wisely envisioned by US President Woodrow Wilson in the 14 points of his speech to Congress on 8 January 1918, after the catastrophe of the First World War. The occupied territories should be cleared everywhere. Wilson attached great importance to the right of self-determination. The peoples of Austria-Hungary should also be „granted the freest opportunity for autonomous development" (item 10). Wilson's vision on the ideal borders in relation to Italy is particularly clear: „A readjustment of the frontiers of Italy should be effected along clearly recognisable lines of nationality" (point 9).

But things turned out differently. The world order after the First World War established borders whose wounds have not healed to this day. The most powerful man in the world failed because of his noble principles. The empire of Austria-Hungary was dismembered, the majority German population of South Tyrol came to Italy, the border runs along the Brenner Pass, without regard to „clearly recognisable lines of nationality". The war-losers had to cede not only South Tyrol, but also many other German-speaking areas, such as the Sudetenland, the Memelland and Gdansk. In the Treaty of Trianon, Hungary, too, had to cede territories that were mainly inhabited by Magyars. Even today, millions of Hungarians live as minorities in the neighbouring states. And so it has happened to hundreds of peoples all over the world in the course of human history.

The Second World War opened further wounds. In the Eastern Bloc, entire peoples were formally imprisoned against their will. A glance at the map of Africa disillusioned our view beyond Europe. The borders seem to have been drawn in an optically ideal way, in a straight line without disturbing curves. In fact they were drawn on the map with a ruler, the fate of the people in these areas was of little interest to the victorious and former colonial powers. Oppression, violence and wars were the result until today. Federalism and territorial autonomy have been applied only minimally in Africa.

The world is no U-Topia. Power and economic interests of the strongest determine the borders. As long as states as a form of organisation are not overcome, they will stand like artificially constructed, iron barriers, separating and hindering people in their activities. They can hardly be moved, if not by war. So the challenging question arises whether a solution for these minorities cannot be found within the states.

The author of this book, Thomas Benedikter, is a member of such a minority, the German-speaking South Tyroleans in Italy. One hundred years ago, the southernmost part of Tyrol was separated from the motherland Austria and turned into Italy. The region has experienced hard fates, fascism, oppression, and a ban on its German language and culture. Even after the World War II there was no return to Austria. Instead, autonomy was intended to protect the minorities. After initially unsatisfactory solutions, protests that led to the UN, bomb attacks and casualties on both sides, a satisfactory compromise solution was finally found at the beginning of the 1970s: Extended autonomy in legislation and administration gave the people of South Tyrol effective opportunities to shape their own community and to create regulations for peaceful coexistence and the participation of all three language groups.

Thomas Benedikter is a special child of this autonomy. His father Alfons, as deputy to Silvius Magnago, the long-standing governor of South Tyrol, and as chief negotiator for South Tyrol in Rome, took part in the struggle for autonomy at the forefront, bringing it to life with hundreds of implementing regulations.

Although much of the autonomy regulations is based on compromise, this new autonomy has not only brought peace and a certain degree of self-government to the province of South Tyrol, but has also enabled it to achieve economic and social advancement, so that today, together with Lombardy, it is one of the most advanced regions in Italy, with the highest per capita income, and one of the most prosperous areas in Europe. The once really poor South Tyrol, for which the Austrian government and many aid organisations in Germany arranged donations to cover the most urgent needs of the people and to preserve their language and culture, is today economically secure and culturally self-confident.

South Tyrol's autonomy is today presented as a model for the solution of minority issues in the world, even though most South Tyroleans now see it as in need of reform and further development. Even the Italian government refers with pride to this peace solution: a model which, although it cannot be transferred one-to-one to other countries, is nevertheless a lesson of history and diplomacy on how to solve minority issues without changing borders.

But Thomas Benedikter did not limit himself to studying this autonomy. In his books he has analysed the fate of many minorities in the world and different models of autonomy. In this book he takes stock, weighs up successes against failures and tries to answer the central question of whether and in what form autonomy can actually be the solution to many problems in the world. He offers a broad panorama of the existing autonomous regions in Europe and beyond and of the struggle of other ethnic or regional communities for more internal self-determination. May this work and the autonomies presented contribute to finding solutions for those minorities and peoples in the world who still have to struggle for freedom and self-determination of their community.

Oskar Peterlini

Oskar Peterlini was the youngest member of parliament at the time, when he was elected to the South Tyrolean parliament in 1978 on behalf of the SVP (South Tyrol's People's Party). From 1978 to 1998 he was a member of the South Tyrolean Parliament and Regional Council Trentino-South Tyrol, and from 2001 to 2013 he served as a Senator of the Republic of Italy. Peterlini is also one of the founders of the regional supplementary insurance PENSPLAN. Since 2011 he has been working as a lecturer for political science and constitutional law at the Free University of Bozen/Bolzano.

Introduction

2021: 100 years of modern territorial autonomy

Why "100 years of territorial autonomy"?

In 1921, Sweden and Finland agreed to grant far-reaching self-government to the Swedish-speaking Åland Islands under Finnish sovereignty. On 24 June 1921, the League of Nations in Geneva approved this solution. On 10. October 1921, ten states signed a convention on the permanent demilitarisation and neutrality of Åland. On 9 June 1922, the Lagting, the islands' directly elected parliament, met for the first time. Therefore, Åland will celebrate 100 years of autonomy in 2021-22. The jubilee year will begin on 9 June 2021 and last until 9 June 2022, exactly 100 years after the first meeting of the Lagting.

In 2021 Åland celebrates 100 years of autonomy

Why "modern" territorial autonomy?

Territorial autonomy means being able to govern oneself democratically as a regional community to the greatest possible extent without being a sovereign state or having to break away from the state of affiliation. The prerequisite for this is a compromise between a democratic constitutional state and the region concerned. The purpose is usually to protect one or more ethnic minorities, a smaller people or a special regional community and to give the minorities equal rights. Territorial autonomy creates a legal-political framework for different degrees of internal self-determination. It is a special territorial form of political organisation which must not be understood as a mere subcategory of federalism, but as a distinctive form of political organisation with distinctive features, based on a specific formula for the relationship between the central state and the regional community. Before 1921, there was no such relationship within a democratic constitutional state. Regional autonomy is a political and constitutional structural element sui generis that deserves specific attention and analysis in theory and practice.

Why this book?

100 years after the legal introduction of the first modern territorial autonomy in a democratic constitutional state, one can take stock and venture an outlook. Has this form of self-government worked and what is the state of autonomy in Europe and worldwide? A sober look at the downsides of the history of territorial autonomy so far should not be missing either: Where has autonomy failed? Where is it in crisis and where is it sought by a regional community but denied by the state concerned? Finally, a look ahead: where could territorial autonomy solve acute conflicts between the state and minorities? Why are so many states reluctant to grant territorial autonomy? Where, on the other hand, is mere autonomy no longer sufficient to fulfil the claim to self-determination of a country or a people?

The world of territorial autonomy is diverse and in flux: regions that are already autonomous today are striving for more autonomy or even independence, others have been struggling for a minimum of autonomy for decades. The volume takes a broad look at existing autonomous regions in all parts of the world. It looks at crises and conflicts surrounding territorial autonomy, based on current analyses of eighteen case studies and supplemented by interviews with prominent political and academic figures from nine of the regions concerned. Some of the interviewees have been in leading positions in autonomous politics for decades, have committed for the autonomy of their home regions for many years, or have made autonomy one of their central research topics. Their answers provide important insights into what autonomy means in political practice.

The original purpose of autonomy: minority protection

The protection of linguistic and ethnic minorities is still in a state of disarray worldwide. Indigenous peoples are threatened not only in their culture and way of life, but often in their very existence. When they are not anymore allowed to own and control their land and natural resources, they will be deprived of their economic livelihood. Language minorities in industrialised countries often lack the legal framework to comprehensive protection and further development of their language. It has been proven that a mere individual ban on discrimination cannot ensure the necessary protection for minority languages. Only collective protection mechanisms on the ancestral settlement territory provide the framework for full equality with the dominant languages or with the state language. This framework is provided by, for example, a separate member state of a federal state, but also by territorial autonomy, in which several languages are recognised as equal official languages. Generally, autonomy can be considered as an efficient tool to ensure the protection of minorities, because the multiplication of states cannot be the solution to cope with cultural diversity. There are worldwide between 3,000 and 5,000 living languages. To grant comprehensive self-determination to the majority population of regions with such languages alone, at least 525 additional states would have to be created (Stephen Ryan,

1997, 2). Territorial autonomy without secession is a viable alternative, but only if it is structured in such a way that the culture, language, way of life, identity and economic livelihoods of the minority or smaller people concerned are permanently protected.

The side effect: more democracy and self-government

Territorial autonomy brings political power closer to the citizens. This creates an area for regional democracy in which citizen participation and political control from below functions far better than in unitary states without regions or federal states with legislative sovereignty. Autonomy provides more political self-rule for special regions and allows the population of a region to govern itself while remaining legally and politically integrated into the state. Without democracy one cannot speak of genuine „self-legislation" (autos=self, nomos=the law). However, where several ethnic-linguistic groups live together - and this is the case in the majority of today's autonomous regions - joint government is required: Consociational democracy is the buzzword that has been used in Switzerland not so much for ethnic reasons as for primordial democratic reasons since the founding of the modern federal state in 1848. This ensures the necessary democratic balance and prevents territorial autonomy from becoming an ethnically exclusive space, i.e. an ethnic reserve or reservation.

What does this book offer?

This book focuses on these problems. It is not just about comparing the diverse experiences with territorial autonomy, which would be empirically costly and theoretically too complex. Rather, it is about an interim balance after the first 100 years of modern territorial autonomy. Starting with the Åland archipelago in Finland, the first experiments with autonomy in Spain and Eastern Europe in the interwar period, and then proceeding with the introduction of autonomy in various countries of Western Europe after the Second World War. No golden bridges were built to territorial autonomy. In most cases years of violent or at least political conflict between the state and a minority, a smaller people, a regional community preceded it. Rarely was autonomy given from above.

In some cases it has not been able to resolve the basic conflict and has failed. This volume also deals with this: where is autonomy in crisis? Where has it failed? Where has it remained incomplete or does it not even deserve this title?

This work traces these questions. It starts from the indispensable clarification of what is meant by „modern" territorial autonomy. Not every territory that describes itself as autonomous is actually autonomous de facto and de jure. On the other hand, various genuine territorial autonomies avoid this designation. Not the label is decisive, but the content.

After a brief history of autonomy, I will go into examples of autonomy that show what autonomy can achieve: from the Åland Islands to South Tyrol, from the

Basque Country to the German-speaking Community of East Belgium to the Bodoland in north-east India. Autonomy has also been introduced in South Asia and South-East Asia, rarely in America and Africa. Indigenous peoples have achieved a certain degree of protection in America, primarily through reservations. The fine distinction between territorial autonomy and ethnic reservation must be kept in mind. Far clearer, however, is the difference between genuine autonomy and pseudo-autonomy or „autonomy-like arrangements".

In recent decades, autonomy systems have also fallen into crisis in various ways, or have not come into existence at all despite intense conflict. In some regions of Europe political movements are fighting for autonomy, in others autonomy is on the negotiating table as a model for conflict resolution. What open conflicts could be resolved with this kind of power-sharing between central state and region? Why territorial autonomy as a concept of internal vertical power sharing is still undervalued? The work explores such questions.

Many regions, minorities and ethnic communities today place their hopes in genuine territorial autonomy. Whether Hungarians from Szeklerland in Romania, Corsicans in France, Muslims in Pattani, Thailand, Tibetans in China, Mapuche in Chile and Kurds in Northern Syria-Rojava: autonomy as a form of democratic self-government without shifting borders and secession is their political dream and project. In other cases, autonomy has reached its limits: on the road to national emancipation, Catalans, Scots and Iraqi Kurds are no longer content with autonomy. The potential of territorial autonomy for resolving open ethnic conflicts is explored in the final outlook.

I would like to express my thanks to all the personalities from politics and academia with whom I have been able to hold talks in the respective autonomous regions. Not all meetings, interviews and discussions from my visits to 20 of the currently 60 functioning autonomous units worldwide are reproduced here. For important suggestions I would like to thank Alessandro Michelucci (Florence), Levente Salat (Cluj-Napoca/Kolozsvár), Andria Fazi (Corte, Corsica), Robert Louvin (Aosta) und Eduardo Ruiz Vieytez (Bilbao). Special thanks to Oskar Peterlini, former Senator a.D. in the Italian Parliament and assistant professor at the Free University of Bozen for the foreword. I would like to thank my wife Hanna Battisti for editing the graphic design and lay-out and the Foundation Südtiroler Sparkasse, which supported the publication financially. I wish you pleasant reading.

Thomas Benedikter, January 2021

1

What actually is territorial autonomy? A clarification

„Tibet Autonomous Region" is the name given to the Western core area of historic Tibet, which has been part of the People's Republic of China since 1950. Hundreds of other territories in China are officially called „autonomous". Are they really autonomous? „Avtonomnye Okrug" and „Avtonomnye Oblast" call themselves sub-regions of the Russian Federation: are they autonomous regions comparable to South Tyrol or the Basque Country? „Autonomous Republic of Karakalpakstan" is the name of a large steppe region in Uzbekistan which enjoys extensive powers of self-government. Can its citizens have a say in the politics of this region?

In the WIKIPEDIA list of autonomous regions worldwide, there are 140 sub-state entities that supposedly have autonomy. However, a considerable part of these territories are autonomous in name only, but not in substance. Other territorial autonomies, such as the German-speaking Community of East Belgium, do not have „autonomy" in their title, but from a constitutional point of view there is no doubt about this quality. They are missing in this list. Still other regions have indeed been granted autonomy on the paper of a state law, but the reality on the ground is quite different.

It is therefore necessary to define precisely what modern territorial autonomy is, and this requires well-founded criteria for determining it. For example, is Corsica, a "territorial collectivity" of France, autonomous, although it is not allowed to adopt its own laws? Is the island of Jeju in South Korea autonomous, whose parliament is not elected but appointed by the state government? Is the Navajo reservation in the USA autonomous and in what sense? Is the vast rainforest region of Western Papua autonomous, although Indonesia acts like a colonial power there?

Some states have a surprising variety of autonomous regions such as Russia, China and Spain. But while China's power structure does not allow for regional democracy, and Russia is a semi-free asymmetric federal state, whose constituent states usually bear this label for historical reasons, regional autonomy has been elevated to the basic principle of Spain's state structure. It is therefore necessary to clarify what territorial autonomy exactly means and, to this end, to draw demarcations from related systems of territorial separation of powers and to establish criteria for defining genuine territorial autonomy. This is a necessary step to clarify what this book is talking about.

Autonomy: a system of territorial power sharing *sui generis*

How can territorial autonomy be defined? Regional territorial autonomy is a form of internal power-sharing between the central state and one or more sub-state entities, in that legislative powers are delegated in a permanent form to an elected regional assembly, while maintaining regional democratic self-government and the territorial integrity of the state as a whole. Autonomy is thus a specific form of vertical division of political decision-making power, tailored to a sub-state entity, transferring legislative and administrative competencies from the central State to the autonomous territory.

This concept transfers a minimum set of legislative and administrative powers from central government to a sub-area of the national territory (region, province or country). This shifts some political decision-making power from the central state, i.e. the capital, to this part of the country and its political representation. Under the Constitution and a special statute, this region will have greater political self-governance and its citizens will have greater opportunities for democratic participation. Autonomy is a form of state organisation that generally ensures the preservation and development of ethnic, cultural and linguistic communities that are distinct from the majority population of the state. At the same time, regional autonomy is aimed to ensure ethnic-cultural diversity and consociational democratic decision-making even within the autonomous region when several ethnic groups or communities share a sub-state-territory.

Territorial autonomy is usually - with the exception of Spain - only granted to one or a few regions of a state with special historical, geographical and ethnic-cultural characteristics. In contrast to the symmetrical regional state, territorial autonomy is always a response to a special political need for regulation of a specific area. Regional autonomy primarily means the endowment with genuine legislative sovereignty, which in some cases is granted to all regions in a symmetrical form (Netherlands) or in a asymmetrical form (Spain). Special autonomies can be established in federal states, unitary states and in regional states. „To speak of a ‚political regional unit', seems to make sense only when legislative powers are assigned to a region, because a regional policy without legislative powers, which must be exercised by a regional legislative body requiring democratic legitimation in a constitutional state, does not seem possible," writes Anna Gamper (Gamper, 2004, 71).

It makes little sense to distinguish between regions with territorial autonomy and symmetrical regional states solely on the basis of the concrete quantitative form of legislative competences, says Anna Gamper. In the present analysis, territorial autonomy is not assumed in the case of the symmetrical regional state, which would rather be defined a symmetrical decentralisation. In this sense, territorial autonomy constitutes a form of vertical separation of powers for particular entities, separate from the granting of legislative sovereignty in symmetrical form to all the regions or provinces of a state. This could also be defined as „special autonomy" (Happacher/Obwexer 2013) or as an „autonomous region with special status". Gamper sums up the difference between federal systems and regional states as follows: „An autonomous region must be represented in the national parliament by representatives elected by the population or democratically legitimised bodies in the region. However, in contrast to the federal state, no institutional participation in the national state legislature is required, i.e. no participation of the regions in legislation at the central level" (Gamper, 2004, 72). In short: In federal systems, the single federated entities have an institutionalised political right to have a say at the central level of government and, together with the parliament, are responsible for competence setting, whereas in regional states they do not.

Territorial autonomy is thus legally distinct from the constituent state in a federal system. However, federal states can also establish territorial autonomy as a second level of government. For example, Belgium and India have autonomous territories at sub-state level, such as Bodoland in the Indian federated state of Assam and the German-speaking Community in the Belgian region of Wallonia. In the federal state of Canada, there are autonomous territories in addition to the provinces (states) which are not equal to the provinces: Nunavut, Yukon and the Northwest Territories. For these areas, territorial autonomy offers a way of doing justice to their ethno-cultural specificity without establishing an ethnic reserve or a separate constituent state.

In terms of state structure, today one often speaks of a multi-level system of governance, especially with regard to the EU with its four levels of legislation and administration. But in most of the world's states there is no multi-level system, at best only two: the central state and a sub-state level of counties or municipalities. With the exception of the 24 states around the world that have a federal constitution, the intermediate level of the regions with legislative sovereignty exists only in a few exceptional cases. Territorial autonomy has also only been applied relatively rarely, namely in about 70 cases in 25 countries, but some former autonomy systems no longer exist today. The dominant state model is still the unitary state, and in 2020 only 110 out of 195 UN-member states are fully democratic.

There is no autonomy in the strict sense of the word in „dependent territories" according to Article 73 of the United Nations Charter. Such territories neither enjoy full independence or sovereignty, nor are they constitutionally an integrated part of a sovereign state. There are various forms of such dependence. In most cases such territories are overseas and are a legacy of the colonial era. Special arrangements for self-government have been put in place for these areas, including legislative powers. Some dependent territories under Article 73 of the UN Charter have also been granted the right to self-determination, which has been exercised in the past and is still pending in other cases.

Furthermore, dependent territories can only govern themselves democratically to a very limited extent. The decision-making bodies of these territories are usually appointed by central governments and not elected by the population of the dependent territories (examples: the British Crown Territories of Gibraltar and

Forms of territorial power sharing in modern states

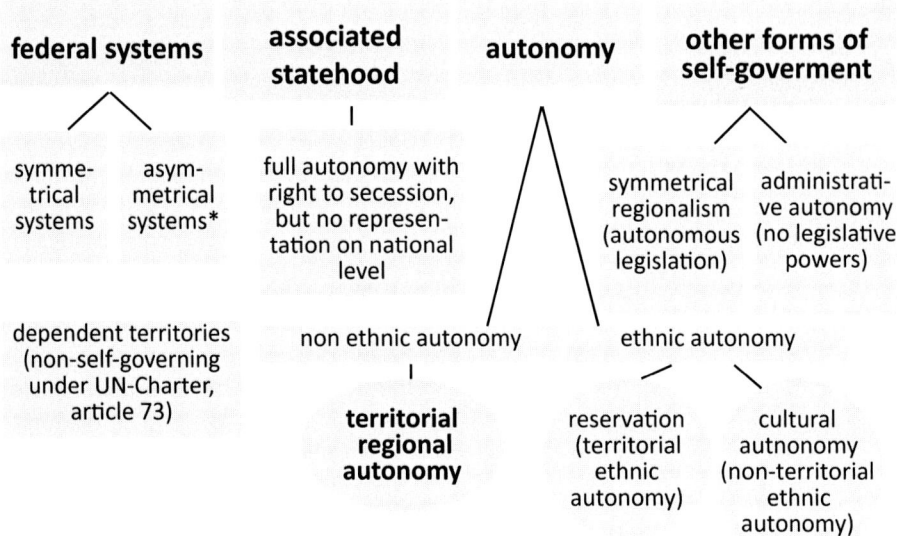

*One or more territories have a different legal position from the ordinary member entities of the federation.

the Falkland Islands, Tokelau in New Zealand, the Bouvet Islands of Norway, the US Virgin Islands). In addition to such „dependent territories" recognised under international law, there are currently various territories which are militarily occupied, which have split off, which are occupied by a liberation movement, and which are therefore de facto independent. All these territories cannot be regarded as modern territorial autonomies.

No territorial autonomies in the strict sense are reservations for indigenous peoples on their ancestral territory. Reserves originate from the idea of a „protected area" with limited sovereignty of the respective titular nation, to which its inhabitants must belong personally as „native peoples". However, reservations remain almost completely excluded from the decision-making processes and democratic institutions of the state as a whole, while the internal political rights of representation in the reservation only belong to the titular ethnic group. Territorial autonomies, on the other hand, form an integral part of the legal order of a state and internally grant the same political and civil rights to all legally resident people. Today's reservations, mostly in the USA, Canada and Brazil, aim to protect the rights of indigenous peoples on their ancestral territory in an exclusive manner consistent with the concept of „ethnic autonomy".

Forms of vertical power sharing (territorial organization of states)

Territorial organisation of states	Description of the arrangement	Examples
Microstate	A micro-state, which has transferred some state functions to neighbouring states, while retaining its sovereignty.	San Marino, Vatican, Liechtenstein
Freely associated state	An arrangement whereby a smaller community or „free state" joins a larger state. The associated state has substantial autonomy in all internal affairs, but has little influence over the larger state. As a rule, each contracting party can dissolve the association at any time.	Cook Islands, Niue, Puerto Rico
Centralist state Unitary state	Legislative sovereignty lies exclusively at the national level, the „national" parliament. The lower levels (regions, provinces) have administrative powers at best, but no legislative powers.	The majority of all souvereign states
Condominium	Via a regional community, two states (neighbouring states) jointly exercise sovereignty over a third (smaller) state, which, however, enjoys internal self-government.	Andorra, New Hebrides
Confederation	A loose but institutionalised cooperation of two or more states that do not enter into federal commitments.	CSI, EU, Serbia-Montenegro (until 2006)
Reservation	Form of self-government of a smaller people on their ancestral territory with a special form of reserve citizenship limited to the members of the recognised titular ethnic groups of the reserve without political equality of all legally resident citizens.	Navajo, Sioux, Hopi (USA), Miqmaq (Canada), Yanomami (Brazil)
Federation Federal state	Two or more constituent units form a common state with common institutions, based on constitutional law. Each constituent unit has the same powers and the central state has limited powers over the constituent units.	Belgium, Germany, Switzerland, Austria, USA, India, Russia, Brazil, Canada, South Africa, Ethiopia

Regional state	A state with two levels of legislative power, central and regional. The State Parliament is the exclusive legislature of the State and constitutional legislation. No „constituent state" of the regions.	Spain, Italy, Kenia
Dependent Territory	„Political dependence" of a region according to Article 73 of the UN Charter means its fiduciary administration by a State without being legally part of that State.	Gibraltar, Virgin Islands, Tokelau etc.
Territorial autonomy	An autonomous region is an integral part of a sovereign state and has legislative and executive powers that are legally valid only for its territory, whose inhabitants have equal political rights and are also represented at national level.	Åland, Eastern Belgium, Gagauzia, Aceh, Greenland, South Tyrol, Basque Country

Source: Thomas Benedikter (2012), The World's Modern Autonomy Systems, EURAC Bozen

No autonomy without the rule of law and democracy

The word autonomy is made up of autós (the subject or bearer of an autonomous entity) and nomós (the law), which refers to legislative sovereignty. A strictly formal legal approach considers autonomy as given, even if this legislation is exercised by an unelected decision-making body, or by a body established without democratic procedure. This is the case, for example, with autonomous units at all levels in China. The democratic legitimacy of the main body of an assembly - the regional parliament (assembly, council) - is secondary from this perspective. What counts is whether decisions are taken locally or not. If one takes such a concept of autonomy as a starting point, territorial autonomies also exist in semi-free states, authoritarian systems or even dictatorships.

In China, regional or local party officials determine the policies of autonomous territories, not freely elected representatives. This makes a huge difference not only for the democratic legitimacy of these decisions, but for political life as a whole. Since in countries like China, Pakistan, Azerbaijan, Tajikistan and Uzbekistan, only people without democratic legitimacy are ruling regions formally designated as autonomous, no real self-government is given. Yet, without basic democratic freedoms and political rights, it is of little relevance to the people whether party bosses in the state or their lackeys on the ground in the region decide. In principle, territorial autonomy must be democratically constituted, or it does not allow „internal self-determination" of the population of the area concerned. Genuine autonomy is about both: the legal competence of the autonomous territorial unit and the democratic process of political decision-making in its organs. Like all citizens in democratic states, true territorial autonomy requires all citizens of the region to have a say in the decision-making process, not rulers who haven't been freely elected. Therefore, there is no real autonomy without a working democracy.

Is the autonomous region not only de jure but also de facto part of the state? Do the decision-making bodies of the region concerned and of the State of nationality recognise each other? Only when a state exercises state sovereignty over a territory and guarantees the constitutional legal order can one speak of territorial autonomy. The „republics" proclaimed after an illegal secession are just as "self-ruled" as territories freed from resistance movements. The large territories of the FARC in Colombia were no more autonomous than the breakaway territory of Transnistria in Moldova or the Taliban-controlled areas of Afghanistan.

Thus state sovereignty must be recognised by the population of an autonomous region and its legitimate representatives; regional autonomy must exist de jure and de facto and be enshrined in the legal, possibly constitutional order of the state. An independent judicial system at regional and state level (constitutional court) must ensure that autonomy is respected. Disputes between the central government and the autonomous entities must be heard by independent judges in these bodies. There can be no modern territorial autonomy without a properly functioning rule of law.

Finally, it is important to stress an aspect relating to the rights of the inhabitants of the autonomous community as citizens. Although some of them are members of a recognised national minority, they have the same citizenship as the national majority of the State. Citizens of an autonomous region have to have the same rights and duties at State level as all other citizens in any other part of the State. They take part in general elections, have access to the labour market and the civil service throughout the national territory, are subject to compulsory military service and the same State tax laws. In their autonomous region they are subject to autonomous legislation under autonomous and State laws. All citizens who immigrate to the autonomous area from another part of the national territory have the same political rights and obligations as other citizens of this autonomous region. The principle of equal rights for citizens therefore applies equally to political representation at national and regional level. As a rule, the freely elected representatives of autonomous territories in the national parliament must also have full voting rights.

Two other citizens' rights can make this aspect even clearer: the right to vote for all citizens resident in the autonomous region and the right of free establishment in the region (with certain limits). America's Indian reservations cannot be considered modern territorial autonomies, since certain civil rights within the self-governing territory are linked to the personal affiliation with a recognised tribe or people. Freedom of access and settlement in the reservation's territory are limited. The equality of citizens in political rights in an autonomous region thus distinguishes territorial autonomy from other forms of self-government. This criterion serves to distinguish the concept of territorial autonomy from freely associated territories and reservations of indigenous peoples (on ethnic autonomy see „Ethnic autonomy versus territorial autonomy").

Let us note that territories or regions are to be classified as autonomous regions in the sense of state and constitutional law if they comply with the following four conditions:

1. **Democracy:** a pluralist system at national and regional level with full respect for civil liberties and fundamental political rights. These include, in particular, free and fair elections.

2. **The rule of law:** a constitutional and legal order recognised and applied by the central State and the region concerned. The legally established status of autonomy must be in force and applied. The rule of law also requires the separation of powers and an independent judiciary.

3. **Legislative sovereignty:** An autonomous region must have a minimum level of legislative powers. Merely administrative powers or a right to propose regional laws are not enough.

4. **Equality of civil rights** for all legal residents of the autonomous area. They enjoy all civil rights at national level and, conversely, all civil and political rights in the autonomous region.

Territorial autonomy, based on the rule of law and democracy, creates a legal framework for the internal self-government of a regional community, limited to that territory and to clearly defined policy areas, without changing national borders. Territorial autonomy usually means a special solution tailored to the individual case.

On the basis of these four criteria, it is possible to filter out from the multitude of so-called „autonomous territories" those areas which do not have genuine territorial autonomy. These criteria are crucial for both the theoretical clarity and the political utility of the concept of territorial autonomy. In the event of conflict, it is not to the advantage of national minorities, minority peoples or regions, nor of central states and other parties to the conflict, if basic concepts and proposed solutions remain ambiguous. If we look at existing autonomies, both parties should have a common view of what „territorial autonomy" in a modern, comprehensive sense means in the first place and what expectations can be formed at grassroots level in this respect.

On the basis of these criteria, it is possible to identify fairly clearly those autonomous regions which today enjoy genuine territorial autonomy. There are currently (early 2021) 60 sub-state entities (regions, provinces, districts) with territorial autonomy in 19 states.

Regions or sub-state units with modern territorial autonomy in 2020

State	Autonomous territory	capital	population	area km²
Italy	Sicily	Palermo	5.026.989	25.426
	Sardinia	Cagliari	1.630.474	24.089
	Friuli Venezia Giulia	Udine	1.211.357	7.856
	Trentino-South Tyrol	Trento	1.074.819	13.606
	Aosta Valley	Aosta	125.501	3.263
Spain	Andalusia	Sevilla	8.414.240	87.268
	Catalonia	Barcelona	7.675.217	32.091
	Madrid	Madrid	3.266.126	605
	Valencia	Valencia	5.003.769	23.255
	Galicia	Santiago de C.	2.699.499	29.574
	Castile and Leon	Valladolid	2.399.548	94.223
	Basque Country	Vitoria/Gasteiz	2.207.776	7.234
	Canary Islands	Las Palmas	2.153.389	7.492
	Castilla-La Mancha	Toledo	2.032.863	79.463
	Murcia	Murcia	1.493.898	11.314
	Aragon	Zaragoza	1.319.291	47.698
	Extremadura	Mérida	1.067.710	41.634
	Asturia	Oviedo	1.022.800	10.602
	Balearic Islands	Palma de M.	1.149.460	4.992
	Navarra	Pamplona	654.214	10.390
	Cantabria	Santander	581.078	5.321
	La Rioja	Logrono	316.798	5.045
United Kingdom	Scotland	Edinburgh	5.438.100	77.910
	Wales	Cardiff	3.138.631	20.735
	Northern Ireland	Belfast	1.881.641	13.843
	Isle of Man	Douglas	84.314	572
	Guernsey	Saint Peter Port	62.307	78
	Jersey	Saint Helier	102.700	119
Finland	Åland Islands	Mariehamn	30.074	1.580
Denmark	Greenland	Nuuk	56.081	2.166.000
	Faroer Islands	Torshavn	51.371	1.395
Belgium	German Community	Eupen	77.949	854
France	New Caledonia	Nouméa	280.460	18.576
	French Polynesia	Papeete	283.007	4.167
Moldavia	Gagauzia	Comrat	134.535	1.832
Serbia	Vojvodina	Novi Sad	1.913.889	21.506
Portugal	Azores	Ponta Delgada	245.766	2.351
	Madeira	Funchal	254.368	740

Canada	Nunavut	Iqaluit	35.944	2.093.190
	Yukon	Whitehorse	35.874	482.443
	Northwest-Territory	Yellowknife	41.768	1.346.106
Panama	Guna Yala	San Blas	36.000	2.370
	Emberá-Wounaan	Union Chocó	9.000	4.398
	Ngobe-Buglé	Chichica	121.000	6.673
Tanzania	Zanzibar	Zanzibar	1.155.065	2.654
Georgia	Adjara	Batumi	333.953	2.900
Iraq	Autonomous Region Kurdistan	Erbil	5.895.052	46.861
Philippines	Bangsamoro Autonomous Region	Marawi	3.781.387	12.711
Papua New Guinea	Bougainville	Arawa	249.358	8.800
Indonesia	Aceh	Banda Aceh	247.257	55.392
India (only Autonomous Districts under the 6th Schedule of the Constitution)	Bodoland	Kokrajhar	3.155.359	8.821
	Karbi Anglong	Diphu	965.280	10.434
	Dima Hasao	Haflong	213.529	4.853
	Garo Hills	Tura	865.045	8.167
	Jaintia Hills	Jowai	295.692	3.819
	Khasi Hills	Shillong	1.060.923	7.995
	Chakma ADC	Kamalanagar	45.307	686
	Lai ADC	Lwangtlai	75.477	1.870
	Mara ADC	Siaha	55.000	1.445
	Tripura Tribal Areas	Khumulwng	679.720	7.132
Total	**60**			

Source: [www.istat.it]; [www.wikipedia.org]; [http://en.wikipedia.org]; latest data of population census or official estimated figures.

Notes: The autonomous regions are classified according to the criteria for determining modern territorial autonomy set out in this volume. Pseudo-autonomy or quasi-autonomy is not taken into account here. „Autonomy" is always referred to the constitutional legal status of a territory, not to the degree of freedom of political decisions of a political body whatsoever.

The Bangsamoro Autonomous Region was created in 2018 as an extension of the „Autonomous Region Muslim Mindanao".

The Autonomous Region of Bougainville (Papua New Guinea) will become independent in the coming years, following the decision for independence by referendum in December 2019.

The Crimean Autonomous Region of Ukraine seceded from Ukraine after an unconstitutional referendum in March 2014 and was incorporated into Russia, where it does not enjoy autonomy.

There are also two autonomous cities in Spain, Ceuta and Melilla, but without legislative powers. The „Territorial Collectivity of Corsica" also has no real legislative powers and is therefore not listed here.

The Caribbean Region North and the Caribbean Region South in Nicaragua can currently no longer be regarded as functioning territorial autonomies, because Nicaragua as a whole is no longer a democratic state with free and fair elections (Freedomhouse) and therefore democracy is not guaranteed at regional level.

Numerous other only nominally „autonomous" areas are not taken into account here because of the lack of democracy. The states of Moldova, Georgia, Serbia and Tanzania are classified by Freedomhouse as „partially free", which is why their territorial autonomies are included in this table.

The two once autonomous hill districts of Leh and Kargil in the state of Jammu&Kashmir in India were converted into a union territory in 2019, a status that cannot be classified as territorial autonomy. Officially, there are 25 autonomous units in India. Only those Autonomous Districts are listed here established according to the 6th Annex of the Constitution of India, which have sufficient legislative powers. Not listed are the ADCs with mere administrative autonomy set up by the federated states.

The Georgian region of Adjara is a borderline case in the classification of regions with territorial autonomy worldwide. The region has autonomous status under the Constitution of Georgia and the Basic Law of Adjara. There is a freely elected parliament (Supreme Council) and a government elected by it. But the President of the Government (head of the executive) is proposed by the President of Georgia (not by the Regional Parliament of Adjara). Moreover, the President of the Republic can dissolve the regional parliament of Adjara at any time. Despite these restrictions, Adjara can be counted as an autonomous region de facto and de jure.

Under the aspect of legal-political classification, the „Autonomous Units" of the Russian Federation can be classified both as units of an asymmetrical federal system and under the category „Territorial autonomy at sub-state level within federal states". Here the former approach has been chosen. For further details see: Thomas Benedikter, The World's Modern Autonomy Systems, EURAC Bozen 2012

The scope of autonomous powers - Three examples

The scope of the legislative powers of an autonomous entity is at the heart of every territorial autonomy. The existing autonomous regions show a different amount of competences, but is difficult to display a ranking of autonomy system according to the scope of autonomous powers. This table provides for a blunt comparison of 3 autonomous regions with regard to some special powers (except ordinary autonomous powers as listed in the autonomy statutes).

Area of legislative and/or executive power	South Tyrol	Catalonia	Åland
Regional police/internal security forces	No	Yes	Yes
Penal/penitentiary system	No	Yes	No
Tax collection/tax agencies	No	Yes	No
Consumer protection and bilingual product labels	No	Yes	No
External representation offices – Right to missions abroad	Partially	Yes	Yes
Primary competence for vocational training	No	Yes	Yes
Primary competence for the education system	No	Yes	Yes
Primary competence for toponymy/geographical names without restrictions	No	Yes	Yes
Regulation of professional chambers and liberal professions	No	Yes	No
Statutory power (right to elaborate and approve one's own autonomy statute, in accordance with national parliament)	No	Yes	Yes
Co-determination rights for the regulation of immigration	No	Yes	Yes
Competence for the regulation of banks and insurances	Partially	Yes	Yes
Regional citizenship reserving some civil rights for residents	No	Yes	Yes
The right to opt out from the application of certain categories of international treaties	No	Yes	Yes
Partial responsibility in civil law	No	Yes	No
Administration of the judiciary	No	Yes	No
Autonomous court of auditors	No	Yes	No
Council of safeguarding the autonomy	No	Yes	No
Autonomous Supreme Court	No	Yes	No
Exclusive power for autonomous audio-visual media stations	No	Yes	Yes
Exclusive competence for the municipal code	No	Yes	Yes
Shared competence for the social insurance system	No	Yes	Yes
Participation to the central state's negotiation with the EU	No	Yes	Yes
Right to be involved in the negotiation of international treaties whenever autonomous powers are concerned	No	Yes	Yes
Shared competences for saving banks	No	Yes	No
Primary competence for the health system	No	Yes	Yes
Postal service/postal system	No	No	Yes
Limitation for non-residents without regional citizenship in the acquisition of land and real estate	No	No	Yes

Source: Thomas Benedikter (2020), Mehr Autonomie wagen. Südtirols Autonomie heute und morgen. POLITiS, p. 26; respective autonomy statutes.

2

Fake autonomy: when the label is deceptive

WIKIPEDIA brings under the entry „Autonomous Regions" a colourful list of territories with autonomous status, including Mount Athos, Gorno-Badakhshan (Tajikistan), the Palestinian Autonomous Territories, the region of Puntland and the Republic of Somaliland, the Province of Friesland, the British Overseas Territories, Spain's autonomous cities of Ceuta and Melilla and some more. A wide variety of territories and entities have been grouped together here without clearly defined criteria for designation. Territorial units with exclusively administrative powers can be found alongside the autonomous communities of Spain and the regions with special status in Italy, but also „dependent territories" according to Art. 73 of the UN Charter. Genuine autonomous regions such as the Faroe Islands and Åland are found in the company of self-governing territories in authoritarian states such as Uzbekistan, Tajikistan and Azerbaijan.

This is due to the fact that „autonomy" is on the one hand positively loaded, but on the other hand neither political science nor state and constitutional law define sufficiently clearly what standards territorial autonomy has to meet. Many local authorities are declared „autonomous", although their leadership can at best initiate some decrees and legal acts, but never approve bills and laws. Other areas managed as „autonomous entities" do have legislative powers, but are part of a state that is either authoritarian or not democratic at all. As explained in Chapter 1, for the citizens of a region that is autonomous in name only, it makes little difference whether the omnipotent nomenklatura in the capital or the local party cadres take democratically not legitimised decisions over their heads. Even the top-down nomination of the head of the executive branch of an „autonomous" territorial entity makes the democratic character of such a territory appear questionable.

The question of „quasi-autonomy" is somewhat more complex in the case of ethnic reservations, which are also included in the WIKIPEDIA list of autonomous territories. As explained before, the decisive factor here is the equality of civil and political rights for the people legally resident in the autonomous area. If in the territory designated as autonomous political rights are only granted to members of the titular ethnic group - the only recognised ethnic communities or indigenous people - this does not meet the requirements of modern democratic territorial autonomy.

By way of example see these three cases of supposedly autonomous regions in Asia. Karakalpakstan calls itself an autonomous republic of Uzbekistan with its own constitution and parliament. This Central Asian steppe region is governed by a Council of Ministers, whose President is an ex-officio member of the Government of the Republic of Uzbekistan. Karakalpakstan is free to regulate its internal organisation and administrative structure and even has the right to secession on the basis of a referendum on self-determination. The current level of basic democratic rights and political freedoms in Uzbekistan and in the region does not allow for any talk of territorial autonomy, even remotely democratically legitimised and governed.

In February 2006, a special law introduced the „Self-government of Jeju-do Province" in South Korea. This gave the island an autonomous status that distinguishes it from the other provinces of the state. There is a 41-member provincial council, which is not elected by the population of the island, but appointed by the central government. Three members of this council act as political advisers to the provincial government. Some administrative powers are now being transferred in stages from the central government to Jeju province. Jeju will have its own local police force and tax system. However, the South Korean parliament has the right to unilaterally amend the special laws at any time. These regulations do not correspond to the concept of a modern territorial autonomy.

The mountainous region of Gorno-Badakhshan of the Republic of Tajikistan has its own regional assembly with some legislative sovereignty. The powers of this autonomous region are regulated by a constitutional law. The borders of Gorno-Badakhshan can only be changed with the consent of this regional parliament. The members of its regional assembly are elected in accordance with the regional electoral law. Gorno-Badakhshan also has its own judicial system. However, the executive branch of the region is appointed, not elected, by the President of Tajikistan. Overall, the region cannot be classified as a „modern autonomy system" because neither Tajikistan at large nor the supposedly autonomous region does not meet minimum standards of democratic rights and fundamental freedoms.

This finding applies, in differentiated gradation, to all arrangements of territorial separation of powers in the states of Central Asia (Uzbekistan, Azerbaijan, Tajikistan), Pakistan, Bangladesh and the People's Republic of China. Either there is no democratic system at all (China) or democratic procedures are not sufficiently free and fair (Azerbaijan), or the allegedly autonomous entity has no political representation independent of the central government (Pakistan). As stated above, the lack of genuine democratic institutions, fundamental rights and procedures prevents the population from substantial self-government. In other words, it makes no substantial difference to the people of an officially „autonomous region" whether certain governmental functions are exercised by central ministries or by members of a nationwide power elite appointed by the central state, who may come from the region concerned, but who are neither freely elected nor politically accountable to the regional population.

Other „autonomy-like arrangements", while meeting the criterion of a functioning rule of law at central and regional level, are not modern autonomy systems for other reasons. Such arrangements exist in the US (US Samoa and the Virgin Islands), New Zealand (Cook Islands, Tokelau and Niue), Australia (Norfolk Islands) and the United Kingdom (Gibraltar, Falkland Islands). From the point of view of constitutional and international law, most of these arrangements correspond to the status of a dependent territory under Article 73 of the UN Charter. In contrast to the territorial autonomies discussed here, these territories - like the British Crown Colonies - are not constitutionally part of the respective national territory. Although these territories enjoy special arrangements and are managed autonomously either as dependent territories or as associated entities, they usually have no legislative power and no political representatives freely elected on the spot, not nominated by the state of affiliation. In most cases, the inhabitants of these territories are deprived of the suffrage for the State's parliament. The central government, on the other hand, is the highest decision-making authority with regard to amending, enacting or blocking decisions taken by the legislative or executive authorities of the territory. This is typically the case in the dependent territories of the USA and United Kingdom.

There is no doubt that there is a high degree of self-government in the political practice and day-to-day business of these territorial units and that interference by the trustee states in internal affairs (e.g. by the USA, Great Britain, Australia and New Zealand) is limited to the necessary minimum as long as state security interests are safeguarded. However, a modern territorial autonomy is structured differently. The economic and financial dependence of such former colonial territories is also a decisive factor in determining autonomous political decision-making power.

In the legalistic approach to defining modern systems of autonomy adopted here, a fine but clearly discernible dividing line can be drawn, for example, between New Caledonia (an autonomous overseas "territorial Collectivity", fully integrated into the Republic of France) and Niue (an entity freely associated with New Zealand) and American Samoa (a dependent territory under Article 73 of the UN Charter) and again St. Pierre and Miquelon (a French overseas départment without legislative sovereignty). If we take as a benchmark the conflict resolution potential of forms of autonomous self-government as a form of state organisation relevant for the future, it is not the status of a „dependent territory according to Art. 73 UN Charter", a relic of the colonial era of the great colonial powers, that can be desirable for regional communities all over the world, but only a modern system of territorial autonomy that fully meets all the criteria for determining genuine territorial autonomy and allowing self-rule. For future negotiations between regional communities and central states on the introduction of territorial autonomy, it is required to share the clearest and most precise definition of autonomy possible, as otherwise misunderstandings and failure of the process would be inevitable.

In some cases, territorial autonomy has been agreed between the conflict parties as a transitional solution, as for instance in the so-called peace process between Palestine and Israel. In 2020 the state of Palestine was recognised by 138 UN member states. But 27 years after the start of the Oslo peace process it has become clear that independence is a bitter illusion for the Palestinians and not genuine territorial autonomy, but military occupation will continue indefinitely. In almost all territorial autonomies functioning today, however, the status of autonomy is not merely a temporary solution, but permanent. A few autonomy statutes, such as those of Greenland and the Faroe Islands, explicitly provide for the right and procedure to exercise the right of self-determination.

The territories included in the WIKIPEDIA list can thus be considered at best as „autonomy-like" arrangements of internal decentralisation. In particular, the lack of democratic decision-making procedures and in the composition of political representation bodies and the absence of legislative powers make the term „autonomous" appear unjustified in many cases. Of course, there are also clear differences between authoritarian states, for example between China and Pakistan, between Azerbaijan and Uzbekistan. The democratic standard of political systems varies, and the text of the constitution and political reality often diverge sharply. Nicaragua, for example, is currently governed in disregard of fundamental political rights. Under these conditions, even the autonomy of Nicaragua's Caribbean Coast cannot really function democratically and under the rule of law. These sub-regions could be described as „quasi-autonomous", as the political decisions are not taken by freely elected local political representatives. But the door to autonomy is open: if the state of affiliation observes democratic rules of the game, it delegates a minimum of legislative powers to the region, and if the regional parliament is freely and fairly elected, the leap to autonomy is done.

The label „autonomous" must therefore not be allowed to obscure the political reality behind it. If the people of an autonomous region are not free to choose their political representatives or even to assemble and express their opinions freely, the basis for regional democracy is missing. If the elected regional assembly meets only to approve decisions taken by the executive or local representatives of the regime, there is no democratically legitimate legislation. Even if the ministers and heads of government of an autonomous entity are selected and appointed from above, i.e. by the President of the Republic or the central government, one cannot speak of autonomous institutions of territorial autonomy. Only clear and theoretically well-founded criteria allow a clear definition of territorial autonomy. Anything else is label fraud.

3

From Åland to Bangsamoro: A brief history of territorial autonomy

Starting from a precise definition of territorial autonomy (cf. Chapter 1), which presupposes a democratic constitutional state, its history only begins in 1921 with the adoption of the Åland Islands Autonomy Act in the Parliament of the Republic of Finland. In the history before 1921, there are indeed autonomy-like arrangements of territorial self-government, but in most cases neither the rule of law nor democracy existed as basic requirements. In addition, the few democratic constitutional states that existed before World War I did not have territorial autonomy. In other words: even if different states had granted forms of autonomy to some single sub-areas, this did not take place under the constitutional conditions that would have allowed democratic self-government. In various states, part of the state power and thus of the political decision-making powers was indeed transferred to subordinate rulers. In the absence of democracy, however, one can at best speak of local exercise of power, not of democratically founded autonomy.

In Europe there have been precursors of political autonomy since the 16th century, especially in the sense of cultural autonomy. Religious minorities such as the Protestants in some Catholic-dominated regions, the Jews in numerous European cities, the Muslims in Christian Orthodox areas of Eastern and South-Eastern Europe enjoyed rights of self-government. In the Ottoman Empire, Christians and Jews had a kind of cultural autonomy as religious communities. This system of minority protection, known as „millet-system", remained in place until the end of the Ottoman Empire in 1918. It gave Jews and Christians their own family law system, their own courts and schools and the right to freely practise their religion and customs. These communities were often subject to their own tax system, which required them to pay higher taxes than Muslims.

In the first half of the 20th century, territorial autonomy was established in various European states to contain political conflicts resulting from shifting borders after the First World War. Some areas with German-speaking minorities in Central and Eastern Europe were given special status by the victorious powers of the World War to replace self-determination, e.g. the free city of Gdansk, the Memel-Klaipéda area in Lithuania (1924-1926) and the Saarland from 1920 to 1935. However, the solutions adopted were inadequate and their shortcomings provided the German Reich, which had been under Nazi rule since 1933, with the pretext of building up irredentist threats, preparing military aggression and finally carrying out annexations.

In Catalonia, the first autonomy statute was approved on 20 June 1931 (Estatut de Núria), and confirmed by 99 percent of the Catalan voters in a popular referendum. After being curtailed by the Spanish Parliament it was adopted on 9 September 1932 in the Cortes of Madrid. This autonomy had a short life as with the beginning of the Spanish Civil War in 1936 it could not any more operate and was definitely crushed by the Franco regime in 1939. The same happened to the Basque autonomy established with the Statute of Autonomy for Álava, Gipuzkoa and Biscay, which came to be enforced in October 1936 just in Biscay, with the Spanish Civil War already raging, and which was automatically abolished when the Spanish nationalist troops occupied the territory.

Although most of the territorial autonomies only came into existence after the World War II, previous conflicts and forms of self-government sometimes prepared the ground for this. Zanzibar, for example, had been part of the Sultanate of Oman in colonial times, then briefly independent, which was saved in the form of territorial autonomy in the state union with Tanganyika, which was founded in 1964. The princely state of Jammu and Kashmir enjoyed extensive autonomy within British India even under British colonial rule. The Atlantic coast of Nicaragua with the Miskito and Rama had never been under Spanish colonial rule. The Miskito people had already extracted self-government from the British Empire in the 18th century. This was confirmed in two follow-up agreements of 1860 and 1905 between the independent Nicaragua and the United Kingdom. The Muslim region of Bangsamoro in Mindanao succeeds the historical Sultanate of Maguindanao. The autonomy of Vojvodina dates back to the time of the Austro-Hungarian monarchy, but was structured differently than today. At that time Serbian nationalists in Vojvodina fought for more autonomy from the Kingdom of Hungary. In Tito Yugoslavia it was then the various minorities, mainly Hungarians, Germans and Croats, who claimed a special autonomous status for Vojvodina within Serbia.

In the second post-war period there were initially unfavourable conditions for a broad political discussion on autonomy. Although on 10 December 1948 the right of all peoples to self-determination was enshrined as a fundamental principle of international law in the Charter of the United Nations and was later entrenched in the UN Covenants on Civil and Political Rights in 1966, its application was limited to peoples dominated by the classical colonial powers. New forms of colonialism exercised by newly independent developing countries were overlooked. Indigenous peoples were not even recognised as such.

The applicability and concrete implementation of the right of self-determination of peoples and other communities was never precisely defined in international law. In most cases national minorities, ethnic groups and indigenous peoples were denied this right. But even territorial autonomy as a substitute for independent statehood was viewed with distrust by state elites in the post-war period. Since there were more than 100 national minorities in Europe due to the drawing of new or existing borders before 1945, territorial autonomy was not seen as a measure of pacification but rather as a step towards a possible revision of existing borders. Also outside Europe autonomy as a collective right was perceived rather as a threat to existing state borders, as in Africa, for example, where the hegemonic titular ethnic groups of the newly independent states behaved as new nation states. A collective right to autonomy was not seen as a substitute for state sovereignty, but rather as an invitation to question the nation states. Nationalist state elites still view this concept with deep mistrust today.

Nevertheless, in the post-war period some states in Western and Northern Europe found their way to a policy of recognising and protecting national minorities in national and constitutional law. A growing trend towards general decentralisation and regionalisation (Italy, United Kingdom, Spain, Belgium) encouraged this process of granting autonomy. In addition to the oldest territorial autonomy in Europe, the Åland Islands in Finland, special autonomies were established after 1948 in Italy, the Netherlands and Denmark. Belgium provided an example of how a previously centralised state can be gradually transformed into a federal state. This process provided for two of Belgium's three linguistic communities, the Flemish and the Walloons, a constituent federated state, and territorial autonomy within the Region of Wallonia to the German-speaking minority on the eastern border of Belgium. In Spain, the 1978 Constitution aimed to do justice to the historic smaller nations oppressed by the Franco regime and enshrined the right of all regional communities to autonomy (Article 2 of the Spanish Constitution). In recent decades, this previously centralised state has become a quasi-federal state, but this has not ended the push for statehood in Catalonia and the Basque Country.

However, autonomy regulations in Europe have also been heavy births on several occasions. In Great Britain, Northern Ireland had to wait until 1998 to find an internationally agreed solution based on the devolution of a broad range of powers to the parliament and government in Belfast. In France, the demands of national minorities such as the Corsicans, Bretons, Basques and Alsatians for territorial or at least cultural autonomy have been stubbornly rejected so far. France insists on the principle that there is only one nation and has only granted real territorial autonomy to the two overseas regions of New Caledonia and French Polynesia. Italy, founded as a regional state in 1948, established five regions with special status due to the presence of national minorities for ethnic and historical reasons (Valle d'Aosta, Trentino-South Tyrol, Sardinia and Friuli Venezia Giulia). In Sicily, a strong regional movement established extensive autonomy immediately after the end of the war. The other regions were also to be given limited legislative sovereignty, but this did not come into effect until 1970.

In Kosovo, an autonomous province of the constituent republic of Serbia, a radical renewal of the autonomy that had been in force since 1948 was adopted in 1974, putting the Albanian majority population almost on an equal footing with the Serbs. The multicultural region of Vojvodina also enjoyed extensive autonomy within Serbia and Yugoslavia's socialist and federal state structure. But in 1989, when Eastern Europe heralded the transition to democracy and freed itself from the USSR, Serbian leader Slobodan Milošević turned back the clock and began to abolish Serbia's two territorial autonomies. It was not autonomy as such that failed in Kosovo, but the nationalist policy of denying old minority rights. As a result, the entire ethnic balance of the Tito state collapsed, culminating in the wars in Croatia in 1992, Bosnia-Herzegovina in 1992-95 and Kosovo in 1998-99. The result is well known: apart from the secession of all member republics, Montenegro seceded from Serbia in 2006, Kosovo became independent in 2008, and the province of Vojvodina regained its autonomy in 2009. New state borders have not led to national homogeneity in the 28 states of Central and Eastern Europe, but to an increase in ethnic minorities. Against this background, cultural or territorial autonomy is once again gaining in importance for national and ethnic minorities in this region.

Autonomy has also failed in some cases in Eastern Europe and the Caucasus: in Georgia it was the abolition of the autonomy granted under the Soviet Union that triggered the uprising and separation of two regions, Abkhazia and South Ossetia. In Ukraine, the multi-ethnic Crimea had a distinct autonomy status since 1994. Nevertheless, a Russian Irredenta in 2014 carried out a questionable process of self-determination, which was enforced with the help of military support from Russia and led to annexation to Russia. In Moldova, on the other hand, Gagauzia's autonomy has lasted since 1994, whereas Transnistria was not satisfied with such a status. In many member states of the Council of Europe there are still strong reservations about autonomy in any form. There is widespread fear of a hypothetical spiral of „cultural autonomy, self-government, secession".

The only experience of territorial autonomy in Africa immediately after decolonisation was the arrangement between Ethiopia and Eritrea, based on a decision of the UN General Assembly, which lasted from 1952 to 1961. This autonomy failed miserably, leading to three decades of armed resistance by Eritreans. Even the first autonomy granted to Southern Sudan by the Government of Sudan in 1972 remained on paper, and its failure triggered two decades of bloodshed in 1983. Under the partnership between Tanganyika and Zanzibar, established in 1964, the archipelago of Zanzibar has become an autonomous state of Tanzania. In post-colonial Africa, however, centralised states became the rule, federal states and territorial autonomy the rare exception.

In Asia, autonomy was introduced for Kurdistan in Iraq in 1970, but was crushed by Saddam Hussein's regime in 1974. Only in 1991 after the 1st Gulf War were the Kurds of Iraq able to regain their autonomy. In India, after independence in 1947, the former principality of Jammu and Kashmir was granted a special status, which was definitely abolished in 2019. Territorial autonomy later took on a certain importance as a result of decentralisation within some member states of the Indian Union, particularly in the multi-ethnic Northeast (Assam, Meghalaya, Tripura). In Bangladesh, however, the autonomy promised to the indigenous peoples of the Chittagong mountain regions turned out to be a bitter illusion. In the Philippines and Indonesia, it was not until the 1990s that autonomy was seen as a viable concept for resolving conflicts with minority peoples in Mindanao, West Papua and Aceh. The Muslims in Mindanao had to fight a long battle against the Philippine state until their region was granted autonomy in 2014 under a peace treaty with the government, which was expanded in 2019 to become the Bangsamoro Autonomous Region of Muslim Mindanao. The granting of autonomy to the province of Aceh in the far west of Sumatra was preceded by decades of bloody conflict. In the far east, Indonesia occupied and colonised the western part of Papua New Guinea, after committing genocide in neighbouring East Timor in the 1970s.

In Oceania, an island belonging to France was granted special autonomous status for the first time in 1999, namely New Caledonia. In two referenda in 2018 and 2020, this „collectivity sui generis" voted for maintaining the status quo as an autonomous territory rather than independence. On the other hand, the island of Bougainville, which has been autonomous since 2002, voted by a large majority for secession of Papua New Guinea in 2019.

A different type of territorial autonomy emerged in the People's Republic of China, which recognised in its constitution the right to territorial autonomy at three levels (regions, prefectures, counties) and created over 300 such territories to protect the rights of national minorities or minority peoples. In an authoritarian one-party state, however, autonomy is rather a fake.

In America, the concept and practice of autonomy is closely linked to the history of the subjugation and forced assimilation of the Indian peoples. While the colonial powers in Latin America adopted the strategy of mixing European cultures and indigenous cultures in a process of mestizisation that was anything but peaceful, the indigenous peoples of North America were largely exterminated or forced into reservations in the most inhospitable areas. The creation of reservations for the indigenous peoples of America goes back to the bloody campaigns of subjugation and extermination by the colonial powers which continued into the 19th century in North and South America. In lengthy processes of demarcation, indigenous peoples were able to secure at least some last areas of retreat in which they were safe from oppression and discrimination. However, indigenous peoples' reservations differ from territorial autonomy in terms of their legal status and internal structure. Only in recent history Canada (Nunavut), Nicaragua (Caribbean region) and Panama (Guna Yala, first law on self-rule in 1938, new „Ley Organica" on autonomy in 1953) in some cases have granted territorial autonomy, as a means to preserve the fundamental rights of the indigenous peoples of these areas.

If we look at the emergence of territorial autonomies that are functioning today, we can identify at least four circumstances that have historically favoured the establishment of autonomy. First, autonomy came into being when the state itself underwent a period of upheaval, as Spain after the end of the Franco era in 1975-78, the Philippines after the fall of the Marcos regime in 1985, Moldova and Ukraine after the dissolution of the Soviet Union in 1991, Italy and Portugal in 1948 and 1974, when dictatorial and centralised systems gave way to democratic and regionalist structures. The same happened in Nicaragua after the end of the Somoza regime in 1979, but only after severe conflicts with the Sandinista central government.

A second circumstance is the granting of autonomy in the course of a decolonization process when either full independence was not desired by the population concerned or the community was not yet found to be ready for full statehood. This has happened in Greenland, Nunavut, the province of Guna Yala, the Netherlands Antilles, Bougainville and New Caledonia. The Faroe Islands had also declared their support for full sovereignty in 1946, but then resigned themselves to territorial autonomy within Denmark.

In the third group of existing autonomies, this was granted as part of a negotiation process between the central state and the region concerned, in conjunction with pressure from neighbouring „protecting power" states (South Tyrol, Åland Islands, Crimea, Northern Ireland), in order to protect ethnic minorities and ethnic groups in a targeted manner.

Fourthly and finally, autonomy was only granted after tough disputes, which often escalated into violent conflicts. The military conflict in Aceh in Indonesia lasted from 1976 to 2005, the wars in Southern Sudan from 1983 to 2002, and in Mindanao, Muslim Moros have been fighting for autonomy or independence since 1969. The armed struggle between the Sandinista government and the indigenous peoples of the Caribbean region lasted four years and was taken over by the anti-Sandinista counter-guerrilla. Violence prevailed in Bougainville from 1989 to 2001 and in New Caledonia from 1985 to 1998. In Europe, the Basque Country was struck by violence of this kind (900 victims between 1969 and 2003), Northern Ireland (almost 3,300 victims between 1972 and 2005) and in Corsica there was political violence from the mid-1970s until the self-dissolution of the FLNC in 2014. The struggle for self-determination and autonomy is still being fought violently in many cases in various states.

How has territorial autonomy affected these first 100 years of its application? There is no doubt that this concept of sharing political power between the central state and a sub-region has been successful in most cases: it has pacified some militarily fought conflicts (Northern Ireland, Corsica, Basque Country, Caribbean coast of Nicaragua, New Caledonia, Aceh, Bodoland, Bangsamoro, Bougainville) and at least shifted the conflict to the political level, if not resolved it. Territorial autonomy has led to the protection of ethnic-linguistic minorities and indigenous peoples in about 35 cases, making secession unnecessary. Political stability has been achieved in most autonomous regions and positive economic development has been initiated. Only in a few cases has territorial autonomy failed as a long-term solution, as in Eritrea, Kosovo, the Memel region of Lithuania, Abkhazia, South Ossetia, Southern Sudan, Crimea, the Indian administered part of Jammu and Kashmir.

In some cases, territorial autonomy was conceived as a transitional solution with the option of choosing between independence and autonomy. Bougainville, the Netherlands Antilles, Southern Sudan have opted for statehood or another status vis-à-vis the mother state (e.g. free association). In some other autonomous regions, such decisions are still pending, such as Catalonia, Scotland and Iraqi Kurdistan. Historically, territorial autonomy cannot be seen as a static, definitive solution: autonomy statutes and by-laws of autonomous regions have often been developed further, thus extending and completing the whole autonomy. In the territories occupied by Israel, so-called autonomy was supposed to prepare the foundation of a Palestinian state as a transitional phase. Apart from the fact that there can be no real territorial autonomy in a military occupation regime, Israel has not yet fulfilled its duty to grant self-determination to the Palestinians.

Thus, in a historical perspective, territorial autonomy has served above all to pacify conflicts between central states and national minorities and thus to protect minorities. But apart from this main reason, two general trends have additionally promoted this kind of vertical division of powers, one of a political nature and the other of a more social nature. The democratisation of many states in the world since the 1970s, and then again in the 1990s after the end of the Soviet bloc, has triggered growing popular pressure for greater political representation and effective participation in politics. The extension of democracy to lower levels was also seen as a counterbalance to the danger of a return of authoritarian tendencies in the central state. More democracy at lower levels of government - both regional and local - not only serves to protect ethnic minorities, but also creates more democracy for the population at large. In multi-ethnic regions, however, concordance-democratic rules and rights of representation for all must be ensured in order not to provoke new conflicts within autonomous regions.

A broader social development towards decentralisation has become noticeable in many regions of the world in recent decades. In addition to the growing awareness of ethnic and cultural identity, which in turn gives impetus to demands for minority protection and autonomy, there is a general need for regional cultural roots in compensation for the dissolution of boundaries in many areas of life in a globalised world. The attraction of centralised and large-scale organisations such as national parties and trade unions is diminishing, while local and regional reference groups are increasing in popularity. People feel less and less like parts of a large, centralised organisation, but identify themselves with local communities. This has led to a tendency that has been described as „re-territorialisation" of politics, although the supranational level is also becoming increasingly important. Territorial autonomy in this sense can be seen as a special form of the general decentralisation of state power.

In retrospect and in light of the territorial autonomies which have been functioning and newly established for some time now, it can be assessed whether this concept has actually led to secession or, on the contrary, has met legitimate demands and interests of national minorities without changing state borders. Many conflicts in Europe and on other continents could have been prevented with a clear entrenchment of minority rights and autonomy concepts. In this sense, the international community would be called upon to codify minority rights even better and to regulate territorial autonomy as an „internal form of self-determination" under international law. Today, autonomy is demanded in various states, but hardly any new territorial autonomies are established.

Timeline of territorial autonomy 1920-2020

Year	Event
6.5.1920	First Finnish autonomy law for the Åland Islands.
24.6.1921	The League of Nations decides on the relevance of the Åland issue under international law leaving Åland under Finnish sovereignty.
27.6.1921	Finland and Sweden sign the „Åland Agreement".
9.6.1922	First session of the directly elected Parliament of Åland.
9.9.1932	1st Statute of Autonomy of Catalonia adopted by the *Cortes* (Estatut de Núria)
October 1936	Statute of Autonomy for Álava, Gipuzkoa and Biscay. Election of the first Autonomous Council and Government of the Basque Country.
1938	Official foundation of the autonomous Comarca de San Blas, later „Comarca Guna Yala" in Panama (re-established in 1953).
1939	Abrogation of the autonomy of Catalonia and the Basque Country by the Franco regime.
5.9.1946	The Paris Treaty between Italy and Austria grants autonomy to South Tyrol.
1948	Autonomy for the Faroe Islands of Denmark.
1948	Creation of four regions with special autonomous status in Italy (Friuli Venezia Giulia later in 1963).
1952	The UN decrees that Ethiopia must grant autonomous status to the province of Eritrea.
1961	Dissolution of the autonomous parliament of Eritrea. Armed resistance.
April 1964	Establishment of the autonomy of Zanzibar as a part of the Republic of Tanzania
1966	Adoption of the UN Covenants on Civil and Political Rights, recognising the right to self-determination of peoples.
20.1.1972	Entry into force of the 2nd Autonomy Statute of Trentino South Tyrol (Italy).
1975/76	The Azores and Madeira are granted autonomy in Portugal.
1.5.1979	Autonomy for Greenland as part of Denmark enters into force.

1979	New Statute of Autonomy for Catalonia adopted, based on the Spanish Constitution of 1978.
1979	The second autonomy of the Basque Country enters into force.
30.1.1984	Foundation of the German-speaking Community of East Belgium.
1987	Establishment of the autonomy of the Atlantic coast of Nicaragua (now the Caribbean Coast North and South).
1.8.1989	The Autonomous Region of Muslim Mindanao legally established by the Parliament of the Philippines.
1991	Adoption of the ILO Convention on the rights of indigenous peoples.
25.6.1992	Adoption by the Council of Europe of the „European Charter for Regional and Minority Languages" (in force on 1.3.1998).
4.10.1992	Establishment of the "Federal State of Kurdistan" by the first elected Parliament of Kurdistan in Iraq.
5.11.1992	European Framework Convention on the Protection of National Minorities" approved by the Council of Europe
18.12.1992	UN-Declaration on the Rights of Persons Belonging to National or Ethnic, Religious and Linguistic Minorities.
12.5.1994	The FUEN submits a draft for a „Special Convention on the Rights to Autonomy of Ethnic Groups in Europe" to the Council of Europe.
23.12.1994	Gagauzia is established as an „autonomous territorial unit" in Moldova.
1.7.1997	Establishment of the „Hong Kong Special Administrative Region" as part of the People's Republic of China.
1997	The Scottish people vote for a separate parliament with limited powers within the United Kingdom (autonomy).
10.4.1998	Good Friday Agreement between the United Kingdom, the Republic of Ireland and Northern Ireland to establish autonomy.
1998	Entry into force of the „Scotland Act" for Scotland's autonomy.
5.5.1998	The Nouméa Convention establishes the autonomy of New Caledonia.
1999	The Canadian province of Nunavut is granted territorial autonomy.
1999	Adoption of the OSCE's Lund Recommendations on the effective participation of national minorities in public life.

2001	Following the peace agreement with Papua New Guinea, the province of Bougainville is granted autonomy.
9.8.2001	The province of Aceh in Sumatra is granted autonomy status.
2003	French Polynesia receives a new Statute of Autonomy.
2003	First autonomy regime for "Bodoland Territorial Area District" (Assam, India).
6.7.2003	The majority of the Corsican electorate votes against the Matignon process for limited autonomy.
2003	With the „Yukon Act" the Yukon Territory obtains autonomy in Canada.
1.7.2007	The Netherlands Antilles shift from territorial autonomy to another status (free association - overseas municipality) splitting up in different entities.
13.9.2007	The UN adopts the „Declaration of the Rights of Indigenous Peoples" recognising the right of autonomy or self-government of these peoples in areas of their internal or local affairs.
14.12.2009	Proclamation of the new autonomy of Vojvodina in Serbia.
2011	End of transitional autonomy for Southern Sudan. Popular referendum with decision for independence.
March 2014	Through annexation to the Russian Federation, Crimea loses its autonomy within Ukraine.
27.3.2014	The Bangsamoro Autonomous Region (Philippines) is re-established with an extended autonomy and territory.
18.9.2014	Referendum on the independence of Scotland. Independence rejected.
25.9.2017	Referendum on the independence of the Autonomous Region of Kurdistan (Iraq), not recognized.
1.10.2017	Referendum in Catalonia on the separation from Spain, suspension of the autonomy status for several months.
23.11.-7.12.2019	In a referendum, Bougainville decides by a large majority in favour of independence.
27.1.2020	The autonomy of Bodoland (Assam, India) is significantly extended.
4.10.2020	2nd referendum in New Caledonia. For the second time, the independence of the region and separation from France has been rejected.

From the Memelland to Crimea: failed autonomies

In the history of the 20th century, territorial autonomies have been set up in various continents, but some of them were short-lived. Here are the most important examples of failed autonomies.

The historical autonomy of the Memelland

The Memelland in what is now Lithuania was previously part of East Prussia. The 2,656 km² area along the Memel River had been under German rule for 500 years since the time of the Teutonic Order in the Middle Ages and had been settled by Germans. The border between the Memelland and Lithuania had remained largely unchanged from 1422 to 1920. After the First World War, according to the Treaty of Versailles this part of East Prussia was partitioned off and placed under French administration as a mandate area. At that time about half the population of the Memelland was Lithuanian.

Poland annexed the Memelland in 1922, but Lithuania also claimed Klaipéda, as the area is called in Lithuanian, because of the language of its inhabitants. The French then proposed the creation of a Free State of Memelland. As a result, 1000 Lithuanians in one coup on 10 January 1923 occupied the Memelland and the city of Memel (the "Klaipéda revolt"). The French forces left the country as late as January 1923. The Conference of Ambassadors recognised the annexation of the Memel area as a fact and thus handed it over to Lithuania.

In May 1924, the annexation was also recognised by the League of Nations in the Memel Convention, on condition that the Memelland shall be granted autonomy. The statute of autonomy adopted by the Lithuanian Parliament on 8 May 1924 established the second territorial autonomy in Europe after that of the Åland Islands. The German citizens lost their German nationality and became Lithuanians. But as early as December 1926, the autonomy of the Memelland was revoked by martial law.

On 22 March 1939, one week after the German Wehrmacht invaded Prague, Hitler's Germany gave Lithuania an ultimatum, forcing it to give up the Memelland. It once again became a province of East Prussia. In October 1944, the entire German-speaking population of the Memelland was evacuated to Germany before the approaching Red Army.

The Silesian Voivodship (4,216 km²) was an administrative unit that included parts of Upper Silesia that had been ceded to Poland by Austria-Hungary after the First World War in 1920 and by the German Reich in 1922. It was an autonomous voivodship (province) in the Second Polish Republic from 1922 to 1939, with Katowice as its capital. This voivodship was abolished on 3 September 1939 with the beginning of the German occupation in the Second World War. In postwar communist Poland no kind of autonomy has ever been established. The city of Gdansk (Danzig), on the other hand, from 1920 to 1939 was not an autonomous region, but a „free city" under the mandate and supervision of the League of Nations. After World War II, almost all Germans were expelled from Danzig.

Eritrea

Following a decision by the UN General Assembly, the former Italian colony of Eritrea was granted as an autonomous province to the Abyssinian Empire in 1945. But Ethiopian emperor Haile Selassie increasingly eroded the political rights of the Eritrean population from 1952 onwards. In 1960, the Eritrean regional government was downgraded to a mere administrative authority, and the regional parliament in the Eritrean capital Asmara was dissolved. Finally, Eritrea was militarily occupied by Ethiopia and incorporated into the state as a normal province. Eritreans fought back as early as 1961, and the resistance grew into a broad independence movement. The uprising against Ethiopia has been spreading since the fall of the monarchy in 1974, supported primarily by the Eritrean People's Liberation Front (EPLF). In 1987, the government of the Ethiopian People's Democratic Republic declared Eritrea an autonomous region. Too late, because the Eritreans were no longer satisfied with such an arrangement. After another four years of war with high casualties, the EPLF took the capital Asmara on 24 May 1991 and proclaimed independence. The war of independence had lasted 30 years.

South Ossetia

The small Caucasian region of South Ossetia was occupied and annexed by the independent state of Georgia after the war that lasted from 1918 to 1920. Tens of thousands of Ossetians were killed or displaced. Shortly afterwards, Soviet Russia occupied all of Georgia and established an „Autonomous Oblast" (region) on the territory of South Ossetia. This region became part of the Soviet Republic of Georgia on 20 April 1922 as the „South Ossetian Autonomous Region" and enjoyed extensive cultural rights. After Stalinism, the autonomy rights were re-established in the 1950ies. Nothwithstanding some interruptions a certain degree of autonomy status under communist rule existed from 1922 to 1989.

In August 1989, Georgia adopted a „Programme for the Georgian Language", which aimed not only to promote the Georgian language, but also to resettle ethnic Georgians in areas inhabited by ethnic minorities and to establish military units to which only ethnic Georgians could be admitted. The country's ethnic minorities felt threatened by this nationalist policy. In late 1989 the first riots broke out in some parts of Georgia, including South Ossetia and Abkhazia.

On 10 November 1989, the South Ossetians decided to establish the South Ossetian Soviet Autonomous Republic, which would have resulted in significantly increased autonomy rights. The decision was immediately annulled by the Georgian government. The first violent conflict in South Ossetia ensued, which lasted until January 1990. Georgian nationalists laid siege to the South Ossetian capital

Tskhinvali, while troops from the Soviet Ministry of the Interior attempted to separate the enemy sides. On 20 September 1990, South Ossetia declared itself independent as a Soviet Democratic Republic. In 2005 and most recently in 2008 there were further short wars with thousands of dead and displaced persons. With Russian military support, South Ossetia was able to defend itself. Today a good 90 percent of the population of this tiny region are ethnic Ossetians, since most of the Georgian minority left after the fighting. In referendums, the remaining population of South Ossetia has repeatedly spoken out in favour of independence, but is actually seeking admission to the Russian Federation and unification with North Ossetia.

South Sudan

When the Republic of Sudan was founded in 1956, many Southern Sudanese felt ignored, later marginalised and oppressed. From 1958 to 1972, rebels fought for the independence of the black African South of Sudan. From 1972 to 1983, Southern Sudan was granted autonomy under the 1972 peace agreement, but the central government in Khartoum always intervened strongly in the autonomy of the South. From 1983 to 2005, Southern Sudan's People's Liberation Army (SPLA) waged a war with an estimated two million casualties. It was not until 2005 that a peace agreement was signed in Khartoum. It recognised the right of self-determination for South Sudan, which covers almost 620,000 km2, and granted the country territorial autonomy as a transitional solution. In the referendum on independence held from 9 to 15 January 2011, 99 percent of voters voted in favour of independence for South Sudan. The autonomy of South Sudan was thus history, but not the war, as the new Republic of South Sudan experienced a civil war between the largest ethnic groups of the Dinka and Nuer from 2013 to 2018. South Sudan is the youngest independent and officially recognised state in Africa.

Kosovo

Kosovo on 3 September 1945 became part of the Socialist Republic of Serbia within the Federal Republic of Yugoslavia as the „Autonomous Region of Kosovo and Metohija". Although the region had already been largely populated by Albanians since its annexation to Serbia in 1913, had been denied the status of a constituent republic of Yugoslavia. Like Vojvodina in the north, Kosovo was granted territorial autonomy in the south of the republic. For nationally-minded Serbs, even the establishment of two autonomous regions in Serbia, namely Kosovo and Vojvodina, meant a weakening of the state.

In 1963, Kosovo was transformed into an autonomous province, which meant a better position. However, it was not until 1974 that Kosovo's autonomy rights were decisively extended and the province's right of self-rule within the Republic of Serbia and the Yugoslav Federation extended. However, tensions grew increasingly acute. Kosovo's Serbs felt disadvantaged by the majority Albanian provincial government, while Albanian Kosovo felt discriminated against by Serbia and aspired to the status of a constituent republic of Yugoslavia. After the seizure of power by Milosević in 1989, Kosovo's autonomous status was abolished. Albanian politicians then called for a boycott of all Serbian institutions. For almost a decade, Albanian society in Kosovo engaged in non-violent resistance, until the uprising of the Albanian Liberation Front (UCK) in 1998, which initiated the independence process. In 1999, following the expulsion of a large part of the Albanian population by Serbia, Kosovo was liberated in a NATO intervention. Kosovo's independence had already been declared in 1992 following an unofficial referendum, which was only recognised by Albania. Independence was officially proclaimed by the Kosovo Parliament on 17 February 2008. 114 of the 193 UN member states have so far recognised this youngest European state.

Crimea

From 1946 to 1954 the Crimean peninsula had been a region within the Russian Federation. The then head of the Communist Party and President of the USSR Khrushchev annexed Crimea to the Ukrainian Soviet Republic in 1954, allegedly for purely economic reasons. For Khrushchev, it was inconceivable at that time that a state border would ever run between Russia and Ukraine. On 20.1.1991, 93 percent of the inhabitants of the Crimea were in favour of re-founding the „Autonomous Soviet Socialist Republic of Crimea". The Supreme Soviet of Ukraine agreed to this, but as a part of Ukraine. On 24.8.1991 Ukraine became independent within its existing borders, including the Crimea. However, in December 1991, only 54 percent of Crimean voters voted for Ukrainian independence. It was mainly to accommodate the Russian-speaking population that the peninsula was declared an Autonomous Republic of Crimea in 1992. In its constitution (Statute of Autonomy), Ukrainian, Russian and Crimean Tatar were declared the official and equal languages of Crimea.

In March 2014 a kind of coup d'état took place in Crimea with covert military support from Russia. On 16.3.2014, a referendum on self-determination was held in violation of the constitution of the autonomous Crimea and Ukraine: 96,77 percent of the voters voted for accession to Russia. According to independent reports, however, only 30-50 percent of the inhabitants of Crimea had taken part, of whom about 60 percent had voted for the Anschluss. Immediately afterwards, an application for membership was submitted to Russia, which was accepted by the Russian Duma and the Council of the Federation. After ratification of the treaty and after the Constitutional Court of the Russian Federation had declared the legitimacy of the integration treaty, Russian President Vladimir Putin signed the constitutional-altering law on 21 March 2014 to admit the Crimea as a federal subject named "Republic of Crimea" and city of federal rank Sevastopol to the Russian Federation. The autonomy of the Crimean peninsula was thus history.

4

The first modern territorial autonomy: the Åland Islands

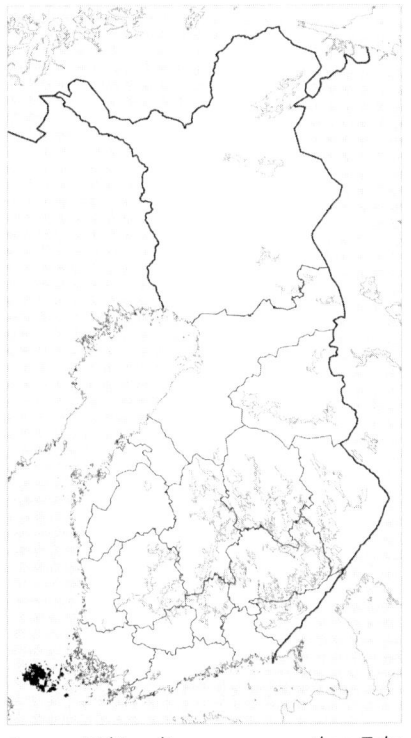

Source: Wikimedia commons, author: Tubs

The «Åland archipelago» consists of around 6,500 islands between Finland and Sweden with a land area of 1,527 km². The archipelago has just 30,000 inhabitants, half of whom live in the capital Mariehamn alone. Åland is a very special region: autonomous, demilitarised, neutral, Swedish in language and culture and yet part of Finland. Since 1921, Åland has been autonomous due to an agreement between Sweden and Finland and a Finnish state law, making it the world›s oldest «modern territorial autonomy» as part of a democratic constitutional state. This form of self-government of the Ålanders was also approved by the League of Nations on 24 June 1921, and it began with the first session of the Åland Parliament on 9 June 1922. Like South Tyrol›s autonomy, the autonomy of Åland is based on an agreement under international convention, or to be more precise customary international law.

How did the autonomy of the Åland Islands come about?

Åland's autonomy, like that of various other regions of Europe, has its origins in a shifting of borders as a result of war. Åland has been inhabited by Swedes since the Middle Ages and was part of the Kingdom of Sweden from 1362 to 1809, together with the whole of Finland. In 1809, after the Napoleonic Wars and 650 years of Swedish rule Sweden had to cede the whole of Finland, including the Åland Islands, to the Tsarist Empire. Under Russian rule, the islands became an outpost of Russian national defence. The Ålanders were a small Swedish minority in the Grand Duchy of Finland, which in turn enjoyed a kind of autonomy - without democracy - in Tsarist Russia. Finland maintained Swedish as its official language during this period. It was only towards the middle of the 19th century that Finnish was given equal status within the Grand Duchy.

The Åland Islands were of great military interest to Russia because of their location off the coast of Sweden, which greatly expanded the fortifications on the archipelago. During the Crimean War in 1856 the most important Russian fortress was destroyed by the French and British navies. Even then France, Russia and Great Britain agreed to the complete demilitarisation of the islands.

In 1917, after the peace treaty between the German Empire and Russia, the Finnish independence movement got its historic chance. On 6.12.1917, the parliament in Helsinki declared independence. After the Swedish and Russian epochs, the Finnish epoch began for Åland. However, the omens for self-determination and autonomy were not at all favourable during the formation of the Finnish nation state: a civil war was raging in Finland. Nationalists did not want to give up the archipelago, while the Ålanders wanted to reunite with Sweden.

On 31.12.1917 the Ålanders held an informal referendum: 95 percent voted for reunification with Sweden. Sweden tried in vain to raise the conflict at the Paris Peace Conference and to enforce the right of self-determination of the Ålanders. The Ålanders themselves submitted a petition for self-determination to the peace conference in Paris, but Finland refused to hold a referendum.

The Ålanders feared that they would be rapidly assimilated into independent Finland. A self-convened Åland Assembly negotiated bilaterally with Sweden and Finland and was also represented at the Peace Conference in Paris in 1919. But the newly independent Finland did not want to cede its sovereignty over the Åland Islands. In May 1920, the Finnish Parliament passed the first law establishing autonomy for the Swedish-speaking Ålanders. This autonomy law literally says: „The Ålanders shall have the opportunity to live as freely as possible in a region that is not a state in its own right". The Ålanders rejected this offer of autonomy, and the dispute was again submitted to the League of Nations. Special rapporteurs examined the case and in 1921 proposed solutions to the League of Nations.

In Geneva on 24 June 1921 the League of Nations then officially decided that

- Finland has sovereignty over the Åland Islands;
- increased protection of the Swedish language and culture should become part of the 1920 Act of Autonomy;
- the whole archipelago should be demilitarised and given a neutral status.

Immediately after with the so-called „Åland Agreement" of 27.6.1921 between Finland and Sweden, the archipelago was granted to Finland as an autonomous region under these conditions. Finland declared its willingness to „allow the people of the Åland Islands to protect the language, culture and local Swedish traditions". The autonomy of the Åland Islands is also enshrined in the Finnish Constitution (Art.120). Their Statute of Autonomy can only be amended by the procedure for amending the Constitution, and any amendment must also be approved by a qualified majority of the Åland Parliament. To date, Åland is the only area in the world that is at once autonomous, demilitarised and neutral. In October 1921, a convention for the complete demilitarisation of the islands was

The Parliament of Åland (Source: Lagtinget)

adopted, which was confirmed by the 1946 Paris Peace Conference. Because of this demilitarisation, the Åland Islands are often referred to as „islands of peace".

Three conditions seem to have favoured this autonomy solution:

- The conflict did not escalate because all parties were willing to compromise.
- The League of Nations and other countries successfully mediated.
- Finland became a democratic state governed by the rule of law, which guaranteed its commitment to implement autonomy.

Åland's autonomy was a compromise between Finland's claim to sovereignty and the Swedish and Ålanders' claim to self-determination. In the second half of the 19th century, the Ålanders had sought to join Sweden. After 1921, they initially struggled with autonomy, which was only gradually accepted. The tendency to see themselves primarily as Swedes remained until the 2nd World War. After 1945 the Ålanders began to develop their own regional identity. It is said that most Ålanders answer the question of their identity with the sentence: „Neither Finn nor Swede, but Ålanders consciously and decisively". At the same time, Finland has always had a special relationship with its neighbour Sweden because of its centuries-long affiliation with Sweden. Swedish is still recognised as the second national language in Finland, but far more Swedes live as a recognised minority on the south coast of Finland than on the Åland Islands. Today most Ålanders are proud of their autonomy.

A comprehensive autonomy

Åland is the only region in the unitary state of Finland with very extensive legislative powers. It is also the only region of Finland with Swedish as its exclusive official language, while Swedish is recognised as a minority language in the rest of Finland. It is also the only completely demilitarised region in Europe. These three basic features characterise the „Åland model": extensive self-government, the status of the regional language as only official language, neutrality and demilitarisation.

The core of any autonomy is the extent of its legislative and administrative powers. Åland's parliament, the Lagting, is allowed to pass its own laws in a wide range of areas of competence, with the exception of foreign policy, civil and criminal law, justice, the monetary system, labour law and most of the tax law. Parliament consists of 30 members. The right to vote and stand for election is granted to all Finnish citizens of full age who enjoy the Hembygdsrätt, literally „right of domicile". This form of regional citizenship is a prerequisite for exercising the right to vote, the right to purchase real estate and the right to conduct an independent business. In order to acquire this right of domicile, an applicant must have both Finnish citizenship and sufficient knowledge of Swedish and must prove that he or she has been resident on the islands for at least 5 years.

The Åland Islands' political parties are completely independent of the Finnish parties, although there are ideological affinities. Åland also has a party for independence in the form of „Åland's Future". The Åland Islands form their own constituency in the national elections and send a deputy who, regardless of party affiliation, traditionally joins the Swedish People's Party, the strongest political force in the Swedish minority in Finland.

The laws adopted by Åland's Parliament are forwarded to the President of Finland. The President may exercise a right of veto after consulting the Supreme Court, but in only two cases: When the Parliament in Mariehamn has exceeded its competence; and when the law affects the external and internal security of the State. The right of veto is normally based on the opinion of the so-called Åland delegation, which is made up equally of members nominated by the Finnish Government and the Åland Parliament.

The Åland Islands have spending sovereignty, but Finland collects its taxes, customs duties and levies on the islands. 0.45 percent of the annual state budget is returned to Åland in a lump sum. The Åland Parliament then decides quite autonomously on the use of the allocated funds. Only the municipal taxes can regulate the Åland Islands autonomously. 200 civil servants are enough to manage Åland's autonomy.

A special feature is also the „Åland delegation" which coordinates cooperation with the State: two of the five members are appointed by the Finnish Government, two by the Lagting, while the chairman is appointed by the President of Finland. Its main task today is to examine the constitutionality and compatibility of Åland's laws with European Union law and the Finnish Constitution. It forwards its opinions to the Finnish Supreme Court, which in turn informs the President of the Republic.

Åland has been a demilitarised and neutral zone since 1921. This means that no military may be stationed on the islands and no military installations may be built. The Ålanders themselves are exempt from compulsory military service, but they are required to do alternative civilian service on the islands. The Åland Islands have their own flag and are allowed to issue their own stamps. Since 1993 the islands have had their own postal system.

There are also special features in the area of external relations. The Åland Islands have had their own seat on the Nordic Council, to which all Scandinavian countries belong, since 1970. Finland's accession to the EU could only be completed after the Åland Islands had been approved. The special arrangements of the Åland Islands regarding basic transport rights and freedom of trade have been maintained. According to the Autonomy Act, Åland must be consulted if an international agreement affecting its competences is to enter into force in Åland. On the other hand, the representatives of the Åland Islands have the right to be consulted when drafting the Finnish position on new EU regulations and directives.

Åland also has a very special arrangement in the field of language policy. As early as the turn of the century 1900, one of Finland's first language decrees stipulated that Finnish and Swedish were to have equal status. This language equality even goes so far that the laws discussed in the Finnish Parliament are presented at the same time as Finnish and Swedish texts. In the Åland Islands, both the administration and the education system are monolingual in Swedish. English is compulsory, Finnish and other languages are optional.

What about the autonomy of the Åland Islands today?

In 1921 the League of Nations' decision for autonomy was a compromise. All parties had to give in. After that they made the best of it. Today the Åland Islands are regarded internationally as a model of territorial autonomy for the protection of minorities and conflict resolution. The Ålanders are well protected in their culture and language, and there have been no significant conflicts between the Åland Islands and the Finnish state. In addition, autonomy has already been extended twice (1951 and 1991). On the one hand, there is a high degree of stability in the relationship between the state and the autonomous region, and on the other hand, autonomy is still being developed, as the Ålanders now insist on obtaining further powers.

This is the case, for example, with regard to the financing of autonomy, on which Helsinki and Mariehamn could not reach an agreement yet. Finland does not want to concede the Åland Islands a separate tax system, while Åland complains about too little room for manoeuvre in tax and economic policy. The Åland Islands also insist on being allowed to operate exclusively within their competences. Experts, on the other hand, argue that autonomy gives only a partial right to self-government, while the actual sovereignty remains with the state. Under the autonomy statute, the Åland Islands are on an equal footing with the central state.

In the relationship between central government and autonomous regions, tensions are inherent in the nature of things. The question of how such conflicts are dealt with is crucial for the quality of autonomy. Helsinki also does not want to allow international mediators to settle differences of opinion. According to Helsinki, the current reform process of autonomy is a domestic issue that does not require international legal assistance. Sweden has traditionally kept out of this process.

The previous reforms of the autonomy law in 1951 and 1991 have only been negotiated domestically between Åland and the Finnish state. Now the Åland Islands are seeking to revive international guarantees, in particular to introduce symmetrical monitoring of legislation. It turned out that there is no international organisation that could play such a guarantor and mediator role. Even on the Åland Islands themselves, it is controversial whether the development of the autonomy should be pursued only in a bilateral dialogue with Helsinki or whether international support should also be sought. It is true that there were three parties involved in the settlement of the Åland issue in the 1920s: the Åland Islands, Finland and Sweden. Russia, France and the United Kingdom were marginally involved because of their security interests. But it is not clear whether these states can act as „guarantor powers" today.

A further reform of Åland's autonomy?

What are the objectives of the Åland Islands and Finland in reforming autonomy? A Åland Parliamentary Commission has already concluded in 2010 that the 1991 Statute of Autonomy is outdated in content and structure. Reforms would be needed, in particular, in the regulation of funding, the division of responsibilities between the state and the autonomous region, the method of transferring new responsibilities to the Åland Islands, and state control of autonomous legislation.

In terms of responsibilities, only the powers of the State should be listed, while the Åland Islands should be able to regulate everything else autonomously. The transfer of further powers should be simplified. As regards financing, the Commission proposes that in future a high proportion of local tax revenue, i.e. tax revenue generated on the islands, should be retained.

The mixed Finland-Åland Commission reached a compromise in June 2017, which resulted in a government proposal for a new Statute of Autonomy. However, the Åland requirements were only partially met. For the time being, the demarcation of state and autonomous competences will not be changed. However, the Finnish state can now transfer further powers to the autonomous

Ålands Lagtinget: the Parliament of Åland in 2021 (Source: Lagtinget)

islands without amending the constitution. The financing system will be made somewhat more flexible in the future.

The regionalisation of Finland and the reform of the health care system will also affect the Åland Islands, although this is an autonomous competence. This will require coordination with central government. The Ålanders will also be able to study at Swedish universities with automatic recognition of their qualifications. Swedish doctors will be able to work in the Åland Islands without a licence from Helsinki. The Åland Islands also want their own seat in the European Parliament, what has not yet been accepted by Helsinki.

The relationship between the Åland Islands' statute of autonomy and the Finnish constitution and the role of the so-called „Åland Delegation" is still open. This third reform of the autonomy law is to be adopted by both parliaments in Helsinki and Mariehamn on the occasion of the 100th anniversary of the Åland autonomy, but there will be no new autonomy statute in the current legislature.

The Åland Islands: a prototype for territorial autonomy?

The Åland Islands are an example of successful conflict resolution through territorial autonomy with the help of an international organisation. Although one of the most developed territorial autonomies in the world, Åland's autonomy is not yet complete and will soon be expanded. In today's political context, more and more power is being transferred to the supranational level of the EU, while on the other hand more subsidiarity is being demanded on sub-state level by strengthening the regions and municipalities. In the Åland Islands, too, it has been noticed that membership of the EU in particular is increasingly setting limits on political autonomy at sub-state level.

Overall, Åland's autonomy is now considered a success. A number of key factors have been decisive in this: a sufficient scope of legislative and administrative responsibilities; an autonomy not only implemented immediately, but also expanded in several steps; then the international recognition of this solution both by the League of Nations and by Sweden; a functioning democratic constitutional state and the fact that the conflict was not carried out by force. The rights of the autonomous Åland Islands in foreign relations are also very far-reaching: not only are they represented in the Nordic Council on an equal footing with other states and autonomous regions of Denmark, but they also have a major say in Finland's relations with the EU.

Other factors favouring Åland's autonomy are rarely transferable. The Åland Islands have a very homogeneous cultural background, with 95 percent of the population being Swedish-speaking nationals and a very small population of 30,000 people. This facilitates a compromise solution, as complex procedures for consociational democracy and proportional representation of ethnolinguistic groups are not required. The territorial autonomy of Åland 100 years after its introduction can serve as a model for many other autonomous regions that have only been able to realise a fraction of possible territorial autonomy. However, for this model case of territorial autonomy, the favourable internal, national and international context played a decisive role, which is seldom the case in other conflict situations.

5

Rescuing a language through autonomy: the Basque Country

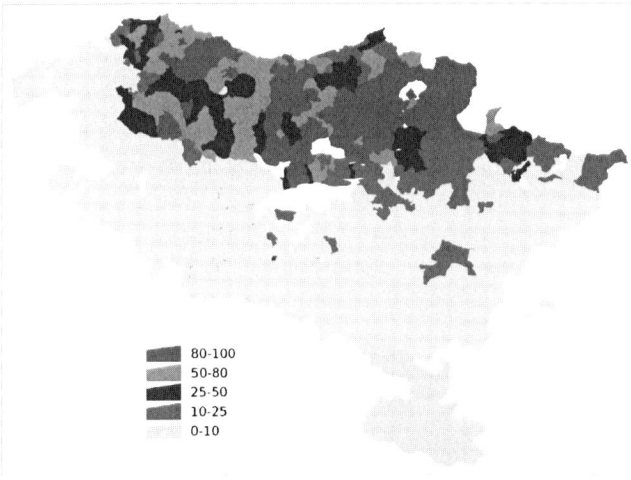

■ 80-100
▨ 50-80
■ 25-50
■ 10-25
░ 0-10

Source: Barasoaindarra. - Navarra: Censo de población de 2001, Instituto de Estadística de Navarra.Euskadi: Mapa sociolingüístico 2001, Gobierno Vasco., CC BY-SA 2.5, 2.0,1.0

Percentage of Basque speakers in the Autonomous Communities of the Basque Country and Navarra.

The Basque Country had enjoyed special rights, the so-called Fueros, since the Middle Ages. Fueros are the legal systems of the various Christian empires on the Iberian Peninsula, which have been in force until modern times, and the local special rights which also came into being during this period. For the Spanish-Castilian nationalists the Fueros were a thorn in the side. This nationalism became more and more pronounced during the 19th century in the wake of the Carlist Wars. The Basque special rights were abolished by laws passed in 1839 and 1876, and the Basque Country was largely brought into line. In response, Basque nationalism developed touching a milestone in 1895 when the Basque National Party (PNV) was founded.

Violence and counterviolence

The beginnings of the Basque Country's territorial autonomy date back to the 1930s. While Catalonia had already been granted autonomy in 1932, the first statute of autonomy of the Basque Country (Euskadi) came into force on 6 October 1936. Immediately afterwards, this first Basque autonomy was lost in the Spanish Civil War: the Basques, united on the side of the Republicans, were defeated. Franco's regime took revenge with harsh repression and the suppression of everything Basque. This in turn provoked resistance on a political and cultural level, but also with violence. 1962 saw the foundation of the Basque paramilitary organization ETA (Euskadi Ta Askatasuna - Basque Homeland and Freedom).

In the 1978 referendum on the new Spanish Constitution, the Basque Country was the only Autonomous Community which rejected it. Only 30 percent of the Basque population voted in favour of the new Constitution because it did not recognise central rights of the Basques. However, the Statute of Autonomy of the Basque Country, an „organic law of the State" based on Article 81 of the Constitution, was approved by a majority in the Basque Country in 1979. Both the Parliament in Madrid and the Regional Assembly and the people of the Basque Country must approve the Statute and any reforms to it.

The neighbouring province of Navarre, which is culturally and historically part of the Basque Country as a whole (Euskalherria), has been given its own Autonomous Community in accordance with the wishes of its dominant political forces. In Navarre, a much smaller proportion of the population considers itself Basque. Both the Spanish Constitution and the Statute of the Basque Country allow Navarre to become part of the Autonomous Community of the Basque Country. Both Autonomous Communities derive their claim to autonomy from the historical special rights of the Fueros, which were explicitly recognised by the 1978 Spanish Constitution. Unlike the other 15 Communities, the Basque Country and Navarre have a partially autonomous tax system, collect taxes themselves and transfer to the State each year an agreed share of the regional tax revenue.

ETA's actions and attacks after autonomy was granted in 1979 were an echo of the repression under the Franco regime, but were increasingly rejected by the Basques themselves. ETA's long-standing political arm, the Herri Batasuna party (later Batasuna), which is committed to self-determination, won 18 percent of the vote in the Autonomous Community of the Basque Country in 1998, but only 9 percent in 2009. After almost 50 years of armed conflict, the vast majority of the Basque population was finally fed up by the terror and counter-terrorism of the Spanish state. In 2011, the remaining ETA fighters finally declared the dissolution of the formation. But the Spanish state did not let up with trials against Basque parties, lawyers and activists, against Basque media and organisations. Usually, the Basque convicts had to serve their sentences far away from their home region, separated from relatives and friends. The painful consequences of the long armed conflict: some 900 deaths, more than 600 political prisoners, torture, ill-treatment, extortion, a climate of violence and fear.

Nevertheless, the will for self-determination remained broadly entrenched in the Basque Country. For a long time the political landscape of the Basque Country was divided into three parts. On the one hand, the strict opponents of the Basques' right to self-determination in the form of the offshoots of the Spanish parties, on the other hand, the advocates of the gradual expansion of territorial autonomy without renouncing the right to self-determination (PNV and others), and then Batasuna and other left-wing parties who did not clearly distance themselves from the violence of ETA. The Basque National Party (PNV), founded in 1895, has been insisting on autonomy since 1979 and has always been the party with the largest number of votes. In addition, there is traditionally a broad left-wing nationalist movement (izquierda abertzale), which has long been fragmented. It was above all the question of the use of force and the relationship with the underground movement ETA that divided the left forces. Only after the ETA finally stopped the armed struggle in 2011 and announced its dissolution these parties came together in a joint political front called EH Bildu (Basque Country Unite).

A significant proportion of the Basques consider autonomy only as an interim solution and seek independence or a loose confederation with Spain. While for the offshoots of the Spanish parties in the Basque Country the current statute grants the maximum possible autonomy, the Basque parties want to extend this autonomy without renouncing self-determination - the „right to decide". The Spanish Constitution, in turn, sets strict limits to this aspiration.

The political debate on autonomy and sovereignty

Surveys in the Basque Country have repeatedly shown that the majority of the population is not satisfied with the achieved autonomy status. In 2003, the Ibarretxe (PNV) government launched a first attempt to reform the autonomy of 1979, which not only provided for increased autonomy with the transfer of all transferable powers to the Autonomous Community, but also redefined the constitutional relationship between the Basque Country and Spain in the form of a free association. Only defence, civil, commercial and criminal law, the merchant navy, the regulation of migration and asylum, production, trade, possession of arms and explosives, air surveillance and foreign policy would have been excluded whenever this reform would have been approved. But the „Plan Ibarretxe" was rejected by the Spanish Parliament by 313 votes to 29 (see end note).

On 27.6.2008, the Parliament of the Basque Country decided to hold a referendum on the future of the region in October 2008. The aim was to open negotiations with Madrid with a view to voting on independence by 2010 at the latest. Again, this law was rejected by the Spanish Constitutional Court as unconstitutional. Under the current legal system, only Madrid has the competence to decide whether to allow referendums in the Autonomous Communities. Since then, this request has not been any more raised by the Basque parties as Spain's constitutional system does not allow it.

The conflict between the Basque Country and the Spanish State is not only sparked by the latter's strict refusal to allow a democratic process of self-determination, but also by the implementation of autonomy. The central state repeatedly intervenes in Basque autonomy through laws and regulations. In legal proceedings, the Constitutional Court, which is appointed quite unilaterally by Madrid, usually decides in favour of the state. Until 2009, some important responsibilities (employment policy, prison administration, social security) had not even been transferred to the Autonomous Community as provided by the Statute, and the further expansion of the autonomy was not even conceivable. Against this background, the Basque parties tend to be frustrated by the real possibilities offered by autonomy. While the conservative Partido Popular rejects any expansion, the Social Democratic Party PSOE can at best imagine a moderate adaptation of the statute, but not even a symbolic entrenchment of the right to self-determination. There is no common political basis between the two political camps, the Basque parties and the parties of the State, and there is no obligation for concordance government, just as there is no obligation in other autonomous regions of Europe.

The PNV won a relative majority in all nine elections to the Basque Country Parliament, but on several occasions had to form coalitions with either the PSOE or the Basque Left. Only from 1.3.2009 to 2012 did Spanish parties in the Basque Country govern without the PNV and provide the President of the Basque Country. This was because Batasuna had been banned and as a result its voters boycotted the elections (9 percent invalid votes). In 2012, this government failed and the PNV returned to power. In 2012, the Basque parties PNV and EH Bildu together won 58 percent of the vote (48 out of 75 seats in the regional parliament) and 46 seats in 2016. In the election of 12.7.2020, the Basque „sovereignty" parties PNV and Bildu obtained a solid two-thirds majority in the Basque Parliament, with almost 66.9 percent of the votes and 52 of 75 seats. The Basque „national camp" emerged stronger from these elections, also under the impression of the central government's harsh approach to Catalonia's independence aspirations.

The Basque language: prohibited and discriminated against

The Basque language is accompanied by a touch of mystery. It is the only isolated language in Europe, a language not related to the Indo-European languages. The Basque Country has maintained this language since time immemorial. The real mystery of Basque is not so much its origin as the fact that the Basques have been able to preserve their language, they say. How is it possible that a language that for decades was only spoken within families and between friends, that has a very limited literary and written tradition and was completely banned from the public domain for 40 years, survives in this freshness?

For more than a century, the Basque language had experienced a decline. In 1868, 69 percent of the inhabitants of the Spanish Basque Country still spoke Basque, but by 1981 the figure had fallen to 21.9 percent and even these people had not been alphabetized in Basque, so they were mostly unable to write in Basque. The only official language and language of the public was Castilian. Basque was recognised as a second official language in the 1st Autonomy Statute of 1936, but with the Franco dictatorship it was banned. With the prohibition of Basque at school, in the media world, in administration, judiciary and politics, it lost its role in public life and fell into the status of a language of the peasant world without social prestige. Basque was not considered at all suitable for adapting and developing in the modern world. The number of Basque speakers decreased steadily, while more and more Basques learned Spanish and only spoke Spanish. Basque lost essential domains of communication, was no longer

The headquarter of the Government of the Basque Country in Gasteiz/Vitoria.

present in the media and in the modern world of work. Moreover, around a third of the current population of the Basque Country immigrated from the rest of Spain only in the second half of the 20th century, mainly because of the need for labour in the heavy industry of the Basque Country.

The renaissance of the Basque language

The revitalisation of the Basque language has been underway since 1982, based on the new autonomy statute. Basque has survived because the Basques believed in their language. However, it was only when the new autonomy came into force in 1979 that the political and legal framework for the emancipation of Basque was established. Basque has been recognised as a co-official language in the Autonomous Community of the Basque Country (AC Basque Country) in Spain since 1979. In the Autonomous Community of Navarre (AC Navarra) it has been a co-official language since 1986, but only in the predominantly Basque speaking municipalities. In France, Basque is recognised as a „regional language" and thus as a cultural heritage worthy of protection with constitutional status. However, the Basque speakers in France cannot derive any concrete legal claim from this. Thanks to its autonomous status, the spread of Basque in the Autonomous Community has not only been stabilised for over 40 years, but has been strengthened in almost all the main areas. Today, at least 750,000 people speak Basque in this area (cf. Britannica, Basque Language). In addition, there are some 90 000 emigrated Basque speakers living outside the historic Basque Country.

Euskal Herria, the Basque Country at large in its historical context, comprises three regions: the Autonomous Community of Euskadi and the Autonomous Community of Navarre in Spain and the French Basque Country. Each of these regions has different conditions as regards language development and the use of Basque is subject to three different legal regimes.

Basque is the „lengua propia y específica" of the Basque Country. It is the official language in the AC Basque Country, but only in parts of the AG Navarra, where only about 10 percent of the population (about 60,000 people) consider themselves part of the Basque cultural community. In France, despite official recognition, the Basque language speakers do not have specific rights. In these three regions, Basque has undergone a completely different development over the past 40 years, mainly because of differences in the legal regulations and, consequently, in the social recognition and use of the language by the population.

Throughout Euskal Herria there were 751,500 Basque speakers in 2016, or 28.4 percent of the total population. Between 1991 and 2016, the number of Basque speakers increased by 223,000, mainly due to the language policy of the Autonomous Community of the Basque Country. In Navarre, the increase was only 28,700, while in the French Basque Country the number of speakers fell by 17,900. If the entire population were counted, including minors, the number of Basque speakers today could be much higher, at around one million. Whereas only 24.1 people in the Autonomous Basque Country called themselves Basque speakers in 1991, by 2016 the figure had risen to 33.9 percent. Passive Basque speakers accounted for 19.1 percent of the population in 2016. Altogether 53 percent have an active or passive knowledge of the Basque language. Between 1991 and 2016, the number of people who have an active or passive knowledge of the Basque language increased by 420,000. In 2016, 325,000 people in the Basque Country spoke mainly Basque in everyday life. 140,000 people have learned Basque as adults in these 25 years.

The public's attitude towards the use of Basque is predominantly positive, as is the attitude of the people towards the promotion of the Basque language by Basque Country policy. While 50 percent in the French Basque Country are neither for nor against, two thirds of the inhabitants of the AC Basque Country 2016 were clearly in favour. In the AC Navarre, however, there are more opponents than supporters of this kind of language policy. This clearly shows the different appreciation of Basque by the population of the three regions of the historical Euskal Herria. The revitalisation of Basque is the official line of government in the Basque Country, is only half-heartedly pursued in Navarre and is not supported at all in the French Basque Country.

At the beginning of the 1980s, on the basis of the Statute of Autonomy of 1979, the political leaders of the Basque Country developed a language policy to safeguard the existence and development of the Basque language, known in Spanish as „normalisation". The development of the language, which is managed by the Autonomous Community, has been one of the factors behind the amazing sociolinguistic changes in the Basque Country over the last forty years. The Basque language policy deals with two main areas: firstly, the language itself, its standardization and modernization; secondly, the status and regulation of the use of the Basque language. The latter covers the position of Basque in the administration, the educational system, the media, cultural life, work and business, adult education, digital media. The AC Basque Country, based on its autonomous powers, has always sought to consistently increase the importance and the dissemination, the quantitative and qualitative weight of the Basque language.

Future challenges for the Basque language policy

Despite the dominance of the economically stronger languages (Spanish, French and, to an increasing extent, English), the „euskaldunisation", i.e. the promotion of the Basque language in all areas of life in the Basque Country, has made great progress. The official language policy aims to promote the use of Basque, to strengthen families in the intergenerational transmission of the Euskera (Basque language), to motivate non-Basque speaking citizens to learn Basque and to encourage migrants to learn Basque in addition to the State's official language. An essential prerequisite for this is the autonomy of the Basque Country, with the appropriate language policy regulatory competence, with the provision of the necessary financial resources for language promotion and with a basic political consensus on language issues among the majority of the Basque Country's political parties.

Basque is now spoken by an increasing number of people as a habit in everyday life and has proved its worth as a means of communication in all areas of life: „The key factors for the successful revitalisation of Basque in the Basque Country so far are the following: the willingness of citizens to actively support this policy; the targeted and long-term policy of the regional government; the high degree of social and political consensus on language policy; the variety of initiatives from society in private-public cooperation and the creation of a single standard language" (Galparsoro, 2019, 96).

Overall, the situation of the Basque language today seems promising. The assessment of what has been achieved depends on general expectations. According to the Basque expert Galparsoro, the social health of the Basque language is stronger than some would like to admit, but not yet as far advanced as many Basques wish. However, the Basque language today is stronger than some friends of the Basque country could have imagined 40 years ago. But there is still much to be done, if only to preserve what has been achieved. A „critical optimism" is appropriate (Galparsoro 2019, 139). The revitalisation of the Basque Country is still an unfinished process and what has been achieved so far needs to be further consolidated. Language policy must respond to new sociolinguistic conditions and to the needs of new Basque speakers, because any politically supported language planning also has its limits.

What does the Basque language need to be strengthened further? „What Basque needs is that we need them," says Galparsoro, „we are the only ones the language can count on (literally: "El euskara necesita que lo necesitemos", Galparsoro 2019, 139). The communicative benefit of the language must be cultivated and preserved. Speaking Basque must increasingly become the rule in the everyday life of hundreds of thousands of Basques. The new challenges of digitalisation must be met immediately in order to adapt the language to the communication needs of today's time and generation. The Basque language remains above all a concern of Basque speakers, not of the whole society, because Basque speakers and Basque people (inhabitants of the Basque Country) are not the same. At present, in everyday life still only about one third of the population of the Basque Country speaks more or less the Basque language in the same extent as Spanish or French. The central question for the future development of this language is the extent to which Basque is used as a first language. The renaissance of Basque, the „Euskarabatua", is a great community work of the Basques, which is well on its way, also thanks to autonomy.

Note:

The Ibarretxe Plan provided for a new Statute of Autonomy based on three pillars:

- *The Basque people are a European people with their own identity.*
- *The right of the Basque people to decide their own future, understood as the right to self-determination, is recognised.*
- *The decisions of the citizens of each region of the Basque Country (Autonomous Community of the Basque Country, Navarre, French Basque Country) should be accepted by the other peoples of Europe.*

It also proposes a series of reforms:

- *Freedom of relations with Navarre and the French Basque Country, based on the choices made by each of the regions.*
- *An autonomous jurisdiction.*
- *Spain should guarantee direct representation in the EU.*
- *Spain shall guarantee that the new staff regulations cannot be unilaterally restricted or cancelled. To this end, the Spanish Constitutional Court will be adapted and a bilateral commission for conflict resolution will be created; treaties and international agreements affecting the Basque Country will have to be approved by the latter before they enter into force.*
- *Recognition of the Basque citizenship and nationality of all the inhabitants of this Community so that they may acquire dual Spanish and Basque citizenship. Acquiring one or other nationality does not diminish or increase the rights and obligations of citizens.*
- *Official Basque sports elections.*
- *Exclusive competence in public administration, education, culture, sport, language policy, finance, housing, environment, infrastructure, transport, public security, employment and social security.*

"In the eyes of most Spanish citizens to be a Basque is the wrong way to be Spanish, however you are Spanish."

Interview with Prof. Eduardo J. Ruiz Vieytez, University of Deusto, Bilbao

E. Ruiz Vieytez is a professor of Constitutional Law at the University of Deusto (Bilbao), where he has served as dean of the Faculty of Social and Human Sciences, and previously as director of the Human Rights Institute. He was legal adviser of the Basque Ombudsman and the president of an NGO working on the promotion of immigrants' rights in the Basque Country (1993-1999). He has also been a member of the Spanish Council for the Integration of Migrants, and participated in several country missions of the Council of Europe concerning linguistic and national minorities.

According to the Basque autonomy statute of 1979 the status of the Basque language is one of full equality with Spanish in the public area. Today, is the Basque language really on equal footing with the State language with regard to every sector of public administration and services including the judiciary?

Vieytez: No, legally speaking it should be on equal footing for the whole Basque Autonomous Community (BAC), including all public administration. In practice, equal rights are not achieved yet. And judiciary is the sector, in which Basque is used less, sometimes it is even impossible to claim its use. There are still many obstacles. To begin with, the judges and attorneys are members of national corps, the vast majority has no knowledge of Basque language. The maximum what you can get as a citizen of the BAC is to use the Basque language in court and claim translation, which could turn out as a disadvantage in legal procedures. Some judges may not react very sympathetically. The presence of Basque language in the State sector of public administration is also low. In the BAC, in provincial governments and in municipalities the use of Basque is significant, but surely not dominant. Maybe Basque is prevailing in the municipalities of the Basque speaking area, especially in Gipuzkoa. But most internal documents are still produced in Spanish, and only then translated into Basque.

Are all citizens entitled to interact with the public administration in one of the two official languages of the Basque Country?

Vieytez: Yes, as a principle, they are but often the linguistic rights are not respected in practice as the administration and other public services are not prepared to respond in Basque. You have to wait, it leads to complications for the citizens, and this has a deterring effect for the citizens. In some sectors and some places you don't even dare to use Basque unless you want to provoke an uncomfortable situation.

In the BAC Is there any official certificate of bilingualism especially regarding the degree of knowledge of Basque which every applicant for a public sector job has to submit before being admitted to a competition? Is this required just for the Autonomous Community jobs or also for all State administration jobs located in the Basque Country?

Vieytez: There are official certificates on the knowledge of Basque language. But no official certificate has to be produced when you apply to a public job. It depends on the concrete position for which you apply, as there are different requirements. Basically, if you apply for jobs in the educational sector, you will be asked to hold a C1 level of Basque; also in some administrative positions. But in general terms, the knowledge of Basque will provide you a complementary allowance in the merits to get the position, but it will not be a compulsory prerequisite. A physician of a public hospital, for instance, will earn some additional points, maybe 8 percent more, if he or she proves to have a C1 level in Basque, but it is not an excluding requirement most of the times.

Today schools of type D using Basque as medium language are the most popular type of school with almost 68 percent of all pupils enrolled. Why has the bilingual school (type B) with just 19 percent of pupils not gained such an acceptance, as it would match somehow better the sociolinguistic reality of the Basque Country, as most families still use Spanish at home.

Ruiz Vieytez: The reason is precisely this factor. Bilbao for instance is a Spanish speaking city. Probably one fourth of its population can speak Basque, but Spanish is absolutely dominant. If people want their children to be bilingual, the best they can do is to send them to a Basque speaking school. On the other hand, Spanish is given for granted, as there will be no problem to learn it well. So the challenge is to put children in a milieu as much Basque as possible. Even in type D some students end up with an insufficient fluency in Basque language, when their daily life milieu is Spanish speaking. In the Basque speaking area also with type B you could achieve fluency, but not in predominantly Spanish speaking areas, although even most of the teachers will not be native speakers of Basque. The B model works just as a substitution of type A. Another reason is also this one: parents also choose the school thinking about who will be the friends and mates of their children. Quality and social prestige play an important role as well. In type D schools there will be more native speakers of Basque, in type A more foreign immigrants. Type D has become the privileged type of school in terms of social prestige and quality of education.

As reported, 52 percent of University students in the Basque Country follow courses of study with Basque as medium language. To which extent is this pos-

sible? Are there just some lectures in Basque or are there complete courses of study held in Basque as main medium language?

Ruiz Vieytez: Yes, many high school graduates from a Basque speaking school prefer to go on with Basque also in their University studies. Some academic degrees can be completed in Basque, others are organised partially in Basque, partially in other languages. You have to combine two or three languages. Generally, the public university can provide for more courses fully held in Basque language.

According to the Encuesta Sociolinguistica 2016 34 percent of the population of the BAC use Basque as the first language, but passive knowledge of the language since 1991 is increasing. In 2016, 19 percent have got such knowledges. What is it about?

Ruiz Vieytez: 34 percent with Basque language as the main language in daily life may be too optimistic. 34 percent of the BAC's population can be considered bilingual, but the people who use Basque in daily life as first language will be about one quarter and not more. Not all of those 34 percent have got the opportunity to use it in daily life. In Alava the main language is Spanish in every sector. Thus there would not even by the chance to use Basque so frequently. In a meeting, in order to speak Basque, everybody is required to understand it. But this happens in one meeting out of 10. Passive knowledge means that you formally have got a degree, maybe B2, probably you are not very fluent in speaking Basque, but one can read and understand the language. You will understand most of the text on media, but you might not be able to communicate, especially not in a written form. This is very typical for native Spanish speakers, who have learned the language as adults or have graduated from schools of type B or even D in Spanish-speaking zones.

What's about the future, when the majority of the Basque population will be perfectly bilingual?

Ruiz Vieytez: Indeed, today almost all Basque-speaking people have become bilingual. Once in history the Basque language in some areas of Euskadi was granted, and just the doctor, the teacher and the priest knew Spanish, but the rest of the people where still native Basque speakers, even in the first half of the 20th century. Until 1950 the Basque language was quite safe in these environments, but what happens if everybody is bilingual? It is easy to shift to the State language whenever it appears more comfortable. Most of the media, TV, radio, Internet is broadcasted in Spanish. When there is a regime of full bilingualism the question is, which language will be chosen for communication? There is a risk that just one language will emerge as the main tool for communication due to simple utilitarian behaviour.

In the initial draft of the Autonomy Statute the Basque Autonomous Community was allowed to maintain official relations with Basque-speaking authorities in Navarra and in Iparralde in France. But this later has been rejected by Madrid. Today, how can the government of the BAC co-operate on linguistic-cultural projects with partners abroad?

Ruiz Vieytez: The Basque Royal Academy (Euskaltzaindia) is allowed to have international cooperation. They are funded for such purposes, basically financed by the BAC. Now in the French Basque Country there a new institution, la Communauté d l'Agglomeration Pays Basque, composed by all the Basque municipalities, which is entitled to carry out transborder cooperation too. There are small projects. Also some indirect financing of schools in Basque medium language is possible. For the Basque people this is of great symbolical importance. Sometimes Spanish political parties challenge such forms of cooperation, as they regard it as not legitimate.

In the elections of the Basque Parliament of 12 July 2020 the Basque parties have increased their votes. Now EH Bildu holds 21 seats and PNV 31 seats out of 75 in total. This is a majority of two thirds. Does this have any significance for the parliamentary procedures? Which coalition will rule the BAC?

Ruiz Vieytez: Not really. The PNV (Partido Nacionalista Vasco) will keep its governing coalition with the Spanish Partido Socialista (PSOE). Basically the coalition will be the same as in the previous mandate. The PNV has no intention today to emulate the Catalan way, as it doesn't want to risk anything. Bildu would like to take up some initiatives for pushing the right to decide, but the PNV is not keen of confrontation. They don't want to go to jail or in exile for this purpose, or risk the current autonomy.

The Spanish government of Pedro Sanchez has struck an agreement with the Catalan ERC. Do they have such an agreement with the PNV as well?

Ruiz Vieytez: The PNV is a stable partner of the central government. The current political situation at State level is the most comfortable situation for the PNV. There is no overwhelming majority of the Spanish parties in the Cortes, so they need the PNV and a Catalan party to preserve the majority. So PNV by supporting this government can negotiate on a range of issues and can get some advantages in exchange. In the Basque Country the PNV then presents itself as the true and efficient guardian of Basque interests in Madrid. That's the traditional role of the PNV in the Spanish parliament.

Since 1979 the Basque statute of autonomy has not been amended at any time. The Plan Ibarretxe of 2003, rejected by the Spanish Parliament, encompassed the right of the population of Euzkadi to decide and the possibility to form a kind of free association with Spain. Did it also contain an extension of the territorial autonomy in terms of exclusive powers and resources of the Autonomous Community? It is said that 37 competences listed in the Autonomy Act haven't been transferred yet.

Ruiz Vieytez: Generally speaking, the Statute should be updated and powers extended. In 2003 the Basque Parliament in the so-called Ibarretxe-plan tried to include some more powers which had not been included in the statute of 1979. Only some basic powers should be left to the State, whereas all the rest should be in the responsibility of the BAC. But the main issue of the Ibarretxe-plan was the so called right to decide. Moreover, it encompassed the recognition of a kind of regional citizenship of the Autonomous Community by giving the option of declaring oneself to be Basque, on a voluntary basis. But from the perspective of the Spanish parties such a right would have automatically created two communities on the same territory. Instead of considering it a progressive step forward to dissociate citizenship and identities, they regard it as a risky segregation into two separate groups. The political and cultural approach from the two national identities tend to exclude and misunderstand each other.

Another proposal included in the Ibarretxe-plan was a new relationship between the Autonomous Community and Spain, similar to associated statehood. What is this about?

Ruiz Vieytez: Yes, but the proposed new status of association should not be confused with freely associated statehood as Puerto Rico with the USA. The idea was that the new legal status should be based on the will of the Basque people, and of the Spanish people of course. Therefore, the proposal was to recognise the Basque people as a sovereign people, but willing to remain in the Spanish State, excluding independence. This would have been a voluntary act of mutual recognition, in the sense that in return for renouncing on independence there would be a free will to remain within Spain. This would be similar to a form of confederation, not to associated statehood under international law.

Is the right to secession an indispensable component of a good autonomy statute?

Ruiz Vieytez: There are several examples of autonomy statutes that include, more or less explicitly, this right such as Greenland, the Faroer, Gagauzia, Québec, New Caledonia, Saint Kitts and Nevis, Northern Ireland, and some other regions which once have been autonomous and are now independent as South Sudan, Montenegro, Eritrea…. Generally, the most successful way of solving sovereignty conflicts so far has been independence. In Slovenia, Estonia, Slovakia or Montenegro nobody speaks about sovereignty conflicts any more. But coming back to the concrete questions, the answer is negative. If the final goal is just to ensure a good autonomous status, then the recognition of a right to self-determination or to sovereignty is not necessary. The challenge is when, according to the democratic electoral free expression of the citizens that happens to be insufficient.

Several States would be prone to establish territorial autonomy for some special cases, if they could be sure that autonomy will not be the first step to secession. How can such States be assured to maintain their territorial integrity?

Ruiz Vieytez: In my opinion, it would be a good idea to constitutionalize or regulate the process of secession, to establish appropriate guarantees and limits for both sides, the State and the community seeking sovereignty. The autonomous community might request secession and be independent one day, but only following a given process, because previously they have agreed on it. As long as this process is not completed, self-determination is not going to happen. The autonomous community doesn't have to renounce on self-determination by introducing such a regulation in the legal order. This could help to solve the conflict and to give a big load of stability and trust. It is similar to Canada's clarity act with regard to Québec. It is very difficult for existing nation states to reach that point, but in cases of a true conflict that cannot last for ever, this could be an efficient instrument for accommodation, making possible to keep territorial integrity precisely because there is a legal way to challenge it.

Would it help to rule out in legal constitutional terms ever possibility of secession? Could this help States to establish territorial autonomy?

Ruiz Vieytez: It depends on the elements of the concrete conflict. In some cases, this will not be sufficient as the conflict will remain as long as there is a popular will to be recognized. Then, if you do not offer a possibility to accommodate or to regulate a secession process, the only alternative for that consistent will might be independence. I think that regulating such processes can be a solution to avoid many problems. If autonomy works, secession will not be on the agenda. But if it doesn't work, the alternative of independence must remain as an alternative option. This happened in Catalonia. The Spanish State has a huge power to repress such movements, but for a democratic state it is not acceptable in the long term to throw the president, vice-president or other democratically elected representatives of Catalonia in jail because they pursued a democratic referendum. At least half of the Catalans don't wish to be part of Spain and they should have the fundamental right to express this will in a democratic referendum. Repression is no solution, as the Catalan citizens will not give up this goal. Maybe they get exhausted for several years, but if the political problem is not really recognised and dealt with, it will reappear sooner or later.

Catalans and Basques consider themselves as different nations. Thus Spain's population can be seen as an "uneven multinational reality", as you define it. As Juan Linz said: "Spain is a state for all Spaniards, a nation-state for a large part of the Spanish population, and only a state but not their nation for important minorities." Should this reality be recognized in Spain's constitution?

Ruiz Vieytez: There is a centralistic view at the Basque and Catalans as "Spaniards", as populations of Communities on the same political ground as those of all other Autonomous Communities. If you ask average Italians whether they consider Sardinians, Friulians and Sicilians as Italians, sometimes using different languages or dialects, there will be no doubt. In the same way, a vast majority of Spanish people see the Basque and Catalans. On the other hand, Italians don't consider the South Tyroleans to be true Italians, rather you are regarded "as a people on the wrong side of the border". But in Spain there is not such a parallel understanding for the Basques or the Catalans. The average Spanish citizen will not have the perception of diverse nations living in Spain, only a majority of the Basques and Catalans have. Probably you will get the answer: "To be a Basque is the wrong way to be Spanish, however you are Spanish; that is what your ID card says."

Today in Spain Catalan and Basque self-determination movements claim to have full recognition of asymmetry, but the State is reluctant to award this. The Spanish political forces favour a symmetrical structure of vertical power sharing. Other Autonomous Communities try to neutralize the national project of Catalonia and the Basque Country. How to break out of this vicious cycle?

Ruiz Vieytez: It is very difficult because the territorial issue, which is obviously a national identity issue, is extremely sensitive for the vast majority of the citizens. It is difficult for a nation like Spain to recognise the obvious fact that there are, at least, two other successful national projects in the country. They can see it election after election in both the Basque Country and Catalonia, but there is a strong resistance to recognise this asymmetry. From this perspective, these two regions are just two out of 17 Spanish regions and must not be regarded as national projects with the same legitimate aspiration as the Spanish one, which is obviously much bigger and powerful enough to have its own state. The recognition of Spain as a plurinational country, as the UK or Canada for instance, is still a significant taboo for the majority of the Spanish political parties and their electorates. In this context, if you do not develop a national strategy for the majority to assume this plurality, to assume the linguistic, cultural, national plurality as a common heritage of all and not as a handicap against unity, it is not possible to bring it into the legal order. This work can only be done by the Spanish political forces in common as a way to give stability, enhance and strength the State, but they seem to be far way from sharing this view.

Would an extension of the autonomy of the Basque Country and Catalonia still be considered as a privilege by the majority of the Spanish citizens?

Ruiz Vieytez: Spanish people in general don't look at the Catalans as privileged people. Rather they consider just the Basque country and Navarra as privileged, because of their special economic and fiscal agreements with the State. Catalonia in financial terms is not privileged. It has to be said, that when Catalonia's first statute was settled, the Catalan representatives were offered a similar system of fiscal agreement as the BAC and Navarra got recognised due to the historical fueros regime. But the Catalans did not accept it in that moment. After some years they realized that they made a big mistake. The belief was: who collects the taxes from the citizens is the bad guy. The good guy should just spend the money. Later they claimed something similar as the concierto economico, but it was too late. Of course it is better to negotiate with any counterpart when you have the money in your pocket.

What's about the quest of a new political status for the Basque Country?

Ruiz Vieytez: That this could turn into an amendment of the Statute within the constitutional framework is, at the very least, complicated to envisage. Only by going down the route of the historic rights argument could an original solution of this kind be reached without pro-State positions being concerned about the threat of such a system being extended to other nationalities and regions within the State. However, the current social and political conditions are very different from those which in 1979 made a truly bilateral negotiation of the Statute possible, and there is no indication that Spain is on the way to genuinely reforming its autonomy model in such a way that its symmetrical nature is altered. How the Catalan dispute is settled in this legislature may provide a guide for the future on the level of territorial reform that the Spanish State is prepared to accept and, consequently, on how a new agreement on self-government for the Basque Country could be articulated. Nevertheless, at the moment the forecast is for there to be an ongoing clash between two distinct political majorities who, unless there are significant constitutional moves that enable the situation to become unblocked, are unable to reach satisfactory agreement between them.

The right to decide for any regional community: which would be the effect in the long term? Current nation states would risk to be broken off?

Ruiz Vieytez: The right to decide has to be recognized whenever a regional community emerges as a political subject through a clear, consistent and legitimate electoral expression. That is proved by concrete facts and data. These facts and data in democratic systems are produced by electoral processes. If in a given territory you register a consistent pattern of voting in favour of an alternative configuration of power, something must be done. But this happens in Europe in a very limited number of cases. Most of Europe's regions do not even think about independence. Recognizing the right to decide helps to solve such conflicts in a democratic way. The legal system is required to recognize such emerging regional communities as a new political subject, as it happened in history with the women and the black people. In Switzerland the women obtained the right to vote only in 1974, and only men were entitled to decide on it. From this perspective new subjects should be recognized and be given the right to decide freely.

When claiming recognition as a new political subject, should a regional community be composed by peoples or ethnic groups different from the State's dominant titular nation?

Ruiz Vieytez: No, in my opinion this should not be a prerequisite at all. The international law does not define what is a people, nor what is a different language, religion or ethnicity. And it must not. There might be different criteria to justify a political aspiration, but in democracy, the only truth is political will, expressed in free elections in a way that is clear, consistent and solid.

Now in Spain more centralism can be observed. More Spanish people in favour of a centralized State. In this context, would it be more difficult to achieve amendments of the Constitution or will there be a permanent tension on this issue as a growing majority of Spain's political forces are opposing it?

Ruiz Vieytez: Indeed, more centralism is much likely to happen as maybe 30 years ago. If there would be a second political crisis to justify a second period of constitutional reform, it could happen. But this is very unlikely. The end of the 1970ies was the moment of decentralisation, and everyone was in favour. But now the times have changed. The majorities of Catalonia and the Basque Country still want to expand their self-government. But the majorities of the other Spanish Communities that in 1978 were in favour of decentralization as a guarantee for more democracy, have to some extent shifted. Today many sectors think: we went too far, we should walk back and recentralise some of the powers. But minority nations they want to head on this way, towards more self-government. The two dynamics that in 1978 were convergent, seem today divergent. Thus, the historical moment is not propitious to reach such an agreement.

Catalonia and the Basque Country share various features and the basic legal and political framework of the Spanish State, but they show also many structural differences. You mention that even their national political projects are quite different. Why?

Ruiz Vieytez: Yes, but the origin of the national projects in both countries and also the political strategies are different. Basque and Catalan parties haven't coordinated themselves. The one community plays A, when the other plays B, in order to get more benefits. Now for instance PNV supports the government in Madrid. Catalonia and the Basque Country share the vision of Spain as a multinational country, but they do no care much about the rest, or even about Catalonia. Apart from that they are quite different in origin. Basque national project has always been more radical, dogmatic, in a certain sense more "Germanic" and the Catalan one more pragmatic, more "Mediterranean". There are also significant differences on sociocultural and linguistic grounds.

Why did Galicia, although culturally, linguistically, politically different from the rest of Spain, never express a strong national movement as Catalonia and the Basque Country?

Ruiz Vieytez: Galicia has got a different socio-economic history as an economically backward region. In Galicia only the left forces developed a certain commitment for national issues from the 60ies, but not the conservative and centre-right parties as in Catalonia with the CiU and in Euskadi with the PNV in the late XIXth century or beginning of XXth century. Galicia has not been industrialized in the same degree, agriculture and fishery remained the economic pillars for long time. There wasn't any such significant urban middle class to build up a nationalist project as happened in the Basque Country and in Catalonia.

Catalonia is an ongoing conflict. In your opinion, only by establishing procedures and institutions for self-determination for single smaller nations in the Constitution and in the Autonomy Statute will provide conflict solution and more stability of the system at large. Which way out of the political stalemate in Catalonia after the referendum on independence of 2017?

Ruiz Vieytez: At the moment, it is very difficult to see any feasible solution, or a minimum common point to think of a stable scenario for Catalonia. The fact is that 50 percent of the Catalans are voting repeatedly for breaking out from Spain. This is a serious problem for any country, considering the economic and political weight of Catalonia in Spain. At the same time, for a vast majority of the Spaniards, self-determination is out of question since challenging the unity of the sovereignty is not even subject to debate. Being like this, there is no political or legal solution and it will remain a combat of forces. It might reach a moment of weakness of the state that the Catalan secession movement could use but it is difficult to foresee. At the same time, the current situation cannot be maintained as it is, since it does not make any sense for any democratic country, and it is exhausting for both sides. In my opinion, and having reached to this point (that could have been avoided should the state have adopted a more inclusive and intelligent strategy in the last 10 years), the only way out for a generation is to prepare a decision process in Catalonia that can be organised and developed with a minimum agreement by the majority of Catalan political sectors. This should end in a way or another in a referendum that may set up the issue for a period of 25 years, bringing back some stability and breaking the current gridlock.

6

Italy's rocky road to greater regional autonomy

For years, political Italy has been experiencing a tug-of-war between the central state and some regions in the north, especially Veneto, Lombardy and Emilia-Romagna. The Lega (formerly Lega Nord), which governs almost everywhere in the north, has set its sights on extending the autonomy of these regions, but the forces of obstruction are strong. Why does it not want to succeed in introducing „differentiated autonomy" by region in Italy? Why does the South resist more autonomy? Why are the regions with a special statute denied the expansion of their autonomy?

Source: de.wikimedia.commons, author: TUBS

Regionalism with the hand brake on

Italy's republican constitution of 1948 established the state as a regional state, but in 1948 only four regions with special status were initially able to start operating: Sicily, Valle d'Aosta, Sardinia and Trentino-Alto Adige. It was not until 1963 that Friuli Venezia Giulia became the fifth autonomous region, as it was first necessary to wait for a solution to the dispute over Trieste with Tito's Yugoslavia. Sicily and the Aosta Valley had already been granted special status in 1945. In the case of South Tyrol, there was even an obligation under international law to do so under the Paris Treaty of 1946. Sardinia was able to assert its cultural and geographical particularity.

The 15 regions with regular statutes, however, were not activated until 1970. The constitutional fathers thus wanted, on the one hand, to accommodate the regions with linguistic minorities and Sicily with differentiated autonomy regulations first and, on the other hand, to give all other regions limited legislative sovereignty and administrative autonomy in a symmetrical, i.e. uniform manner.

The North-South divide proved to be a major brake on the implementation of this regional state concept, which since the founding of the state has required a permanent transfer of considerable public resources from the industrialised, prosperous North to the economically backward South. This also led to conflicting interests within the normal regions and within the parties: while the northern Italian regions with normal statutes repeatedly pressed for the expansion of the institution „region", the South emphasised the role of the central state, which was to ensure the constant flow of resources from North to South in the name of national solidarity. The situation was made more difficult by the fact that, even from 1970 onwards, the regions of southern Italy did not show great efficiency in the management of their competences and financial resources.

As a result, politicians from various parties tried to take the bull by the horns: after the traditional parties and the whole „political class" had been hit by a deep crisis at the beginning of the 1990s and the second half of the 1990s had seen long and fruitless discussions about Italy's transformation into a federal state, the reform of the state structure was carried out in 1999 after lengthy deliberations in various special parliamentary commissions. This constitutional reform was supplemented by another reform in 2001, that of the regions with a special autonomy statute.

What innovations of the 1999 constitutional reform for the ordinary regions?

The 1999 reform granted statutory sovereignty to the regions with an ordinary statute. These regions were given more power, could draw up their own statute and regulate their own form of government, e.g. by directly electing the president of the region. The exclusive powers of the State were listed in the new version of Article 117(2) of the Constitution, while all other powers are vested in the regions. The national interest, a cheap instrument in the hands of the government to encroach on regional powers, was abolished. In the case of competing powers (Art. 117, 3), the State dictates the principles. The creation of a Chamber of Regions, a kind of federal council instead of the Senate, could not be implemented in 1999. Nor was the coordinating State-Regions Conference enshrined in the constitution.

Although this reform gave the regions more weight, disillusionment followed soon after the 2001 reform. There was a gap between state legislation and the case law of the Constitutional Court. The reallocation of powers to the State and the regions under the new Article 117 of the Constitution was not fully implemented. The transfer of administrative powers under Article 118 with the allocation of the corresponding finances to the regions under Article 119 was not carried out. The supreme principle of State unity continued to prevail, allowing the State to intervene at any time in regional powers. The originally intended strengthening of the autonomy of the ordinary regions was thus considerably weakened. Parliament often acted in its legislation as if the constitutional reforms of 1999 and 2001 had not even existed.

On the other hand, challenges to regional laws before the Constitutional Court have become increasingly frequent. The state often regained jurisdiction by means of simple laws, redefining jurisdiction ad hoc in state laws themselves (dematerialisation of legislative matters). The Constitutional Court interpreted various state competences as „transversal matters" under Article 117(2), which also allowed for detailed rules to be laid down by the central government. Only the criterion of proportionality and appropriateness remained.

What happened to the autonomous regions? The constitutional reform of 2001 left the statutes of the five autonomous regions enshrined in the Constitution untouched. In Italy, any reform of the special statutes must be carried out by Parliament in agreement with the regions concerned. The possibility of exercising extended rights of autonomy opened up by Constitutional Law No 3/2001 also applied to the five Autonomous Regions. The restrictions applicable to the ordinary regions did not apply. However, it was necessary to enshrine these new freedoms in terms of rights and powers in the special statutes themselves. To date, this has not been done for any of the five regions with special statutes and carries a high risk that the extensions of the autonomy of the regions with special statutes introduced in 2001 will be reversed by a further, but more restrictive reform. This would indeed have happened with the centralist constitutional reform of the Renzi government in 2016. However, this plan was overturned by the people in a confirming referendum on 4 December 2016 with a very clear majority against Renzi's amendment project.

In the conflict between the central state and the regions over the application of constitutional reform, the Constitutional Court has repeatedly distinguished itself not only as a mediator but also as a regulatory body. With the help of its judgements, the rules which the legislator had made too general and imprecise were usually interpreted to the detriment of the regions. From 2005, the Constitutional Court introduced the criterion of the primacy of the State law, later called the „supremacy clause", which can always be applied in favour of the State. The State itself increasingly regulated questions of competing powers in an exhaustive and detailed manner, leaving the regions no room for manoeuvre. The State's „substitute provision" (Articles 120 and 127 of the Constitution) was often used to ensure legal uniformity throughout the national territory, even though this was only intended for exceptional cases.

As the „national interest" had been deleted from the text of the Constitution itself, the Constitutional Court replaced the State in its role of supervising the supreme principle of centralised uniformity. The postulated „loyal cooperation" between the regions and the state became less and less effective. The state seemed to mistrust the regions as legislators on principle, and the regions shied away from the conflict before the Constitutional Court. Thus, the constitutional reforms of 1999 and 2001 created more problems than they solved: Inefficiency and waste of resources in regional administrations, more and more conflicts between the state and the regions, lack of transitional provisions, no clear role for the State-Regions Conference, a lack of representation of the regions in the Constitutional Court itself. Overall, the 2001 reform had brought little progress for the regional state of Italy.

Towards the development of the autonomy of the regions with ordinary statute

A new attempt to reform the Constitution to increase the powers of the regions (devolution) was adopted under the Berlusconi government but was overturned in the constitutional referendum of 25 and 26 June 2006. As a result, in 2007 Lombardy and Veneto requested to make use of article 116, paragraph 3 of the Constitution to grant differentiated autonomy in order to obtain 12 additional powers. Again without immediate success.

In 2016, the Parliament adopted a far-reaching constitutional reform initiated by the Renzi government, which would have led to a considerable reduction of the legislative sovereignty of the regions. The reform also provided for the transformation of the Senate into a „Senate of the Regions", which, however, did not correspond to a body such as the Bundesrat of the German federal system, but rather to a second chamber indirectly elected in the regions with greatly reduced co-determination rights. This constitutional reform was rejected in a referendum on 4 December 2016 by around 60 percent of voters.

The negotiations received new impetus from the referendums of 22 October 2017 in Lombardy and Veneto. In these referendums 98.1 percent of the Venetian voters (voter turnout 57.2 percent) and 95.1 percent of the Lombard voters (voter turnout 38.34 percent) were in favour of more autonomy. There was no vote in Emilia-Romagna, but the Regional Council agreed with the demands of neighbouring regions.

The new Article 116, paragraph 3, allows the 15 regions with normal statute to extend their legislative sovereignty in a differentiated manner. In many areas, they could be given legislative leeway comparable to that of the regions with special status. According to Article 117(3) of the Constitution, the regions with ordinary status could be given as primary powers all those competences which are currently listed in the Constitution as „areas of competing legislation". In addition, the Regions could also secure some exclusive competences such as the courts of peace, the education system, environmental protection and monument protection. The same State law must also specify all the financial resources to cover the expenditure for the new regional competences. Art. 117, para.3 of the Constitution does indeed offer the ordinary regions the chance to develop their autonomy, but it must be demonstrated that the existing competing legislation is not sufficient for the intended purpose.

This reform of the autonomy of the ordinary regions will be carried out by State law on the basis of agreements with the regions concerned. To this end, these regions would have to negotiate separately with the State and, after consulting their local authorities, negotiate an agreement with the Government. This agreement would come into force by means of a so-called „strengthened State law", i.e. a more demanding procedure. Neither the State nor the region concerned could subsequently unilaterally withdraw from the agreement reached. The necessary finances will be determined subsequently. If no agreement is reached on the financing of the additional regional competences, the historical development of public expenditure will have to be taken as a basis.

The Lega under its leader Matteo Salvini is pushing for more territorial autonomy of Italy's northern regions. Electoral campaign in Bozen, South Tyrol, 2015

This option was initially only used by the regions of Lombardy, Veneto and Emilia-Romagna. In the meantime, a total of nine regions have expressed interest in more powers: Lombardy, Emilia-Romagna, Veneto, Piedmont, Liguria, Tuscany, Marche, Umbria and Campania. The other regions of the South could still join. But only with Veneto, Lombardy, Emilia Romagna and Piedmont has the government already concluded preliminary agreements.

After a survey phase by the 2017 bicameral commission for regional issues and several rounds of negotiations between the state and, at that time, three regions specifically interested, on 28 February 2018 three „preliminary agreements" were concluded between the government and Lombardy, Veneto and Emilia-Romagna. There was a general agreement to strengthen these three regions considerably. However, this should not be at the expense of the uniformity of the legal system and the solidarity and balance between the regions. The squaring of the circle, because the transfer of new tasks will inevitably require the transfer of the corresponding financial resources.

The granting of differentiated autonomy to Lombardy, Veneto and Emilia-Romagna received a new impetus with the entry into government of the Lega in June 2018 and became a cornerstone of the coalition agreement with the M5S. Despite the Lega's departure from the government in summer 2019, Minister Boccia presented a draft law for differentiated autonomy in November 2019. But the Corona crisis brought the project to a standstill since March 2020.

What do the regions of Northern Italy want?

The powers sought by the three regions can be grouped into „broad areas". Priority will be given to health, the education system and labour market policy. In addition, environmental protection, energy policy, supplementary social security, cross-border cooperation and the courts of peace are also concerned. At least some core areas of public services are of general interest for the regions.

In all regions, health care alone represents the largest expenditure item in the regional budget. The effects of regionalisation would be particularly far-reaching in the school and university sector. The education system could thus be much better tailored to the needs and social context of each region. New types of schools such as universities of applied sciences could be established. Competitions for teaching staff would be organised at regional level, with staff being able to choose between a state or regional core role. In vocational training and higher education, regions could tailor their offer much more closely to the needs of their own companies. Not only school construction and personnel management, but also student hostels, study grants and student transport would be managed directly by the regions. Veneto and Lombardy are also striving to have their own school system in terms of content. In the field of research, these regions want to act more autonomously and carry the project-related cooperation themselves.

In the field of employment, it covers active labour market policies, the organisation of employment offices, job placement services and many complementary services. The transfer of large parts of the civil servants in health care, schools, higher education, labour market services and social services would greatly strengthen the role of the regions as collective bargaining parties and employers. Regional supplementary pension insurance is also of growing importance. As regards the Courts of Peace, the regions would relieve the burden on the state Ministry of Justice.

Other important areas which the regions want to regulate are landscape and monument protection, environmental protection, regional planning, regional transport policy and mobility, civil protection and water management, including energy policy. Italy's main industrial regions also want more room for manoeuvre in the regulation and promotion of industry.

In its proposal, the Veneto Region asked for all the powers authorised by the Constitution to be transferred and, in order to finance these tasks, for the transfer of 90 percent of the tax revenue of IVA (value added tax), IRPEF (income tax) and IRES (company's profit tax) generated on its territory and for participation in all the public funds for the areas transferred. This, in turn, has fuelled suspicions in the southern regions that the economically strong regions of the Po Valley are seeking to decouple themselves financially from the State.

A secession of the rich?

The autonomy aspirations of the northern Italian regions with ordinary statutes are viewed with suspicion in southern Italy. Centralist right-wing parties and political forces, which have their strongest voter base in the south, such as M5S, have raised more and more concerns. The spectre of 20 different school systems was painted on the wall and the reform project was seen as an attack on the unity of the state. It is presumed that different standards of public services would be created, differing from region to region. Bureaucracy would be doubled at regional level, and the regions would have to cut spending in health, education and social services. The main concerns stem from fears that state funding for regions with low tax revenues would be drastically reduced. Indeed, the regions aspiring to „differentiated autonomy" are demanding a higher share of state tax revenue collected in their territory to finance the new competences. This would entail a reduction in the resources available in the State budget for the South, which in turn could lead to a reduction in the scope and quality of public services in the South of Italy. In short, the transfer of funds from the North to the South (regions with ordinary status) would inevitably be curbed. More autonomy in the North would lead to less money for the South.

The crux of the reform is therefore the arrangements for financing the regions with ordinary status, which claim to be strengthened in their powers. In accordance with the preliminary agreement of 28.2.2018, this would be based on the assumption that the three interested regions would receive an appropriate share of the regional tax revenue. Lombardy, Veneto and Emilia-Romagna would like to be able to retain most of their annual „net contribution" (residuo fiscale, the balance between the revenue from state taxes and the financial benefits received by the state in relation to the territory of a region) themselves. This would meet the wish of the citizens and taxpayers of the region to be able to expand the performance of the region in accordance with their own tax payments. The State, on the other hand, insists on setting uniform standard needs throughout Italy so that it can then continue to incur most of this expenditure on the basis of „historical development". This would not, however, confer any significant advantage on the northern regions, which are interested in a qualitative leap forward for their citizens. The regions would also be able to collect additional regional taxes and would be given responsibility for the local finances to finance the municipalities.

In 2016, the so-called net fiscal surplus (residuo fiscale) of the three northern regions interested in differentiated autonomy is estimated at 88.324 billion euros: this is the net amount that the three regions pay into the state treasury to finance the central state and the South. With a net fiscal surplus of 54 billion euros, Lombardy alone could cover the deficits of all the regions of southern Italy.

If the richer regions of northern Italy retain a much higher proportion of state revenue to cover their costs, the state may lack the resources to make financial transfers to the south. It is feared that the solidarity-based financial equalisation between northern and southern Italy would be substantially weakened. While the regions of Italy's north are demanding a maximum financial contribution of 90 percent of their respective regional tax revenues - based on the financing system of the regions with special status Sicily, Valle d'Aosta and Trentino-Alto Adige - the other regions are resisting: the rich north should not be allowed to shirk its obligation of solidarity with the south and with the central state. No „secession of the rich" should be allowed.

Between the North-South divide and „differentiated autonomy"

Negotiations between some regions of northern Italy and the State have been delayed by the pandemic, but have not been suspended. The basic concern to gain more political autonomy is still being pursued and they intend to make full use of the room for manoeuvre in negotiations with the State. The scope for interpretation of Article 5 of the Constitution, which grants autonomy but requires equality, will have to be explored to the limit.

The question also arises as to the extent of the „asymmetrical differentiation" of the Italian regional system. All Italian regions differ in structural features. Italy, more than Germany, would have been predestined for a federal system since its foundation. Now it seems to be accepted that each region can and does choose its own menu of additional responsibilities. The basic concern of regionalism, however, is not to identify individual regional characteristics from which a few competences can then be derived. Political autonomy in the sense of more room for democratic self-government should be considered as the organising principle of state-building.

Financial equalisation between the economically stronger and weaker would have to be carried out separately on the basis of objective criteria. A far-reaching differentiation would paradoxically lead to an Italy with 20 regions with special status, would significantly increase the complexity of the system, which in turn would reduce its efficiency.

As Robert Louvin points out in the interview hereafter, Central and Southern Italy do not have a regionalist culture or a leadership that is seriously committed to more rights for the regions. In northern Italy, this culture has tended to take root, but often guided by short-sighted, more economic interests. This is where Italy needs to start again now: namely with the long-term interests of these regional communities, sustainable development, environmental and climate protection, generational justice. The autonomy demands of these regions, Louvin confirms, have nothing earth-shattering about them. The crux of the matter is the financial resources, which the central state does not want to give up, just as little as its role as a distributor of wealth.

Today, a different coalition is ruling than in 2018, which has slowed down reform plans. For the Movimento 5 Stelle (M5S), the Lega's advance on behalf of the North was too far anyway, especially since the M5S has a stronger voter base especially in the South. The social democratic Partito Democratico will not accept regional autonomy, which weakens the solidarity-based financial transfer in favour of the poorer regions. The M5S insists that differentiated autonomy should not affect the minimum level of public services throughout the national territory, especially in the areas of health, education and social services.

Finally, the whole project could also fail because of a centralised interpretation of the Constitution by the Constitutional Court, which places the principle of unity and indivisibility of the Republic (Article 5 of the Constitution) and the uniformity of living conditions throughout the national territory above the right of self-government of the regions. Thus the project stands and falls with the willingness of politicians to allow differentiated (asymmetrical) regional autonomy and thus differentiated development of the country.

If a region with a normal statute cannot provide more resources than before for the political shaping of a newly acquired task, autonomy would not have enough fuel from the outset. If such a region cannot to a certain extent spend its tax revenue on services and infrastructure for the citizens in the region, autonomy can only be implemented through regulation. Autonomy, however, necessarily requires financial autonomy, without prejudice to the duty of solidarity-based financial equalisation between prosperous and weaker regions.

Italy's approach to differentiated autonomy could probably fail precisely because of this issue, namely the central state's refusal to give a little more resources to the regions of northern Italy and the state's inability to partially regionalise its tax system. Each region would then be at least partly responsible for its own financing and, according to democratic preferences, would demand higher taxes in return for better public services. Just as no federal state can function without fiscal federalism, regional autonomy cannot be sustainable without such a system of sharing responsibility for covering regional expenditure.

Italy is therefore faced with this fundamental question: should the regions become a financially autonomous area of regional democracy, in which citizens and taxpayers have a minimum say in taxes, public revenue and expenditure, and political representatives have some room for autonomous decision-making? Or does Italy, with its chronic North-South divide, want to remain with the model of redistribution from North to South, which brings permanent discontent in the North and structural financial dependence and inefficiency in the South?

The structural causes in the system of Italian regionalism should be examined. Why do we want to give the regions legislative sovereignty if we do not want to give them any political room for manoeuvre through elected regional assemblies? In Italy there are no regions that claim to be nations in their own right. Although the Lega has in the past threatened to secede from Lombardy and Veneto or the whole of northern Italy, the situation is different from that in Spain and the United Kingdom. It is rather a question of decentralising state power in the sense of „good governance", i.e. ensuring a more efficient, less costly and citizen-oriented administration, in order to give the efficient regions the chance to manage themselves better. Finally, to give the citizens of the region more democratic influence over the concrete policies and public services in their region: one of the basic concerns of territorial autonomy.

"Let's link the issue of autonomy with the communities' and territories' long term political challenges."

Interview with Prof. Robert Louvin, former president of the Autonomous Region of Aosta Valley

Robert Louvin, a lawyer from Valle d'Aosta, was President of the Autonomous Region of Valle d'Aosta from 2002-2003, previously President of the Regional Council and Regional Assessor for Education (1993-1998). He was regional councillor for Union Valdôtaine from 1988 to 2003, from which he separated in 2005 and was re-elected in 2008 for Vallée d'Aoste Vive. He is now President of the Valle d'Aosta-State Bilateral Joint Commission. In addition to numerous publications Louvin is also the author of the standard work „La Valle d'Aosta. Genesi, attualità e prospettive di un ordinamento autonomo" (Aosta 1997). With Prof. Louvin we take a look to the smallest autonomous region in Italia and the chances for „differentiated autonomy".

The Aosta Valley has been Italy's first region to demand self-determination, initially in 1945, and then to receive a kind of provisional autonomy statute as early as September 1945. The relationship between the Aosta Valley and the Italian state was much less conflictual than that between Rome and South Tyrol. Can we say that your autonomy is a success story that does not need any major reform?

Louvin: In an overall assessment of these 75 years of autonomy of the Aosta Valley we may say that this experiment all in all has succeeded. Some difficult tasks could be solved in the reconstruction after the war. There has been significant economic and social development. Our autonomy model based on the statute of 1948 has produced positive results at least until the first 2000s.

Then, factors of confusion and disorientation arose: the political system, which since the 1970 was dominated by the Union Valdôtain, has entered in a crisis. The defence and the usage of the French language and culture has lost momentum in the political class and even the financial setting founded in 1981 went in crisis. In the same time the revenues of the Casino of Saint Vincent crashed dramatically.

The autonomist proud we once experienced, aimed at alternative ways for self-government instead of being just executors of Rome's political will, all of a sudden had suffered. What once has been a model of self-government, appreciated by all, has grown old and has missed the chance to master new challenges both on institutional and economic level. Thus, it won't be enough to talk about some partial amendment of the autonomy: we have to think about rethinking and reforming the whole approach to autonomy. Even the way how the recent Covid-19 pandemic has confirmed that the regional administration is not any more fit enough.

Initially in 1945 France has also envisaged the annexation of the Aosta Valley to France. Later France always declined to be involved as a protector state of the francophone minority in Italy. Has this French position weakened your efforts to enlarge your autonomy?

Louvin: France indeed has renounced not only on its claims of annexation of the years 1944-45, but also on a role as protector state. This has strongly reduced our negotiation force. Its initial claim, however, has been the trigger to achieve the autonomy immediately. And we were prepared for that. But due to this French position the Aosta Valley has suffered a kind of cultural isolation towards the francophone area regarding opportunities of higher education, of integration in the French media world and cultural exchange of any kind. Our linguistic peculiarity has been cultivated like a small and closed backyard with rather disappointing results. The number of Valdostans ready to use French in both the professional and private life has considerably shrunken. Among the population at large, due to the bilingual education system, a minimum level of French language skills is ensured. But this remains just a palliative which cannot compensate all missed opportunities of potentially being an extension of the francophone area of France and Switzerland.

Recently the Aosta Valley internally is hit by a series of scandals which drove the region in a deep political crisis. The regional government stepped down in April 2020 and in September 2020 midterm elections had to be held. How do you explain this kind of degeneration of the Autonomous Region and which are its main causes?

Louvin: In the last years there have been alarming events linked to politicians victims of infiltration of the organized crime. For both regional and local institutions the effects have been devastating. It cannot be of any comfort that such phenomena have also affected our neighbour regions as Piedmont, Liguria and Lombardy. The peculiar feature of the Aosta Valley is linked to two convergent factors. The first one is an excessive tendency of politicians to a clientelist way of gaining electoral consensus. The small scale of our region has favoured the mutual exchange of favours between electors and elected. Thus, step by step the sense of legality and impartiality of the administration has been undermined.

The second, both in the traditional milieu and in the immigrated communities of Aosta Valley systematically has been organized a kind of political barter deprived of any ideological or programmatic content, but just relying on personal friendship, neighbourhood and mutual profit. The cultural and ideal value served as a façade for such practises. By this way the parties including the autonomist movement have lost their role of leaders ready to empower the society in cultural and political terms.

When considering the political landscape the Aosta Valley likewise South Tyrol for decades has been dominated by one autonomist party. Only later after 20 years the arena has become more pluralistic with a growing number of parties. Which effect has had this new fragmentation of the Valdostan politics on the joined political claims for more autonomy?

Louvin: As far as the Aosta Valley is concerned, the substantial monopoly position of the Union Valdôtain which lasted since the end of the 1970ies until 2013, then has definitely ceased to exist. The guiding principles were not held up anymore: the electoral consensus and the administrative pragmatism has turned to be the real religion of the local political class. It is the same as with the money. The bad one scares away the good one. When the clarity and power of positions and strategies of the Union Valdôtain was gone, all could freely declare themselves "autonomist forces", but with no real coherence. In the relationship with Rome, both on political level and legislative dynamics, we could say that the flag of autonomy has been brought down since a long time. Even when there are deeper dissent politicians try to avoid any conflict and thus also avoid to tackle big social challenges. What today prevails is parish nationalism and political tactics.

As the two autonomous provinces of Trento and Bozen also the Aosta Valley has the right to amend freely its form of government and is allowed to establish new forms of direct democracy. Thus, it is in the forefront of new instruments of referendum rights which later have been applied several times. Today, to which point have you got? The Valdostans now can launch popular initiatives and referendums as your Swiss neighbours?

Louvin: This kind of referendum practice in the first 1990ies has been pushed by a political minority of the green left. The autonomist majority looked on that with suspicion and concern, but this innovation could be established after the constitutional reform of 2001. With a popular initiative in 2011 for the first time in Italy ever since a regional bill has been approved directly by the people. And this has proved that direct democracy can be a strong tool of participation, than decisions imposed from above without the consent of the people can be blocked, as it happened with the waste incineration plant. Today, 5 percent of the electors of the region can submit a draft bill to the regional council. Whenever this popular initiative would not be approved by the council, a popular referendum has to be organized. The draft bill will be approved when at least 50 percent of the turnout of the last regional elections are scored with a majority of Yes-votes. This is not just a theoretical success, but a very useful tool which in the future will foster democratic participation.

But besides the problematic issue of the minimum turnout of voters, there is another obstacle: the central government can challenge a posteriori a popular initiative approved by the people of the Aosta Valley. This a very serious fault of the system, which nevertheless has been recognized even by the constitutional court. Indeed, the legal control of the Region's competence on the referendum's issue should be carried out before the vote not afterwards.

Also the Aosta Valley in the past strived for a more robust and complete autonomy, extending its legislative powers enshrined in the Statute of 1948. Recently, priority is given to Italy's northern regions with ordinary statute which claim a differentiated autonomy. So, along with other Regions with a special statute, the Aosta Valley will have to wait for having its autonomy completed? Are there some new proposals on the table?

Louvin: The extension of our legislative rights is currently not on the political agenda of the parties. The debate is fully focused on internal institutional reforms. But, this won't have immediate effects as the system is still blocked by the will to protect the narrow-minded interests of single political groups. There are no organic proposals of completing and innovating the autonomy on the horizon. Also the current setting of powers is partially contested by national political forces and the central state's apparatus. I am referring to the role of the regional president who in Aosta Valley is also in charge of the powers of a prefect. This now is frequently criticized even by regional politicians.

What has been done in the last years in Aosta Valley to develop its model of special autonomy? The experiment of these 30 years have provided to be not successful. The third attempt to reform your autonomy statute by a participatory approach dates back to 2006-08, but was to no avail. Is there any organic reform proposed by the Regional Council or isn't there any particular wish for such a project?

Louvin: After three attempts to reform the statute of the Aosta Valley, no political force comes forward with such proposals anymore. Today, they are fully focused on the electoral laws, it's like as nobody would get aware of the statute growing older and older, which since 1948 has never been substantially amended. Among the population economic concerns are prevailing today, especially after the crisis of 2008-9. The debate about the bilingualism is kept covered, on institutional level there are some discussions about electing the president of the Region directly by the electorate. But this option hasn't gained much consent among the Valdostan parties. The current mushrooming of political parties and the decreasing capacity to enter in stable coalitions proves that this political system has arrived to a dead end, and hasn't yet found a way out.

Statutory reform once more: which are the most visible gaps of your statute or the most nasty encroachment of the central state into the autonomous powers? And which would be the 4-5 most important points of innovation of the Aosta Valley's autonomy statute?

Louvin: I have got the impression that the means to defend ourselves have got the same power as bayonets and fencing swords in front of machine guns and tanks. The reform of 2001 has been termed as "quasi-federalist", but it provided some very useful tools to the central state to gain more ground. This refers particularly to some state powers in financial affairs, in environmental protection and civil service regulation. In reality, today state controls, which apparently where abolished 20 years ago, have resurfaced in other forms, and even more powerful. The government challenges our regional laws five times more frequently than before 2001. The court of auditors once had no power to administrative control, but today it can intervene massively and challenge also general political decisions of the regional council.

I am convinced that the statute of autonomy should be redrafted in a more detailed way, ensuring more space for autonomous decision making, but also empowering the democratic counterbalance and local level of administration. We have also to take into account the structural limits of the Region which counts just 128.000 inhabitants. It has to renovate its apparatus, has to improve its performance and capacities. 20 years ago everybody thought that the Region would be ready to act more swiftly and efficiently than the state. Today it is not anymore the same and the people's distrust towards the regional administration has grown. In some cases, which might appear paradoxical, the Region itself has renounced on exercising his normative powers provided by the statute: thus it is to no avail to claim some new powers if we are not able to use those tools already in our hands.

After the referendum of 22 October 2017 in Veneto and Lombardy and the first government Conte in June 2018 the process of according a differentiated autonomy to 3 or 4 northern regions with ordinary statute has been pushed forward, but has lost momentum after the exit of the LEGA from the government and after the pandemic. Which will be the fate of this reform of Italy's regionalism in this legislature?

Louvin: I can't predict the future. Too often in Italy we have seen regionalist and autonomist attempts, also federalist and even separatist claims, which after short time cooled down or vanished. There are various interests and also the pandemic has shown that the country reacts in a geographically different pattern with different performances. Southern Italy has no regionalist culture, nor has it leaders prone to develop a strong regionalist setting. In northern Italy this political culture is more deeply rooted, but often guided by short sighted ambitions or purely economic interests. There is a come and go between political tactics vis-á-vis Rome and the effort to gain more power on national level is fuelled by a strong wave of nationalist populism. This all does not comply with a sound federalist spirit which for a while was living also in Italy's constituent assembly embodied by politicians like Emilio Lussu and Adriano Olivetti. From this legacy we have to start linking the issue of autonomy with the communities' and territories' long term political challenges: the economic sustainability, the protection of the environment and of the climate, the solidarity among the generations as our responsibilities for the future.

The four regions of Italy's Northern part with ordinary statute substantially don't claim nothing more than the transfer of some important powers like

health care system, the environmental politics, some more freedom regarding interregional activities, the management of local entities, the urban planning, the education system etc.. Mostly powers governed by the Regions with special statute since many years with good results. How do you explain the strong resistance of some political parties, media voices and even the academic world towards a kind of decentralization successful in both several Italian regions and other regionalist and federal countries?

Louvin: Substantially, the claims raised by those regions are not so revolutionary at all. The real reason behind this resistance are the financial resources which the central state is not ready to surrender as this would mean to renounce on its role of distributor of wealth and controller of resources. The culture of federalism encompasses a high degree of maturity, the capacity to keep away from populism, the recognition of diversity and of the common good. The historical experience of the Italian state has not produced such exciting results in this regard. The constitution contains some important principles: autonomy and decentralization, protection of linguistic minorities, subsidiarity. But the deep state machinery never has absorbed this approach and values. They are not willing to transfer some decision making powers from the centre. Unfortunately, in this regard Italy is similar to Spain, which recently has reacted with violence and judicial means to the claims of the Catalan people expressed by purely democratic means.

Let's come to the future of the Regions with special statute. In 2012 after a referendum the region of Sardinia has claimed a constituent assembly to approve a completely new autonomy statute. In 2004 and 2005 the Region Friuli Venezia Giulia has organized a participatory process to elaborate and approve e new statute of autonomy, which later never was discussed in Parliament. In 2016-17 the Autonomous Province of Bozen has called for a convention on its autonomy, whose final documents contains a long list of proposals for the amendment of its autonomy statute. But since more than 3 years the provincial council never took up the issue. Such attempts to exercise some pressure on Parliament through citizens' participation are bound to fail? If statutory sovereignty could help Italy's autonomous region, in which way could this be established in in the constitutional system?

Louvin: I have followed carefully the three experiences you cited, which have different features and different degrees of people's participation. In some cases there has been too much rhetoric about, so the initiatives ultimately remained an elite's affair without involving the greater public. So, there has been nothing of revolutionary in these procedures. The reform of the statutes, on the other hand, do not affect the issue of the fundamental rights and of the financial system of these regions. What this is about, is to reconstitute the rules for the State-Regions relationship. Such questions do not raise much enthusiasm, sometimes are legally complex and difficult to be explained. Such processes can have a strong impact only when backed by a huge popular mobilisation, as happened in 2006 in Catalonia when its autonomy statute was reformed. In Italy there is nothing similar so far, although there are three hot spots of independence movements which should be taken seriously. I refer to Sardinia, Veneto and South Tyrol. The history after some decades will tell us whether the fire smouldering in those regions has been definitely extinguished or is going to burn up again.

The fate of Italy's special autonomies will be just a defensive game? When even the big regions with ordinary statute are hitting on so strong obstacles when trying some more autonomy, the autonomous region inevitably will have to wait until the strengthening of the "ordinary" regions is over?

Louvin: I am not sure that the regions with ordinary statute will really be empowered at the end of the day. But, if the regions with special statute think they should keep silent in the meanwhile, this would be a very serious mistake. The life of autonomous regions, no matter which size or legal form they take, is made of permanent conflict with the Parliament, the government, the central administration. It's like driving a bike: if you quit pedalling, you'll lose the balance and fall. Thus, one should always keep the pressure high, set clear goals of increasing the autonomy in terms of quality and quantity, evaluate carefully what has been accomplished and never assume that such success will last for ever. History teaches that institutions are like human beings, they may decay and sometimes even disappear, or shift to completely different forms. This can happen for Italy's regions too, which today are already different compared with the first decades of the Republic. However, on one point I'm sure: nobody can remain in an isolated marginal position. The choice of other regions always have an influence on the general framework and a far-sighted leadership never will choose isolation, but stay in touch with the other entities.

7

A much-vaunted but incomplete autonomy: South Tyrol

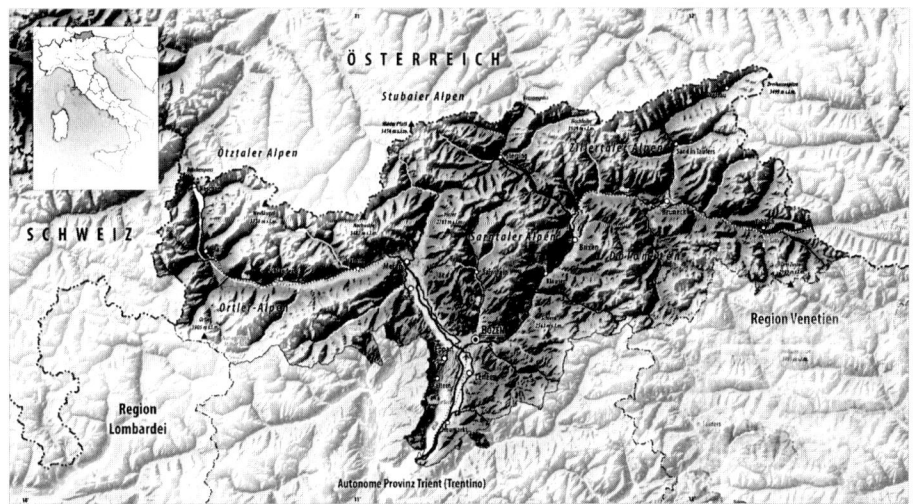

Source: wikipedia.org; author: Tschubby, CC-BY-SA 3.0

South Tyrol's autonomy is regarded worldwide as a model of territorial autonomy. Every year, scholars, journalists and delegations of ethnic minorities from numerous countries visit this province in Italy to learn about the development of this form of territorial autonomy on the spot. Researchers study the success factors, politicians praise the South Tyrol model and when the presidents of Austria and Italy meet, this autonomy is praised almost ritually. But is this territorial autonomy really as complete as it is usually presented to the outside world?

The 1972 Statute of Autonomy: a compromise

South Tyrol's autonomy is one of the few in the world based on an international treaty, namely the „Treaty of Paris" signed on 5 September 1946, which came into force in February 1947 as part of the peace treaty between Italy and Austria. Italy tried to fulfil its obligations under this treaty by means of the 1st Statute of Autonomy, which was adopted by the Constituent Assembly on 31 January 1948. Despite strong opposition from South Tyrolean representatives, this autonomy, which should have applied only to South Tyrol, was extended to the neighbouring Italian-speaking province of Trentino. The new region „Trentino-Tyrolean Etschland" had a clear Italian majority and was given far more power than the province of Bozen, the actual minority area. The 1st Autonomy Statute was a false start. The resistance of the South Tyroleans, some of which was articulated by force, led to years of unrest, then international negotiations and finally to a breakthrough: on 23 November 1969 the general assembly of the South Tyrolean People's Party (SVP) in Meran approved the new statute by a narrow majority.

The autonomy enshrined in the 2nd Autonomy Statute of 1972 was a compromise solution between the Italian state and the SVP. More than 20 years of tough negotiations between Bozen and Rome went by until this statute was converted into applicable law. Eventually in mid-1992, Italy and Austria before the UN were able to declare the dispute over South Tyrol to be settled. Even after the so-called declaration of dispute settlement, the autonomy of South Tyrol has continued to develop dynamically. The powers of the region and the two provinces were redefined, with the region being greatly undermined. A wealth of new provisions improved core areas of minority protection, for example in the education system, ethnic representation in public service, and in political decision-making processes. The new statute aimed on the one hand at the preservation and development of the two national minorities of South Tyrol, the German speaking South Tyroleans and the Ladins, and on the other hand at the functioning of territorial autonomy with consociational democracy mechanisms for the benefit of all inhabitants of the country.

49 years after the entry into force of the 2nd statute, the existence of the German and Ladin cultural community within Italy can no longer be considered as endangered. Since 1972 South Tyrol has experienced constant economic growth and a modernisation boom, also thanks to its autonomy, and has risen to become one of the most prosperous regions in Europe with a high quality of life. The state is no longer considered an enemy in South Tyrol, although there is a widespread unease with its centralist attacks, its cumbersome administrative apparatus and its complicated tax legislation. Added to this is the distrust of Italy's financial and economic stability, which is admittedly widespread not only in South Tyrol.

A majority of the Italian language group also welcomes the autonomy, which was not the case in 1972. If it is the minimum level of self-government for the South Tyroleans, it was then an inevitable compromise for the Italians of South Tyrol, which required the renunciation of a number of advantages and privileges. Later, all language groups and a steadily growing number of migrants since 1990 have benefited from the growth of the economy and employment, from a well-developed social system, a functioning civil service and a well-funded provincial administration.

The South Tyrol autonomy of 1972, based on the so-called "South Tyrol package", was a compromise between the SVP and the Italian state: numerous demands of the South Tyroleans remained unfulfilled or could not be enforced. The autonomous South Tyrol, for example, remained inserted into the unloved superstructure of the Trentino-Alto Adige region. Subsequently, the "package autonomy" was somewhat improved by means of implementing provisions and the direct transfer of responsibilities by the state. The status quo of the autonomy as in 1992 is guaranteed under international law, and further development is at the discretion of the Italian State. Restrictions, on the other hand, are legally questionable, but after 30 years of expansion (without any change in the Statute) this would in any case be a step backwards. EU law has also become increasingly evident as a legal limit and restriction on autonomous policy-making on provincial level.

Up to now, South Tyrol has not had a „general overhaul" of its Autonomy Statute as other autonomous regions in Europe (Catalonia, Åland, Greenland). As much as this autonomy is praised as a model: it is incomplete and in great need of reform. A reform of the 2nd Statute is therefore a question both of enshrining in the Statute what has been achieved since 1992 along with restoring previously lost competences and, finally, of extending the scope of the 1972 autonomy. The full potential of possible territorial autonomy under the Italian constitutional system is far from exhausted.

The 2001 constitutional reform: a double-edged sword

Following the comprehensive reform of the Italian Constitution in 1999 and 2001, the autonomous regions with special status have had to accept significant setbacks. This constitutional reform was intended to extend the powers of all the regions and limit the legislative powers of the State. Anything not expressly assigned to the State was to fall within the competence of the regions. More fiscal federalism should also be introduced. Any improvement in the status of the regions with ordinary statute which did not yet apply to the five autonomous regions of Italy should be automatically extended to them. The constitutional reform of 2001 gave the ordinary regions, in particular, the chance to extend their modest power. However, 20 years after this reform, not even the regions with ordinary statute in northern Italy, such as Lombardy, Veneto and Emilia-Romagna, have achieved this goal.

The 2001 constitutional reform was also used by the central state to encroach upon the exclusive competences of the autonomous provinces. The State was given so-called transversal competences whenever it was necessary to defend „national interests". These transversal powers, which are superior to autonomous law, allow the state legislator to intervene in the national competences in areas such as trade, tourism and public procurement, for example, for reasons of protection of competition. South Tyrol's autonomy has also been limited in administrative procedures, in regional urban planning and in the organisation of its staff. The central State's transversal responsibility for the protection of the environment and the ecosystem allows Rome to interfere in a number of exclusive provincial competences such as landscape conservation, civil protection and hunting. Through the back door, the legislative powers of all regions with special statutes were thus again restricted in favour of the central State.

The scope of regional legislative powers is at the heart of territorial autonomy. Since 1992, some powers have remained in place, others have been extended in some cases and others have been significantly reduced. In the case of state delegations, there have been increases in civil protection, road construction, the education system, the use of public waters, and hydroelectric power generation. However, competences just delegated by the state can also be revoked, as they have not yet been definitely entrenched in the Statute of Autonomy as original regional competences.

The constitutional reform of 2001 should also only have a positive effect on South Tyrol, for example by removing the prior control of provincial laws by the government. Nevertheless, this reform has had a negative impact on legislative and administrative autonomy, mainly due to the jurisdiction of the Constitutional Court. European Union law, for its part, has restricted the space of autonomous legislation by laying down rules on public procurement, trade, tourism and energy and, more generally, by requiring respect for fundamental freedoms and the general prohibition of discrimination on grounds of nationality. While on the one hand European Union law limits the extent of autonomous policy-making, it has also created new opportunities for cross-border cooperation through the European Grouping of Territorial Cooperation EGTC.

„Overall, the check on the state of autonomy has, in purely quantitative terms, produced a balanced picture between restrictions and extensions. However, it should be noted that qualitatively, the 2001 constitutional reform has brought about a significant change in favour of the requirements of the state legislator. Some of these restrictions could be reversed through implementing regulations in negotiations with Rome in 2016 and 2017, for example in regional planning, trade and hunting", Professors Happacher and Obwexer explained in a detailed expert opinion on the effects of the 2001 constitutional reform on the autonomy of South Tyrol (Happacher/Obexer, Innsbruck 2015). Thus, the full restoration of these competences is an important issue in negotiations on autonomy reform.

New attempts to reform the Autonomy Statute

The 2nd Autonomy Statute, the basis of South Tyrol's autonomy, in 2021 is 49 years old. The social, economic and cultural development of the province has not stood still since then. On the contrary: the overall context has changed in favour of South Tyrol. Austria joined the EU, the border beams at Brenner, Reschen and Winnebach fell in 1995 thanks to the Schengen Agreement and since 2001 Italy and Austria have been part of the euro zone. Also in 2001, Italy extended the autonomy of the regions with special status by a constitutional reform. However, the statute of the Autonomous Region Trentino-South Tyrol of 1972 has not been adapted or even renewed.

Autonomy did not remain static; instead, current issues often had to be resolved in the joint bilateral commissions, new legal aspects had to be dealt with in the context of the implementation of EU standards, and constitutional court rulings had to be reacted to by amending the existing law. South Tyrol's of both policy definition and practical implementation of solutions has thus partly been extended, partly - as for example with the new financial regulations for 2009 and 2014 - setbacks had to be accepted.

In South Tyrol today it is less a question of protecting minorities than of completing its scope of self-rule as an autonomous entity. In various areas, the autonomy of 1972 left much to be desired, and by far not all of the missing elements could be gained in the course of the SVP's policy of small steps. It is not without reason that the SVP presented a concept for achieving so-called full autonomy as early as September 2011. The autonomy of 1972 was to be substantially extended, leaving the central state with only the classic central government functions: judiciary, defence, foreign policy, monetary policy, the overarching economic policy and civil and criminal law. South Tyrol was also to be given the provincial police force, primary responsibility for the health system, the education system and fiscal sovereignty. "Full autonomy", as the SVP termed its proposal, initially remained an empty formula, which even the SVP representatives in the Roman parliament never made a condition of coalition agreement with the respective government majority.

In order to get down to business, the SVP senators submitted a draft constitutional law to Parliament in March 2013, which amends the majority of articles in the 1972 Statute of Autonomy of the Trentino-Alto Adige Region (newly introduced by the SVP senators as DDL No.43/2018 on 23.3.2018). Here are some essential points of this legislative proposal, which has not yet been dealt with:

- The Region Trentino-Alto Adige/Südtirol would become a mere „body for consultation, planning and coordination" of the two provinces, an institution without legislative powers.
- The statute would entrench the Province's competence to grant concessions for hydropower electricity generation. It would also take account of the liberalisation of the electricity market (Articles 12 and 13).
- The delegation of powers from the State to the province may be effected by Government decree. The two autonomous provinces Trent and Bozen may also delegate powers to the region, both legislative and administrative (Articles 17 and 18).
- Art. 19 on the education system would be rationalised and the principle of mother-tongue schools would be maintained, transferring education to the provinces as a primary power.
- The region would in future be financed by the two provinces and would no longer have its own revenues (Art.33).
- The revenues of the autonomous provinces would be reorganised: the provinces would assign to the State the shares of the tax revenues collected on their territories to which they are entitled, not the other way round as is currently the case (Art. 75).
- The provinces are given primary responsibility for municipal finances (Art. 38).
- For the Ladins, too, the so-called procedure for budget-guarantees would be established and a corresponding commission of the Provincial Assembly (Landtag) would exercise a right of veto (Art. 42).
- The government commissioner, no longer mandatory under the constitution since 2001, would be removed from the autonomy statute for the provinces

of Bozen and Trento. His powers would be transferred to the Governor, as is already the case in the Region of Valle d'Aosta (Art. 42 and 43).
- The provincial administrative court would also include a Ladin judge (art. 44).

While this draft law has been ignored in the Italian parliament so far, similar to other proposals by autonomous regions to reform their statutes, the South Tyrolean provincial assembly also wanted to make a new attempt at a general overhaul of the statute in 2015, with a new type of participatory democracy. For the first time, the reform of the Autonomy Statute was no longer to be negotiated only at the highest level in exclusive party and expert circles, but in a participatory process involving the citizens. The Provincial Assembly set up an „Autonomy Convention", in which citizens, experts and politicians were to work together to submit well-founded proposals for the reform of the Autonomy Statute of 1972.

The Autonomy Convention confirms the need for reform

On 16 January 2016, the Landtag opened this new participatory process. The convention was a novelty in the history of South Tyrol, also as a form of deliberative citizen participation. The Autonomy Convention was operative for one and a half years (February 2016 to September 2017). It was clearly evident that the topic of autonomy was of particular interest to German speaking South Tyroleans, far less to the members of the Italian speaking community and the Ladins. For one and a half years, this convention, composed by 33 members nominated by the Provincial Assembly, met and finally presented a comprehensive package of demands in September 2017. Naturally, it was not possible to reach a consensus across language groups, thus some Italian-speaking members of the Convention presented minority reports. However, this attempt to reform the Autonomy Statute with citizen participation has so far been in vain, as since September 2017 neither the Assembly nor the Regional Council has taken up the Convention's proposals in order to subsequently submit a joint proposal to the Italian Parliament based on the so-called regional initiative.

The final document of the autonomy convention has raised a broad public debate in South Tyrol's society. Later, the autonomy reform also played a minor role in the parliamentary elections in March 2018 and the provincial elections in autumn 2018. Neither the citizens nor the direct participants of the Convention and the Forum of 100 have so far urged the Provincial Assembly to finally start discussing their results. It looks as if a real Convention would have to consist of directly elected citizens in order to exert real pressure on representative bodies with democratic legitimacy.

The widespread desire among the South Tyrolean population for more autonomy and more democracy has, however, been very well articulated and has received broad support in the course of the 2016/17 Autonomy Convention. But that any of its proposals is will reach the parliament in Rome is still anyone's guess at the moment. It is not to be expected that the constitutional conditions will be created by the State to ensure that the will of the citizens is taken more seriously. In fact, there is one important element missing in Italy's general constitutional system for this: the statutory sovereignty (autonomia statutaria) of the regions with a special autonomy statute, i.e. the legal competence of these five regions to approve its own statute, which would subsequently after accordance with the national parliament would be adopted as a constitutional law.

The Autonomy Convention also proposed to grant South Tyrol a right to decide on its political status within the framework of its statute, in other words: the right of self-determination. Apart from the extremely slim chances of enforcing such a provision in the Parliament in Rome, this would require prior amendment of a central constitutional principle, namely the unity and indivisibility of the Republic (Article 5 of the Constitution), which is at the heart of the constitutional text.

Areas of South Tyrol's autonomy in need of reform

What is the need for reform of the autonomy of South Tyrol? The following is an incomplete list of single areas of the 2nd Autonomy Statute which, from the author's point of view, require amendments in order to extend the autonomy of the province of South Tyrol:

- The Ladin language group must be put on an equal footing with the larger two language groups in various respects. Despite some improvements since 2001, the Ladins are still not completely equal, e.g. there is still no clear-cut right of representation of the Ladin language group in the provincial government. Ladins are not represented neither in the administrative court nor in the supreme body of administrative judiciary of the state nor in the arbitration commission for the so-called balance guarantee in the South Tyrolean assembly.
- The transfer of the autonomous regulatory competence of the province in matters of direct democracy, citizen participation and voting rights is insufficiently regulated.
- In contrast to the regions with ordinary statute, Italy's regions with special statute do not have „statutory sovereignty" (the power to approve its own statute). Only the Parliament in Rome is authorised to amend the special statutes. Many autonomous regions, such as those of Spain and Denmark, have the right to draw up their own autonomy statute, which must subsequently be ratified by the respective national parliament.
- An important pillar of cultural autonomy and the protection of minorities is the local responsibility for education. South Tyrol also has only secondary competence in this area.
- South Tyrol can be constituted as a separate autonomous region independent of the Autonomous Province of Trento, with which it has been forced into a kind of forced marriage since 1948. The Autonomous Region of Trentino-Alto Adige has not only already lost most of its legislative and administrative duties, but is perceived by all German-speaking political forces in South

The opening session of South Tyrol's autonomy convention, EURAC Bozen, February 2016

Tyrol as an annoying block on the leg of the further expansion of autonomy. However, the Trentino province vehemently resists the further erosion or even abolition of the region.
- Ethnic proportional representation as a regulatory mode of equal access to the public service can be regulated more efficiently by introducing bilingual competition procedures for public service jobs.
- As an autonomous region, South Tyrol must be more effectively involved in the formation and implementation of European Union law insofar as its legal competences are affected.
- The government commissioner's office representing the Italian State can be abolished and its powers can be transferred to the Governor, as is the case in other Italian regions with special statutes.
- The financing of autonomy (the revenues of the Province of Bozen-South Tyrol) must be better secured by making the relevant agreements between the State and the Province a genuine part of the Statute of Autonomy.
- Since genuine tax autonomy of the autonomous province (as for example in the Basque Country and Navarre) seems illusory in Italy, South Tyrol should at least be given the responsibility for tax collection with autonomous tax offices. In addition, the Province may be given greater leeway in the collection of its own taxes.
- There is a great need to clear up the 1972 Statute of Autonomy, many of which have become obsolete as a result of legal and political developments over the last 49 years.
- South Tyrol must be explicitly excluded in the statute and national constitution from the application of the central state's right to intervention based on so-called transversal state competences.

- All competing legislative competences should become primary competences, for which only the constitution, international obligations and Union law should apply as barriers. This would largely eliminate a source of conflict between the central government and the autonomous province before the Constitutional Court.
- South Tyrol could be given more scope for action in external relations, following the example of the autonomous regions of Scandinavia: cross-border cooperation and the „European Grouping of Territorial Cooperation" could be strengthened. South Tyrol could be given the right to interact with the EU Commission itself, to engage in independent development cooperation, and to join international organisations in the field of sport and culture.
- South Tyrol could be substantially improved in the judiciary being given the power its own higher regional court, and thus be able to administer the judiciary more efficiently itself.
- The composition and functioning of the joint State-Province commissions must be more democratically regulated. As these commissions are quasi-legislative, they must be the an expression of the parliaments at national and state level and must be given more democratic legitimacy and transparency.
- Essential competences are still lacking in the field of economic and social policy.
- South Tyrol can retain primary competence for toponyms without being obliged to maintain the place names imposed during the Fascist period in 1922-1943.
- Austria's protective power function would be explicitly anchored in the preamble of the statute.

That this need for reform of the South Tyrolean autonomy statute exists is not only proven by the political practice of the past 29 years since the declaration of the settlement of disputes in 1992, which marked the time of the full implementation of the "South Tyrol package". Countless times up to 2001, the government in Rome directly vetoed provincial laws by refusing to approve them, and from 2001 onwards challenged them before the Constitutional Court. In the majority of these cases, the central government retained the upper hand. The need for reform is also clearly demonstrated by the SVP's draft Constitutional Law No 43/2018 on the amendment of the Statute, which was tabled in Parliament. The need for reform of the South Tyrolean autonomy is also demonstrated by the extensive catalogue of proposals contained in the final document of the South Tyrolean Convention, which met in Bozen from February 2016 to September 2017.

However, any reform of South Tyrol's autonomy must be based on a consent among the three ethnic groups of the Province. At least the majority of all three language groups should agree on the reform of the statute, because Rome will grant more autonomy the sooner all language groups pull together.

Now Austria and Italy have stated in the 1992 "Dispute Settlement Declaration" that Italy's obligations towards South Tyrol have been fulfilled. How, then, can an extension of the existing autonomy be justified? On the one hand, the very special position of South Tyrol in the Italian regional system is undisputable as its autonomy is guaranteed under international law, with a consociational democracy based on this principle of three distinct language groups. In addition, the Province has proven that it handles this autonomy responsibly, uses its resources efficiently, is concerned about equal rights between the language groups, and can thus cope with a higher level of self-government. A right to more autonomy also arises for democratic reasons. If a large majority of the country's population requests such an extension, the central government must take this into account. However, this political will must first be articulated on the ground, and democratically legitimised reform proposals must be driven forward by a broad political platform.

The example of South Tyrol also highlights a delicate aspect of any territorial autonomy: financing. Also thanks to a relatively favourable financing key combined with an efficient administration, the autonomous province has not only been able to successfully exercise its powers, but has also a steady economic growth that has made it the most prosperous province in Italy. However, funding can be unilaterally altered by the state without constitutional amendment, as it is not a fixed part of the Statute of Autonomy. This happened after the financial crisis of 2008/9, when South Tyrol was pushed to a new financial agreement with the government. Fundamental interests risk to be subordinated to the steady flow of flow of public revenues towards the region Trentino-South Tyrol and the two autonomous provinces, as the public funds available on regional level are the decisive lever for maintaining power. South Tyrol's public budget only to a very small share is fed by its own tax revenues. Any territorial autonomy must be based on a stable and secure financial foundation. Otherwise, there are two dangers: on the one hand, an autonomous province can be financially starved, on the other hand, it can become financially and thus also politically dependent. Both are dangerous for genuine political autonomy.

The example of South Tyrol's autonomy, in force since 1972, shows in many ways what modern territorial autonomy can achieve. On the other hand, even in this „showcase autonomy" the too narrow limits are clearly visible. In a comparison of the range of autonomous powers and the scope of internal self-rule of an autonomous entity, South Tyrol is at most in the upper middle range of the existing autonomy systems. South Tyrol is not the non-plus-ultra of autonomy, and a general overhaul of its statute is overdue. Proposals for this are on the table, a participation procedure for reform has already been initiated. But so far without result.

„We must have the courage to demand what we want".

An interview with Luis Durnwalder, former Governor of the Autonomous Province of South Tyrol

Born on 23 September 1941 in Pfalzen, Luis Durnwalder was director of the South Tyrolean Farmers' Union from 1968 to 1979, and mayor of Pfalzen from 1969 to 1973. Since 1973 member of the Provincial Assembly, from 1973 to 1978 Regional Assessor, from 1976 to 1978 Vice-President of the South Tyrolean Provincial Assembly, from 1979 to 1989 Provincial Minister for Agriculture and Forestry, Hunting and Fishing. Durnwalder was Governor of South Tyrol from 1989 to 2013. In the regional elections of 1998 and 2003, he was able to garner more than 100,000 preferential votes from South Tyroleans of all language groups. He was later also consulted as a mediator in several intra-state conflicts abroad.

The Autonomy Convention ended in September 2017, and since then there has been complete silence. As a member of the Convention of 33, you submitted a lot of proposals for the reform of the statute and were one of the most active members of the Convention. What will now become of the results of the Convention?

Durnwalder: A wrong assumption was made from the very outset. The current provincial governor thought that a reform proposal submitted by the Convention would immediately be approved by the provincial assemblies in Bozen and Trent and then submitted to the parliament in Rome. Then the Convention raised the bar higher than had been assumed. The Convention was nothing more than a stocktaking of the inadequacies of the current autonomy and the wishes of the people for further expansion. It raised the question: Where does autonomy need to be completed? In the SVP, one believes that many of these demands will not pass in Trent, first of all the deconstruction of the region. But they don't have the courage to say: this is what our people want and this is what we demand. But as early as 1992, we agreed to the declaration of settlement of the international dispute on the condition that it would be possible to continue in the form of a dynamic autonomy. To this day, far too little use has been made of this possibility.

„Get rid of Trent" was the slogan of the large-scale rally at Sigmundskron in

1957. With the 2nd Statute in 1972, this was only partially achieved. Should South Tyrol become its own autonomous region and how could this be enforced against the Trentino province?

Durnwalder: In its current form, the region Trentino-South Tyrol no longer has any meaning. Today it is just a legally protected sink of public money. Of course we need to cooperate with Trentino, but this does not have to be done by force through this empty box, but can also be carried out voluntarily by the two provinces. One should have the courage to demand a region of South Tyrol on its own and a separate region of Trentino. All competences remaining with the current region should be transferred to the two new regions. Originally, one wanted to be sure that only South Tyrol would get autonomy. Then Degasperi prevailed, who also wanted to give autonomy to Trentino. Today people no longer have the courage to demand the abolition of the region.

Is Trentino's fear of losing its special autonomy if the region is abolished justified?

Durnwalder: Trentino clings to South Tyrol because it assumes that this is the only way to preserve its autonomy. But the Trentino people would also have to muster as much will to assert themselves as all the other autonomous regions in Italy and Europe, which have no international protection of their autonomy, but are at least secured by the constitution. The Trentino people must stand up for their rights themselves and not just rely on getting everything that South Tyrol gets in terms of autonomy rights. South Tyrol is a different reality. As SVP we have tried everything to undermine the region. After 1992, more competences have been delegated from the region to the two provinces, such as the fire brigade, the credit system, the chamber of commerce. Some things have been improved by the constitutional reform of 2001, and now the two provinces together form the region and not vice versa. I am in favour of the autonomy of Trentino and of cooperation with Trentino. When two political institutions pull together, it is easier, but not in a forced association like the current region.

The constitutional reform of 2001 has also brought disadvantages to South Tyrol. One has the impression that in the development of autonomy one always takes one step forward and one step back....

Durnwalder: Since the constitutional reform of 2001, autonomy has been silently eroded. Professors Happacher and Obwexer proved in a 600-page expert report from 2014 that autonomy has been restricted in various areas since then. In some areas there has been an increase, but in others there has been regression. The so-called transversal state competences have turned out to be a real stumbling block. On the basis of overriding principles, e.g. protection of competition or protection against discrimination, the state can restrict competences in trade, in public procurement and even in administrative procedures, in building law and in other areas. One has, for example, invented the transversal state competence of environmental protection. Thus hunting has been allocated to environmental protection. Thus, South Tyrol's primary competence for hunting has been restricted and subordinated to this superior state competence. These transversal competences have led to more and more legal challenges of our provincial laws before the Constitutional Court and in most cases since 2001 the government has had the upper hand.

How should South Tyrol autonomy be expanded? What should be expanded?

Durnwalder: For South Tyrol, one must abolish the national interest. To avoid conflicts between the state and the province, all concurrent or shared competences should be transformed into primary ones. All new substantive issues should be transferred to the province. In the 1960s, certain political subject areas did not even exist, for example in the energy sector, in environmental and climate protection, even in telecommunications: nobody talked about broadband connections back then. What is being done about the postal service, for example? Eight years ago, we were already much further ahead than we are today. If we had jurisdiction over the post office, we could run it much better. The Carabinieri could also become the provincial police, although other departments of the state police could well remain with the state to fight crime. It is the same with the public service broadcasting RAI. After the first attempt to take over RAI, nothing happened, even though we already pay 20 million a year for RAI services according to the Milan Agreement. But what we need is an independent regional broadcaster with an independent board of directors.

Will the regions with a special statute have to wait until the northern Italian regions with an ordinary statute have received their „differentiated" autonomy first?

Durnwalder: We must support every initiative towards federalisation or regionalisation of Italy. The central state should cede more competences to all regions. At the moment, however, we are experiencing a centralist spirit. Since 2001, there has been talk of transferring important competences to regions, for example in the police, health and education. In the state-region conference, I raised the question of whether South Tyrol could then form its own regional police force. The Lega ministers at the time immediately back-pedalled. The 2001 reform also provided for the most-favoured-clause: all that the regions with ordinary statutes receive should also be given to the autonomous regions. But this only happened in part. Today, these projects to strengthen the regions are stuck. The opposite of federalisation is happening, namely more centralisation, and this also affects South Tyrol.

How should South Tyrol proceed with the reform of the autonomy statute? Should all regions with a special statute stand together for more autonomy or should they march separately?

Durnwalder: It is imperative to resume negotiations with Rome. Essential questions are at stake. We must have the courage to put legitimate demands on the table. We should create an additional level in the negotiation strategy. In Italy's current situation, there are actually three different types of regions. Some regions with an ordinary statute want to increase their competences. Then there are four regions with special statute with their needs, and then as a special case the Trentino and South Tyrol, because our autonomy was created on the basis of an international treaty. The constitution can be amended at will, but international treaties must be respected. All the autonomy granted until 1992 must remain in place unless Austria agrees to change it. We have a different legal basis, because the other regions with a special statute rely only on the constitution. Thus, we have to negotiate on three levels. If we negotiate separately, our autonomy tends to be extended, because the state does not feel obliged to grant the same extensions to all the other regions with a special statute. If we negotiate together, then all negotiating partners will receive just as much or just as little.

Does South Tyrol need the sovereignty for approving its own statute, like the autonomous communities of Spain, for example, which are allowed to negotiate their statutes with the central parliament?

Durnwalder: We don't have a provincial constitution in that sense, but the autonomy statute forms part of the constitution. If we see that Trento does not go along with new demands, we would still have to clearly articulate our ideas. In this case, a cuddly approach is useless. In any case, we need the support of the people. If there is no pressure from below, then the political representatives will also have a harder time asserting this at the negotiating table. As a rule, not everything is conceded immediately, but gradually. In the 1990s, we only received more rights and responsibilities because we demanded it.

In 2013 and then again in 2018, the SVP tabled a constitutional bill in parliament to reform the Statute of Autonomy, which amends the Statute in the majority of its articles. The chances of it coming up in this legislature are slim. But why is the SVP not campaigning for this bill to be dealt with?

Durnwalder: One must have the courage to make the treatment of this proposal a precondition for coalitions in Rome. You won't get anywhere with a cuddly approach. The SVP should make it clear: we support this or that government, but these are our demands. If there is no willingness to negotiate, then we cannot support the government.

Funding is a sticking point of any autonomy. You achieved the Milan Agreement in 2009. In 2014 Kompatscher negotiated the so-called safeguard agreement, with which South Tyrol seems to be able to cope well. Today, a net 72-73 percent of the state's tax revenue collected in our territory remains in the province. In 2022, this agreement must be renegotiated. Would it be a success to go on with the current mode?

Durnwalder: It was a step forward in 2009 to define exactly which state revenues we participate in. In the meantime, the state taxes are collected from us, our share remains in the province and the share due to Rome is passed on. But actually, the tax agencies should also be transferred to the autonomous province. Moreover, the current statute already provides for us to have a say in the collection of taxes. However, this has never been implemented. With the 2014 safeguard pact, we are also contributing our share to the consolidation of the state budget. This mode can also be continued, but the conditions imposed by the state in terms of the stability pact must be dropped. We must be able to manage the province's revenues according to our own political preferences.

You were a member of the Committee of the Regions (CoR) of the EU representing South Tyrol for 20 years. The Committee of the Regions has repeatedly called for more co-determination rights and complained that the regions have too little influence in EU policy. How could the Committee of the Regions be upgraded? How can it actually be involved in EU legislation?

Durnwalder: Initially, I assumed that we would be able to submit initiative motions to the EU-Council and European Parliament on behalf of the regions. The CoR should have its own say in EU directives and regulations. I thought I could make a difference, but I was sorely disappointed. I found out that the CoR is not taken seriously, but is more of a fig leaf. There is no real participation. The role of the regions in the EU should be significantly strengthened. We also need a reform of the Parliament, the Council and the Commission, which means: the separation of powers in the EU as a whole needs to be reorganised. But even if the CoR is strengthened, a major problem remains: the regions are positioned very differently in the EU at national level. A considerable number of EU members have no regions with legislative power at all. Centralist states like France and Romania have yet to implement such reforms.

Is it therefore pointless to set up a kind of third chamber of the regions alongside the Parliament and the Council as long as not all EU member states have regions with legislative sovereignty?

Durnwalder: Germany and Austria have proposed to form a separate EU committee only of legislative regions, but they did not get their way. In the CoR, we assumed we would be a fully-fledged EU institution alongside the Parliament and the Commission. But this is not the case. Moreover, the CoR brings together a wide range of local and regional authorities, including municipalities and cities. But often the regions are superordinate to the municipalities as direct supervisory bodies, as is the case here in South Tyrol. In that case, there is no need for the subordinate regional authorities to have their own representation in the same EU committee.

The Dalai Lama has been a guest of yours several times. South Tyrol has actively supported the Tibetan government-in-exile in its proposal for genuine autonomy for Tibet within China. But does that even go together: a democratically governed autonomous region in an authoritarian state system?

Durnwalder: The Dalai Lama described the South Tyrolean autonomy model as largely transferable to Tibet. He assumed at the time that China could grant Tibet a kind of partial sovereignty. The government-in-exile later stopped insisting on any kind of sovereignty, but only on genuine autonomy, also hoping of a democratisation of the Chinese state as a whole in the long term. Meanwhile, China is pumping more and more Chinese immigrants into Tibet, which will sooner or later make Tibetans a minority in their own country. Then even a referendum on the status of the Tibet Autonomous Region would no longer make sense.

You have been invited by the self-declared republics of Donetsk and Luhansk in eastern Ukraine as a mediator. With what result?

Durnwalder: In the Donbass, Russia could actually be the protecting power of the Russian ethnic group, but there is no bilateral treaty there. The Russians make up at least two thirds of the population there and demand a special status for the Donbass. At the time, I asked to be invited as a mediator by both the EU and Russia. When I received that, I flew in via Moscow to reach the crisis area. That is why I am now persona non grata in Ukraine. Ukraine has officially protested to the Italian Foreign Minister against my visit. Yet in my proposals I have always advocated the preservation of Ukraine's full sovereignty. The Russians of Donetsk and Luhansk would be in favour of autonomy, but not a second-tier autonomy. The president of this self-declared republic told me: we want a sovereign state. I suggested that Donetsk and Luhansk should rather become autonomous sub-territories of Ukraine with a special status, and that one should strive for an agreement with Ukraine. However, in the whole Ukraine issue, the dispute between the USA and Russia plays a decisive role, and that makes a solution more complicated.

International protection and Austria's role as a protecting power were also decisive for the success of South Tyrol's autonomy. Only very few autonomous regions can count on such a kind of protection. Could the international organisations play as a substitute guarantee powers for autonomy?

Durnwalder: There is no doubt that we have achieved more than the others. This was not solely due to us, but also because the situation is different. We have the advantage that as a national minority we have the majority in South Tyrol and that our autonomy is entrenched on international level. In many other regions, the ethnic groups or minorities have no outside support behind them. Now there are various conventions for the protection of minorities both in Europe and worldwide. But these are interpreted by states entirely as they see fit. The same applies to the protection of indigenous peoples, where states do not consistently implement their obligations. There, it is up to the organisations themselves to show claws. The Council of Europe has always had the courage to adopt various innovations. But this is received and implemented very differently by the member states.

In 2014 and 2017, there were two important referendums in autonomous regions in Europe: Catalonia and Scotland. In Scotland, legally in line with the central state and against independence in the result; in Catalonia, legally not in line with the Spanish constitution, but for independence in the result. Today, in 2020, there seems to be a majority for statehood in both cases. How can these two conflicts be resolved?

Durnwalder: These conflicts can only be resolved in agreement with the state, or with a state with a protecting power function. The majority of Catalans are

Luis Durnwalder in one of his weekly press conferences as Landeshauptmann (chief minister of the Autonomous Province of South Tyrol). Foto: Thomas Benedikter

certainly in favour of independence. But if the central state does not agree, the whole process is blocked constitutionally, even if a clear majority in the region votes for independence. So one has to create clear legal conditions. If one were to hold a referendum today on the political status of South Tyrol, the result would depend entirely on whether the legal framework is constitutionally correct and the result is also implemented. If this is not clearly regulated, no large voter turnout can be expected in such referendums, and no majority will be reached. But if Austria and Italy reach an agreement on implementation beforehand, there would be a majority for Austria. I am convinced of that. But the parties would have to show their colours. If it is not ensured that a referendum is fully implemented, the majority would rather be for stability, i.e. for the status quo.

In a global perspective territorial autonomy has been given in very few cases. Only broad political movements of minorities have succeeded in making progress. Today, various regions are fighting for autonomy, such as the Szeklerland in Romania, the Corsicans in France, the Kurds in Turkey and Syria. How can autonomy be wrested from these states?

Durnwalder: Only if the people of these regions have the courage to stand up again after defeats and persistently continue to stand up for it. We South Tyroleans have not allowed ourselves to be discouraged and have sought allies. Thus, with time, the realisation could mature among the states: we have to do something, for our own benefit and inner peace. This will always be difficult with authoritarian nation states like Turkey, because the framework conditions are different. South Tyrol is an example of how minority problems can be solved, but certainly not the only example. Unfortunately, we still have the old centralist spirit in many countries in Europe, but there are also opportunities for autonomy. It takes patience, perseverance and tenacity to push it through.

Reserves for indigenous peoples of America

Ethnic reservations or territorial autonomy?

88 deputies representing 110 communities of the Navajo Nation meet regularly in the round pavilion of the Council building in Window Rock, the capital of the Navajo Reservation in Arizona. Partly in the Navajo language, the deputies debate current issues and new regulations for their people. In 1991, the Reservation Statute was revised and now provides for a clear separation of powers between government, legislative body and judiciary. The Navajo Reservation has a considerable range of political responsibilities, from health care, education and social welfare to police and local jurisdiction. Between plenary sessions of the Navajo Nation Council (National Council), 12 standing commissions deal with these areas and subjects. The Navajo reservation is Arizona's only reservation originally established by contract. In fact, it is older than the state of Arizona itself, which only became the 48th state in 1912. At 67,339 km2, the Navajo Reservation is also the largest in the USA, almost as large as Bavaria, but sparsely populated with only 270,000 inhabitants. The reserve has existed in this extension since 1923, when more and more oil companies wanted to lease Navajo land for oil exploration. The reserve has become a model of Indian self-government. Is this kind of autonomy not equivalent to that of South Tyrol and many other territorial autonomies? What distinguishes a reserve from a modern territorial autonomy?

Reserves: own territory „on revocation"

Most of the indigenous peoples of North America now live on reservations with special legal status. They cover barely 2,3 percent of the land area of the United States (about 225,000 km2), but most reservations are quite small. 65 percent of the reservations are smaller than 100 km2, and only 7 percent are larger than 2,500 km2. On the other hand, nine of the 304 reservations exceed the smallest US state of Delaware (5,375 km2). In 2016, 566 Indian peoples were legally recognized at the federal level, but only 304 have their own reservation. A slight majority of the two million or so Indians in the USA (0,6 percent of the total population) live outside the reservations, mainly in the cities.

In the 1980s and 1990s, thanks to some reforms, the Indians were able to recover some 15,400 km2 of lost land. 93 percent of the reservations are now located in just 11 US states, mainly in the southwest (Arizona, Utah, Montana and South Dakota), while only 3 percent of these reservations are located east of the Mississippi River. The expansion of the white settlers has ended, but the Indian nations have been pushed into the most inhospitable and barren areas of the USA. The formerly self-sustaining and sustainable economy of the Indians has been destroyed and this has made most reservations dependent on public subsidies and their inhabitants dependent on social benefits.

The idea of Indian reservations in the USA goes back to the time of segregation politics before independence declared in 1776. As the USA expanded westward, the Native Americans were forced into remote and inhospitable areas. The long process of Indian resettlement began in the 1820s and continued until the end of the 19th century. Increasingly, the US government took steps to establish reservations where the surviving Native Americans would live in small areas under the supervision of the US Army and a new Native American administration. Thus, the First Nations finally lost their status as nominally sovereign nations with the right to self-determination. Most reservations were established in the second half of the 19th century on the basis of treaties with the US government. The Indian peoples were given the right to a „territory revoked", and Washington quite often revoked land rights that had been contractually guaranteed in advance. The lion's share of the Indian land had been annexed or privatised by the state and sold for individual ownership, often resulting in its subsequent resale to non-Indians.

The ability of Native Americans to actually rule on their own is limited. The right of a tribe to self-government is called „inherent" on the one hand, and „residual" on the other. In practice, these legal terms mean that Indians' rights are limited to those areas that have not yet been taken away from them by the US Congress. The power of Congress over First Nations reservations is further defined as „comprehensive" (plenary). This means that Congress is also able to break treaties and dissolve tribal governments or entire reservations.

Strong external control even today

Today it is part of the normal picture of the US reservations of native Americans that local police and civil courts, housing programmes and health care are run directly by the reservation. However, the Bureau of Indian Affairs (BIA) still has an important influence on the use of the reserves' natural resources. Indian land, with all its natural resources, is the property of the state, and is left to the Indians only for their use. 10 percent of gas and oil reserves, 33 percent of low-sulphur coal reserves and 55 percent of uranium in the USA are on Indian land (cf. Klaus Frantz 1995, 40). Within the Indian reservations, 80 percent of the land is still tribal owned property, while 19 percent is private property, owned by individual Indians but also by non-Indian private owners. The remaining one percent belongs to the federal government, mostly for public infrastructure and services such as roads, schools, hospitals. Neither the individual owner nor the titular tribe of the reservation are allowed to sell the land, but in return they are exempt from the property tax levied by the states. A large portion of the reservation land is now leased to white US citizens or agricultural companies.

Over the last 30 years, the indigenous nations have sought not only to consolidate their land holdings, but also to preserve the remaining elements of their political sovereignty and traditional rights to exploit the resources of their territories. Such rights had often been enshrined in treaties, for example in the use

The Parliament of the Navajo nation in Window Rock (Arizona)

of watercourses. But Indians continue to clash with white farmers and other interests under strong state pressure. An important goal of the policy of the Indian nations was not only to preserve and revitalise their cultural heritage, but also to prevent the further fragmentation of their land due to the division of inheritance.

What are reservations from a legal point of view?

From a legal point of view, there are different types of reserves. The most important is the Treaty Reservation on public land, which is granted by the US government to a recognised people or tribe. The second most important form is a reservation that is privately owned by the Native Americans.

What legal sovereignty do Indians have within the reservations? Although all reservations belong to one of the 50 member states of the United States, they are not subject to the political, administrative and tax systems of the respective state. Reserves also have their own system of jurisdiction. To this day they have been able to preserve some elements of their former sovereignty. They are not integrated into the political system of the districts (county), nor do they elect their own members of parliament, neither to the parliament of the respective state nor to the federal parliament, the US Congress in Washington. The members of the reservations elect the „Tribal Council" and a governor or president. The administrative authorities of the Reserves issue regulations that apply to all residents of the Reserves, regardless of their membership of a First Nation. However, it is quite complicated for non-Indians to even obtain permission to settle within a reserve. Indians are entitled to vote as US citizens, but as resident on a Reservation they do not participate in any state political election, only for US federal authorities.

Although the Indian reservations are often not compact, geographically contiguous and ethnically homogeneous territorial units, they form separate territories in terms of tax legislation, administration and political participation (right to vote, political representation bodies). The remaining sovereignty of the First Nations is mainly reflected in the political system, tax legislation and local jurisdiction. In principle, the inhabitants of a reserve are exempt from state and federal taxes, but not completely. For those US states with a larger share of reserve land, this tax exemption of the reserves means a considerable loss of property tax revenue. Members of an Indian nation are also exempt from federal taxes, while white landowners within a reservation must pay US taxes. On the other hand, reservations are allowed to collect their own taxes within certain limits.

There are also some relics of former sovereignty in the jurisdiction. Since the „Termination Law" of 1953, the reservation courts have largely been replaced by state courts. But in some other states, such as Arizona, Nevada, Colorado, New Mexico, Utah, Wyoming and Dakota, Indians have their own status due to the special legal relationship between the reservations and the federal government. Reserves have their own tribal courts with jurisdiction for minor crimes with the possibility of appeal to a federal court. However, US courts have ruled that Indian tribes may not exercise jurisdiction over US citizens who live on the reservation and have purchased land.

From these considerations, it can be concluded that the US reservations - and this also applies to a large extent to Canada - do not constitute territorial autonomies in the sense of the criteria applied here. The main differences lie in the political representation at regional and state level and in the special „ethnic reservation citizenship", which is linked to membership of a recognised tribe. Furthermore, in the USA there is no constitutional basis for the territorial autonomy of the Indian reservations. Some parts of their territory, which belong to certain legal categories, can also be sold in private property transactions. Thus, although America's reservations share some basic characteristics of classical territorial autonomies, some essential aspects are regulated differently compared to the new territorial autonomies of indigenous peoples in Canada (Nunavut, Yukon), in Nicaragua (Caribbean regions), in Europe (Greenland). More closely related is the system of US reservations with the territorial autonomies of India and the preferential status of „scheduled tribes" (recognised tribal communities).

Ethnic autonomy differs from territorial autonomy

The US and Canadian reservations are based on the concept of „ethnic autonomy", which grants exclusive self-government to an indigenous ethnic group in an area. This is done with good reason and according to democratic and constitutional principles. This means that democratic participation and political representation is reserved for the members of the titular ethnic group to be protected. Only tribal people can claim these political rights, while non-indigenous US citizens or Canadians can move into a reservation and settle down with some effort, but are not granted political rights. This arrangement is a safeguard that is perfectly justified in light of the history of North American Indians. The Native Americans, and only they, should be able to govern themselves in the last territories remaining under their responsibility, within the limits of their competences. No non-Indians should be allowed to have a say in this. For their part, the citizens of the reservation do not or hardly care about the fate of the USA. The influx of non-Indians into these reservations is also strictly controlled and is only possible to a very limited extent.

This is not the case in modern territorial autonomies. Every other citizen and, within the EU, every other EU citizen can move to the respective autonomous region on the basis of freedom of establishment. Third-country nationals can also settle anywhere in the EU as legal migrants, whether autonomous or not. National citizens and EU citizens can exercise their electoral and representation rights everywhere, at least at local level, if necessary after a short transitional period.

In principle, modern territorial autonomies are open: Immigration and emigration can only be encouraged or limited by social and economic incentives and measures. The regulation of citizenship law is in the hands of the state. Only the autonomous Åland Islands have so far been able to introduce their own „regional citizenship". The lack of control over migration can also be to the disadvantage of an ethnic minority in an autonomous region. The state can, regardless of the objections of local politicians, promote immigration to the autonomous region in a targeted and massive manner in order to outnumber a minority on its traditional territory. The Papuan people in West Papua (Indonesia) and the indigenous peoples of the Chittagong mountain areas (Bangladesh), the Sahrawi people in Western Sahara, the Uighurs and Mongols in the People's Republic of China have thus become a minority in their own country, despite formal autonomy. Ethnic autonomy is therefore legitimate in order to provide effective long-term protection for indigenous peoples on their territory. The citizens of a modern territorial autonomy, on the other hand, are not subject to any ethnic „club pressure" and mostly form inclusive regional communities. They form a territorially based community whose ethnic composition may also change, but which is in principle open to immigration from the rest of the national territory and from abroad. Reserves for indigenous people are areas reserved for the titular ethnic group, who exercise exclusive political power linked to the ethnicity of their voters and elected representatives for their protection.

8

Conflict resolution through autonomy: Northern Ireland

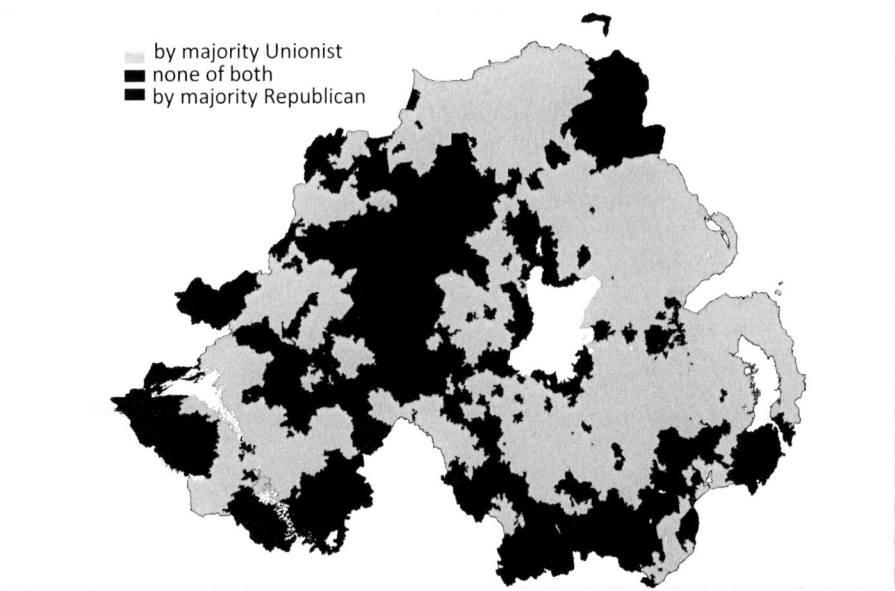

Predominant national identity in Northern Ireland in 2011 (Census data). Source: Wikimedia, author: SkateTier - Own work, CC BY-SA 3.0,

For Ireland 1921 was the year of partition. In 1920 the British Parliament passed the "Government of Ireland Act", which came into force on 3 May 1921 dividing the island and creating Northern Ireland. In June 1921 Northern Ireland's first devolved government was formed, but hardly it can be termed as a "modern territorial autonomy". After the civil war of 1921-22 this part of Ireland was ruled by the Unionist majority, causing growing discontent and frustration among the Catholic Irish. Eventually, for more than 30 years Northern Ireland has experienced one of the most violent conflicts in post-war Europe. Between 1969 and 1998 the politically motivated violence in Northern Ireland, the Troubles, claimed at least 3.245 victims. The conflict had its roots in the subjugation and colonisation of Ireland by the Britishers, the partition of 1921, the tensions between Protestant unionists and Irish nationalists, the way in which the United Kingdom ruled this part of the country. Northern Ireland for decades has been the epitome of a divided society, a bitter conflict between two opposing camps, a symbol of terrorist violence and harsh military repression by an EU member state at home. The political affiliation of the northern part of Ireland was at stake: Unionists fought to remain with Britain, while the majority Catholic republicans fought to reunite Northern Ireland with the Republic of Ireland. Since the Good Friday Agreement of 1998 and the granting of autonomy to Northern Ireland, the bloody conflict has not been finally resolved but has shifted to a political level.

Breakthrough with the Good Friday Agreement

The peace process in Northern Ireland began back in 1991 when the British Secretary of State for Northern Ireland, Peter Brooke, launched all-party talks, excluding Sinn Féin. This was the first step towards the Belfast Agreement. Finally, in 1998, after almost thirty years of bloody conflict, representatives of the opposing camps met under the mediation of the USA and Ireland to negotiate a peaceful solution to the conflict. The process culminated in the „Good Friday Agreement", which was signed on 10 April 1998 by the main parties on both sides. It leads to the creation - in fact a revival - of a national parliament with broad powers and a consociational form of shared responsibility in government. The agreement reached had to be confirmed in a referendum in both Northern Ireland and the Republic of Ireland. In the Republic of Ireland the Treaty was approved by a large majority.

In Northern Ireland the strongest Unionist force in the country, the Democratic Unionist Party (DUP), opposed the agreement. In the end, supporters won by 71 percent of the popular vote, although the Protestants' support was only just over 50 percent. This clear „yes" from the electorate gave the Good Friday Agreement lasting political legitimacy. Violence fell massively and, step by step, constructive relations were established between the opposing groups. The example of Northern Ireland shows that referendums can also make a decisive contribution to the sustainable defusing of conflicts. If a negotiated solution receives broad support from both parties to the conflict, the opposition, on the other hand, loses momentum right from the start.

Disarmament and police reform

Disarmament was an important part of the peace process. An international commission (Commission for Decommissioning) had to oversee the disarmament of the paramilitary units, but this was very slow. Why? Neither side wanted to take the first step. The IRA felt that disarmament was a kind of surrender. Moreover, many feared the resumption of armed struggle. Finally, there were also groups that completely refused to renounce violence. The Provisional IRA is the only organisation that has surrendered its entire arsenal of weapons. The issue of disarmament has been the biggest stumbling block in the formation of the Northern Ireland governments and for the whole peace process.

It was not until July 2005 that the British government began to normalise security arrangements. The military was partly withdrawn and many security installations were dismantled. Northern Ireland was gradually demilitarised. The British army left the task of maintaining internal security to the new autonomous police force. Today all Irish people can move freely around the island and do not have to fear constant harassment from the British military or police. Terrorist attacks have almost ceased. During the period of violence, even going out in the evening and attending a cultural event was a risky business.

The Belfast Agreement paved the way for the reform of the Northern Ireland police force, which before 1998 had only been accepted by the Protestant community. The Irish Republican side had demanded the disbanding of the police units and the establishment of a completely new autonomous police force. Finally, the British police, supported by the army, had been perceived as an essential and partisan player in the Northern Ireland conflict. An important step towards this was the increased recruitment of Catholics as police officers. This was followed by a new name, new uniforms, new vehicles: the Police Service of Northern Ireland (PSNI) also changed its face externally. Overall the police reform was a real success story. In January 2007 even Sinn Féin supported the new police force and stated that the PSNI could be trusted. Cooperation between the community and the police has improved considerably and today the police force is accepted in both communities.

More trust through independent courts and human rights commissions

The Human Rights Commission and the Equality Commission of Northern Ireland have rewritten basic rules of coexistence between the two communities, thereby making a significant contribution to peace. The institutional role of the Human Rights Commission is to uphold human and civil rights and prevent discrimination. Police training, school programmes on peace education and human rights and the drafting of a Charter of Fundamental Rights for Northern Ireland are just some of its achievements. But it also cares about migrants and the rights of other vulnerable groups. This has allowed a culture of human rights to gradually develop in Northern Ireland.

The Equality Commission for Northern Ireland (ECNI) is another public institution crucial for the peace process. It fights discrimination and unequal treatment, especially between Protestants and Catholics, and should restore confidence in the institutions and between groups. Former prisoners were also involved in this process, and the willingness to engage in conflict between Catholics and Protestants did indeed gradually diminish. However, the two groups remained essentially separate and Northern Ireland's society remains deeply divided. Today, this Commission also addresses the rights of other minorities such as homosexuals, LGBTs and migrants. Unequal treatment of this kind still exists in Northern Ireland society and its work is far from over.

The Good Friday Agreement has partially transferred jurisdiction to the Autonomous Region. Its transparency and accountability has improved considerably since then. This step has also strengthened the population's confidence in the judiciary and in public institutions as a whole. The first concern was the large number of prisoners from the Troubles. According to the Belfast Agreement, paramilitary prisoners had to be released early from prison. This was essentially a concession to the respective paramilitary organizations, but was essential to secure the entire peace process. Without this reintegration of the prisoners of both sides, the Belfast Agreement would probably not have been concluded.

The majority of the prisoners were able to return home, some even devoted themselves to conflict transformation and peace work, were involved in youth work and in improving relations between the two communities.

Reconciliation: a long process

Dealing with the violence of the past can only be tackled with functioning institutions in stable political conditions. Right after 1998 it was too early to embark on reconciliation between the two communities. It is difficult to judge whether reconciliation and harmony have really taken root in Northern Ireland's society. There is no doubt that a degree of rapprochement and reconciliation at the elite level has taken place. After all, since May 2007, the former arch-enemies DUP and Sinn Féin have been ruling together. Cooperation works far less at the grassroots and middle levels, e.g. in the field of civil associations. Most people still live in separate settlement areas, and more than 90 percent of the pupils attend schools separated by denomination. People meet at work, at the university, the young generation also in joint clubs where politics hardly plays a role. Complete reconciliation needs time, patience and commitment.

Overall, most of the provisions of the Good Friday Agreement have actually been implemented: the peace process in Northern Ireland has been a success. On 10 December 1998, David Trimble of the Protestant UUP, together with John Hume (Republican SDLP), was awarded the Nobel Peace Prize on behalf of all the actors in the Northern Ireland peace process, including the governments of Britain and Ireland as well as Gerry Adams and Martin McGuinness, who played a major role in the IRA ceasefire.

The autonomy of Northern Ireland

From 1921 to 1972 there had already been a „Parliament of Northern Ireland" with limited powers. The Catholics, however, were severely disadvantaged in this assembly. After the „Bloody Sunday" in March 1972 it was suspended and dissolved in 1973. Northern Ireland was governed directly from London from 1972 to 1990. The „Northern Ireland Assembly", the Northern Ireland Parliament in the Stormont district of Belfast, has extensive legislative powers in all those areas not reserved for the British Parliament. It elects the government of the Autonomous Region. It was created by the 1998 Good Friday Agreement and met for the first time on 1 July 1998. Each member of Parliament must register at the beginning of the parliamentary term in one of three groups: unionists, nationalists and others. A member of Parliament may not change group more than once per term of office. In 2020, there are currently 40 unionists, 39 nationalists and 11 others in the Stormont Parliament. The party landscape is traditionally sectarian, while the British parties play hardly any role at all.

There are three areas of autonomous powers: delegated competence lies exclusively with the Northern Ireland Assembly; „reserved" competences are still

Northern Ireland's Parliament in Stormont, Belfast

exercised by Westminster but can be delegated to Northern Ireland; and exceptional competences are reserved for London. Only foreign and defence policy, citizenship, immigration and asylum, state taxation, electoral law, currency and succession to the throne remain with the State. There are only exclusive powers and no powers shared between Belfast and London. The powers not yet transferred remain with the State. Northern Ireland's autonomy is guaranteed not only by national law but also by international law. The UK-Ireland Agreement was signed by Northern Ireland, the United Kingdom and the Republic of Ireland.

The Northern Ireland Assembly operates under the principle of concordance (consociational model). The vast majority of the 90 MPs are in the governing coalition, currently 82 out of 90 MPs from 5 parties: two unionist, two nationalist and 1 other. The First Minister and his Deputy are elected by concordance. The rest of the ministers are not elected; instead, the governing parties propose a number of members of the government corresponding to their number of MPs. Every time this political agreement could not be established, the region fell into a political crisis, for example from October 2002 to May 2007. The Northern Ireland Government was suspended several times, and the region was then governed directly from London. The region came to a standstill again in 2017. Only when the British and Irish prime ministers considered new elections in January 2020 as the only way out, the parties in Northern Ireland agreed on a new government. In the 2019 general election, the Republican parties won more seats than the Unionists for the first time in history.

The key elements of conflict resolution

Although the Good Friday Agreement has significant shortcomings and the Northern Ireland Parliament was suspended four times, it was fully implemented after 10 years. Sinn Féin and the DUP, the strongest force among Protestant unionists, have ruled Northern Ireland together since 2007. The British army has withdrawn, and more and more Irish Catholics have joined the police. The judiciary and police have been transferred to Northern Ireland as autonomous powers. The conflict has been transformed into institutionalised consensus building for regional political tasks.

A crucial factor in the success of the peace process was the creation of a nonviolent space for politics, namely the establishment of dialogue at all levels. The renunciation of violence and the ability of all parties to compromise were basic conditions for peace. This meant first of all a ceasefire with the IRA, then a readiness to disarm all paramilitary groups and finally the establishment of a new police force. Terrorism had traumatised the entire society. The constant attacks had marginalised politics. First, all paramilitary groups had to recognise the advantage of renouncing violence and realise that there could be no military solution.

Conflict resolution in Northern Ireland was facilitated by an improvement in regional and global conditions. The United Kingdom and the Republic of Ireland joined the EU in 1973. In 1997 Tony Blair led the Labour Party to a landslide victory. As Irish Prime Minister, Bertie Ahern put pressure on the peace process in Northern Ireland. Also the USA under president Bill Clinton supported a lasting autonomy solution. Blair and Ahern were the pioneers of conflict resolution in both states. The Cold War was over and Great Britain stressed that it had no power interests of its own in Northern Ireland. If a majority of the population wanted it, Ireland and Northern Ireland should be reunited peacefully. Blair, Ahern and Bill Clinton were willing to work together in a coordinated strategy to solve the Northern Ireland problem.

The challenge was to find a political framework that would allow the political leaders of both sides to govern together without compromising their fundamental identities. A consensual model of government with a broad range of responsibilities was to provide the opportunity and the salutary compulsion to share power. Political personalities also played a major role in the constant struggle for compromise. Relations of trust between leaders of both camps were needed. David Trimble came forward as a compromise leader of the unionists, Hume as head of the SDLP of the republicans. The Belfast Agreement held because both extremes were at the table: Ian Paisley of the Protestant DUP and Gerry Adams for the Republican Sinn Féin. Finally, a large majority of the population voted in favour of the agreement in a referendum.

It was the political will to reach agreement that was decisive. In Northern Ireland, the aim was not only to create more territorial autonomy from London, but to establish lasting peace and reconciliation between the groups on the ground.

For example, police regulation, demilitarisation, the disarmament of paramilitary groups, the question of prisoners and amnesty, victimisation, respect for human rights and equality between the two religious communities played a far greater role than in other autonomy processes in the UK and Europe at large, with the exception of the Basque Country. Reform of the police, release of prisoners and disarmament of paramilitaries, equality and consociational government were at the heart of the peace agreements. Gradually the overall security situation in Northern Ireland changed: the British Army withdrew, watchtowers on the borders were demolished, emergency legislation was abolished. This led to an economic upturn in the region with increasing foreign investment. The peace process and autonomy provided the framework for Northern Ireland's economic relaunch.

A special Dispute Settlement Commission also contributed to confidence-building. There is a minority veto right in the Parliament, i.e. qualified majority decisions in the plenary session of the Parliament are required specifically for the election of the head of government and his deputy. The regular judiciary of Northern Ireland has jurisdiction in disputes, followed by the British-Irish Intergovernmental Conference. Secession of Northern Ireland is only possible after a referendum, which must be accepted by the Parliament in Westminster. Any amendment to the Good Friday Agreement requires the assent of the Northern Ireland Assembly.

How have these relations changed in the 23 years since the Belfast Agreement? At first it seemed that the two communities were drifting apart. The June 1998 elections were won by the moderate UUP and SDLP, but since 2003 the more radical forces on both sides have been in the majority. Since mid-May 2007, the republican Sinn Féin and the unionist DUP have even been ruling together, which is half a miracle. Various actors in the peace process have changed significantly in the course of this process, both political parties such as the DUP and Sinn Féin, and paramilitary groups. A Unionist hardliner, Pastor Ian Paisley, even became Prime Minister of the Autonomous Region. Sinn Féin and the DUP agreed to govern together in 2007. In 1998, after the Belfast Agreement, the DUP had rejected this strictly and left the all-party negotiations. Sinn Féin, however, welcomed the agreement and supported the new autonomy.

The two moderate parties, the Ulster Unionist Party and the Social Democrat and Labour Party SDLP, later lost a lot of votes. A return to political violence has now become unlikely. The most notable change, however, occurred in the IRA, which abandoned the armed struggle and handed over weapons to the authorities.

No conflict-free society

Anyone visiting Northern Ireland today will notice the many flags along the way. They mark the fact that the street, neighbourhood or town belongs to a particular group: the British Union Jack indicates that Protestants live here, the Irish flag stands for a Catholic settlement. In some areas the inhabitants have even painted the walls of houses or curbs with their colours. This strict separation of the settlement areas is an example of the way of life of most of the inhabitants of Northern Ireland.

Mixed denominational schools are still a rarity. Catholics usually attend church schools, while Protestants study at state schools. Thus, children see themselves as members of different religious communities from an early age. In the field of education and schools, the Belfast Agreement has not brought about any major changes. The joint education and training of Protestant and Irish pupils in the same school would undoubtedly promote understanding and coexistence, especially as they all speak the same language. Such interdenominational „integrated schools" do exist and fewer and fewer pupils want to attend separate schools. Northern Ireland's school policy is currently refusing to allocate more resources to this type of school, mainly because of resistance from the Catholic Church.

Leisure activities also offer little opportunity for interdenominational encounters. Most Catholics play Gaelic football, while the Protestant population prefers rugby. In the world of work, the integration of the two groups is more advanced. Although an institution has already been set up to promote equal rights in the private sector, in many companies, members of one denomination are among themselves. Marriages between members of different communities are also still rare. Unionist and republican parades remain popular and still lead to clashes between groups. There is a growing sense of alienation within the Protestant community.

On 19 January 2019, violence in Northern Ireland returned with a car bomb exploding outside the courthouse in Derry. The following day the British police arrested two suspects and blamed the so-called New IRA, which split from the IRA in 2012, for the attack. Back in Derry, on 18 April 2019, during serious clashes between demonstrators and police, the journalist Lyra McKee was shot and subsequently died in hospital. The New IRA claimed responsibility for the attack.

Brexit creates new tensions

Northern Ireland's economy has developed well thanks to the peace process and autonomy. Following the 1998 Belfast Agreement, a strategy for the economic development of Northern Ireland was drawn up, as it was clear that only a stable economy would provide the social basis for overcoming the conflict in Northern Ireland. However, since June 2016, a completely unexpected repositioning of the United Kingdom has brought new threats to the Northern Ireland economy: the Brexit.

When the United Kingdom voted on 23 June 2016 on the Brexit, Northern Ireland and Scotland voted strongly against: 55.8 percent of Northern Ireland wanted to remain in the EU. In response, Irish Prime Minister Enda Kenny, the leader of Ireland's main opposition party Fianna Fail, Michael Martin, and the leader of Northern Ireland's Sinn Féin, Gerry Adams, spoke about holding a referendum on the unification of Northern Ireland with the Republic of Ireland. While Sinn Féin had campaigned to stay in the EU, the largest party of Protestant Unionists, the DUP, was in favour of Brexit.

In early February 2019, on the eve of the UK's withdrawal from the EU on 31.1.2020, Mary Lou McDonald, the leader of Sinn Féin, called for the reunification referendum provided for in the 1998 Good Friday Agreement to be held. She recalled that the Northern Ireland population as a whole had not voted for the Brexit and certainly not for a hard border with Ireland. But this vote had been ignored by the British Government in London, which did not care about the local people. With the Brexit, Northern Ireland is not only losing billions in EU aid, but also the at least economic unification of the island in the course of the single market. There is still a struggle to resolve border controls between the Republic of Ireland and Northern Ireland and between the latter and the rest of the Kingdom. In 2022 the Northern Ireland Assembly will be re-elected and in 2024 this assembly is expected to vote on the continuation of the application of the Protocol of 1998 (Good Friday Agreement). As in Scotland, territorial autonomy in Northern Ireland not necessarily is made for eternity.

What can autonomy do? The Good Friday Agreement, the basis for Northern Ireland's autonomy, has not only brought political autonomy to that part of the country but above all has resolved a deep conflict. Important elements of the agreement such as disarmament, the principle of concordance in Parliament, veto rights of the two groups, police reform, the Human Rights Commission, international guarantees have played a decisive role in this. „The rifts in Northern Irish society, which were created centuries ago and deepened by the violent conflict, will only have closed in several generations," wrote British politician Peter Hain in 2009, „but what counts is to have set in motion a process on an exclusively political basis. This is the real triumph of recent years, and I hope that this can serve as inspiration to those parts of the world that do not even see the starting point for resolving their conflicts" (Peter Hain 2009, 10).

9

Corsica on the way to autonomy

In ancient times the island was colonised by Carthaginians, Etruscans, Greeks and then by the Romans. Together with Sardinia, Corsica was a Roman province for centuries. In the Middle Ages first the maritime republic of Pisa (1072-1284), then the maritime republic of Genoa took possession of the island for almost 500 years from 1284 to 1755. In 1755 the rebel and statesman Pasquale Paoli expelled the Genoese and proclaimed the independent republic of Corsica. He created a constitution that went down in history as the first democratic constitution, even before the American (1776) and French (1791) constitutions. Paoli is the Corsican national hero par excellence: „U babbu di a patria". In Italy too, many streets and squares are named after him.

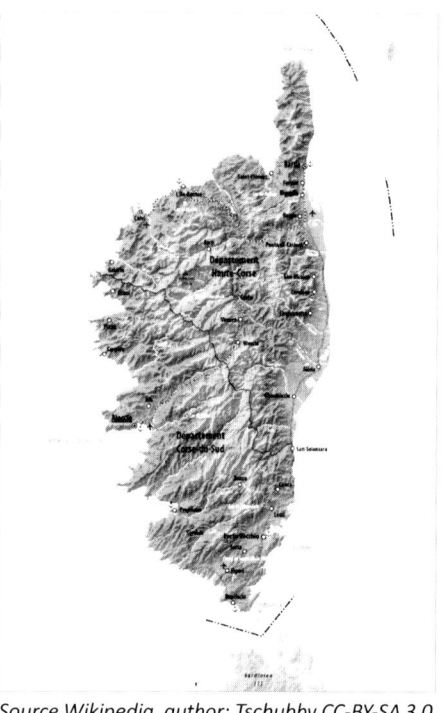

Source Wikipedia, author: Tschubby CC-BY-SA 3.0

The history of a rebellious island in a time lapse

In 1768 Genoa, which did not control Corsica at all, sold it to France and gave a carte blanche for the next stage of the colonization of the island. France's invasion was not long in coming. In 1769 the heroic resistance of Paoli's far inferior troops was broken by the French troops at the battle of Pontenovu. After a brief intermezzo of union with the United Kingdom following an uprising against France, Corsica was declared an integral part of the French Republic in 1789 and remains so today.

But Corsica remained restless and rebellious. While France asserted its national language in all spheres of life, Corsican intellectuals sought to draw closer to Italy. During the World War I, Corsica paid a high blood duty. Some 12,000 Corsicans fell in the fight against the central powers. After Mussolini's seizure of power, Corsica also experienced irredentist activities, but the vast majority of Corsicans wanted nothing to do with the Italian fascists. This is one of the reasons why the occupation of the island by German and Italian troops in 1942/43 remained only a short episode. The Corsicans rejected the Italian claims on the island and formed resistance units themselves.

In the post-war period, Paris promised to do more for the development of the impoverished and backward island. Nevertheless, hundreds of thousands of Corsicans were forced to emigrate to France, driven by poverty, unemployment and the lack of arable land. Corsican nationalism received a new impetus in the 1960s when, following the Algerian debacle, Paris settled 17,000 Algerian French people in Corsica from 1962 onwards. As the immigration of Italians to South Tyrol under the fascism regime, it was a matter of a state-ordered and subsidised settlement of people from the majority population in order to make the Corsicans a minority in their own country.

The errors and omissions of French policy towards Corsica and the lack of any form of self-government forced more and more Corsicans into radicalisation. Initially, the Corsican nationalists only wanted to better protect the Corsican language, introduce local self-government and tax benefits. However, in relation to Corsica, Paris has always interpreted Article 2 of the Constitution („France is an indivisible republic") very strictly in the sense that regional autonomy would also run counter to this dogma. Moreover, despite its small population, Corsica was divided into two départements from 15.9.1975 to 31.12.2017. On 5.5.1976, the „Frontu di Liberazione Naziunale Corsu" (FLNC) was founded, which took up the armed struggle against France. The aim was to press France to grant independence by attacking state institutions and murdering state representatives. But the political violence hardened the fronts instead of convincing Paris to sit down for negotiations for a genuine autonomy. In Corsica's history for 3000 years, there have been 19 ruling powers, 37 different names for the island, 37 revolts and 7 periods of anarchy (Edmond Simeoni 2019, Corsica!). The island people seems to have deserved a little more territorial autonomy and regional democracy.

Corsica's language is threatened

An important part of the Corsican identity is the language. Corsican is a neo-Latin language which developed from Old Tuscan Italian and is particularly closely related to the northern Sardinian dialect of Gallurese. Gallurese, although spoken in Sardinia, is considered a variety of Corsican and not Sardinian (WIKIPEDIA). Corsican is now spoken by an estimated 100,000 people in Corsica, and by an estimated 33,000 Corsicans in mainland France. In Sardinia, around 100,000 people speak Gallurese and 150,000 speak the similar Sassarese. Worldwide, the number of Corsican and Gallurese speakers, including second speakers, is estimated at up to 400,000. The figures for the number of Corsican speakers vary considerably or sometimes contradict each other. Other sources mention only 60,000 speakers of Corsican on the island, other estimates are much more optimistic with 200,000 speakers.

Purely according to linguistic criteria, Corsican does not necessarily have to be considered as an independent language, as it is very closely related to the Central Italian dialects and is largely mutually understandable with these. Corsican is much more closely related to present-day Tuscan than, for example, Tuscan is to the southern Italian dialects, not to mention the Galloitalian dialects of northern Italy. Nevertheless, also due to the political separation from Italy since 1755, the view that the lingua corsa is a language in its own right has gained ground. „The situation is, so to speak, a mirror image of that of Sardinian, which linguistically is so far removed from Italian that it must undoubtedly be a language in its own right, but is often considered an Italian dialect because of Sardinia's political affiliation with Italy" (WIKIPEDIA).

In 1974, Corsican was recognised by the French state as a so-called regional language in the context of the amendment of the Loi Deixonne and is now taught in schools to a limited extent. However, it is still not an official language in Corsica. Thus, many Corsicans are striving for a further institutionalisation of their language and thus a situation of official bilingualism. In December 2015, the newly elected President of the Corsican Regional Parliament, Jean-Guy Talamoni, attracted a lot of attention when he delivered a speech in Corsican at the opening of the Parliament. The regional elections had previously been won by the moderate nationalists (Femu a Corsica) and the radical nationalists (Corsica libera), which includes Talamoni, with 24 of 41 seats. Many French politicians condemned less the content of the speech than the fact that it had been delivered in Corsican instead of French. French is absolutely dominant in education, the media, politics and business in Corsica. According to a 2003 survey, Corsican has far too little weight in everyday life: only 2 percent of the population of Corsica use Corsican as their only everyday language, 14 percent use it at the same time as French, the rest use mainly French. If today only 16 percent of Corsican families pass on the language to the next generation, it is not surprising that UNESCO currently classifies Corsican as a potentially endangered language.

The survival of a language depends on its use in schools and education. As early as 1973, Jean Rocchi founded the scola aperta, voluntary summer schools for children who wanted to learn Corsican, which was forbidden at school. According to current statistics, around 98 percent of Corsican primary school pupils have at least one and a half hours of Corsican lessons per week. At secondary schools, a good 59 percent of pupils in lower secondary education (collège, cullegiu) and some 22 percent in upper secondary education (lycée, liceu) study Corsican as a language subject. In lower secondary education there are a few bilingual schools, but also many schools with only three hours of Corsican per week. At the upper secondary level, the Corsican language plays only a marginal role. In order to develop Corsican language teaching, the region needs above all legislative competence and more teachers trained to teach Corsican. Although many Corsicans are in favour of official bilingualism, previous attempts in this direction have failed due to the veto of the French central government.

The Corsican language has been recognised as a regional language since 1974. Regional languages are enshrined in Art. 75 (1) of the French Constitution, but this has only symbolic value, as concrete rights are hardly linked to it. It can be used vis-à-vis the authorities, but only if Corsican officials are powerful there. Now, the equality of a minority language as an official language presupposes the bilingualism obligation of the officials, i.e. the ability to communicate orally and in written form with the citizens. In addition, Corsican technical terminology would have to be developed in various areas. According to the autonomists, if Corsican is to survive, it must become the second official language on the island, otherwise the cultural decline will be unstoppable. The Corsican cultural movement received a certain boost from the Corsican University of Corte, founded in 1982, and from a traditionally rich and modernising folk culture, but the situation of the Corsican language remains critical.

Between political violence and economic backwardness

At the end of the 1960s, Max and Edmond Simeoni founded the ARC (Azzione pe a Rinascita Corsa), which sought to achieve autonomy by non-violent, democratic means. The 1975 Aleria incident marked a tragic turning point. A group led by the Simeoni brothers had occupied a large farm of a Frenchman near Aleria. Two people were killed in the shoot-out with the police. Edmond Simeoni was sentenced to life imprisonment, but thousands of Corsicans showed solidarity with him. Edmond Simeoni was released after a year in prison and is still considered a national hero in Corsica. The ARC was banned, but replaced by the UPC (Unione di u Populu Corsu), which has been fighting for Corsican interests in the political arena since 1976. The FLNC (Frontu di Liberazione Naziunale Corsu) was also founded in 1976 as an armed liberation front. The FLNC demanded independence and carried out a series of attacks, trying to avoid casualties. The Simeoni brothers and the UPC condemned the violence and wanted to achieve autonomy by democratic means, but without ever being able to rally the majority of the Corsican population behind them. Only on 25 June 2014 did the FLNC proclaim the end of the armed resistance and its own dissolution.

The socialist president F. Mitterand granted a first "special statute" in 1982, which somewhat strengthened the administrative powers of the Corsican regional assembly. This statute was reformed on 13 May 1991 promoting Corsica to a "Collectivité territorial" without giving the region real legislative sovereignty. However, the Constitutional Council in Paris decided that it was unconstitutional to use the term „peuple corse, composante du peuple français" in this statute. Its statement was clear: any legal attribution of special collective rights to a minority or regional community was deemed incompatible with the French Constitution and its doctrine of unity. However, a special status of the island was considered to be permissible.

In the 1990s, the Corsican nationalist movement split into several groups which at times fought each other. The resistance against France seemed at times to be drowned in bloody internal feuds. In 1998 the newly appointed French prefect of Corsica, Claude Erignac, was shot dead in the street in Ajaccio. This in turn intensified French repression. On the other hand, Prime Minister Jospin wanted to strengthen the autonomous powers initiating the so-called Matignon process. Among other things, the Corsican language was to be taught in public schools. The all-French right was strictly against it because it did not want to set a precedent for other minority languages in France (Basque Country, Brittany, Alsace, Occitania).

A third project for granting autonomy was launched in 2002. Paris wanted to create a single department of Corsica with the possibility of adapting state laws to the needs of the island. However, this third attempt also failed: the proposal in 2003 was rejected by 50.98 percent of the electorate in a referendum. This defeat of the autonomists is a reminder of the various home-made problems of Corsican society: excessive immigration, the clan system, clientelism, corruption.

The clan system is a centuries-old plague of Corsica. Some influential clans and their political henchmen hold power. Like the mafia in southern Italy, the clans have their hands in public procurement and appointments. As accomplices to state power, they have always been tolerated by Paris or even used to divide the Corsican nationalists. The clan system not only led to corruption, nepotism, blackmail, but was extremely detrimental to Corsican democracy. Only since 2014, when Gilles Simeoni was elected mayor in Bastia, the clans have been gradually pushed back. Today, the majority of Corsicans want a transparent and honest policy without influence of the clans. Only with transparent administration and clean governance will the autonomy parties be able to maintain the trust of the voters.

From a social and economic point of view, Corsica's development has not been entirely positive, although the economy has grown strongly since 1970. The Corsican economy suffers from structural handicaps: the lack of modern infrastructure and expensive transport, the low presence of industrial firms, seasonal and over-reliance on second homes for tourism, disadvantaged agriculture and a lack of vocational training. This has led to unemployment above the average for France and, as a result, to the emigration of tens of thousands of Corsicans to the mainland. Corsica did not have the chance to develop its economy according to its own priorities, such as more organic farming, settlement of small and medium-sized enterprises, tourism in its own hands, promotion of renewable energies. In 2017, Corsica had 22,000 unemployed and 50,000 people in relative poverty. The regional assembly then demanded preferential treatment for Corsicans when they entered the public service. The French prefect in Ajaccio immediately rejected the demand. This is compounded by financial dependence, since Corsica does not have the slightest financial autonomy.

„The central question must finally be addressed," said Edmond Simeoni in 2017, „does the Corsican people exist or not? Do they have the right to live in peace and self-determination?" If they do, they must be recognised and at least have autonomy. „France colonised Corsica", says the old fighter for the autonomy of Corsica who died at the end of 2018, „since 1966, Max and I have been saying this. Decades of struggle have passed, over 200 dead, thousands of attacks, special laws and repression with political prisoners" (Edmond Simeoni, Corsica!, 2019).

Autonomists on the advance

In recent years, the political movement for autonomy has experienced a new upswing. The autonomous forces of Corsica have been re-forming since 2013 and the successes have not been lacking. In 2014, the lawyer Gilles Simeoni, a son of Edmond Simeoni, was elected mayor of Bastia on a United List of the Corsican Left. In the elections for the Regional Assembly at the end of 2015, the autonomy movement obtained 35 percent of the votes with Pè a Corsica in the form of a self-confident alliance of autonomous (Femu a Corsica, FaC) and separatist (Corsica Libera, CL) movements. The regionalist forces took over governmental responsibility for the first time. Gilles Simeoni was elected chairman of the Corsican regional assembly and in 2017 he was elected head of the regional government. Jean-Guy Talamoni was elected President of the Regional Assembly (see interview).

After about two years of autonomous administration, the election of the 63 deputies to the new unified regional parliament took place on 3 and 10 December 2017. For the first time, the Corsicans were able to elect a united regional parliament, as the island had previously been administratively divided into two départements. The movement Pè a Corsica (For Corsica) led by Jean-Guy Talamoni and the popular mayor of Bastia Gilles Simeoni obtained 45.36 percent of the votes, the right-wing regionalist party of Jean-Martin Mondolini 14.97 percent and the independence movement Rinnovu Nazionale 6.69 percent. Due to the 7 percent hurdle, U Rinnovu was unable to run in the run-off vote, but her voters helped Pè a Corsica to a solid majority. Pe a Corsica received 56.49 percent of the votes in the second round, 20 percent more than in 2015.

Never before had a list with the declared aim of „more autonomy" achieved an absolute majority in Corsican regional elections. Similar election results for single pro-autonomy-parties only existed in the Basque Country, Greenland, Valle d'Aosta and South Tyrol. „With this vote," said Jean-Guy Talamoni, President of the Parliament, „the Corsican people have shown that Corsica is not just a piece of France, but a nation with its own language, culture and way of being in the world". The Paris National Assembly now also includes three Corsican deputies from the autonomy movement and no longer the local vassals of national parties.

A spirit of optimism about autonomy

On 1.1.2018 the new „Collettività Territuriale di Corsica" (Collectivité de Corse) came into force in Corsica, which now manages Corsica as a whole. On 2.1.2018 both presidents of the Assembly and the government took the oath on the preamble of the Corsican Constitution of 1755 (Pasquale Paoli). On 18.1.2018, a constitutional law expert was commissioned to draw up a new autonomy proposal for Paris. On 8.3.2018, the Assembly passed a solemn resolution by 48:1 votes to recognise the rights of the Corsican people. On 29.3.2018, the Corsican Regional Assembly adopted a visionary programme entitled „Corsica 2035 - Pru-

The castle of Corte, a stronghold of Corsican resistance. Foto Thomas Benedikter

gettu di sucietà" on which five permanent working groups had worked. Corsica's autonomists now wanted to get down to business.

The aim of the Corsican autonomy movement is a new autonomy statute with more legislative rights and the full recognition of Corsican as a co-official language. This is to be implemented within 10 years, after which the Corsican population should be able to decide in a direct democratic manner whether this statute is sufficient or whether devolution should be further developed. Although the regional parliament can present legislative proposals in a relatively limited number of areas, these only become law when they are adopted by the government in Paris. Although Corsica is a territorial collectivity with more rights than other regions in France, it still lags far behind the autonomous communities of Spain or the regions with special statute in Italy.

In Pe a Corsica's programme „Autonomy in three years", with an implementation phase in another three years. Pe a Corsica (For Corsica) wants autonomy „de plein droit e de plein exercise". This should not only adapt state laws, but also give the region legislative sovereignty in a dozen areas. This category of law already exists, it is called „national law" (Lois du pays) in French Polynesia. Now Paris must recognize Corsica's specificity and deliver, according to the autonomists. Since January 2018, a new dialogue on this issue has been initiated with Paris, but it is developing only slowly. On 7 April 2017, President Macron said in Furiani during his first visit to Corsica: „The French Republic is strong enough to take account of specific features of its interior". This statement has not yet had any concrete consequences. Macron was only prepared to allow Corsica to adapt its national legislation. This is not enough for Corsica. The government has refused to grant amnesty to nationalist prisoners, to make Corsican the official language and to make the purchase of real estate conditional on several years' residence in Corsica. Corsica is not a priority for Macron. There is also a majority of the right-wingers in the Senate who have traditionally been very hostile to the autonomy of Corsica.

Thus, the mood of optimism in Corsica suffered a serious setback as early as the end of June 2018: the French National Assembly rejected Corsica's demand for an autonomy statute enshrined in the constitution. It is about autonomy, not independence, the three Corsican MPs affirmed. With a separate constitutional article, Corsica was to be given autonomy because of its geographical, social and economic specificity, thus aligning Corsica with the status of overseas collectivities. The negotiations were now blocked. „A historic opportunity to settle the Corsica question is being missed", declared Gilles Simeoni, head of the regional government, „this blockade will lead us into a dead end".

A project for genuine territorial autonomy in the framework of France

Since 1.1.2018, Corsica, as a unified „territorial collectivity", is administratively a single entity. However, it still has no territorial autonomy in the sense of regional legislative sovereignty. Art. 72 of the Constitution grants Corsica a special status, but this position is ambiguous, because no special rights are derived from it. Only two overseas territories in France have so far been granted real territorial autonomy, namely New Caledonia and French Polynesia. Corsica's new autonomous majority demands autonomy at least to the extent of New Caledonia. To this end, the French constitution must be amended, which is only possible with a three-fifths majority in Congress (National Assembly and Senate in joint session). The prospects for this are currently poor.

However, the results of the last two regional elections sent a clear message: Corsica wants to obtain special autonomy as part of France. „Only in this way can the population's expectation of real participation be met," the regional assembly made clear in its resolution of 10.3.2018, „the Corsicans know their own peculiarities best and are best placed to regulate them themselves." The Corsican regional government commissioned constitutional law expert Wanda Mastor to draft such a constitutional amendment at the beginning of 2018. On this basis, the Regional Assembly in Ajaccio addressed a new resolution to the Parliament and Government in Paris. What does Corsica propose?

The „Mastor proposal" recalls that the concept of regional autonomy in no way violates the principle of the indivisibility of the Republic, which is sacrosanct in France. As the examples of Spain and Italy show, all regions could have a statute of autonomy without jeopardising the unity of the State. Two qualities are essential for this: first, such a region needs a directly elected regional assembly and regional government. On the other hand, legislative powers and financial resources would have to be transferred to the region, while general powers would remain with the central state. The autonomy of some regions with special status in Italy, Spain and Portugal would derive solely from their island character, as in Sicily, the Balearic and Canary Islands, Madeira and the Azores. Other regions would have been granted autonomy because of their ethnic-cultural specificity. In Corsica, both requirements coincide. Corsica has this in common with the highly developed autonomous islands in the north: Åland Islands, Faroe Islands, Greenland. And France itself has granted real territorial autonomy to two former colonies in Oceania. Lastly, Corsica not only has a special language and culture, but is also a special case in economic terms, with particular development needs.

Wanda Mastor emphasises that no autonomous region has absolute legislative sovereignty that limits the sovereignty of the state. Autonomous legislation would only be exercised in the competences transferred and would have to comply with the Constitution. Permanent control of the law is exercised by a central organ of the State in Paris: the Constitutional Council. As President Macron himself declared on 24 November 2017: „This energy that I want to give to the territories presupposes that we allow ourselves to break with equal treatment. Equality in the Republic is a noble principle, but this does not have to mean uniformity of norms, because the territories are not in the same situation. Today, the need to adapt norms, to give the regions the capacity to set norms in order to respond to the challenges of our territories, arises".

In the past, it was often thought that Corsica already had such regional powers, especially since it was granted the status of „territorial collectivity" in 1982 and 1991. The 2002 draft law would have provided for a certain legislative sovereignty, but was rejected in the 2003 referendum. With today's clear majority of Pè a Corsica in the Regional Assembly, the time is ripe for a new start, say the autonomists. The constitutional recognition of Corsica's special role would only be the anchoring of a long-standing de facto state of affairs that would have to be shaped constitutionally.

What should the future autonomy of Corsica look like?

The Regional Assembly, a consolidated democratic institution, should be given a number of legislative powers. To date, the Corsican Regional Assembly has only a right of proposal, but no right of initiative. The law of 22.2.2002, art.L, reads as follows: „The Corsican Assembly may submit amendments concerning the competences, organisation and functioning of the territorial collectivity of Corsica". This right of proposal is currently non-binding, as the Prime Minister is not even obliged to respond to it within a set deadline. In short, no specific legislative powers are derived from the recognition of the specificity of Corsica, which has already been legally recognised. According to the Corsican autonomists, it is no longer acceptable to elect a regional assembly for representative and administrative purposes only.

But what powers should Corsica be allowed to exercise autonomously? Wanda Mastor is in favour of the variant used in the French autonomous overseas territories. Corsica would be given the same powers as French Polynesia, but in three main areas: the arrangements for the acquisition of real estate, the region's finances and the language policy. A new constitutional article would clearly list these competences. In addition, Corsica requires competences in social housing, environmental protection, education, employment, health, finance and taxation of real estate. Only the French Constitutional Council should be empowered to ensure the constitutionality of Corsican laws.

Control of the property market and land transactions is particularly important for Corsica, as the island is suffering from a rise in second home tourism. At least 70,000 homes are occupied by mainland French residents for a few weeks' holiday each year. The increasing acquisition of second homes by non-residents has inflated property prices, preventing locals from finding affordable housing. Here, a creeping expropriation of the island population would take place. Corsica claims to be allowed to resolve this vital issue autonomously. In the financial field, Corsica claims more resources, flexibility and the right to collect its own fees and taxes, for example on inheritances and real estate transfer.

The autonomists have demanded preferential treatment for residents when they enter the public service, which the State has refused to grant. Despite 22,000 unemployed (2017), 3,000-4,000 people migrate from the mainland each year and the Corsican labour market is no longer able to absorb them. The autonomists want to raise Corsica's particular problems with the EU and France.

Would autonomy for Corsica trigger a domino effect for further demands for autonomy in France? No, the Corsican autonomists claim that there are hardly any organised autonomy movements at the political level in other regions of France. Only 0.5 percent of France's population lives in Corsica, the island contributes 0.4 percent of France's GDP and 0.015 percent of French exports. Such a reform would in no way jeopardise the indivisibility of France. Corsica would have a special autonomy like the Canary Islands, Sardinia, the Azores or New Caledonia. Nor would France have to become a regional state as a whole. „Egalité" does not mean „uniformité", but unequal things should not be treated equally, nor would autonomy be a revolutionary break in France's state structure when two overseas territories have already been granted autonomy.

The Corsican autonomy movement demands from Paris that the vote of the electorate should finally be taken seriously and that concrete negotiations for a new, genuine autonomy statute should be initiated. A modern territorial autonomy would not only give Corsica more democratic room for manoeuvre, but also prevent the Corsican language from disappearing in the foreseeable future.

„We are not masters in our own house."

Interview with Jean-Guy Talamoni, President of the Regional Assembly of Corsica (Assemblée de Corse)

Jean-Guy Talamoni (born 1960) is a leading representative of Corsican nationalism, active above all in the movement „Corsica Nazione Indipendente" movement. In the Corsican Regional Assembly (Assemblée de Corse), he led the parliamentary group of the Corsica Libera party. On 17.12.2015 he was elected president of the assembly. Talamoni was also a member of the Bastia City Council. Committed for many years to the preservation of Corsican language and culture, in 2007 he founded the Corsican-language magazine „A Nazione" (The Nation) in 2007.

Since 1 January 2018 in Corsica there is just one Collectivity, which has replaced the two Départements and the previous Territorial Collectivity. The regional elections of December 2017 have resulted in a victory of the nationalist parties. The majority of the Corsican population supports your autonomy project. Is the French state ready to enter in negotiations with Corsica's institutions?

Talamoni: There is no political opening up by the French government. Now you have got just one unitary Collectivity of Corsica, which has taken over all responsibilities and resources of the predecessors. Until the mid of 2018 we have talked about the statute of the new Collectivity after the fusion of the three previous institutions. Starting from our electoral success in December 2017 and from our fundamental proposals we have invited the government to open up a dialogue with us.

How has the government reacted? Have there been some constructive talks?

Talamoni: It has been extremely difficult. We were discussing about autonomy issues already with president Hollande since 2015. He made some first concessions, but was not available to amend the French constitution for establishing autonomy for Corsica as he had no majority of three fifths in the national parliament. Addressing the Corsican Regional Assembly Hollande said that Corsica could not obtain a new autonomy statute. President Macron in a first stage was very open minded, but since his first visit on the island all these promises are forgotten. So far, since December 2017 nothing has changed, although now as nationalist parties we are backed by a large absolute majority of the voters. We have got a strong democratic legitimacy for our proposals and claim the formal start of negotiations with the French government. Based on our geographical, historical, cultural and linguistic peculiarity we reiterated our proposal to amend the Constitution inserting a new article referring to Corsica's autonomy. But Paris on this issue remains inaccessible. Neither in the issue of the real estate market, nor in that of the prisoners, nor of the financial autonomy nor of the co-officiality of the Corsican language some progress can be reported. On contrary, the State has retaken some powers. Recently, the prefect has launched a new council of mayors, which will be in direct competition with the existing council of Corsica's municipalities.

Besides these basic claims of the Corsican nationalist parties do you already have a detailed draft of an autonomy statute, perhaps drawing from the proposal of legal adviser Wanda Mastor?

Talamoni: I myself as president of the Regional Assembly have appointed Mrs Mastor with working out this proposal. What she proposes is an amendment of the Constitution identical to the art. 74 of the Constitution referring to New Caledonia, today an autonomous territory on the way to independence. We claim a similar article, but Paris rejects that. Also Femu a Corsica, our allied partner in the majority, fully agrees on that proposal for a territorial autonomy. My party Corsica libera is committed to autonomy as an intermediate step, but later on we should go beyond that. Wanda Mastor's report shows the legal way to achieve this goal.

In which policy area Corsica's nationalist parties perceive the major need of self-government, thus the need of more autonomous legislative and executive powers?

Talamoni: The control of the real estate market is very urgent for us, as the Corsican people are literally expelled out of their homeland by wealthy people from outside. Almost 40 percent of all houses on Corsica are used as second homes. Due to the market dynamics the prices of real estates are growing relentlessly and poorer Corsican families are unable to keep the pace with. The prices of real estate assets directly affect the rents of apartments. Thus, many Corsicans cannot any more find some flats at affordable prices. A growing number of Corsicans leaves the island to find a job and living somewhere else in France and abroad. We need a special power to control the real estate market as the price level grows more than in similar regions of the mainland. Thus, some restrictions must be adopted for accessing real estate property in Corsica. For example, whoever wants to buy a real estate should prove to have been legally residing on Corsica for at least 5 years.

Which other political legislative powers in the hand of the Collectivity of Corsica do you miss most?

Talamoni: As Collectivity we are already responsible for a number of public duties, in compliance with the principle of subsidiarity. For instance in the education sector, in cultural policy, in language affairs excluding the recognition of Corsican as second official language. The education system is not doing so well, social inequalities are high as reported by the PISA assessments. But lacking autonomy we cannot intervene substantially. There are some more reasons why social inequality keeps on growing in Corsica. Thus, I made the proposal to establish a general basic social allowance for all families, but not without prerequisites. In the health sector, the urban planning, the labour policy and environmental protection we need more autonomous powers. We should be in the position to legislate in all such policy areas.

Currently the Collectivity is only allowed to formulate some proposals to be submitted to the government in Paris. If this does not agree?

Talamoni: This possibility exists already since 1981, when president Mitterand granted some few powers to our Regional Assembly. Most of such proposals have been advanced in the 1980ies, but seldom with success. Regularly such proposals ended up as waste paper. It did not work. For that reason we do not recur to this opportunity any more.

Is the Corsican Regional Assembly allowed to approve regulations to adapt national legislation to Corsica's requirements?

Talamoni: What we talk about in this regard are national acts which affect Corsica. According to art. 34 of the Constitution only the government in Paris is entitled to approve acts. As a Regional Assembly we are not allowed to do this, but we can just take decisions within our powers and exercise some rights of consultation. But in the French legal system there is such a hybrid form of regional acts applied in New Caledonia and termed "act of the country" (loi du pays). There is some legal debate whether such acts are real acts. From my point of view as a lawyer these acts are no legal acts, but just decisions in application of their powers as a Collectivity.

Now, our Regional Assembly has got more powers than a common assembly of French regions. Looking on our agenda we discuss much more truly political issues rather than just administrative questions. If serious political problems arise we, the chief of the executive board Gilles Simeoni and I, are the first politicians to be addressed by the people, even before the prefect as the real responsible for law and order on the island. But, as Collectivity we do not have any responsibility neither for the police nor for the judiciary. In the perception of the common public unfortunately we are overestimated in our powers. This is risky in so far as a politician can only be held accountable for what he can rule to a minimum extent. But we Corsicans are not the masters in our own house! The most powerful man on the island is the prefect representing the French government.

If this blockade by Paris will last and no progress in the autonomy issue can be achieved, do you risk a new radicalisation in parts of Corsica's society and politics?

Talamoni: The armed struggle for self-determination in 2014 has definitely ceased. The FLNC's decision to end the violence is an irrevocable and fundamental

The author as guest of President Talamoni in Bastia (Corsica)

change in the political strategy. I am convinced of that. But we cannot rule out new political problems and single acts of political violence forever. On the other hand the political pressure of the nationalist movement and the vote of the electorate hasn't triggered any reaction so far. We have been elected by 56 percent of Corsica's voters with a clear political program, but the French state has rejected all our proposals. These is an affront. We have played with their rules of the game set by the State as the electoral law is issued by Paris. We won and are now in charge of applying our political project.

What we should do in such a situation? We have to rule out any return to armed resistance which is out of discussion. I am very happy with the FLNC's renounce on violence in 2014. On the other hand, based on our strength in terms of votes and seats in the Assembly, we should enter in negotiations with Paris. We are also backed by many mayors of Corsica. Personally, in my party Corsica libera I am committed to go even further on. This means that our political representatives should commit some acts of civil disobedience to push the State to a dialogue and serious negotiations. The message what we convey today is this one: it does not matter whether having 56 percent of the votes of Corsicans backing our request of autonomy or maybe 95 percent tomorrow. We simply have got the right to be heard today.

The Corsican language so far has not been recognized as Corsica's second official language. Moreover, it is spoken always less in daily life. The transmission rate of the Corsican language in families continues to decrease. What can you do to step up this recognition?

Talamoni: Without co-officiality the use of the language will further decrease, in both daily life, politics and media. The Regional Assembly already in 2005 committed an inquiry to the University of Corte to check the state of the Corsican language. The result of this report was very clear: whenever Corsican would not be declared co-official language soon, it is bound to disappear. This is a conclusion drawn by social scientists based on facts and data. On the one hand, the daily use of Corsican is declining, on the other hand the awareness about the necessity to cherish our language recently is growing. Thus, today we have a high linguistic awareness, but a weak practice. As a young man in the 1970ies I had much more conversation partners in Corsican as I have today. Unfortunately, since the 1960ies and 1970ies a large part of the Corsican ceased to use the language as they retained it useless. Today, when we put on vote the issue of recognizing Corsican as second official language, all are in favour no matter from the right or from the left wing parties. In Corsica there is a large consensus on the recognition of Corsican as co-official language of our homeland.

An official language has to be established in its standardized version. What's about the written form of Corsican?

Talamoni: The written Corsican language has been developed in the 20th century only, Before the Corsicans wrote in Italian. There was a diglossia. Italian was used as official language in public life and in literature, and Corsican was the vernacular language of daily life. There were almost no Corsican authors who wrote in Corsican. We had a diglossia with two languages belonging to the same language family. Today we have got a diglossia with French as dominant and only official language, but no coherent bilingualism. Different languages are used for different purposes.

Today we Corsicans claim a new public commitment for the protection of our language. Unfortunately the French language policy is still marked by the same guiding principles as in the times of the French Revolution. The political class of France just speaks one language: French. The revolutionary France even strived to eliminate all forms of patois, the dialects and minority languages. The position of French as the State's only official language has become a dogma. Thus, all our requests for co-officiality are currently blocked.

In 2007 the Corsican Regional Assembly has decided to strengthen the bilingual teaching in the schools. According to most recent available data just 16,2 percent of the pupils of primary and secondary level of the colleges are enrolled in such schools. What can be done to strengthen the role of Corsican in the education system?

Talamoni: Indeed, there are too few pupils enrolled in the bilingual schools. What we could do as first step is to establish Corsican as a compulsory subject for everybody in our schools, in the framework of a new autonomy statute, as usual for all officially recognized minority languages in other countries. Today Corsican is only optional, whereas all subjects throughout France are taught in French medium language. What does it mean for the school? If ever the school would be an optional, for sure not all children would attend it. By law there is a compulsory education and the region's own language should also be compulsory in the public schools. It is not enough to teach Corsican just as an optional subject, although this is of utmost importance, but Corsican should be a compulsory medium language. For that purpose we need many more teachers in Corsican language.

Would such a provision change the overall importance of the Corsican language in the society and public life?

Talamoni: For sure this is not sufficient. We have to think about the use of the language in the society at large. In many regions with ethnic minorities the members of such minority communities do not keep their mother tongue in high esteem. The century long cultural colonization has produced a kind of self-disdain, which is not easy to tackle. We Corsicans should appreciate our language more. To be an official language means that the language is accepted also as a part of professional skills and career, as a means for social promotion, first of all in public service. Still in Corsica we have got a significant number of migrants from both the mainland and from abroad, whose children do not learn Corsican at all as they do not deem it useful in any sense. But migrants in Catalonia learn Catalonia, as only Catalan will ensure their social promotion. What about us?

As the president of Corsica's Regional Assembly you have inaugurated the new session with a speech fully in Corsican. This in official France has been depicted as scandal. But in which extent the Corsican language is used in political life in Corsica? In the municipalities for instance?

Talamoni: Although everybody understands Corsican, also in the Regional Assembly the dominant language is French. On the road by far not all people understand Corsican. Even not all elected representatives are able to speak and write it. The nationalist of course speak it, but probably not all members at the grassroots level. I held my speech in Corsican to raise the issue, and I did it to address our core problems and claims towards Paris. This is what counts most, but Paris just took account of the fact that in a Regional Assembly the president held a speech in a language different from the language of the Republic. This has been perceived as a sacrilege. This is the current situation in France. I am an elected member of an institution of the Republic, but I have been elected by Corsicans to represent Corsican requests.

Also in French Polynesia there has been a similar case, which proved the perversion of France's policy in this regard. There has been an amendment of the French constitution to establish French as the only official State language. But this effort was done in defence of French against foreign languages, English first of all, not for fighting against small minority languages as it is Corsican. But exactly this article has been used to challenge the use of Tahitian in Tahiti's institutions in Polynesia. Unbelievable. Today you have got high-school and university courses in English in Paris, in contradiction with the constitution, and even in the stock exchange in Paris the use of English is allowed, but no Corsican in our own Regional Assembly.

Which role has the Corsican language got in the media?

Talamoni: The Collectivity of Corsica supports the public radio and TV in Corsican language in financial terms. There is Radio Corse Frequenza Mora RCFM which is broadcasting a range of programs in Corsican language. The current majority in the Regional Assembly wants to enlarge the media supply in Corsican language. For this purpose today we need a much stronger presence of Corsican language and programs in the media, in particular in TV and digital media at large. Just symbolical political acts are not enough. We definitely need more resources.

What's about the newspapers in Corsican language? Do you plan additional support for the press to get a Corsican newspaper published?

Talamoni: We should do more in this regard. In 2000 I myself founded a newspaper in Corsican. Today we have just got one local newspaper, Corse Matin, with a weekly insert in Corsican language, what is very few. Of course it would be ideal to publish a Corsican newspaper, but in economic terms this is extremely difficult. Even regional newspapers in French language are currently facing huge problems to survive. Some time ago in Corsica we had even two daily newspapers in French. But today, it would be a big economic challenge to release a newspaper in Corsican language only.

Are there some forms of cross-border cooperation between the Collectivity of Corsica and foreign regions, first of all with Italy?

Talamoni: Yes, such a cooperation is working since longer times within the limits of our regional powers. 4 years ago together with the president of the Regional Council of Sardinia, Gianfranco Ganau, I have founded the permanent Corsican-Sardinian Council. The chairpersons of all political groups of both assemblies are members of that council. The new president of Sardinia is close to the Lega, but our cooperation continues on institutional level, especially with regard to cultural affairs. We have got some cooperation on university level, but also we established a common award for literature. Furthermore, there are some projects of economic cooperation. Thus, we have got a quite good relationship with Sardinia.

Generally speaking, the relations between Corsica and Italy since World War II have been deeply compromised for decades. Italy's occupation of the island in 1942/43 has been very brutal and left deep traces. Afterwards the generation of the war did not want to share anything anymore with Italy. The younger generation today is more open minded and more interested in an exchange with Italy.

Thus it seems unconceivable to think about Italy as a protector state with regard to Corsica as a part of France, in the same way as Austria is acting on behalf of South Tyrol, actively committed for its autonomy. But even France in the first years has been acting in this way on behalf of the Aosta Valley.

Talamoni: In the period between the world wars among Corsican intellectuals there have been a few Irredenta clubs voicing up for a "Corsica Italiana", an Italian Corsica. But such groups, due to Mussolini's plans to annex Corsica and due to the occupation during the World War II, have been fully discredited. Today there aren't any such Irredenta-friendly groups any more. In France such groups for a while served to discredit all activists claiming self-determination and autonomy of Corsica. But in the interwar period there has been another Corsican movement committed just for autonomy or independence, whereas only very few people claimed the annexation to Italy. The official politics of France later on has lumped them all together discrediting the whole movement for self-government of Corsica. We have got cultural relations with Italy, and we share a common cultural heritage and history. Thus, I am favouring new partnerships with Italy's region. But seeking Italy's political support for our claims of autonomy could not be advocated here in Corsica.

The French state in its public expenditures seems to be quite generous with Corsica compared with similar regions of Southern France. Of course, we have to keep in mind the much bigger scope of administrative powers run by the Collectivity of Corsica. Nevertheless, are there financial privileges of Corsica?

Talamoni: Corsica in its history has been suffering a lot since the annexation to France. Throughout the 19th century there has been a French law imposing customs duties on exports from Corsica to mainland France, but conversely the imports from France to Corsica were duty free. During World War I masses of Corsicans have been recruited to the French army and about 12.000 young men died on the frontline. The human loss in those times was enormous. Then we suffered the fascist occupation and the island has been bombed severely. After World War II the industrial development of France almost bypassed Corsica, our economy has been neglected for decades. So we suffered a strong emigration and still today the social situation is quite critical. All together there are good reasons for France to keep on with a major financial commitment in Corsica.

10

Hungarians in Transylvania struggle for autonomy: the Szeklerland

The territory proposed by the SNC for an autonomous „Szeklerland"
Source: Author Andrei Nacu, commons.wikimedia.org, public domain.

March 10 is the „Freedom Day of the Szeklers", a day of commemoration that has been celebrated for years with large rallies and demonstrations. On this day, the Hungarian Szeklers commemorate three martyrs who planned a revolt against the Habsburg emperors in 1854 and were executed for it. These rallies are organised by a non-party platform, the Szekler National Council (SZNT or SNC), which has been fighting for the autonomy of Szeklerland and the rights of the Hungarian community since 2003. The scene of the demonstrations is usually Marosvásárhely, in Romanian Targu Mures, in German Neumarkt. Almost as many Hungarians live in this town as Romanians, but recently there has been a Hungarian-language mayor. Since 2012, the „Szekler Freedom Day" has served in particular to make the autonomy demands of the Szekler people heard. The largest demonstration of this kind so far took place in October 2013, when 120,000 people formed a 54-kilometre human chain across the Szeklerland. For nationalist Romanians, however, autonomy is a red rag. In the annual reports of the secret service, the Szekler demands for autonomy are listed as „ethnic extremism", as if territorial autonomy were synonymous with secession or overthrow. The Szekler refer to the many examples of functioning autonomy in Europe: the Romanian state has been playing deaf for three decades.

Who are the Szekler? What is the Szeklerland?

They are militant and tradition-conscious: the Hungarian Szeklers, former border guards of the Kingdom of Hungary, have lived in Szeklerland (Székelyföld) in south-eastern Transylvania since the early Middle Ages. They are named after the „Széks", which means chair in the sense of seat of power. One of them existed in each of the eight sub-areas of historical Szeklerland. For some, the Szeklers are even the „better Hungarians", for others they are backward looking, even victims of jokes. The Szeklers also have their own flag: sun, moon and Venus on a blue background. Alive is also their unique Rovásirás carving, which remotely reminds of Germanic runes.

The Szeklerland roughly corresponds to the present districts of Harghita, Covasna and Mureș. About 13,000 km2 would be the required autonomous Szeklerland, which does not quite correspond to the historical region, because only the eastern third of the district Mureș, which is more populated by Hungarians, should become part of the autonomous area. About 75 percent of the 900,000 people living in these three counties are Szekler native Hungarians, over 20 percent Romanians and the rest are smaller ethnic minorities. In 2002, the proportion of Hungarian Szeklers was 84.6 percent in Harghita, 73.8 percent in Covasna and 39.2 percent in Mureș. Szeklerland is home to only half of the approximately 1.2 million Hungarians in Romania, the country's largest national minority.

Transylvania, which was part of Hungary for centuries, is a rather historically defined but not clearly demarcated large region of Romania. The Hungarians form a majority in Szeklerland, a strong minority in the Northwest border area and a dispersed minority in the rest of Transylvania. In Romania as a whole, about 10 percent of the 20 million inhabitants belong to national minorities. 19 ethnic groups have been officially recognised by the state. The proportion of Hungarians in the population of Transylvania fell steadily during the communist period, as the Ceausescu regime encouraged the immigration of ethnic Romanians through industrialisation and the civil service. The Germans in Transylvania were „ransomed" in large numbers by Germany during the communist period. The majority of the remaining Germans emigrated after the fall of the Berlin Wall in 1989, so that today only a few thousand German speakers live in Transylvania.

Since the change to democracy in 1989, the Szeklers have been demanding autonomy for their region, one could say they want their old autonomy back. For the Hungarians in Szeklerland, this would mean more equality, self-government, better economic development of the region and less fiddling with and dependence on the central state. A larger share of the regional tax revenue could remain in the region, and Hungarians would have a freer hand in language and cultural policy, education and higher education, and genuine equality and equal rights in language use would be guaranteed. In education, although Hungarians already enjoy clearly defined minority rights, there are still disputes between the Hungarian minority and the state authorities.

Self-rule has a long tradition in Szeklerland

Since the 10th century the Szekler were settled by the Hungarian kings as border guards on the western slopes of the Carpathians to keep out invaders. They were silent, stubborn, combative, just like border guards. In return for their services, the Szeklers were granted autonomy rights and did not have to pay taxes to the Kingdom of Hungary. Together with the Hungarian nobility and the Transylvanian Saxons as the dominant social class, the Szeklers formed the „Nations University", a federal constitution with extensive self-administration. It was crushed at the end of the 19th century. In the Kingdom of Hungary from the Middle Ages until 1876, the Szeklers had enjoyed a kind of autonomy. When Hungary had to cede two thirds of its state territory in the 1920 Treaty of Trianon, 3.3 million Hungarians found themselves part of a minority in the neighbouring states, including around 1.7 million in Romania. Along with the whole of Transylvania, the Szeklerland came to Romania in 1920.

The Szeklers did not give up their claim to political independence even as part of Romania. But only between 1952 and 1968 did the area known as the „Magyar Autonomous Region" have certain rights of self-government in communist Romania. Despite increased immigration from the rest of Romania to Transylvania as a whole, the Hungarians in historical Szeklerland remained largely among themselves. This did not change significantly after the fall of the Ceausescu regime. Szeklerland, with its north-western border region, benefits from Hungary's proximity. Hungarian companies are happy to invest in Szeklerland, especially since the accession of both states to the EU. Lower wages, the same language and the good level of education of the workforce have made the region more interesting as a business location.

The autonomy of the Soviet era had been enforced by Stalin against the will of the Romanian Communist Party, which had tried in vain to prevent the autonomy of Hungarians in Transylvania. Stalin, as a Georgian familiar with self-determination conflicts and national minorities, wanted to avoid any conflict between Hungary and Romania. Romania had initially promised to guarantee the protection of its minorities, without then legally implementing this. Thus Stalin insisted on a certain autonomy for Hungarians. This was not about the legislative sovereignty of a region, but rather only about decentralised administration. However, the rights of the Hungarian minority in language use and education were significantly improved compared to the interwar period. Under Stalin's direction, the entire constitution of Romania of 1952 was laid down in Moscow in its essential points, including autonomy for the Hungarians. Before the first parliamentary elections in October 1952, hundreds of thousands of Romanians protested against the autonomy imposed from outside in Transylvania. Five thousand requests from individual citizens for amendments to the Constitution were lodged to the Communist Party.

This autonomy was abolished by the Ceausescu regime in 1968. The issue was revived after the fall of 1989. Romania's Hungarians have endeavoured to develop their minority rights. But Romanian public opinion was reminded of 1952, when autonomy was imposed on Hungarians from outside. The new demand for autonomy met with widespread rejection from Romanian politicians and the majority population from the outset. A political climate of cooperation and trust between the parties involved as a prerequisite for autonomy negotiations did not exist in Romania after reunification.

Efforts to achieve autonomy since the fall of communism in 1989

The „United Front" of the Hungarians of Romania RMDSZ (Democratic Alliance of the Hungarians of Romania) presented its first autonomy proposal for Szeklerland as early as 1993 with a solemn vow in Cluj-Kolozsvár. The RMDSZ took up where it left off with the autonomy proposals of the interwar period, international conventions for the protection of minorities and examples of functioning territorial autonomies in Europe. It introduced a draft law for the protection of national minorities and for the creation of autonomous public corporations for cultural autonomy, but also for local autonomy.

At that time, many Hungarians assumed that democratic Romania was virtually obliged to restore the old autonomy which had been in force until 1968. Moreover, they expected direct pressure on Bucharest from international organisations such as the Council of Europe, the EU and the OSCE. But apart from Hungary, no one abroad actively supported the autonomy of Szeklerland in Romania. When a bilateral agreement between Romania and Hungary emerged in July 1995, the Szeklers tried hard to enshrine their demand for autonomy in it. This agreement was also a precondition for both countries' accession to NATO. The USA made it clear that it supported neither territorial nor autonomy claims in the post-Soviet states and urged Hungary to reach a compromise, renouncing autonomy for Szeklerland.

The Hungarians of Romania were extremely disappointed, as they had always worked towards this goal without violence and by democratic means. At the end of 1995, however, Bosnia's Serbs were „rewarded" for violence, war and expulsion by being given their own federal canton of Bosnia-Herzegovina under the Dayton Agreement brokered by the United States. Hungary remained a kind of „protective power" for the Hungarian minority in Romania, but the Szeklers had to acknowledge that the question of autonomy could only be resolved internally in their relationship with the Romanian state. From 1996 to 2000, the RMDSZ co-ruled in Bucharest as the "overarching" political force of the Hungarians of Romania. Yet, even during this participation in government it became clear that the majority parties of Romania were not responsive to a territorial autonomy in the historical Szeklerland.

What should the autonomy of the Szekler be like?

In the 1990s, the Hungarians of Romania collected 100,000 signatures for a petition for autonomy for the Szeklerland, which was submitted to the Romanian Parliament. „Szeklerland is a region with a very special past", reads the accompanying report, „which has always enjoyed a high degree of autonomy, under whatever rule and with whatever state, even under the communist regime". The proposal was based on the principle of subsidiarity, one of the fundamental values of the European states. All local communities should be able to decide as much as possible on the ground. The promoters criticise the constant delays in the process of regionalisation of Romania. Against this background, an autonomous Szeklerland could be a pilot project for regional autonomy, which is important and necessary for the whole of Romania. This would create a new territorial entity of Romania, which would be able to regulate and manage a number of powers by themselves without questioning the territorial integrity and sovereignty of Romania.

The territory of the future autonomous region would be composed of the current districts of Covasna, Harghita and a part of the district Mureş, which has a significant proportion of Hungarian population. The new region would be divided into eight chairs (Széks, sub-districts). Hungarian would be an equal official language in the autonomous Szeklerland in public administration, education, the judiciary and cultural life. The main institutions of autonomy would be the Legislative Assembly, the Executive Council (regional government) and a President who would be directly elected every four years. Also at the level of the historical „Széks", political representative bodies should be established. The petition also embraced regulations for the relationship between the State and the autonomous region and made provision for the implementation of autonomy and dispute settlement bodies. It was examined by the Constitutional Committee of the Romanian Parliament, but was quickly rejected as unconstitutional.

After the rejection of these proposals, the question of autonomy remained quiet for some time, but the issue did not disappear from the Hungarian political agenda. The RMDSZ's policy was marked by a constant attempt to remain a coalition partner at the state level. However, this fundamental willingness to form a coalition on the part of the Hungarians has not yet opened the way to autonomy for Szeklerland, which the Romanian parties strictly reject.

The Szekler parties repeatedly refer to European models, to regions in which territorial autonomy has worked well for decades: the autonomous regions in Scandinavia, Belgium, Italy, Spain and Portugal. The comparison with South Tyrol is most often made, because international protection with the „mother state" Hungary is also part of the wish list. In order to give the demand broad momentum and legitimacy, the Szekler National Council (SZNT) was founded in 2003, which on 14.3.2008 for the first time jointly demanded the autonomy of the Szeklerland as the core area of Hungary Transylvania. The Szekler National Council sees itself as a non-party platform. In the villages and towns, delegates are elected for local sections on the territory of the historical administrative units, the „Szeks" (chairs). With this procedure, the leadership of the SZNT is elected, which today is headed by Bálázs Izsák (see the interview hereafter). The SZNT organises the annual „Freedom Day" on 10 March, was organizer of the massive human chain in 2013 and other rallies throughout the region.

From December 2006 to February 2008, the SZNT held an unofficial referendum on autonomy in more than 200 municipalities of Szeklerland. Out of a total of 395,008 eligible voters, 209,304 citizens voted, of which 207,864 (99.31 percent) were in favour of territorial autonomy. The SZNT and the Hungarian party MPP aimed at an official, legally binding referendum on 15.3.2009. At rallies in the run-up to this referendum, not only the flags of Szeklerland and Hungary could be seen, but also banners calling for autonomy along the lines of South Tyrol: „Székelyföld - Déltirol" (Szeklerland-South Tyrol).

Every year in Szeklerland, high-profile initiatives and rallies are held for Hungarian rights and autonomy. While the Romanian authorities used to try to prohibit the rallies, the police have been reluctant in recent years. Before 2015, the demonstrators were even registered by name and punished, and the rally was banned. This measure was later successfully challenged in court. Attempts at intimidation in the past would have meant that not as many participants as had been hoped for came to the rallies. As there has been little visible progress at the political level, it has become more difficult for the Hungarian population to see the next meaningful steps in the struggle for autonomy. The RMDSZ accuses the SZNT of taking too moderate a line towards Bucharest. While there is no consensus among the various Hungarian organisations on a specific autonomy proposal, a kind of competition has developed among parties and politicians as to who is the „best autonomy party".

Autonomy: mere profiling in Hungarian party competition or realistic chance?

What significance do these autonomy projects have for Hungarians in Szeklerland and in Romania in general? Since 1990 the RMDSZ (Democratic Alliance of Hungarians in Romania) has been established as the most important and a kind of collecting party of the Hungarians. In 1996 the RMDSZ joined the Romanian government coalition. A representative of the RMDSZ became Minister for National Minorities. After the 2004 parliamentary elections, Béla Markó of the RMDSZ even became Deputy Prime Minister and Minister for Culture, Education and European Integration. As a very moderate party, the RMDSZ tries to balance minority rights and cultural autonomy on the one hand and the demands for territorial autonomy on the other. In 2005, the RMDSZ presented a draft law for the creation of an autonomous region of Szeklerland, which remained on hold for seven years until it was finally rejected by parliament in 2012. Without the RMDSZ, the situation of Hungarians in Romania today, 30 years after the introduction of democracy, would be much worse, given the strong nationalist sentiment in Romania.

A more radical split from the RMDSZ is the Hungarian Civic Party MPP, which split off in 2008. However, the RMDSZ remains the most elected party in Hungary. In addition, the PPMT (Hungarian People's Party in Transylvania) was formed, which, just like the MPP, is committed to the autonomy of Szeklerland.

The last chapter of this conflict took place in April 2020. The MPP member of

Demonstration for autonomy of the Szeklerland in Marosvásárhely (Romania)

parliament had introduced his own draft law for autonomy in Szeklerland. The MPP is running in a list alliance with the RMDSZ in order to pass the 5 percent hurdle, and brought a senator and a deputy into the parliament in Bucharest. After the Chamber of Deputies, due to a deadline lapse, had waved through the MPP deputy's bill for the introduction of autonomy in Szeklerland on 28.4.2020, the Senate immediately rejected the proposal without discussion the next day. In their statements, the Romanian parties surpassed each other in the severity of their rejection. Autonomy is perceived as an attack on the unity of the nation. Even Klaus Iohannis, the President of the Republic of German origin, was tempted to make a derogatory remark about the Szeklers' autonomy proposals.

Thus, the Hungarian political elite had to painfully acknowledge that autonomy for Szeklerland as an immediate solution is rather unrealistic. However, the demand for autonomy remains a prominent issue for the consensus of Hungarian voters. It has virtually become an instrument for profiling the players in the internal competition of Hungarian parties. Today, autonomy also serves the political mobilisation of Hungarians, but a clear common strategy on how to achieve it is missing.

There is a great deal of honest commitment to autonomy at grass roots level, among mayors and activists. But it has become clear that the Romanian side will never go along with any autonomy proposal. In fact, there is widespread distrust of Hungarian autonomy projects among the Romanians of Szeklerland - 20-25 percent of the population of this hypothetical autonomous region. They are afraid of suffering disadvantages, of having to give up privileged positions, of having to accept new language rights for Hungarians. The political decision-making power would also shift to the disadvantage of the internal minority of the Szeklerland. This makes it all the more important for the Hungarian proponents of autonomy to establish consociational democracy and equal rights for the two large groups, as well as guaranteed political representation in all government offices.

Among the Transylvanian Romanians, there is only an occasional open-mindedness towards the demands for autonomy. Although many Romanians are also annoyed about the lack of return of tax money and the disadvantage in public investment, there are only a few voices sympathetic to the idea. In 1998, the journalist and politician Sabin Gherman drew attention to himself with a manifesto calling for more autonomy for Transylvania. In 2015 a new party was formed in Targu Mureș, which argues in a similar direction: the Party of Free People (POL). Its founding member Dan Masca said he could live as a Romanian with an autonomous Szeklerland. More important to him is that all citizens of the country can freely decide on the future of their city and region.

Faced with this wall of rejection in Bucharest, the Szeklers are increasingly trying to win international support for their cause, both from Hungary and the EU. However, the EU has so far disappointed the Szeklers. The EU has not intervened either before Romania's accession or afterwards to meet Hungary's demands for autonomy. Although the protection of national minorities is part of the Copenhagen criteria for EU accession and one of the conditions for each candidate country, the EU has no authority to intervene in the internal structure of the member states. On the basis of the Union Treaties, the EU does indeed have only limited possibilities to press for the granting of territorial autonomy in one of its Member States.

Perspectives of territorial autonomy in Romania

Over the last 20 years, the political representatives of the Hungarians in Romania have presented no fewer than 16 proposals for a Statute of Autonomy, without being able to break the united resistance of the Romanian parties. Nevertheless, is there any possibility of introducing a certain degree of regionalisation throughout Romania and thus granting Szeklerland a kind of special autonomy status, perhaps along the lines of the asymmetric regionalism in Italy and Spain? In fact, under the Basescu government, it was planned to form large regions by merging 4-7 districts in order to create so-called NUTS II regions for the implementation of EU programmes (Structural and Cohesion Funds) in the course of EU accession. While the Szeklerland was to be transformed into an EU development region, the Romanian side wanted to merge the three districts in question into a 7-district Greater Region, in which the Hungarians would only have made up 30 percent of the population. None of the plans were successful. The NUTS II regions have failed. Today, no Romanian party wants real decentralisation of the state as a whole.

Rather, there are plans and discussions in Romania today for recentralisation, for example in education. This would mean depriving the existing districts of finance and decision-making power. These have elected county councils and county presidents, but no legislative powers. No national Romanian party today wants real decentralisation.

On the table is the strengthening of minority rights, especially language rights, including the question of cultural autonomy. A draft law to this effect, submitted by the RMDSZ in 2005, has never been discussed. There are also fears among Hungarians that the RMDSZ could also be institutionalised as a self-governing body, which would encourage even greater concentration of power and clientelism. Cultural autonomy would meet the needs of Hungarians living scattered in smaller communities in western and northern Transylvania. For the Szeklers in the desired autonomous area it would certainly be too little.

What can autonomy provide in such a case? It is not only legislation and administration by the directly elected political representatives on the ground that is needed. The Hungarians of Szeklerland also expect real equality from territorial autonomy, in politics, in economic life, in the civil service, in language rights. They are tired of permanent subordination to the national language, to the central bureaucracy, the guidelines of the central government, which takes all the relevant decisions. A fundamental problem is that, despite minority protection, there is no real equality between Romanians and Hungarians in language rights and education. Romanians almost never learn Hungarian. What bothers the Hungarians of Romania is the indirect discrimination, the lack of real equality, unequal access to higher positions and to the civil service in general. Hungarians want linguistic equality and equal opportunities for social advancement with ethnic Romanians. Hungarians demand real equality in their ancestral region. The framework for this should be territorial autonomy.

"We need to convince the Romanian majority of the basic principles of autonomy."

Interview with Balász Izsák, President of the Szekler National Council

Balász Izsák (1952), an engineer from Sfantu Gheorghe (Romania), has been continuously committed to public life in Transylvania since the fall of the Ceausescu regime. Politically, he was involved with the RMDSZ (Democratic Union of Hungarians of Romania). Then he was the initiator of the Szeklerland Forum and in 2003 co-founder of the Szekler National Council (SZNT). Under Izsák's leadership, the SZNT has developed into a broad movement for the autonomy of Szeklerland, which fights for the rights and interests of Szekler Hungarians at various levels.

The history of autonomy as the right to self-government in Szeklerland is an old one. Not only did the Hungarian Szeklers have extended rights of self-government under the Hungarian Kingdom, but even during Romania's communist era you had a kind of autonomy. Which territory of Szeklerland was covered by that autonomy and why has it been abolished?

Izsák: There was an autonomous province between 1952 and 1968 that covered Szeklerland. During communism, self-government rights could obviously not be exercised. Yet at the same time, we had more rights to use the Hungarian language than we do now. We studied in Hungarian schools; there were functioning Hungarian cultural institutions: theatres, museums, state-funded folk ensembles. Paradoxically, at that time we had more rights than the German-speaking population of South Tyrol. In 1968, Ceausescu abolished the Szekler autonomy as part of an administrative reform. It is shocking that this has been accepted by the international community without a single protesting voice.

The Szekler National Council SNC is the umbrella organization of the Hungarians striving for the protection of their rights as a national minority and for autonomy of the Szeklerland. As Szekler movement today are you interested to restore this kind of autonomy of the period 1956-1968 on the same territory?

Izsák: Today, the historic Szeklerland is split between three counties in Romania: Covasna, Harghita and Mureş counties. Therefore, in the fight for autonomy, we pursue two basic goals. We must first break the fragmentation of Szeklerland, that is, we must create its territorial unity. Secondly, this territorial unity must be endowed with independent decision-making and executive powers, in other words, the Romanian state must recognize the autonomy of this territory.

When travelling through bigger cities with Hungarian minority population such as Temesvár, Kolozsvár and Marosvásárhely the place naming is not comprehensively bilingual and Hungarian place names are scarce. What's about the official status of the Hungarian language in the counties with a Hungarian majority as Covasna and Harghita or others with a significant share of Szekler population? Is the Hungarian language officially recognized on municipal and county level whenever the Hungarian population is over 20 percent of the total population?

Izsák: There is one official language in Romania and that is the Romanian language. This is enshrined in the constitution, despite the fact that the constitution and various laws allow Hungarians to use their language, but at the same time this is obstructed on all levels. It is not possible to submit an application in Hungarian to a Romanian authority, even where the Hungarians form a majority and representatives of the authorities know the Hungarian language. Romania has ratified the Council of Europe's Framework Convention on Regional and Minority Languages, but it's not being applied. For example, there are no bilingual signs at the entrance to settlements, or just very rarely. Road signs are mostly monolingual. At municipal council meetings, the law allows the use of the Hungarian language where Hungarians are the majority, but the conditions for this are not provided, like in Marosvásárhely, for example. You can only speak Hungarian at the council meeting in villages and towns where, due to the composition of the population, there are only Hungarians. Even in instances where it would be vital, the Hungarian language cannot be used, for example instructions for the use of medicines, warnings for hazardous materials, or the labelling of pesticides and insecticides. In cases like these, people's lives may be endangered or even environmental disasters may occur because a Hungarian person cannot read this important information in their mother tongue.

Besides the language, even the Szekler symbols are often prohibited. Hoisting the Szekler flag and other symbols of the Hungarian community is still a contentious issue which often leads to aggressive reactions of Romanian parties and authorities. Are you as Szekler movement now allowed to publicly display such symbols during public manifestations or on buildings?

Izsák: The Romanian state is two-faced on this issue. As a European Member State, they must guarantee freedom of expression. In contrast, they will do everything in their power to prevent the use of our symbols, especially the Szekler flag. Mayors are penalized for hoisting the Szekler flag on a public building, but even for placing it in their study. We use the Szekler and Hungarian flags in all our manifestations, and they are forced to tolerate it. At the same time, we have to face the fact that they are constantly looking for reasons to penalize us. We have gone to court in more than once such case, and we have won lawsuits against the authorities. However, this does not prevent them from imposing further fines at a later stage, as the aim is to intimidate the community.

Every year on 10 March the "Day of Szekler Freedom" is organized by the SNC in Marosvásárhely, the historical capital of Szeklerland, with tens of thousands of participants. There have been some attempts of the authorities even to block the Szekler Freedom Day, also by judicial means. Are you now officially allowed to hold this manifestation?

Izsák: Due to the pandemic, we did not hold the Day of Szekler Freedom in the spring of 2020. This year is special in this respect, as public events had to be cancelled in many countries. In other years, we have faced harassment from the authorities. This was also meant to intimidate us, since the right of assembly must be recognized and its legal conditions guaranteed in all EU Member States. In this respect, the Romanian authorities are in a state of pressure, and they're not hiding it.

In the counties of Covasna and Harghita with a Szekler majority interethnic relations in the past have been stressed and especially in the 1990ies there have been tensions. Today, is there any interest for territorial autonomy also among the ethnic Romanians? Are there any Romanian parties or political associations open to discuss on it?

Izsák: Autonomy is a frightening term for the Romanian citizens of Romania, and they tie it exclusively to the Hungarians. The political culture is not at a level where people realize that the term is used several times in the Romanian constitution. The Romanian state recognizes the autonomy of universities, the autonomy of churches, and the autonomy of local authorities. The Romanian political elite and the Romanian press have invented a term, and describe our autonomy efforts as "ethnicity-based autonomy". They frame it as if we want a privileged position for Hungarians living in a specific area, such as Szeklerland, as if the institution of autonomy does not guarantee full and effective equality for the citizens of the autonomous region. They are trying to frighten the average laymen, claiming that should Szeklerland gained its autonomy, the Romanian language would be banned and the Romanians would be expelled. This is the meaning of "ethnic-based autonomy" in the Romanian extremist view. At the same time, we have not given up on dialogue, on proper information. In our view, the highest forum for social dialogue is the parliament itself, and we believe that the presentation of the Statute of Autonomy to the Parliament always offers an opportunity for an open dialogue. We are aware that it is extremely difficult to overcome prejudices.

In 2004 the SZNT submitted a draft autonomy statute to the Romanian Parliament based on a respective organic law. Is this proposal still valid today?

Izsák: Yes, this proposal is still valid and it's the most important document of the Szekler National Council. There have been multiple drafts on Szeklerland's autonomy, such as the one drafted by the RMDSZ. However, only the Szekler National Council's draft ended up before the Romanian Parliament. It's the only draft that can be read on the webpage of the Romanian Parliament.

According to your draft statute the subject of the proposed territorial auto-

nomy would be the "Community of Szeklerland" not subdivided along linguistic lines in officially recognized language groups as in South Tyrol. Thus, the Hungarian and Romanian groups living together in a potentially autonomous Szeklerland would not be recognized as separate language groups?*

Izsák: The Statute of Autonomy of Catalonia states that all citizens of the Autonomous Community may use both the Spanish and Catalan languages under the same conditions and in the same way. We consider this as an example, and in the autonomous Szeklerland we want to create the possibility for the status of the Hungarian language to be equal to the language of the state.

One strong provision of your draft autonomy has been inspired by the current autonomy regulations of South Tyrol. This is the ethnic quota system for public jobs, for some public resources and for the proportional representation in most political institutions. Such a provision requires an individual declaration of belonging to one of the two groups. Some political forces oppose this system as a mechanism of separation; others favour it as a mechanism for equal opportunities and social justice. Will it be necessary also for an autonomous Szeklerland?

Izsák: Right now the creeping discrimination is a reality all over Romania. If you ask how many Hungarians or other minority members are currently employed in the public administration, the only answer is: we don't know, as the mother tongue of the employees is not recorded for recruiting. But we do know that in Romania there is a structural discrimination against members of minority communities who are interested in a public job. The Hungarians by far are not employed in an extent proportional to their share on the total population of the county. This is a reality. How we can redress this imbalance in a future autonomous region? The most representative party of the Hungarians in the state parliament, the RMDSZ, does not address this issue sufficiently. But before applying such a quota system, we need to have territorial autonomy. Then an individual declaration of affiliation will be required for each candidate.

The alternative way could be – as in Catalonia and in the Basque Country – to provide for a very strict bilingualism in the public sphere. Only bilingual candidates could be hired who would be obliged to provide a certificate of knowledge of both official languages before giving the admission exam.

Izsák: Such a requirement should be mandatory for every public employee also in an autonomous Szeklerland. They should know both official languages, and all citizens should be allowed to address any public office or entity in either language, in our case Hungarian or Romanian. This should be applied in the same way as it is in Catalonia as well as in South Tyrol. The problem is that the Romanian state doesn't want to know about the co-officiality of regional languages.

In your draft autonomy statute also the historical "Széks" would be re-established as local territorial entities with all political bodies required: a council, a president and a chief governor elected by the citizens. Thus the future autonomous Szeklerland would have a multilevel governance with three layers: the region, the Széks and the municipalities. Isn't this a quite complex construction for a region with about 800.000 inhabitants?

Izsák: That is one of the fundaments of our concept of autonomy, which is different from other autonomous regions. For the Hungarians of Szeklerland, the Szék entities are a core feature of our historical identity; that is why we want them. It is an important feature because cultural differences exist even among the different Széks, and it's absolutely necessary to keep this cultural diversity alive. The borders of the single Szék are not merely historical: they are drawn by nature and geography. In other words, within the Szekler identity there are Szék identities, which mean dedication to these cultural regions. These regions are equal, this is what lives on in our consciousness. This is not unlike how in German speaking regions, Bavarian, Saxon, Prussian and Tyrolean are considered separate.

As an alternative for having a Szeklerland geographically composed by the existing counties (Covasna, Harghita and Tirgu Mureş/Marosvásárhely), could you imagine that also each of these existing counties could obtain some territorial autonomy separately and then co-operate on a higher level, thus avoiding to create a new political territorial entity?

Izsák: This will be quite difficult, as we wish to integrate only one third of Mureş County into the autonomous Szeklerland. Only the eastern part of Mureş County has a substantial Hungarian population, therefore this historical part of Szeklerland should be carved out and be integrated in the new autonomous region. On the other hand, all the three entities need to be united in a new greater region more or less covering the historical area of Szeklerland. Achieving some autonomy just for the existing counties will not be enough.

The situation today: Romania's Constitution today in art. 117 (3) allows autonomous administrative units, but apparently no genuine autonomy with legislative powers. Before establishing Szeklerland's autonomy, has the national constitution to be amended to allow such a new form of territorial autonomy based on the transfer of legislative powers to a directly elected regional council and government?

Izsák: Article 117 (3) of the Romanian Constitution allows for the establishment of autonomous administrative authorities. An example of such an autonomous administrative authority is the Council for the Management of the Archives of the Securitate (CNSAS). In our approach, the regional parliament of the autonomous Szeklerland would also be established on the basis of this provision of the constitution. Therefore, there is no need to amend the constitution for the Romanian Parliament to adopt Szeklerland's Statute of Autonomy. Under Article 117 (3), an organic law may establish such an authority. We submitted the Statute of Autonomy to the Romanian Parliament in the knowledge that it would be adopted as an organic law.

In 2004 the Romanian parliament rejected the SZNT's draft autonomy statute stating that the new entity is not identical with the provision given by art 117

Balász Izsák at the „Day of Szekler Freedom" in Szeklerland

of the constitution. This would create an asymmetry between Szeklerland and the rest of the country, and would divide the society along ethnic lines. On the one hand: of course, an autonomy in most cases is established exactly for that purpose, namely to protect a minority and to ensure a national minority some self-government. On the other hand: does has a hypothetical fundamental right to self-government of the Hungarians of Romania first have to be recognized in the Constitution (and maybe also in bilateral agreements with Hungary), from which later would arise the right to establish territorial autonomy?

Izsák: Every time the Romanian Parliament rejects our draft, we read and analyse their justification. We consistently refute the counter-arguments of the Legislative Council of the Romanian Parliament. Romania made a commitment to comply with the Council of Europe's Recommendation 1201/2003, Article 11 of which sets out the right to autonomy of a minority that constitutes a majority in a given area. Romania has not yet fulfilled this commitment, even though it was a condition for accession. We can safely say that international law is on our side. We look at this commitment by Romania as you would look at the Gruber-Degasperi Convention. The latter may be stronger as a source of international law, but it's up to us to ensure that the "pacta sunt servanda" is fulfilled in the case of Romania's commitment as well.

The autonomy request of the Szekler is often depicted as an attempt to undermine the unity, indivisibility and sovereignty of the Romanian state. This is not confirmed by the real development in about 10 EU member countries which have established a territorial autonomy, sometimes since many decades. Why does the Romanian state not acknowledge this basic purpose of a territorial autonomy?

The author met SNC-president Balász Izsák in Marosvásárhely in October 2020.

Izsák: This question can only be answered by looking at the preceding events. As I said earlier the Hungarian Autonomous Province, was permanently abolished in 1968. Prior to that, there was a campaign for the idea of a unified Romanian state. This was typical of communist propaganda. They use strong words, they try to rile up passions, but they don't state the specific goal. However, everyone understood, and whispered among themselves that the new leader - Ceausescu - wanted to abolish the Hungarian Autonomous Province. It was then that the propagandistic overemphasis on state sovereignty and territorial indivisibility began. As third graders, my classmates and I had to learn sentences about the sovereignty of the state, the indivisibility of Romania. This was followed in 1965 by the adoption of a new constitution that included these criteria: sovereignty, independence, the inalienability and indivisibility of the territory, but most importantly, the Hungarian Autonomous Province, which was included in the previous constitution adopted in 1952, was left out. Then came the administrative reform, aimed to abolish the Hungarian Autonomous Province. Its territory was divided between three new counties which did not have any special powers. But this was also the moment of the rebirth of Romanian nationalism. Authors previously qualified as members of the Iron Guard were once again allowed to be published; their books were printed, and taught in schools. Considering all that, why does the Romanian state not recognize this basic purpose of territorial autonomy? It's because of suspicion or even hatred of Hungarians, deeply rooted in the wake of Ceausescu's national ideology.

Maybe some Romanians living in Szeklerland are afraid of being transformed in a powerless minority on political level, and being governed by a politically rather united Hungarian majority. Did you ever think about mechanisms of so-called consociational government with a mandatory representation of both ethnolinguistic groups in the institutions, in the government in particular? Such mechanisms would have to be enshrined also in the statute as in South Tyrol.

Izsák: Regarding the so-called consociational government, and the South Tyrolean practice of territorial autonomy in general, it must be said, that at the current stage of the struggle for autonomy, it is not timely to talk about details that can only be discussed after the basic principles have been adopted, through a dialogue between the two communities. We should keep in mind that the Gruber-De-Gasperi Convention, which established the autonomy of South Tyrol, did not even cover two pages, and contained no such details either. We need to make the Romanian majority accept the basic principles, but obviously pointing out, that further more detailed regulations will follow after the statute's adoption.

The political world of Romania so far seems not accessible neither for a general decentralization nor for special autonomy regimes for the self-government of some particular national minorities. Is there any sign or voice among the Romanian majority raised in favour of such solutions?

Izsák: A lot of studies have been made on decentralization for the whole country, but whenever the government changes, so do the proposals. The right wing parties come up with one idea, which is later rejected by the left wing parties. Among the Romanian parties there is no unified vision for decentralization, and for us, neither version is acceptable. Unfortunately the one thing left and right wing parties of Romania have in common, is the goal to assimilate minorities. Still, it would be unfair if, in answering such a question, we did not mention those intellectuals with significant, serious influence who understood or directly supported Szekler aspirations for autonomy. Without trying to be exhaustive, I would mention Gabriel Andreescu, Sabin Gherman, Smaranda Enache, Tudor Duica, and Valentin Stan.

What can be done to convince more ethnic Romanians and their political representatives about the advantages of a territorial autonomy?

Izsák: Right now we have a lot of discussions with Romanian mayors in Szeklerland, whose municipalities have a Romanian majority. For the most part, they have no concrete knowledge of what territorial autonomy is about. Usually they reply that local entities feel better off depending directly from Bucharest, rather than on a new regional entity, because the central government is more powerful and financially competent. They need to first understand how territorial autonomy works and what advantages such a system has for everybody.

Besides territorial autonomy, what can and should be done to improve the minority rights generally for the Hungarians of Romania at large including such areas where they settle dispersed? Is national cultural autonomy as it works in Hungary and Serbia a viable way for Szeklers too? The Art. 6 Const. allows the "own decision making and executive bodies according to Statute on National Minorities adopted through legislation." Has this led to grant national cultural autonomy for the Hungarians living outside of Szeklerland or in municipalities with less than 20 percent of Hungarians on the total population?

Izsák: Since 1993, there has been a concept known as three-level autonomy. The personal autonomy of the Hungarian national community in Romania would belong to all Hungarians living in Romania. This is in essence a cultural autonomy. The next level is the autonomy of local governments with special legal status, which would provide autonomy to the people living in Hungarian-majority settlements. This autonomy is implemented the local government. The third level is territorial or regional autonomy, which could operate where Hungarian-majority settlements form a compact unit. This is Szeklerland. The Hungarians living in Szeklerland getting only cultural autonomy would not eliminate the economic vulnerability of the region.

In December 2019 the RMDSZ deputies have submitted a draft bill for autonomy of the Szeklerland in the lower house of the Romanian parliament. On 28 April 2020 this bill has been automatically adopted, but on 29 April the Senate has rejected it. Has there been a serious discussion of the issue or are all Romanian parties ideologically opposed to such a project?

Izsák: There hasn't been any discussion about this draft bill at all. I have been present when the issue was treated. In the parliamentary commission only one member mentioned that it would probably be necessary to discuss this draft bill, point by point. But all the rest said NO. So unanimously they rejected the bill without any discussion. Quite disgraceful for democratic country.

Hungary by extending the citizenship to ethnic Hungarians living abroad has ensured some rights to Hungarian minority members in neighbouring countries such as Romania. Which practical advantages has this measure brought about for you as Hungarians in Romania?

Izsák: I waited to receive Hungarian citizenship, but I never thought of expecting practical benefits. For me, this measure is symbolic, but at the same time very important. When our parents and grandparents were separated from Hungary, they automatically lost their Hungarian citizenship. Nobody asked them about it. I am thinking of them when I say: I am a citizen of Hungary. It is a moral gratification, knowing that the Hungarian nation acknowledges me as a part of it.

Which political tools does the SZNT have to mount more political pressure on Romania's Parliament for achieving autonomy? Which are the political perspectives today for achieving this goal? Can Hungary do something more for your cause?

Izsák: The SZNT is working on five different levels. First: we organize the Day of Szekler Freedom to push the Szekler identity and to keep the Hungarian community united behind the autonomy request. Second: we work with local authorities, as the mayors should learn more about the responsibilities on the Szekler

A 54 kilometers long human chain for Szeklerland's autonomy in 2013

issue. Third, we seek to make the Romanian side know more about all our proposals, understand what we want, as they keep rejecting it. Fourth: Hungary should always raise this issue in all bilateral talks and agreements with Romania. We want to pressure Budapest to keep this topic alive. Fifth, this issue can be fostered on the European level and internationally as well, we lobby to bring the agenda before the EU and other European institutions.

Which kind of support for your request of territorial autonomy for Szeklerland do you expect from the European countries, especially from the EU-institutions? Indeed, the EU by the Union Treaty is not allowed to encroach in such internal affairs of member states. Can the EU, however, be involved more strongly in the attempt to achieve some territorial autonomy in Romania?

Izsák: We need to go back to Council of Europe Recommendation 1201/2003. When it was adopted, the Parliamentary Assembly of the European Council proposed an additional protocol to the European Convention on Human Rights. This was not adopted by the Council of Ministers. The codification of the right to autonomy in international law stops here and has stagnated ever since. There were a couple of spectacular outbreak attempts out of this stagnation. For example, Resolution 1334/2003 adopted on the basis of the Andreas Gross report, or Resolution 1811/2007 adopted on the basis of Lluis Maria de Puig's report, and Resolution 1985/2014 adopted on the basis of the report of Ferenc Kalmár, but neither resulted in a universal, binding international law that an additional protocol to the European Convention on Human Rights could have been. We expect European countries to overcome their prejudices, recognize that this stagnation is not good, and make progress in the international codification of autonomy. It would be equally good if the European Charter of Regional Self-Government finally go from draft law to actual legislation.

11

Belgium's German-speaking Community: "The happiest Belgians"

Half an hour's drive southwest of Aachen, in a hilly moor and forest landscape, lies Eupen, the capital of the German-speaking Community (DG) of Belgium. It is a tranquil, tidy little town with a population of just under 20,000 and a well-preserved historic city centre. You could still feel like you were in the middle of Germany if there were not Belgian flags on the official buildings. But even the representation of the Province of Liège presents itself only in German, the place names are monolingual German and the stores are mainly decorated with German names. Since 10 January 1920, this region belongs to Belgium. It is 140 kilometres to Brussels, and the conurbations on the Rhine, Ruhr and Meuse are even closer. In the south the Eifel and Luxembourg. East Belgium is a border region par excellence. The 4-member government resides in a stately townhouse, just opposite the „Ministry", the administrative centre of the autonomous region. On a hill in the middle of the city, the Parliament is enthroned, a former sanatorium, rebuilt and extended for its new purpose.

Source: de.wikipedia.org, author: El Bubi

A look at the history

After the defeat of Napoleon and the collapse of the French Empire, the Congress of Vienna redrew the map of Europe. In 1815, the east of the Duchy of Limburg, and thus today's East Belgium, was assigned to the Rhine province of the Kingdom of Prussia. It was located in the far west of the Prussian Rhine Province and directly on the border to the new Kingdom of the Netherlands. After the foundation of the German Empire in 1871, Prussia was absorbed into the German Empire. In spite of all adjustments, the population of the district of Eupen-Malmedy-St.Vith always remained closely connected to its Roman neighbour. The borders were permeable. The invasion of German troops into Belgium in 1914 was therefore considered an injustice by many East Belgians.

With the First World War, the German Empire collapsed. Among many other decisions, the Treaty of Versailles, which came into force on January 10, 1920, defined the new borders for Germany. The Eupen-Malmedy area was granted to the Kingdom of Belgium, but on condition that a referendum be held on it. This referendum, decreed by the League of Nations and held in 1920, was neither free nor secret. Anyone who voted against the annexation of the territory to Belgium had to sign a public list and was subsequently subjected to repression by the authorities. Only 271 citizens voted in this form against the cession to Belgium. Demands for a new referendum remained unsuccessful. It was no accident that the vote was called „La petite farce belge" (a little Belgian farce). After that, a transitional regime was established in Eupen-Malmedy, administered by General Herman Baltia. There was press censorship and strict control of all political activities.

The integration of Eupen-Malmedy into the Belgian state was not yet definitive. Brussels negotiated with Germany and would have been willing to cede the German-speaking territory for 200 million gold marks. But France did not want to know about such a partial revision of the peace treaties. After that, the fronts in Eupen-Malmedy between opponents and supporters of a revision of the Versailles Treaty hardened visibly. The pro-Belgian and pro-German camps were irreconcilable. In the 1934 elections, the pro-German "Homeland Loyalty Front" won the majority in Eupen, which ran an active campaign for returning the region to the German Reich. In 1939 the pro-Belgian side narrowly won the majority of votes. But the split between pro-Belgian and pro-German citizens poisoned all areas of society.

On May 10, 1940, the Wehrmacht invaded Belgium and was welcomed in East Belgium. Eupen, Malmedy, St. Vith and Maresnet were immediately annexed by Hitler's Germany in violation of international law on May 18, 1940. However, this annexation has never been recognized under international law. Most of the inhabitants of the annexed territory received German citizenship on September 23, 1941. A little later, the first men were recruited into the Wehrmacht. Of the 8000 men recruited, 3000 fell in the war. Parts of East Belgium were heavily destroyed in the battle of the Ardennes in the winter of 1944-45.

The post-war period

The immediate post-war period was characterized by an undifferentiated policy of purge. The Germans were under general suspicion of collaboration. Without taking into account the specific situation of the annexed territory between 1940 and 1944, the courts of war in Eupen and Malmedy proceeded rigorously. Real and suspected collaborators were severely punished. The number of convicted persons in relation to the total population was four times higher than the Belgian national average.

In the post-war period, the national border with Germany was closed. It was not until 1956 that the border disputes with the Germany were settled and border crossing was made easier again. Since 1963, German has been recognized as an official language in Belgium. In the course of various state reforms, the central state of Belgium developed into a federal state, with the demand for a new form of government coming primarily from Flanders. Wallonia and Flanders are also politically different in colour, which repeatedly complicated negotiations and the formation of a government. Since the 1970s, centralism has gradually been replaced by asymmetrical federalism.

In the course of the Belgian state reform of 1968-71, the German Language Community (Deutschsprachige Gemeinschaft DG) received new autonomy rights. The DG's own representative assembly met for the first time on October 23, 1973 and was directly elected for the first time on March 10, 1974. Initially, the DG had only cultural responsibilities: culture, schools and personal social services.

In 1983 Eupen became the seat of the German-speaking Community with its own parliament and government. The first meeting of the parliament of the DG took place on 30.1.1984. In the course of the 2nd state reform of 1983/84, the three communities of Belgium were given greater powers beyond the cultural sphere. The Council of the DG could now pass decrees, i.e. its own laws, which, however, had to be countersigned by ministers at the federal level. The Parliament of the German Community elected its own government, which was no longer appointed by the central government. More and more decisions were taken in the government and parliament in Eupen, for example in the areas of education, monument protection, media, health and care, employment and social policy. After 2009, social housing, municipal finances and municipal supervision also came under the DG.

With growing areas of responsibility and tasks, the East Belgian political landscape has also become increasingly professionalized. Today, 97 percent of German-speaking East Belgians are committed to the state of Belgium, and a good two-thirds of them also consider themselves royalty loyal. The German-speaking population has not questioned its affiliation to Belgium since 1945. Within the framework of the Schengen Agreement, border controls with Germany, the Netherlands and Luxembourg were abolished in 1995. In contrast to South Tyrol, there was never a common militant autonomy movement in East Belgium, but several parties. On constitutional issues such as state reforms, however East Belgians speak as good as with one voice.

East Belgium's autonomy in the slipstream of federal state reforms

It was a long birth. East Belgium's autonomy did not come about with a single legal act, but has developed in six phases since 1963, under the pressure of the Flemish-Walloon disputes, from a central state to a federal state. In 1963, the territory of the German language was created, in 1973 a Council of the German Cultural Community, in 1984 legislative sovereignty was transferred in a few areas and a government sworn in, and in 1989 a German-speaking judicial district was established. From 2012 to 2014 the autonomy of East Belgium was extended for the last time. During this period, the DG took over more and more responsibilities from both the federal state and the Walloon Region. This was a lengthy process of federalization that does not seem to be finished yet. With each reform, the responsibilities and financial resources of the Council of the DG grew, which in 2004 was renamed the „Parliament of the German-speaking Community".

Federalism and subsidiarity were the guiding principles of these reforms. Power passed from the Belgian state to the communities and regions. This is the special feature of the „asymmetrical" Belgian federal state model, namely its duality. Not only the three regions - Flanders, Brussels and Wallonia - have their own parliament, but also the three language communities. The Flemish have merged their two parliaments (regional and community), the Walloons have maintained two separate parliaments. Although the DG East Belgium is a community with a parliament, it is not yet a separate region on its own, but as an autonomous area it is part of the Walloon Region.

Part of the competences - especially in the areas of culture, education and personal social services - went to the three language communities; the competences related to the territory went to the three regions of Brussels, Flanders and Wallonia. According to Art. 139 of the Constitution, the Walloon Region is allowed to cede regional competences to the DG at any time. The DG thus managed all the policies of the French and Flemish Communities and, on its territory, a considerable part of the regional competences of Wallonia.

Thus the DG is still dependent on the goodwill of the two major groups in Belgium, especially the Walloon Region. In the field of economic policy, the DG still lacks some essential competences. Another problem for all the communities in Belgium is their limited financial autonomy. The tax system remains largely centralized in Belgium, and the regions have no tax revenues of their own. The political representation of the DG East Belgium in Wallonia and Brussels is also not yet optimally regulated. The DG does not have its own constituency for elections to the Walloon Regional Council or the Chamber of Deputies at the federal level. The DG has been represented in the Senate by a Community Senator since 1994. On the other hand, the DG has had its own constituency for the European Parliament since 1994 and, despite its low numerical weight, sends its own representative to Brussels.

The German language prevails

German is one of the official languages of Belgium and Belgium counts itself among the „German speaking countries", together with Germany, Austria, Switzerland, Luxembourg and Liechtenstein. In the DG, German is the official language, but the French minority is subject to so-called language facilitations in dealing with the authorities. All in all, German has a relatively strong position in Belgium compared to its small numerical weight. Federal laws and decrees of state laws also have to be translated. In the army, soldiers from the DG are entitled to training in their mother tongue. In the judicial system, there has been a separate judicial district for East Belgium since 1988, with German as the language of proceedings. In the first instance, the German language can be used in criminal and civil proceedings. German has a very strong presence in the public media, the Belgian Radio BRF, which broadcasts from Eupen.

As early as 1970, East Belgium was given responsibility for the education system. Belgium's educational system is based on the territorial principle, which is primarily exercised by the language communities. Unlike South Tyrol, there is only one school system in the DG. In contrast to South Tyrol, East Belgium has preferred to give French a strong position in schools. Thus, especially in secondary school, a good half of the lessons are generally taught in French. With French as a second language, the children begin playfully in kindergarten. French is also strongly emphasized in East Belgium in view of the higher education preferred by the East Belgians. Teachers in particular study at francophone universities, but a significant proportion of East Belgians study in Germany. Due to this decision for the use of medium languages in the educational system the German-speaking East Belgians are the most fluent in all three national languages of Belgium. In everyday life in East Belgium, one gets the impression of being in Germany, because even the place names and public inscriptions are almost entirely in German.

But multilingualism is a central goal of education policy. Since English is also increasingly being learned, East Belgian students have to learn at least four languages. Starting in grade 1 of elementary school, there are 320 minutes of foreign language instruction per week. Applicants for public service in East Belgium must also prove that they have a knowledge of the German language. This is difficult for Francophones, but immigrants from Wallonia must also be able to speak German for the private labour market of East Belgium.

The legal status of the German language and the DG in the Belgian state structure has to do not only with legislation, but also with administrative actions and symbols. For the German-speaking community, it was a decisive step forward when the Belgian king, with the approval of the government, took part for the first time in 2014 in the Assembly of Heads of State of the German-speaking states of Europe: a strong sign that Belgium also sees itself as a German-speaking state. This was of the highest symbolism and has helped the Parliament of the DG a great deal to be accepted into the circle of the national parliaments of the German-speaking states.

The autonomy offers a wide space for self-government

The government in Eupen, the capital of the DG, now administers a wide range of areas of public life quite independently. Its Parliament has a fairly considerable amount of legislative powers. The hallmarks of this autonomous region are manageability, short distances, flat hierarchies, strong international integration and interdependence with neighbouring regions, and now even an innovative form of citizen participation in politics.

East Belgium has 70 well-maintained schools, 4 swimming pools, 40 percent infant care, 823 places in old people's and nursing homes, a dual education model unique in Belgium, its own music academy, a small university, a historically low unemployment rate, and recorded 400,000 overnight stays in tourism in 2017.

In Belgium there are 25 blocks of competence for the communities and regions. By the end of the current legislative period (2024), four-fifths of these will be the responsibility of the DG. Only five of them will then be still under the Walloon Region: public works, environmental protection, economy, agriculture, transport and mobility. „In 2024, Art. 139 of the Constitution will be 40 years old," says Karl-Heinz Lambertz, President of the Parliament of the DG and former head of the government, „by then this goal should have been achieved, and all remaining responsibilities should be taken over. We are on the final spurt. The DG will be able to further extend its autonomy and will have even more opportunities to shape the living conditions of the people in East Belgium".

The autonomy has made it possible to carry out reforms that would be unthinkable elsewhere. In education, bureaucracy has been massively reduced. Significant simplifications have been made in municipal supervision. The DG has assumed responsibility for employment policy and rationalized unemployment benefits. It has placed great emphasis on cooperation both within Belgium and with partners abroad, especially in German-speaking Europe. The DG is the only member state in Belgium that has a balanced budget. A tax system of its own? East Belgium is too small for that and, according to its competences, it may only collect taxes in those areas where neither the state nor the regions already collect taxes.

What is the German speaking community of Belgium?

With its 77,000 inhabitants in nine municipalities, the DG is home to only about 0.7 percent of the Belgian population. The DG is a national minority in the sense of the Council of Europe Convention for the Protection of National Minorities. The German-speaking Community is also a „small member state", a petite entité féderée. The border location is the third unique selling point. East Belgium is a border region par excellence with national borders to Germany, Luxembourg and the Netherlands.

It is certainly not the navel of the world, nor the navel of Belgium, if Belgium has a navel at all, as Karl-Heinz Lambertz puts it. The DG is simply one of the Belgian territorial entities, a part of the Belgian federal state - no more, but also no less. The DG intends not only to defend and consolidate this position, but also to further expand it.

Autonomy began in 1973 with a rather hybrid statute without legislative sovereignty, but with a directly elected council. The DG was the first to have a directly elected parliament at member state level in Belgium. The duality of the Belgian federal state is also the problem of the DG. In 1970, the German-speaking population was denied the status of both community and region, which would have suited their situation best. The DG intends to take over all responsibilities with appropriate financial resources or funding opportunities that the state has transferred or will transfer to the member states. This fundamental positioning has to do with two things: first, with the desire to pursue coherent policies, and second, with the impossibility of being able to shape policy in a truly sensible manner because of the asymmetry in everyday life.

„Since it has had a parliament with legislative sovereignty and its own government, the DG has been striving for tailor-made policy-making. Autonomy is not an end in itself. It must have an added value for people and take into account the existing specifics," Karl-Heinz Lambertz clarifies, „The DG has consistently followed this path since 1984, taking into account a principle that is often misunderstood when autonomous responsibilities are exercised: Autonomy does not necessarily mean always doing everything yourself. Autonomy means being able to decide what should happen. Whether implementation takes place independently or in cooperation with the community level or with partners beyond the language and state borders is a question of expediency. This must be clarified in each individual case with regard to the object and the subject matter. Especially for small communities, cooperation often proves to be the better and more cost-effective way".

Today, many citizens of the DG appreciate that they have many opportunities to participate in political decision-making in a small area. In autumn 2019, for example, an innovative form of citizens' council was launched, with which randomly chosen citizens can discuss current DG issues and develop proposals for parliament and government. With the permanent citizens' council, this small autonomous community is also breaking new ground in terms of citizen participation. „We are not the architects of the Belgian house, but only its inhabitants," says Lambertz. „The DG has always seen its remaining in Belgium as a prerequisite for high-level autonomy." How Belgian federalism develops depends on the compromises between Flemish and Walloons. The only population group that seems to identify strongly with Belgium are the German-speaking East Belgians.

Outlook: Will there be a „Belgium of four"?

In 1998, all the parties represented in the Council of the DG East Belgium adopted a joint resolution for the first time to extend autonomy. In doing so, the German-Belgians declared their willingness to assume all the responsibilities of the Belgian institution „Region" on their territory. Because this demand was only partially met, it is regularly repeated by the parliament in Eupen. In 2007, a unanimous resolution was passed that expressed the vision of the German-speaking Belgians for the future: a region on an equal footing with the other three regions - Flanders, Brussels and Wallonia - as part of the federal state of Belgium, which is paraphrased with the slogan „Belgium four".

In the joint declaration of 15.9.2009 it says: „As a community region, the DG must remain a definitive and equal autonomous part of the Belgian federal state." This vision was reaffirmed in the parliamentary resolution of 27 June 2011: the historical, geographical, linguistic-cultural and economic position of the DG, as well as the efficiency and administrative capacity of the DG, would argue for a broad-based autonomous status. East Belgium should become an equal member state in the future Belgian state structure. The DG is willing and able to assume all responsibilities with adequate financial resources. In addition, the parliament of the DG demands the regulatory competence of its own democracy, provincial powers (within Wallonia the DG belongs to the province of Liège) and a guaranteed representation of the East Belgians in the federal parliament (chamber and senate).

An almost identical resolution was adopted by the parliament in June 2019. All political forces are urging to take this next logical step towards a „Belgium of four", which would make East Belgium an equal region of Belgium. This would have completed its self-government and co-determination, but would no longer be an „autonomous region" in the narrow sense, but a fully-fledged member of a federal state.

The long-standing Prime Minister of the DG Karl-Heinz Lambertz comments: „We German-speaking Belgians know exactly where we want to go, and we are in no hurry at all. We have great patience and we have learned to make progress step by step. In doing so, we must be able to anticipate future developments…It is important to demand the right thing in the right place at the right time. In East Belgium, nobody is calling for a ‚Belgium of four'. What happens to Brussels or the French Community is beyond our influence. In any case, a federal state with four constituent states is the only reasonable solution for a permanent simplification of the state structure."

„We are the last Belgians."

Interview with Karl-Heinz Lambertz, President of the Parliament of the German Community of East Belgium (Deutschsprachige Gemeinschaft Ostbelgien, DG)

Karl-Heinz Lambertz (1952) was Chief Minister of the German-speaking Community of East Belgium from 1999-2014. He has been a member of the Parliament of East Belgium since 1981 and was a minister in the government since 1990. Since 2016, Lambertz has been President of the DG Parliament and represents its interests in the Belgian Senate as a Senator. From July 2017 to December 2019, Lambertz was President of the EU Committee of the Regions. Since 2014, Lambertz has also been Vice-President of the Congress of Local and Regional Authorities at the Council of Europe. The social democratic politician has helped to shape the entire development of the autonomy of East Belgium.

Belgium's DG is referred to as East Belgium. Do you feel as a Belgian?

Lambertz: Yes, here we feel as Belgians, even sometimes we say: "We are the last Belgians", as we were added to Belgium only in 1920. Today as DG we have got many areas of autonomous political powers, due to the existence of Belgium. Whenever Belgium would fall apart, we were forced to keep a part of Wallonia, or to become a part of Luxemburg or Germany or even become a mini-state as Liechtenstein. We would loose all what we have got today based on our autonomy with legislative powers. We could not get it nowhere else. How to define a "Belgian"? That's as difficult as the question "Do you speak Belgian?" The Belgian identity only can be defined starting from the variety of ethnic communities. In Italy this is totally different.

In your speech on 9-1-2020 remembering 100 years of inclusion of the DG into the Kingdom of Belgium you said in the DG's Parliament, the inhabitants of the German speaking area had very good reasons to thank Belgium. Why?

Lambertz: The DG is grateful, that German in Belgium has been recognized as co-official language of the country. Belgium even defines itself as a German speaking state. This has been manifested in the regular participation of the king of Belgium to the informal meetings of the heads of the state with German language of Europe. We are grateful that Belgium also allows to his German speaking minority a guaranteed representation in the European Parliament and in the Belgian Senate. This mandatory representation will soon be established also for the chamber of deputies, so I hope. Finally, we are grateful that the DG during the last six reforms of the state has not been forgotten, has not been simply been skipped as a quantité negligeable, but step by step has been expanded to a member entity on equal footing and almost the same rights as the other two. We have our own parliament and our own government. Our autonomy not only encompasses the community affairs in Belgian terms, but also a remarkable number of regional powers.

Which powers are still missing for completing the autonomy of East Belgium?

Lambertz: In Belgium the legislative and administrative powers are divided between the State, the three communities and the three regions. As DG we have got all powers attributed to the communities, first of all culture, education and social transfers and services short of the pension insurance which is managed ad federal level. The German speaking area is a part of Wallonia. Applying art. 139 of the constitution Wallonia has transferred to us several regional powers. What is still pending is the transfer of the economic policy, the environmental protection, the remaining energy policy, the agriculture and some parts of public infrastructure. In 2019 our Parliament has reiterated a resolution of 2011 declaring our intention to assume all powers of a member state of Belgium. That is the basic position of the German Community. In Belgium there are no concurrent powers. Our goal is to take over all public activities which are not under control of the State, along with the respective financial funding. Step by step the responsibility of the Region of Wallonia on our territory should be phased out completely.

How free is the DG's legislation in reality? The Belgian government or Wallonia's government do have a veto right on decrees approved by the Eastern Belgian Parliament?

Lambertz: Neither the Belgian nor the Walloon government have got a veto right. In Belgium the bills of the federation and the bills of the member entities have got the same rank. They have to obey by the Constitution and be in line with the distribution of powers herein enshrined. It's up to the Constitutional Court to control this.

When will the DG be upgraded to a fully fledged Region?

Lambertz: Once we have got all regional powers, de facto we are a region. What counts is the transfer of powers and sufficient funds to finance those powers, not just to obtain the label "region". To become a fully fledged region we would need an amendment of the Constitution. And then we had to apply the same financial rules as all the other Belgian regions. Whenever we talk about fiscal sovereignty, he have to recall that the income and corporate tax is linked to the residence of the subject. There are so many Belgians who work in Brussels, but are living in Flanders of Wallonia. In the DG, very few move out in the rest of Belgium, but quite many of us are working in Germany or in Luxemburg. Due to bilateral agreements on taxation these commuters have to pay taxes in the country where they work. If ever they become unemployed it's the Belgian unemployment fund and the DG to cover this allowances.

Does the expansion of the DG's autonomy depend on the further federalisation of the Belgian state or just on the political will of Wallonia?

Lambertz: If we discuss the transfer of further powers from the central level to the federal entities, this is an important issue which depends on the compromises struck by the Flemish and the Walloons. Currently, we do not have special requests to take over further powers of the federal state. One exception is the health system, as the division of powers between the federal and regional level could be improved in this sector. Our most substantial requests are addressing Wallonia. There are new challenges. For instance, when environmental protection measures are combined with capacity building and employment promotion, Wallonia cannot carry it out as the employment policy lies with the DG. There is some similar structural overlapping in other areas, too.

Thus, the further expansion of your autonomy depends on Wallonia. But is Wallonia ready to cede some pore powers to the DG?

Lambertz: East Belgium is a part of Belgium. On our territory there are two federal entities with the same legal position, responsible for different political areas: the DG and Wallonia. But there is no subordination. Since an amendment of the constitution of 1983 the transfer of regional powers from Wallonia to the DG is possible with ordinary law and this has been done several times. For instance, we have got the cultural heritage, social housing and urban planning. Of course, Wallonia must be ready not only to give us such powers, but also the respective funds. We have to do much more to convince Wallonia to reach that point. But I am optimistic that in the next years we can achieve further powers.

In the Parliament's resolution of 27.6.2011 the DG formally requests to become an equal federal member of a "Belgium in four", thus on equal footing with Flanders, Wallonia and Brussels?

Lambertz: The path to become a community-region has already been embarked, as it is the logical next step. We officially request to take over all regional affairs, along with the respective financial funds. My forecast is that Belgium will only become a mature federal state, when it will be transformed in a "Belgium in four". This would be a logical evolution, but it is up to Belgium how many regions or entities it will create. Thinking about "Belgium in four" the Gordian knot will always remain Brussels. The French community should be abolished as this creates too much complexity and gives Brussels more powers, because in cultural and educational matters Brussels has its own situation, which it should be able to regulate itself as a Community region.

The „Belgium of four" is actually the easier way to push through our demands at the federal level. We would then no longer need all the mechanisms of bipartition at the member state level in the Belgian federal model. Parts of the Flemish - especially the N-VA - see things differently. They do not want Brussels to become completely autonomous, but rather strive for a confederal model. Belgium would no longer have its own elected parliament, but only a Flemish and a Walloon one. These would then together form the Belgian parliament and the government would consist of ministers from Wallonia and Flanders. Special solutions would have to be found for Brussels and the DG.

"We feel as the German-speaking Belgians, even more since far reaching autonomy has been established," you said in an interview with German scholars Frank Berge and Alexander Grasse in 2003, describing the Germans of Belgium as a well protected minority. Now, however, just like South Tyrol, you want to further extend your autonomy. How do you justify this to Wallonia and Brussels?

Lambertz: The request for a further expansion of East Belgium's autonomy is linked to the evolution of the Belgian model of a federal state. The DG is ready to exercise all powers currently exercised by the Belgian federated entities by itself as a constituent federal entity with equal rights. Only by such a system the DG can govern in a coherent and efficient manner. As DG we are quite a small entity, but this isn't a real obstacle. Autonomy and cooperation is the more effective way.

In East Belgium after World War II never existed an overarching "catch all party" as the SVP in South Tyrol. How have you been able to speak with one voice as DG when autonomy issues were on the table?

Lambertz: First of all, one has to understand the two-tier structure of the Belgian federal state as this explains also 90 percent of the positions of the German speaking minority. Secondly, you have to know that in Belgium there are almost no national State-wide parties. Not only the regional parties, but also the Christian Democrats, Liberals, Greens and Social Democrats are divided along linguistic lines. The power of the parties is anchored in the regions. That's why the regions are so strong in Belgium. These often leads to complex negotiations whenever it comes to form a government. Having such strong regions Belgium can even go on for many months without a working government. In the DG there is one regional party, the ProDG, which is now also the strongest one in terms of votes. All these parties are very independent of their respective Flemish and Walloon sister parties. The politics of East Belgium are decided only here and in no other party head quarter of Wallonia.

Now to Europe. In an interview with DW on 8.9.2017 you said: „Europe really needs to limit itself to the issues where European solutions are needed." And: „Europe was and is in large parts too much of an elite project." The territorial autonomies in the EU, yours, those of Spain, Portugal, Italy, Denmark, are not only limited by the central state, but more and more by EU law. You mention as

The Parliament of East Belgium in Eupen

a problem the „excessive regulatory density of EU norms", which violates the principle of subsidiarity and encroaches on the competences of the regions and federal entities. Must the EU's regulatory competences be scaled back again with a reform of the Treaties? Do all regions have to insist again on more leeway of their own in regulation?

Lambertz: Subsidiarity is not so much a question of shifting competences around, but of the appropriate density of regulation for each policy area. Only that which makes real sense at the respective level should be regulated by law. At the same time, the scope for action of the lower levels should be preserved and more cross-border cooperation should be allowed. That's why we have the EGTC and hopefully soon a new mechanism to apply the legal system of one country for very specific policy areas on the territory of the neighbouring country. A very pragmatic thing in principle, but also a small nuclear explosive for the principle of sovereignty. Luxembourg proposed this mechanism during its Council Presidency. It is currently being examined in the legal service of the Council of Ministers.

You have been a member of the CoR representing the DG since 2001 and its President from 2017 to 2020. On the occasion of the CoR's 25th anniversary celebration on 16.12.2019, you called for more co-determination rights for the CoR, which until now can only issue opinions. Time and again, you as the CoR President, have complained about the lack of influence of the representation of regions and local authorities in EU policies and decision-making processes. Should the CoR be upgraded to a 2nd chamber of the EP and thus directly involved in EU legislation? Or rather should the CoR keep its current position in the institutional structure, but be directly involved in the trialogue process?

Lambertz: Even before the CoR was created in 1994, there was a call for a Senate of the Regions. This would be the third legislative body alongside the European Parliament and the Council of Ministers. However, this proposal has little chance of success, as it would further complicate the already complex European decision-making system. A different system would emerge if the second chamber replaced the Council of Ministers. In a 2018 book, I proposed a bicameral model: the directly elected Parliament and the European Senate, composed of representatives of regional and national parliaments. The Commission would become a real government. The Council of Ministers would be out. This construction would be far less schizophrenic than today and then subsidiarity could also be redefined. A bit utopian? In any case, the regions must be given more weight in EU decision-making. Involving the CoR in the trialogue procedure would be an important step in this direction.

The CoR's composition is quite heterogeneous. In the EU there are 270 regions, but only about a quarter of those regions have got legislative powers, the others not. Moreover the CoR also represent the local entities and municipalities. How can you imagine a Senate of Regions in such a heterogeneous nature of entities? A Senate of Regions doesn't require the existence of regional democracy of that kind in all member countries?

Lambertz: Local authorities form the third governance level of the European polity. At this third level, regions often share responsibility for local authorities. This dimension has recently become much more important because around 70 percent of EU activity is concretely implemented by regional and local authorities. Compared to the situation 25-30 years ago, regional structures are stronger today. This has happened in many ways, because each state has its own order and its own approach. In some centralist states, however, regions have been created on the drawing board in order just to use the EU structural funds. Even without their own legislative sovereignty, those institutions that exist at the regional level should be better integrated into the complex system of multi-level democracy. This is where it is important to respond more intensively to the diversity in the EU.

In another interview you requested more powers for the European Parliament, a real government and a two-chamber-parliament to take the regional perspective fully into account. How could the regions participate to the legislative procedure?

Lambertz: Take the French regions, which have now become really big. The provinces of the Netherlands also have considerable weight, but they cannot approve bills. The basic question is: how should states be constituted at all in the 21st century? The history of each state counts here. It's about finding directions: where should the whole thing develop? For me it is clear: we need more influence of the regions. During my term of office, we launched a pilot project in the CoR to improve subsidiarity control. We want to have more opportunities for dialogue in the preliminary phase of European legislation. Regional parliaments should be given the opportunity to get involved before an EU regulation or directive is deposited. Not as one of countless stakeholders, but in an in-depth dialo-

Karl-Heinz Lambertz in his office in the Parliament of East Belgium.
Foto: Thomas Benedikter

gue between the CoR and the Commission. 30 regions have signed up, including many from Italy.

In your legislature as President of the CoR also the harsh conflict between Catalonia and the Spanish state broke out, on the referendum on independence in October 2017. Which was the CoR's position on that?

Lambertz: Many things have gone wrong in Catalonia in recent years. Calls for secession are always an indication of a lack of balance in the relationship between state and region. The vast majority of Europe's approximately 300 regions and also the 74 regions with legislative powers do not dream of being independent states tomorrow. They want to optimise their autonomy, but always within the state to which they belong. Autonomy issues should be resolved through domestic negotiations and changes in the legal situation. On the other hand, the use of violent means by the state does not help to resolve such conflicts. What matters is the willingness to compromise at the negotiating table, as difficult as that may be.

Mostly, the advocates of territorial autonomy look at this kind of power-sharing in a state only from the perspective of the region concerned. But what does autonomy actually bring to the state as a whole?

Lambertz: The German-speaking Community is a political laboratory of a manageable but realistically feasible scale. As a small federated entity and as the border region of East Belgium, we can try out solution models and forms of co-operation before they are applied elsewhere. Behind this policy approach lies a considerable potential that can be usefully brought to blossom. In a small and manageable territory, pragmatic solution concepts can be implemented in numerous policy fields in close cooperation with local authorities, and experience can be gained that can also be useful elsewhere. I can think of examples from vocational training, employment, education and social policy, as well as from spatial planning and housing. The permanent citizens' dialogue launched last year in the DG, with its citizens' council determined by lot and its citizens' assemblies, is also a good example of solutions from which others can learn.

Territorial autonomy more or less in South Tyrol and in East Belgium have been successful. This is a framework for regional democracy and the protection of minorities. On the other hand, altogether autonomy in the world is not applied so often, when conflicts between States and Regions with ethnic minorities are to be settled.

Lambertz: The autonomy issue is not only a minority issue. Some minorities have autonomy, but some regions claim autonomy without being a minority. In the case of the EU, the big issue is whether and how it can properly incorporate regional and local authorities as a third level in its institutional structure. At the moment, Europe is still an association of nation states. But these do not bring Europe together, but rather apart. If I want to strengthen cohesion in the EU, I have to ensure that regional diversity is preserved. This diversity of regions and cultures must be able to articulate and develop. Whenever there is conflict, it shows a lack of balance between states and regions. If the states succeed in achieving a balance, this is also important for the EU. Europe has always found it difficult to tackle minority issues properly. This was the case with the eastward enlargement and now also with the negotiations with the countries of the Western Balkans.

This was also the case with the European Citizens' Initiative Minority Safepack, where the EU does not seem to care about the protection of minorities seriously enough. The Council of Europe has always been more active in this area. This is a point where the EU and the Council of Europe should work more closely together. The minority issue itself also very often has to do with borders, because minorities often live on borders, for example in Northern Schleswig, South Tyrol, East Belgium. The question always arises whether we find a scattered minority or a compact settlement area of a minority. It depends on this whether I have to define personal rights as with the Sorbs, or whether I can establish territorial autonomy as in East Belgium and South Tyrol. Both of us had the chance of being a small but relatively homogeneous territory of a language minority.

Autonomy in Oceania: New Caledonia and Bougainville

Two large islands in Oceania have enjoyed territorial autonomy in recent decades: Bougainville, which belongs to Papua New Guinea; and the French „collectivity sui generis" New Caledonia, along with French Polynesia which shares the same features of self-rule. The French state avoids the term „autonomy" as much as possible. On both islands, liberation fronts had fought violently for independence for years. Both territories were then granted territorial autonomy by treaty as a transitional solution. Recently, the electorate of these islands was able to decide on the future political status of their island in a free referendum. The result was mixed.

Territorial autonomy has not convinced the people of Bougainville

From 23 November to 7 December 2019, the Bougainvilleans were able to choose between extended autonomy and complete independence from Papua New Guinea. With a turnout of 87.5 percent, 97.7 percent voted for full independence. The referendum was one of the three pillars of the 2001 „Bougainville Peace Agreement", which ended the war that had lasted from 1988 to 1998. A provisional peace agreement was signed in New Zealand in January 1998 after between 15,000 and 20,000 people had been killed by the violence between the state army and the rebel forces. This was followed by the final peace agreement in 2001, which declared Bougainville an autonomous province within Papua New Guinea. On 20 May 2005, elections for an autonomous provincial assembly were held for the first time. However, the 2001 Autonomy Statute has not been fully implemented.

The island of Bougainville, with some associated smaller islands as large as Crete with a population of around 250,000, is located about 1,000 kilometres east of Port Moresby, the capital of Papua New Guinea. Bougainville's cultural identity is clearly Melanesian, but there are a number of different ethnic groups with a total of 19 languages. Bougainville was colonised relatively late. Initially under British-Australian influence, Bougainville fell to Germany in the late 19th century. After the end of World War I, Bougainville became Australia's trust territory, which treated the island as a kind of backyard. Despite the colonial regime, a small political elite developed among the indigenous population thanks to better educational opportunities. Even before Papua New Guinea's independence in 1975, some associations on Bougainville had demanded self-determination. The aim was to achieve complete self-government, tax exemption and a return to traditional leadership structures in the village communities. A political movement for autonomy thus developed. But despite its close historical and cultural ties to neighbouring Solomon Islands, Bougainville was beaten to PNG when the country became independent in 1975.

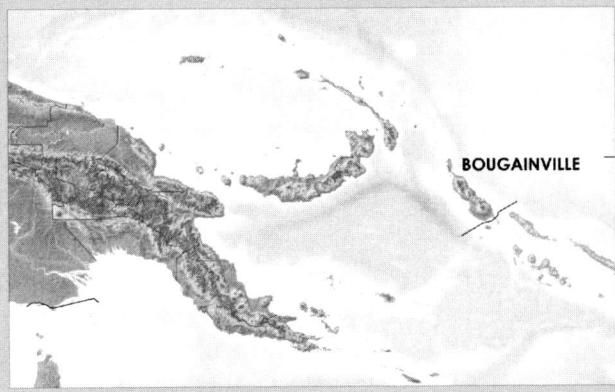
Source: Wikipedia, author: Carport, CC BY-SA 3.0 unported

Meanwhile, negotiations have been initiated to separate Bougainville from Papua New Guinea. But Papua New Guinea is pressing for more time. Despite the clear result, Papua New Guinea is not obliged to release Bougainville into independence immediately. The final word lies with the Parliament of Papua New Guinea, which must ratify independence. There was even talk of a five-year transition period before the new republic was proclaimed. Above all, the island must find solutions to stand on its own feet financially and economically. So far, the Autonomous Region has received 80 percent of its income from the state.

Now Bougainville is faced with the decision to tap into new sources of income, such as the reopening of the huge Panguna copper and gold mine. It is precisely this mine that has caused severe environmental, social and economic damage in the past, and fuelled the conflict between Bougainville and Papua New Guinea. The mine had been operated by the Anglo-Australian mining company Rio Tinto from 1972 to 1989, and had provided Papua New Guinea with considerable income. Most of the jobs had been taken by Papuans from the main island. More than a million tonnes of excavation material had been dumped into the rivers of Bougainville, with devastating consequences for the health of local residents, who had hardly any drinking water left. Rio Tinto had large areas of the island deforested, resulting in mudslides that buried entire settlements. The environmental damage, never paid compensation and discrimination against the locals led to Bougainville's ten-year armed uprising.

Now the Bougainville government is considering reopening copper and gold mining. The copper and gold deposits are said to be worth many billions of dollars. This has aroused covetousness both on the island and among various foreign mining companies. But for many islanders, Panguna still stands for war and the worst environmental disaster in living memory. And by no means all landowners agree with the reopening of the Panguna mine. Now they are considering whether the „Melanesian way" should be preferred, namely a mixture of consultation, negotiation and consensus-seeking. The presumably longer transition period until Bougainville's independence requires great political skill.

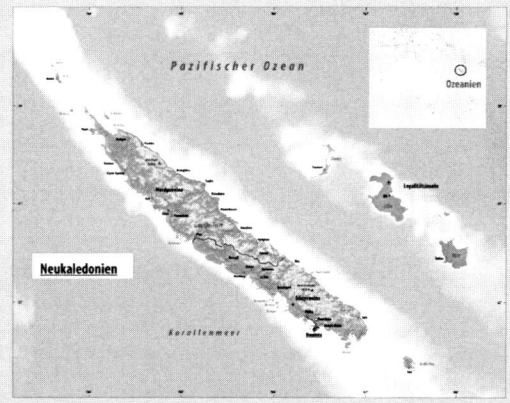

Source: Wikipedia, author: Tschubby, CC BY-SA 3.0

New Caledonia votes for autonomy within France

On 4 November 2018, the 174,000 eligible voters on the large Pacific island of New Caledonia were called upon to decide at the ballot box whether the archipelago should remain under the territorial sovereignty of colonial power France or become an independent state. 56.4 percent of voters voted to keep New Caledonia as an autonomous region under the territorial sovereignty of the French state. Not all French citizens legally resident in New Caledonia were eligible to vote, but only those citizens who lived in New Caledonia before 1994 and who could prove that they had been resident in that autonomous region for at least 20 years.

Because more than a third of the Regional Assembly called for another referendum, a second referendum on independence was held on 4 October 2020. With a turnout of 85 percent, this time 53.3 percent of New Caledonians voted to stay with France. Nevertheless, the issue of independence is not finally off the table, as New Caledonia remains a region that has been managed by the UN as a „dependent non-decolonised territory" since 1986. In French Polynesia, France's second autonomous overseas region, political forces also want to hold such a referendum.

France occupied this island in 1853 and subjugated and colonised its indigenous people, the Melanesian Kanaks. The colonial power encouraged the immigration of French, Asians and Polynesians from other colonial areas, so that today the Kanaks make up only 39 percent of the population. 8 percent are Polynesians from Wallis and Futuna, also French territory. New Caledonia thus has a multi-ethnic society, but almost 60 percent of its inhabitants no longer speak an autochthonous language. Resistance to French rule only began to organise in the 1970s. In 1984, the National Liberation Front of the Kanaks FLNKS was founded, which to this day by political means continues to fight for the self-determination of the island population and a free „Kanaky New Caledonia".

Since the Nouméa peace agreement of 1998, New Caledonia has had genuine territorial autonomy with a directly elected Regional Assembly and a Regional

Government elected by the Assembly. Until 2003, New Caledonia was a so-called overseas territory, and since 2003 it has been a „collectivity sui generis" (region with a special statute), sending two representatives to the National Assembly in Paris. Within this framework, the Regional Assembly can legislate in most policy areas and elect its own government, which, as in Northern Ireland, is supported by all major parties in accordance with the principle of consociational democracy. Autonomous powers do not include defence, justice, monetary policy, police, criminal justice and migration policy. Communications, higher education and some public bodies have not yet been transferred.

New Caledonia's political landscape is divided between opponents (loyalists) and supporters of independence. The indigenous peoples, the socially and economically inferior Kanaks and Polynesians, tend to support independence; the Caldoches, as the descendants of the French immigrants call themselves, are in favour of remaining with France. In New Caledonia, it is primarily the left-wing forces who advocate secession from France, while the Caldoches are generally among the economically privileged. The loyalists are not homogeneous: there are decidedly nationalist forces that even reject any expansion of autonomy. Other forces welcome the common New Caledonian identity and advocate more autonomy without secession. New Caledonia is „a small nation" in the context of France, similar to Scotland in the United Kingdom and Québec in Canada, it is argued. The no to secession is justified by the island's high economic dependence on France, its military security and the high quality of life thanks to French financial support.

In fact, a good 30 percent of New Caledonia's GDP comes from financial allocations from the French state, but a good proportion of these allocations return to France in various forms, solely through the high level of food imports. Proponents of independence point to the large nickel reserves and tourism, which can guarantee economic independence. Today, New Caledonia's GDP per capita is significantly higher than that of its oceanic neighbours such as Vanuatu or the Fiji Islands.

New Caledonia is a multicultural nation, but the FLNKS has also taken up the cause of New Caledonia, albeit as a state-independent community. Since 1963, the Kanaky population has steadily declined due to immigration from France. Although the victory of the opponents of independence was expected, 46.7 percent of New Caledonians voted in favour of separation from France in 2020, more than expected given the island's high economic dependence. The supporters of the idea believe that only an independent state can preserve the Kanak identity. The possibility of freely and jointly determining New Caledonia's social, economic and foreign policy development would only exist with independence, and a special partnership with the former colonial power would be out of the question. No less than 83 percent of those in favour of independence have a good image of France and want to continue the close relations even if the independent state is founded.

There is no reason to fear a new flare-up of political violence in the event of a definitive rejection of independence, since all parties have agreed to continue to hold an institutional debate on the island's common future. The 1998 Nouméa Convention states that the island's autonomy is irreversible. The strongest political force, Caledonie Ensemble, has announced that if the island remains with France, it will enter into new negotiations with Paris to establish a special and permanent statute of autonomy, including the fundamental right to self-determination, the exercise of which will be abandoned in the medium term. Territorial autonomy guarantees New Caledonia both the protection and the economic advantages of belonging to an influential industrial country and the umbilical cord to the „Grande Nation", which is particularly important for the descendants of French immigrants. New Caledonia shares this orientation with the vast majority of French overseas territories, the remnants of its colonial empire, which have democratically chosen to remain with France, but almost always without real territorial autonomy.

12

A state offers autonomy: Morocco and the Western Sahara

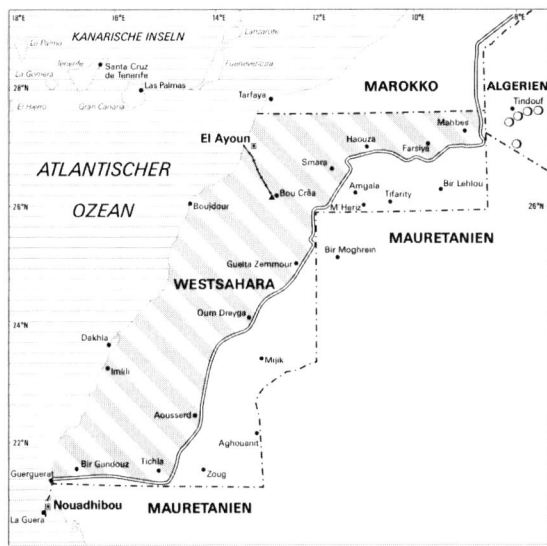

Source: Geographic Institute University of Bern, 2019
Cartography: A. Hermann

For a good forty years, tens of thousands of Moroccan soldiers have piled up a sand wall that stretches 2,400 kilometres through the Western Sahara. The wall has been built by the Kingdom of Morocco since the 1980s to protect the border, probably the second longest border fortification ever built after the Great Wall of China and the Roman Limes. The border wall, secured with barbed wire and countless landmines, divides an area of 266,000 km2 known as Western Sahara, which Morocco calls its „Sahara region". It had been Spanish colonial territory until 1975. After the Spanish left, Mauritania and Morocco moved in and occupied it against the will of the Sahraui, the tribal population of the region.

Morocco annexed the north of Western Sahara in 1976 and the rest in 1979 after Mauritania withdrew. These annexations were not recognised by the United Nations, and to this day Western Sahara is officially listed by the UN as a „Dependent Territory" under Article 73 of the UN Charter. In several resolutions, the UN has affirmed the Sahrawi right to self-determination. The EU Court of Justice has also ruled that Western Sahara does not belong to Morocco under international law and should therefore not be considered part of the national territory under the bilateral treaties between the EU and Morocco. Despite the lack of a legal basis, Morocco claims full sovereignty over its „Sahara region".

In a legal limbo since 45 years

The Popular Front for the Liberation of Western Sahara POLISARIO had been fighting against the Spanish colonial power even before Morocco took over, and after its withdrawal in 1976 it saw itself cheated of the right to self-determination by the neighbouring states. Thus, on 27 February 1976, the POLISARIO nevertheless proclaimed the Sahrawi Arab Democratic Republic and called for a referendum to be held. This republic, recognised by around 50 states, has been a member of the African Union (AU) since 1984. In response to the admission of the Republic of Sahara, Morocco left the AU in the same year and was then the only African country without AU membership for 33 years. The Kingdom only returned to the African umbrella organisation on 31 January 2017. The Republic Sahara has no seat in the UN as the recognition depends on the results of a referendum on the status of the Western Sahara.

For 16 years, POLISARIO waged a guerrilla war against Morocco. It was not until 1991 that a ceasefire was reached. Then came the earth wall, which pushed the POLISARIO and the Sahrawis, who had not fled to Algeria, into the inhospitable, almost uninhabited east of Western Sahara. Morocco now controls about 80 percent of the entire territory. Along with the 1991 ceasefire agreement, it was agreed that the local population would decide on the future of Western Sahara in a referendum in 1992. However, the holding of the referendum failed already in the preparatory phase, as Morocco and the POLISARIO could not agree on who should be entitled to participate in the referendum as a „native".

While POLISARIO considers only Sahrawis who lived in Western Sahara at the time of the end of Spanish colonial rule and their descendants to be eligible to vote, Morocco demands that members of Sahrawi tribes who formerly lived in southern Morocco should also be considered indigenous. A new attempt to organise a referendum in 1997 also came to nothing: after Morocco and the POLISARIO could not reach an agreement on the definition of those entitled to vote, the UN, following the suggestion of the then US Secretary of State James Baker, made a mediation proposal, which was only accepted by the POLISARIO.

James Baker did not give up so quickly. His second plan called for a referendum on future status after a transition period with territorial autonomy. This plan was unanimously approved by the UN Security Council in 2003, but rejected by Morocco because it feared losing the referendum. Under the impression of the events of 11.9.2001 in the USA, King Mohammed was able to convince US President George Bush that an independent Western Sahara would become a staging ground for terrorist militias. Allegedly the POLISARIO is hostile to the West and Western Sahara could become a field of action for jihadists. The POLISARIO is pleased with the US involvement in the issue because for years no one at the international level cared about the conflict. The EU is divided on the Western Sahara issue, as on many others. While several EU member states do not want to alienate Morocco, the EU as such has not recognised the „Sahara region's" affiliation to Morocco under international law and has enshrined corresponding legal reservations in bilateral agreements with Morocco.

It was not until early December 2018 that talks between Morocco and POLISARIO resumed after a long hiatus, encouraged by former Trump administration security adviser John Bolton. Bolton had worked in Western Sahara as part of a UN peacekeeping mission in 1991 and had been a member of James Baker's negotiating team in the late 1990s. Bolton and UN Special Envoy for Western Sahara Horst Köhler, the former German president, managed to gather the main players in the conflict around a table in Geneva on 5 and 6 December 2018: Morocco, Mauritania, Algeria and POLISARIO. It was agreed to continue the talks because no one could be satisfied with the current status. The UN peacekeeping mission was only extended for another 6 months in 2019 under pressure from the USA.

Thus, Western Sahara remains in a diplomatic limbo to this day. The POLISARIO insists on a referendum, while Morocco offers territorial autonomy within the state borders at best. The main point of contention here is the question of whether, in addition to integration into the Moroccan state with autonomy at best, independence of Western Sahara from Morocco should also be an option in this referendum. Although Morocco offered autonomy for the first time in 2007, it still strictly rejects a referendum on the sovereignty of Western Sahara under international law.

The peace negotiations in Geneva have so far remained inconclusive. Morocco is accused of delaying tactics. De facto, it controls the most important part of Western Sahara and hopes that sooner or later this will be recognised by the international community under international law. To date, the international community has not submitted a new proposal. Thus, the final status of the territory remains unresolved to this day. POLISARIO calls its country „Africa's last colony" and accuses Morocco of expulsion and occupation in violation of international law. Thus, Western Sahara is today one of the oldest unresolved self-determination conflicts worldwide.

Forced immigration and development

Even before the annexation of the territory, Morocco invited hundreds of thousands of Moroccans to the „Green March" to Western Sahara in 1975 and settled them there with generous support from the state. Today, almost 600,000 people live in Moroccan-controlled Western Sahara, of whom only about a fifth are Sahrawis. All the top jobs in business and administration are held by Moroccans. Moroccan and foreign companies exploit Western Sahara's greatest resource wealth, the phosphate deposits and the fishing grounds in the Atlantic. The territory is tightly controlled by the Moroccan military, police and secret service, Sahrawi protest rallies are violently dispersed, basic political rights and freedoms are severely restricted. Morocco denies human rights violations and accuses POLISARIO and Algeria of repeatedly stirring up trouble in Western Sahara.

On the other hand, Morocco is trying to convince the population of the advantages of belonging. According to Transparency International, the state has invested 862 billion USD in Western Sahara since 1975. Infrastructures have been built, the few cities have been developed, military security has been provided, resource extraction has been promoted and even tourism has been allowed. King Mohammed IV is quoted as saying that Morocco has invested 7 dirhams of public funds for every dirham of revenue from Western Sahara. In Morocco's Western Sahara, residents pay no taxes and receive generous unemployment benefits. It is said that many Sahrawis have now also come to terms with belonging to Morocco and welcome these development efforts.

In Morocco itself, the majority is firmly convinced that Western Sahara belongs to Morocco. In the Moroccan understanding of the state, the territory has always belonged to the kingdom and anyone who disputes this is considered a kind of traitor to the country. It is said to be a sacred concern of Morocco to have reintegrated this part of the kingdom after the Spanish colonial period.

On the other hand, there is still the big problem of refugees in the camps in Algeria. According to the UN, 170,000 Sahrawis live in the Tindouf area in southwestern Algeria under extremely makeshift conditions in camps named after the largest cities in Western Sahara, 50,000 in Smara alone. Since the late 1970s, the second generation has grown up here, knowing only camp life. UN agencies and other aid organisations look after the camps, whose economic situation seems to have improved in recent years. In this „permanent exile", the Sahrawis cherish the dream of returning to an independent Western Sahara, while Morocco accuses the POLISARIO of using the refugees for its own purposes. But the POLISARIO has introduced a functioning self-government, ensured equal rights for women and abolished slavery. Parts of the Sahrawi youth, however, are becoming increasingly impatient and more radical forces are pushing to resume the armed struggle. Young Sahrawis have already joined the jihadists in northern Mali. Drug trafficking and religious fundamentalism could take hold if a solution is not found soon.

Morocco's offer of autonomy

In April 2007, the Kingdom of Morocco submitted an official proposal to UN Secretary-General Ban Ki-Moon for the establishment of a Sahrawi Autonomous Region, entitled „Moroccan Initiative for the Negotiation of a Statute of Autonomy for the Sahrawi Region". Such a compromise was intended to resolve the conflict between Morocco and the Sahrawi people. Western Sahara was to receive territorial autonomy, and in return the legitimate representatives of the Sahrawi people were to recognise the sovereignty of the Moroccan state. This raises two fundamental questions: first, are the Sahrawis willing to forego a referendum on self-determination in return for identifying themselves as an autonomous part of Morocco? Secondly, is this offer of autonomy at all likely to secure peace, stability, self-government and the protection of the rights of the people of Western Sahara? Indeed, genuine territorial autonomy cannot be established in Morocco's current political system as easily as, say, in a democratic constitutional state in Europe. While France, the USA and some other EU states welcomed Morocco's autonomy proposal, POLISARIO, representing the Sahrawi people, rejected it outright.

This brings us to the second question: does the Moroccan state even offer the necessary framework conditions for a functioning territorial autonomy? As explained in the opening chapter, this would require a fully functioning constitutional state with an independent judiciary, a democracy with protection of all civil liberties and basic political rights, and the abolition of the patronage-based power apparatus in the state and in Western Sahara. Now, the Kingdom of Morocco has made substantial progress towards parliamentary democracy and the rule of law at all levels since the accession of Mohammed IV, but true democracy in its entirety has not yet arrived. Freedomhouse lists Morocco as a „partially free state". Modern territorial autonomy, however, requires a democratic system with the rule of law both in the state as a whole and in the autonomous region. Autonomy rights that cannot be fully enforced in Moroccan courts would make territorial autonomy questionable from the outset. The Moroccan autonomy initiative for Western Sahara could certainly serve to initiate a peace process that, after a transitional phase, would lead to a stable order accepted by a majority of all conflict partners. But what form should such territorial autonomy take in order to fulfil this claim?

Improvements to the autonomy proposal unavoidable

In bilateral negotiations, the parties to the conflict would first have to reach an agreement on the procedure for drafting a statute and creating the autonomous region. The Saharan autonomy arrangement would have to be clarified in detail in these negotiations and the outcome of the negotiations would have to be presented to the entire population of the region in a free referendum. According to the resolutions of the UN General Assembly and the UN Security Council on the Western Sahara conflict, the legitimate inhabitants of Western Sahara should be free to decide whether autonomy in the negotiated form is accepted or not.

However, as with the referendum on the sovereignty of Western Sahara, which POLISARIO has been calling for 45 years, the stumbling block here would also lie in the definition of those entitled to vote: should all Moroccan citizens resident in Western Sahara today be entitled to vote, or only those who can demonstrate a minimum period of residence, or even only those who were legal residents before the annexation of the territory by Morocco in 1976? How should Sahrawi refugees in Algeria participate in the vote? If all current residents were eligible to vote, the indigenous Sahrawi would be outvoted if they rejected the autonomy solution, because they would only form the minority of those eligible to vote.

Another key point of territorial autonomy is the competences transferred to the region. In the case of Western Sahara, Morocco would be willing to cede a considerable part of state powers to this region compared to other Arab states. Nevertheless, important policy areas are missing from Morocco's 2007 offer, such as the control of fishing grounds and the exploitation of mineral resources (especially the rich phosphate deposits), which are enormously important for Western Sahara, energy supply, the self-responsible organisation of the regional administration and the civil service as a whole, and the communication infrastructure, for example in the form of a regional radio-TV station. Responsibility for internal security and regional police is also not mentioned in the 2007 autonomy proposal. In view of the forced immigration on the part of Morocco in recent decades, another competence of crucial importance is missing: the control of immigration. An autonomous region of Western Sahara would have to be allowed to co-regulate the influx of new settlers from Morocco.

What position would the indigenous tribal population of the Sahrawis have in the autonomous region? The Moroccan autonomy proposal assures them a „privileged position" inside and outside the territory and a leading role in the institutions and bodies, which is not further defined. What control could an autonomous Western Sahara exercise over its natural resources? Morocco's autonomy proposal does grant the future autonomous region a share of the revenues of the use of its economic resources, but remains deliberately vague. Such important basic rights must be precisely regulated in an autonomy statute in order to prevent future conflicts: Who is the rightful owner of the region's natural resources? Who grants which concessions of use? What is the autonomous region's share of the total revenue? Such questions must be regulated in detail in an autonomy agreement.

How should the state of Morocco be represented in the Sahara Autonomous Region? According to the Moroccan proposal for a statute, the head of the regional government should also be a representative of the state. He would have to assume a dual function: democratically elected head of the autonomous Western Sahara, but also representative of the state in Western Sahara appointed by the king. However, a clear separation of democratically legitimised governmental responsibility and state supervisory role is required and common in most autonomous regions. The independence of the regional parliament, which is directly elected by the citizens, and its right to freely determine the regional government are among the core institutions of modern democratic territorial autonomy. The state should be able to take legal action against transgressions of competences by an autonomous region through the right of action before the supreme courts, but not through mere instructions to a regional president who is dependent on the king. The areas of responsibility between the state and the autonomous regions must remain clearly separated in a constitutional state.

Morocco's 2007 autonomy proposal also lacks a bilateral body to settle disputes and implement autonomy. In other territorial autonomies it has been shown time and again that such an interface is of enormous importance in conflicts,

The Moroccan state considers the Western Sahara as its „Sahara-Region". At the right hand the royal family. Street board in Rabat. Foto Thomas Benedikter

problems of interpretation, adjustments of legal norms. In Italy, Denmark, Finland, Spain, such state-region commissions have proved very successful. Tasks, composition and working methods would have to be precisely defined in the statute of autonomy.

Similarly, the process of implementing autonomy must be precisely regulated, because experience shows that implementation takes many years. In a conflict case that has been going on for decades with little mutual trust between the conflict parties, it would also have to be ensured that the implementation of the statute is continuously monitored by international institutions (e.g. UN, AU, Arab League) and that a clear time horizon is adhered to.

The international context plays a very important role for the lasting stability of an autonomy solution in the Western Sahara. Today, the greater part of the Sahrawi people live as refugees in neighbouring Algeria. Such factors have played a very decisive role in the success of other territorial autonomies. Not only in the autonomy negotiations, but also in the guarantee of territorial autonomy itself, this neighbouring state would have to be included as a kind of protective power. This role can also be anchored in the autonomy statute without violating Morocco's sovereignty. Algeria would then be the guarantor and supervising authority according to international and Moroccan law, which can be a condition for the Sahrawis' consent to the autonomy solution and a guarantee for lasting peace.

What can autonomy achieve in the case of the disputed Western Sahara? Since the Moroccan autonomy initiative is to be seen as a negotiation offer, there is considerable room for negotiation. Now both sides have to move. Above all, Morocco has to improve the autonomy offer considerably in order to get POLISARIO back to the negotiating table at all. Algeria, too, has an interest in a solution to the conflict: for too long, 170,000 Sahrawis have been harbouring in the Algerian desert; for too long, this desert region has been divided by a mined sand wall and relations with Morocco have been strained. The Sahrawi tribal peoples and the Berber-influenced population of Morocco have much in common besides language and religion. Western Sahara as an autonomous part of Morocco can be advantageous for both sides, as long as democratic self-government and the special position of the indigenous Sahrawis are guaranteed. Territorial autonomy with high standards can be the key to conflict resolution in Western Sahara, but it has to be a genuine autonomy.

13

Autonomy in name only: Xinjiang/East Turkistan and the autonomous entities of China

Source: Britannica. Creative Commons Attribution-Share Alike 3.0 Unported license.

Territorial autonomy for ethnic minorities („National Regional Autonomy") is a fundamental right enshrined in the Chinese constitution (Art. 31): „Regional autonomy for ethnic minorities in China means that autonomy is applied under the united leadership of the state where ethnic minorities live in compact communities. In these areas, organs of self-government have been introduced. The implementation of this policy is crucial to the relationship of equality, unity and mutual assistance between the different ethnic groups" (Chinese Government White Paper 2005, Preamble). However, communist China never recognised „peoples" and embarrassingly avoided the word self-determination, only so-called minzu (nationalities). The Communist Party had already abandoned the idea of self-determination of peoples and a federal republic in 1935.

China's „National Regional Autonomy"

Communist China feared outside interference, especially in the newly conquered border regions with significant smaller peoples such as the Tibetans, Uyghurs and Mongols. On the other hand, the Chinese constitution of 1982 explicitly states that the big-national Han chauvinism and local chauvinisms must be fought.

In China, „minzu" is understood to mean a historically grown community of people united by a common language, territory, economy and culture. Customs and language are the most important characteristics of ethnicity, and more rarely history and religion. Around 400 ethnic minorities were considered „minzu" when the state was founded, but only 55 were recognised. In areas where at least 20 percent of the population belongs to an ethnic minority, territorial autonomy „under united leadership of the state" may be introduced to protect it. Only the new Constitution of 1982 clarified this basic principle; the National Autonomy Act of 1984 implemented it and was amended in 2001. However, no autonomous region can adopt a statute of autonomy by itself.

Starting from these basic principles, regional autonomy has been gradually implemented since 1949, at three levels: at provincial level with 5 autonomous regions, at district level with 30 autonomous prefectures and at county level with 117 autonomous counties. In addition, in the autonomous Inner Mongolia there are three autonomous banners with roughly the size of counties. The European autonomous regions are best represented by prefectures in terms of area, while the five autonomous regions are the size of large territorial states covering alone two thirds of the land area of the People's Republic of China.

Inner Mongolia was the first to be established as an autonomous region as early as 1947, two years before the proclamation of the People's Republic of China. Today, however, the Mongols form a smaller minority (17 percent) than the Han Chinese (79 percent). Nevertheless, more ethnic Mongolians live in Inner Mongolia than in the Republic of Mongolia. The Uyghur Autonomous Region in Xinjiang was founded in 1955, Ningxia and Guangxi became autonomous in 1957 and Tibet was the last region to receive territorial autonomy in 1965. Among the five autonomous regions of China, only Tibet has an absolute majority of the titular ethnic group. In Xinjiang, the Uyghurs currently still form the relative majority.

There are no autonomous prefectures or counties within the four autonomous regions of Tibet, Inner Mongolia, Ningxia and Guangxi. Only in the more multi-ethnic Xinjiang (East Turkestan) is there administrative autonomy for other minorities in the form of six autonomous counties of Tajiks, Kazakhs, Mongols, Hui and Xibe. In theory, the autonomous regions can make independent decisions in numerous policy areas, but the central government's guidelines for „unity, harmony and socialist development" always take precedence.

China's system of territorial autonomy is based on the State Law on „Regional National Autonomy" of 1984, which was amended in 2001, and the Implementing Law of 2005. The People's Congress and the People's Government of the respective level are the governing powers. The autonomous regions, prefectures and counties are responsible for regulating local and ethnic issues, and have a degree of self-government in education, language, customs and cultural policy. They also have special funding rights. Legislative control, if any, is the responsibility of the central government in Beijing. However, the real political power in the Chinese system clearly lies with the Communist Party and its local structures.

In the case of multi-ethnic autonomous units, all ethnic groups must be adequately represented in the People's Autonomous People's Congress and the People's Government, as proportionally as possible to their share of the population. If this proportion is less than 50 percent, the ethnic minority must even be disproportionately represented. The heads of government of the autonomous units must belong to the respective titular ethnic group, which is not very important in view of the one-party rule. In most cases, the CCP tried to somehow co-opt the elites of these peoples and ethnic groups.

The Chinese system of autonomy has proved its worth on the cultural level in many cases, preserving the identity of minorities, securing language rights, preventing assimilation. China thus has a basically positive approach to minority protection considering territorial autonomy as a means of limited self-rule. The empire had already maintained good relations with many minorities. Autonomy is thus regarded as a historically developed right and a form of state organisation for the protection of minorities. After all, even in the fight against colonial invaders in the 19th and 20th centuries there was almost always a political consensus between the Han Chinese and the minorities. The systemic limit of this kind of autonomy is the profoundly authoritarian system of this state.

Real autonomy in the People's Republic of China?

Can the forms of territorial autonomy in China be classified as „modern autonomy"? Doubts are justified from both a constitutional and a political point of view. Although the legislative body of the autonomous regions (the „Autonomous People's Congresses") and the executive body ("People's Governments") can pass or amend laws, any act must be countersigned by the central government. This greatly limits substantial autonomy in legislation and administration. The principle of unity and the general interests of the State always prevails over autonomy in the end.

An example of this softening and relativization of autonomy is provided by Article 7 of the Law on Regional National Autonomy, which states that „the organs of self-government of the ethnic autonomous territories must put the interests of the State as a whole above any other interest and make positive efforts to achieve the objectives set by superior state organs" (Art.7 Law on RNA). In this context, a fundamental aspect of China's state structure must always be kept in mind: the party hierarchy forms a parallel power structure which dominates the political representative bodies and severely limits their decision-making scope from the outset.

This means that decision-making procedures independent of the party are not guaranteed or that decisions contrary to the interests of the party are not even possible. Even though some powers have been formally transferred to the autonomous units, two central criteria for genuine autonomy are not met in China's constitutional order: free political decision-making by political representatives directly elected by the people, and full compliance with the rule of law with independent courts and separation of powers.

It is impossible to determine the degree of acceptance by China's ethnic minorities of the present autonomy arrangements. Independent researchers also confirm that China's minority policy has improved the concrete situation of minorities in many areas compared to the past in the Empire (Shuping Wang 2004). On the other hand, the ancestral territories of the minorities are among the poorest and economically most backward areas in China. The economic disparities between the minority regions and other provinces, especially the booming coastal regions, cause some minorities to revolt. Recently, the Chinese government has sought to promote the economic development of the central and western regions where most minority populations live. In the meantime, however, overheated economic growth has raised new problems, such as the more intensive use of land, water, forests and the large-scale mining of mineral resources in the minority regions, which threatens the living space of minorities.

There is also criticism of autonomy regulations by the Han majority population. In many autonomous areas, minorities are also numerically in a minority in their traditional territory, but enjoy preferential treatment in various respects (positive discrimination, disproportionate representation in the civil service, other forms of promotion). This in turn is perceived as discrimination by many Han Chinese. The need for an autonomous entity has been questioned in several cases where a national minority is also in a local or regional minority. This is now the case in three of the five autonomous regions, namely Guangxi, Ningxia and Inner Mongolia. Others regard the existence of autonomous regions as a threat to China's national unity in general.

Xinjiang: A strategy of cultural extinction

The Chinese use „Xinjiang" (western borderland) to refer to East Turkistan, the historic settlement area of the Uyghur Turkic people. Before the invasion of the Red Army in 1949, East Turkistan had been independent for a short period of time on two occasions, then it was incorporated into the People's Republic in defiance of the right to self-determination. In 1955 China constituted the „Xinjiang Uyghur Autonomous Region" (XUAR). Already in the 1950s, purges were carried out among the intellectuals of East Turkestan, which worsened during the Cultural Revolution. Starting in the 1960s, the CCP pursued a resettlement policy to break up the Uyghurs' compact settlement pattern in the countryside and force them to migrate to the cities. The Uyghurs used the period of opening up China under Deng Xiao Ping and Hu Yaobang to demand genuine autonomy and an end to the multiple discrimination. On several occasions, such protests were violently suppressed, whereupon radicalised groups carried out attacks. In Eastern Turkestan, serious unrest and tensions between Han and Uyghurs have been recurring since 1997. In 2009, hundreds of people died in riots in Urumqi.

The state tried to portray the Uyghur resistance as a problem of terror that must be dealt with severely.

Even before that, namely since the turn of the millennium, China has switched to a strategy of assimilating the Uyghurs through increased immigration. According to government figures, 75 percent of the population of Xinjiang were Uyghurs and only 6 percent Han Chinese in 1953. According to the latest official data, the Uyghurs make up 45 percent of the population, the Han Chinese 41 percent. In the capital Urumqi - similar to Lhasa - more than three quarters of the population since long time are Han-Chinese. This immigration from the East, systematically encouraged by the state, has completely transformed the economic, social and cultural life of East Turkestan. The national culture has been replaced by Chinese-dominated life and Chinese-dominated institutions and business life. In the foreseeable future, the Uyghurs will become a minority in their own country.

The religious customs and traditions, literary production, art, culture and architecture of the Uyghurs are dismissed as backward in this sense. The Chinese mainstream is portrayed as culturally superior and modern, not only in technological terms. As in many other minority areas, the expression of Uyghur folk culture is barely tolerated as folklore. This assimilation project becomes visible to the outside world in the new architecture in Xinjiang: while on the one hand the old Uyghur towns are being rolled down as unhygienic, the new high-rise housing estates are transforming East Turkestan into any Chinese province. The irretrievable destruction of the old Uyghur building culture can best be observed in Kashgar on the Silk Road. While the Han Chinese, who migrated to the former Qing Empire, still built their quarters separately from the older Uyghur buildings, things are different today: in architecture, too, everything Uyghur must give way to the Chinese model of modernisation.

Uyghurs have long been excluded from political decision-making processes, apart from compliant collaborators in the CCP, who are selected and nominated from above. Immigration from China's eastern provinces, together with cultural alienation, is leading to an ethnically segregated society. Han Chinese get the best jobs, all leading positions and also dominate the educational system. Uyghurs and smaller minorities suffer systematic discrimination on linguistic grounds alone. The renunciation of genuine equality and further development of the Uyghur language, the suppression of religious life, the suppression of Uyghur culture from public and private life, the exclusion of the Uyghurs from political decision-making processes have since been part of the Chinese „modernisation programme" of the Far West. China's aim is to prevent the Uyghurs' cultural reorientation towards Islamic Central Asia, to integrate them fully into hand-dominated China, and ultimately to eradicate the Uyghurs' independent cultural identity. Today they are under pressure as a whole to subordinate themselves to a development model propagated by the state, disseminated by Han Chinese and enforced by local authorities. This leaves only two options open to Uyghurs: Adaptation and assimilation combined with some economic advantages or resistance under the general suspicion of extremism and separatism.

Total surveillance and repression

Since the Uyghurs did not succumb without resistance to this policy, which has lasted for decades, the state resorted to measures of obligatory indoctrination and repression of all resistance. A comprehensive surveillance and control apparatus with high-tech methods has been set up. Human rights violations have culminated in the establishment of re-education camps for more than one million Uyghurs.

The trend towards surveillance has been steadily growing in China and has intensified since Xi Jinping took office. The target groups are various social and ethnic groups such as civil rights activists, religious minorities, university professors, but also a whole people: the Uyghurs. Xinjiang has now become a police and surveillance state that is unparalleled worldwide. As Dolkun Isa, the President of the World Uyghur Congress, reports, thousands of surveillance cameras, a finely woven network of road checkpoints and systematic monitoring of communications on the Internet and mobile phones are key elements of surveillance. Then there are the re-education camps. The „China Cables" smuggled into the West by independent journalists, a wealth of official documents from the innermost reaches of the CCP's power apparatus, have confirmed this strategy: China has set up „educational facilities for the Uyghurs" throughout Xinjiang. Of course, these are not educational institutions, but internment camps. The detainees have to undergo prescribed training in order to be released at all. The training programme includes Chinese, party doctrine and the teachings of Xi Jinping.

Why does China rely on this rigorous repression of the Uighurs? Because it believes that this is the only way to achieve the security and stability the CCP wants. The oppression of the Uyghurs is not really new, but has taken on new dimensions since 2014. It is about general state oppression, not just the individual persecution of political activists. The principles of regional autonomy and the protection of ethnic minorities, which are enshrined in the Chinese constitution and state laws, are being taken ad absurdum in East Turkestan.

No autonomy without democracy

China has established a differentiated system of regional and local territorial autonomy to meet the demands and wishes of its 55 national minorities, which in reality are often smaller peoples. There are justifiable doubts as to whether these entities can be considered „autonomous regions", especially since one essential quality is lacking: democracy. Furthermore, the rule of law and the observance of numerous human rights are not present, even if these „national autonomies" do cover certain needs and interests of the minority peoples. Legal protection mechanisms are underdeveloped in the judicial system of the PRC.

To speak of genuine territorial autonomy, another basic prerequisite is missing: basic democratic rights, decision-making procedures and representative bodies. This does not necessarily include party pluralism in the Western sense, but it must respect fundamental democratic rights and political freedoms, in particular the right to freely elect political representatives in the Regional Assembly and the right to freely stand as a citizen in any election. Other important fundamental political rights enshrined in the UN Charter of Fundamental Rights, the ICCPR and ICSER of 1966 are not respected in China. Today, the most blatant examples of violations not only of basic democratic rights but also of fundamental human rights are XUAR (Xinjiang/East Turkestan) and the Tibet Autonomous Region.

In regulating autonomy, constant reference is made to „socialist development", which must govern the policies of the autonomous regions. Autonomy is thus embedded in a framework of national laws, rules and institutions. But there is no constitutional mechanism for controlling the vertical separation of powers. The communist party retains general control. There is no provision for direct participation by the population of the territory, except in elections at the lowest level. The weak establishment of the rule of law in China and the absence of a democratic system, together with the overriding objectives of unity and control of economic development, prevents genuine territorial autonomy, even in regions where there are no widespread human rights violations, such as Guangxi and Ningxia. In the words of Yash Ghai: „There is no independent authority to monitor the borders, so there is no clear protection against interference with autonomy. The Communist Party retains full control and within the party there is no requirement for local participation or autonomy" (Ghai, 2000, 91).

When discussing the issue of „autonomy in China", it must first of all be borne in mind that autonomy has a different status in this system than in a democratic context. In China, autonomy is decoupled from political pluralism and the rule of law in the Western sense. It is about a form of government in which ethnic groups, together with members of the majority population, are given more power in political decision-making processes (executive and legislative). The Chinese state recognises the peculiarities of the ethnic and minority cultures on its territory and is also clearly interested in promoting their political participation and social and economic development. However, all autonomy provisions have to move within the framework of the superior state laws and institutions and ultimately within the framework of the ruling power structure. This considerably restricts the freedom and scope of movement of subordinate communities and institutions.

Territorial autonomy from the Chinese perspective

From the perspective of the elite in power in China today, there is another „necessary" limitation to the concept of territorial autonomy. There must be ethnic legitimation and a minority demand for autonomy, but the granting of autonomy is made conditional on loyalty to the Chinese state and subordination to the overall interests of the state. Language, culture and education are protected to a certain extent, as long as ethnic identity does not lead to a different, „non-state" political self-esteem. The leading class of Han Chinese is aware of the historical experience of Han chauvinism and the assimilation of many minority cultures into the dominant culture. Thus they respect their history, traditions and customs to the extent that they see themselves as part of the „history of China as a whole".

But whenever minority peoples do not want to be forced into this overriding political scheme, autonomy becomes a threat. For example, Tibetan Buddhism and Xinjiang's Islam, based on their respective religious identities, have different world views than the Chinese Communist Party. A narrowly limited scope for political decision-making under strict control from above: that is all. This applies less to the former communist regulation of society and the current surveillance state than to the basic concepts of value systems, human development and human rights.

In many regions of the world today, the religious basis of ethnic identity is more strongly affected by market-economic dynamics than by Marxist-Leninist dogmas. In China, too, the strong emphasis on economic modernisation is now threatening the way of life of minority peoples more than ever before, as they are ever more integrated into the overall economic system and their natural resources are being opened up even more to external access. This has led to serious environmental impacts and huge migratory movements of Han Chinese. Such dangerous developments can be observed above all in Xinjiang and parts of Tibet. When the autonomous administration of such a region becomes „ethnic" in a strict sense, autonomy is quickly curtailed or the parallel power structure of the Communist Party intervenes with appropriate corrections. Autonomy seems to be tolerated only to the extent that it does not disturb the overall project of the Communist Party. Sovereignty, national unity and non-interference from outside are the central pivotal points. The claim to „internal self-determination" remains suspicious to those in power, not only from a political point of view, but especially when it is expressed as a claim to civilisation.

This understanding of autonomy is closely linked to the emergence of the concept of autonomy in the history of the Communist Party, where free negotiations between minority peoples and their legitimate representatives and the representatives of the majority people of the state never took place on an equal footing. However, despite the fundamental objections to the existence of autonomy in non-democratic systems, it must be noted that China, compared with other democratically governed mega-states such as India, Indonesia, Brazil and Nigeria, has also made considerable achievements in the implementation of autonomous administration and cultural protection of minorities. At least to some extent it has accommodated the needs and interests of some of the 55 officially recognised minority peoples.

"There is no real autonomy neither in East Turkestan nor in China at large."

Interview with Dolkun Isa, President of the World Uyghur Congress WUC

Dolkun Isa, 52, was born and raised in East Turkestan (Xinjiang). As a university student in 1984-1988, he became aware of the extent of the disenfranchisement of his people, the Uyghurs, whereupon he became committed to more democracy and equal rights. In 1988, Isa organised a large student rally in Urumqi, which was violently broken up by the police. Isa was expelled from the university and persecuted for years. In 1994, he fled to Turkey and applied for political asylum in Germany in 1996. He has been a German citizen since 2006. After his arrival in Germany, Dolkun founded the World Uyghur Congress (WUC), the umbrella organisation of 32 Uyghur organisations in 18 countries. In 2017, Dolkun Isa was elected president of the WUC.

There is a report from first hand by Uyghur lady Asiye Abdulaheb, who has also supported the release of the so-called „China Cables" on China's strategy in Xinjiang. What's about the forced detention centers in Xinjiang-East Turkestan?

Dolkun Isa: This eyewitness reports about appalling conditions. The living conditions vary from camp to camp, as there are about one thousand of such centres in the whole region. In some of these detention centers 20-30 people are forced to share one room with just one toilet for all. They sleep on the concrete pavement. The hygienic situation is miserable, there is a lack of water and food. The inmates are forced to work hard, many of them die soon. By force and torture they are forced to self-criticism, to admit misbehaviour and to pledge obedience. But most of them do not even know why they are kept in detention. Private visits are allowed for not more than 20 minutes, every phone call is registered.

What is happening today in East Turkestan at large?

Dolkun Isa: Not only those camps are the problem, but the whole region. East Turkistan today is a kind of „open-air-prison" for more than ten million people. East Turkestan has turned into a police state, probably you cannot find another example in the world where systematic surveillance by electronic means is so wide spread and highly organized. Not only there are everywhere cameras, but also the cell phones and the internet communication is under constant surveillance. Now also emotional recognition cameras are tested to control the citizens. China uses East Turkistan as a test area for developing new observation technologies, which later will be exported to third countries. Besides the physical monitoring today digital data control is even more important. In Tibet since 2011 an fine-mesh net of police checkpoints has been set up, now the same has been established in East Turkistan. There are thousands of police monitoring station all over the country, only in Urumchi 960 police monitoring station were built by Chen Quanguo, CCP's Regional chief. Moreover since 2016 all citizens have to download a special app to be tracked on their cell phone for 24 on 24 hours.

Looking to your country East Turkestan, the Chinese Constitution of 1982, the Law on regional national autonomy of 1984 and the act on the implementation of the LRNA of 2005 have established a kind of territorial autonomy, but China apparently is not in compliance with its own law. Additionally up to 2012 there have not been any regional acts released by the Autonomous Regions of China and subsequently approved by the standing committee of the National People's Congress, as it is required by the Chinese constitution. Have regional acts of the XUAR ever been approved by Beijing?

Dolkun Isa: Indeed, the Chinese government has to approve the draft acts approved by the Regional People's Congress of the Autonomous Regions. The People's Congress of Xinjiang is the supreme political institution of the XUAR. But in East Turkestan everything draft act is worked out by the national CCP in the interplay with the regional politbureau of the CCP. Only then the Regional People's Congress is ordered to proceed with formal discussion and approval of regional acts. This is no parliament in the European sense. It gathers just twice a year and the parliamentary process is like a show, like under telecommand by the local and national CCP.

Who are the members of the Regional People's Congress? Do all of them have to be members of the CCP?

Dolkun Isa: In a democratic society the members of a Parliamentary Assembly should all be elected by the citizens. I used to live in East Turkestan up to 1994, then I was compelled to leave my country. I have never seen an election of the Regional People's Congress of Xinjiang. Its members are just selected and appointed by the regional CCP according to their loyalty to the regional and national communist party. Every regional CCP has a party secretary, the same happens on prefecture, county and municipality level. They are the main watchdog on party loyalty.

Who can stand for election? Some scholars say, that in China on municipal level also independent citizens are allowed to stand for election.

Dolkun Isa: There are no elections, just the nomination of candidates and the appointment of the chosen delegates. I have never heard about independent candidates in the municipalities nor have I ever seen an election campaign of such candidates for a seat at any level. No formal elections are being held.

Nevertheless, some representatives of the National People's Congress are not members of the CCP. Among the members of the Xinjiang delegation there have been some imams as representatives of religious communities, who however have to recognize the leadership of the CCP.

One basic rule in China: in autonomous regions, prefectures and counties the chief governor has to be a member of the ethnic minority group of that territory. Which significance does this regulation have?

Dolkun Isa: According to autonomous law of the XUAR the governor must be an Uyghur, but these Uyghurs are never elected by the citizens, but just chosen by Xinjiang's CCP-politbureau and then appointed by Beijing. The Chinese security service, before selecting such a personality, searches his whole personal background 4 or 5 generations back. If they find any relative not really co-operative with the system, the person will not be appointed. Moreover, every candidate for higher party ranks has to complete successfully the CCP-school of party cadres in Beijing. After 2-3 years the students are graduated and tested once more before embarking a political career.

Have there ever been Uyghurs appointed as CCP-chiefs on regional, prefectural, county level in Xinjiang? Who is in charge of the local party section?

Dolkun Isa: The party secretary in all regions and provinces is definitely a Han Chinese. In East Turkestan in every public institution and also in public enterprises you have got two bosses. One is the executive director, the main decision maker. At his side there is a party cadre as a kind of watchdog. Even some private companies have got such CCP-cadres as adjoint directors. The official governor of the XUAR cannot do anything without consulting the CCP officials, who always prevail in the instruction and decision preparation. Thus, there is always a double leadership, the officially responsible head and the party official at his side. Without his approval nothing can be done.

Between the foundation of XUAR in 1955 and the crackdown of the first mass demonstrations against Chinese rule in 1988 and later in Ghulja in 1997 has there been any period when Xinjiang's autonomy was working in a limited sense?

Dolkun Isa: After Mao's death in 1976 and the end of the 1980ies we could see some kind of signs of autonomy. After ousting the "Gang of Four" Deng Xiao Ping could push forward a new strategy for China. China opened the door to the world, everything was more liberal, even before Hu Yao Bang coming to power. In the beginning of the 1980ies up to the mid 1990ies there were some signs of autonomy. Quite a lot of Uyghurs were released from jail and had some chances to professional and political careers. They could freely go to the mosque, attend schools in Uyghur language, which was the second official language of the XUAR. After Tien An Men in 1989 the wind changed and also for ethnic peoples and autonomous regions civic rights and freedoms were ever more cut back.

The author with the president of the World Uyghur Congress, Dolkun Isa, Munich 2020.

After 9/11/2001 China systematically used terrorist attacks elsewhere and some violent acts of resistance in East Turkestan as a pretext for their policy of control and assimilation in XUAR. In those years did Uyghurs ever push actively for self-determination? Has there been an organization for the liberation of East Turkestan?

Dolkun Isa: In the 1980ies the Uyghur protest was mostly peaceful. When I studied from 1984 to 1988, we could freely gather and discuss. Later in 1988 15-20.000 of us in a public rally demanded more autonomy, a stop of nuclear testing in Xinjiang and a stop to the systematic population transfer from China to our country. We also claimed democratic elections. But all of this just in compliance with the Uyghur people's right to autonomy, in other words with Chinese laws. In 1988 I led this demonstration in Urumqi. Then I was arrested and excluded from the University. After 1989 China applied new restrictions leaving anymore space to spontaneously express our protest. China also send military forces to crackdown popular protest. 8000 people, most of them civilians, were killed in the first revolt in the 1990ies. In 1997 in Ghulja peaceful demonstrations for religious freedom were suppressed in a bloody crackdown with 300 people killed as Amnesty International reported. Later China not only blamed alleged terrorist groups, but directly attacked the religious communities in East Turkestan.

What happened to family planning in Xinjiang?

Dolkun Isa: Up to 1984 in East Turkestan the one-child-policy has been applied, whereas for national minorities two children were allowed. But this has been applied in a very restrictive manner. The rule was: as a family of a national minority you are allowed to get a second child, but after the first one you have to wait at least for 3 years. The authorities not only fined families who got more children, but later even applied forced sterilization to Uyghur women. No wonder that family planning offices were attacked by angry people, who claimed freedom of decision on the number of children.

Has there been any protest against the continuous immigration of Han Chinese people to East Turkestan?

Dolkun Isa: Since 1985 the issue of stopping the population transfer from China to East Turkistan was a core issue. At that time the central dogma of family planning was the 2-children-policy for national minority peoples. But China argued that XUAR has got a big territory and a small population so that it could absorb further people. If a higher population was required in our own country, why China did not allow us Uyghurs and other minorities to have more children? This is what outraged the local population. The CCP enforces a policy to transform the Uyghurs into a minority in their own country. 1949 before Communist rule Han Chinese population in East Turkestan has been just 4-5 percent of the total population, including the military and police forces. Today, according to official data, Han Chinese are more than 40 percent. We know that Chinese statistics are not very reliable, but in this case the Government tends rather to underestimate the figures of Han people living in East Turkistan.

If we consider XUAR's autonomous powers the scope of the so-called autonomy on paper is quite big embracing many single sectors including language policy, science, culture, education and high school. Has the Uyghur language still an official position on equal footing with the Chinese language?

Dolkun Isa: According to the China's law, even today Uyghur language is the official language of the XUAR. Even on Chinese money our language appears along other languages of the autonomous regions. Until the first 1990ies the Uyghur language had equal rights and the Uyghur could use it before courts and public authorities. They could use their mother tongue everywhere and were entitled to have interpreters if necessary. Since about 30 years the role of the Uyghur language has strongly been reduced, step by step. When I was a student Chinese students were taught in Chinese and Uyghur and other minority like Kazakhs, Kyrgyz students were taught in Uyghur language. Since 2006 Uyghur is not any more used as a medium of teaching, but just a subject with some hours twice a week, even in the kindergarten. Now university students in the first year have to learn just Chinese language, later in the main course just Chinese is allowed as medium of instruction. Even Uyghur professors to Uyghur students have to teach in Chinese. This even violates Chinese law and constitution.

Which legal remedy do Uyghur people have in such cases? Has the Autonomous Region or the citizens of the XUAR any right to challenge such a measure before the Chinese supreme court?

Dolkun Isa: The head of the Court must be a member of the CCP, this is very telling about its independence. There is a double presidency as in all leading positions in China: one is the president of the court, the other the appointed party secretary. This is how the system works. The supreme power always lies with the CCP.

Can we imagine a working territorial autonomy in the framework of an authoritarian state with one-party-rule as it happens in China? Tibet's exiled government claimed for a "genuine autonomy", but could this ever be combined with China's political system?

Dolkun Isa: There is this proposal of the exile government of Tibet for genuine autonomy also claiming to treat Tibet along the principle of "One country, two systems". This proposal has been rejected by Beijing. As they did in Tibet the Red Army has captured and occupied East Turkestan, which has been an independent Republic, fully disregarding the right to self-determination of the Uyghur people and other smaller national groups. Then in 1955 China has accepted regional autonomy for Xinjiang. The same happened to Tibet which until 1949 has been a sovereign nation with a special relationship with China. Tibet later made several proposals for autonomy. There have been several meetings between Chinese government and the exile government of Tibet. According to Deng Xiao Ping's motto China first stated: we can discuss about everything, short of independence. China met the Dalai Lama's delegation for several years, but later after 2006 the whole process was stopped.

Why?

Dolkun Isa: China since the 1980ies opened up to the world and the global market, its economy was growing fast by exporting to the whole world. At that time it needed the co-operation with Western countries especially for technological exchange. Now China is almost the strongest economy in the world and doesn't need the Western countries anymore in the same degree. Thus, China took off the mask. On the other hand, now the world is interested to keep Chinese markets, to have good relationships, to benefit by Chinese investments.

Did the WUC ever propose anything similar as "genuine autonomy" for East Turkestan? Can you imagine such a compromise with China?

Dolkun Isa: According to Tibet's experience our former leaders were also calling for a dialogue with China, based on the right to self-determination. We held a big conference in the European Parliament on the topic of "self-determination" in 2010. Then we called on China's government to enter into a dialogue, but Beijing never responded. China's goals in East Turkestan are very clear: full assimilation, full control, no real autonomy, over 3 million of Uyghurs in re-education camps, all kinds of discrimination and repression of Uyghurs. Our official position as WUC is to seek freedom for the Uyghur people through peaceful, nonviolent, and democratic means in order to determine their political future independently as Uyghur people. We have completely lost trust in the Chinese state. China had ensured to grant autonomy, but has never complied with this obligation. We have the so called XUAR, but all decision making power lies with the Chinese state and the CCP.

Do you think China will ever enter into negotiations with the WUC?

Dolkun Isa: If the Chinese leadership would like to enter in a real and honest negotiation with us they had first of all to stop immediately the most serious human rights violations of millions of Uyghur people and accomplish with their international and constitutional obligations for minority protection and self-government. Before this doesn't happen, it would be senseless to talk.

Is the current development in Hong Kong a further proof that the principle of "one country, two systems" doesn't work?

Dolkun Isa: The young democracy activists in Hong Kong since about two years displayed exactly such banners "If we don't act now, tomorrow we will live like Xinjiang". Since about two years this is a widespread slogan in Hong Kong. But China doesn't care and passed the new security law. We can state without doubt: even in Hong Kong autonomy is over. Until Xi Jinping took the power, Hong Kong still had some democratic institutions, freedom of speech, media, freedom of assembly and partial democratic elections were allowed. But then step by step Beijing has increased its interference. However, the Hong Kong parliament has never been elected in fully democratic manner. Now, step by step China is tightening the noose, not taking care about international opinion.

Do you still have any contact with your family back home?

Dolkun Isa: No, most of the members of my family are held in forced detention. This is for sure for my two brothers. I don't know what's about my sister. My mother died in such a re-education camp two years ago. Recently I learnt from a Chinese newspaper report that also my father passed away. He was already over 80 years old and probably he could not survive the hard living conditions in this kind of centres. But I don't have any details about his death.

Since 1996 you are living in Germany in exile, but for many years you have been placed on Interpol's wanting list. Due to China's pressure you were wanted as a "terrorist". Are you still persecuted?

Dolkun Isa: Yes, and I do not travel in countries which are actively collaborating with China. This applies to most Asian countries, but also many other countries. I run the risk of being arrested and extradited. I am also blackmailed, and I get threats that my relatives still living in China will suffer and aren't any more safe. In the last 20 years I often have been blocked during public demonstrations in Western countries and on airports, as in Geneva, Seoul and even once in Rome. The Chinese authorities still try to hamper our activities wherever they can.

„One Country - Two Systems" in Hong Kong?

Hong Kong, which is part of the People's Republic of China, represents a special case of political-territorial autonomy. This autonomy has not been established to protect ethnic minorities, as Hong Kong is inhabited by the vast majority of Han Chinese. Rather, this autonomy serves the coexistence and integration of another economic and political system, that of the former crown colony of Hong Kong, into the „mother state" China. This autonomy is based on the Sino-British Treaty of 1984, the Assignment Agreement of 19 December 1984, which aims to preserve the special character of the area. The Hong Kong Special Administrative Region (HKSAR) of the People's Republic of China was established on 1 July 1997 on the basis of the principles of „one country, two systems" and „Hong Kong administer Hong Kong". These principles are enshrined in the Basic Law, the HKSAR Constitution. This gives Hong Kong a „high degree of autonomy".

Has Hong Kong really been granted autonomy following the transfer of sovereignty from Britain to the PRC on 1 July 1997? China has given Hong Kong guarantees that it will be a „Special Administrative Region" with special legislative and executive and judicial powers, except for foreign and defence policy. Thanks to Hong Kong's leading position as a world trading centre and its economic success, China declared its intention to leave Hong Kong's government untouched despite the transfer of sovereignty. This historically unique operation took place against the background of the accelerated transformation of the Chinese economy into a market economy, but without granting the population democratic rights and freedoms by Western standards. The Sino-British Declaration of 1984 established the principle of „one country, two systems" and is supposed to be valid from 1997 to 2047. During this period, China's socialist system may not be introduced in the HKSAR.

Today, Hong Kong can be described as a modern capitalist state with internal self-government under the sovereignty of the PRC, which is empowered to maintain national unity and territorial integrity throughout the motherland. The constitutional document of Hong Kong is the Basic Law, which was enacted by the Chinese People's Congress on 1 July 1997 („Basic Law of the Hong Kong Administrative Region of the People's Republic of China").

It endows Hong Kong with a high degree of autonomy, declares its capitalist system untouchable and maintains the separation of powers between the legislature, the executive and the judiciary. All laws previously in force in Hong Kong should remain in force unless they are in flagrant contradiction with the Basic Law. This type of constitution recognises all resident citizens of Hong Kong, the right to freedom of expression, freedom of the media, the right of assembly and demonstration, the right to free information, the right to practice religion, and also the right to strike and form trade unions. The basic norms of the International Covenants on Civil and Political Rights and the International Covenants on Economic, Social and Cultural Rights of 1966 remain in force. In addition, Hong

Kong remains an open harbour and customs territory with its own currency. The Basic Law states that free flow of capital is granted and that China may not levy taxes in Hong Kong. The Government of Hong Kong remains responsible for public order, while the People's Liberation Army is stationed in Hong Kong only for external defence.

The People's Congress of the People's Republic of China is the only institution authorised to interpret and amend the Basic Law of Hong Kong. Neither the Parliament nor the citizens of Hong Kong have this right. Hong Kong is represented in the National People's Congress by 35 MPs, all of whom are selected by Beijing. The Government of Hong Kong is accountable only to the Central People's Government in Beijing. Moreover, China has intervened several times in the autonomous Hong Kong's sphere of freedom, for example when the right to demonstrate was retroactively amended and demonstrations have to be authorised by the government in Beijing. Parties which Beijing says threaten internal security can be banned. Anti-subversion laws" are designed to prevent excessive criticism of the Chinese government. Freedom of expression can be restricted for very vaguely named reasons of national security. In the summer of 2019, a so-called law on the extradition of persons deemed criminal or a threat from Hong Kong to Beijing triggered huge mass protests directed against the Beijing-oriented government of Carrie Lam. After bitter disputes, this government was forced to withdraw this extradition law on 23.10.2019. At the local elections in November 2019 the pro-democracy camp achieved a landslide victory. The central government then took the next step to restrict autonomy and democracy in Hong Kong. On May 28, 2020, after prolonged protests and unrest, the National People's Congress of China passed a new „Security Law" for Hong Kong, giving state authorities direct access to Hong Kong citizens and new rights of intervention on Hong Kong territory.

Is Hong Kong an example of real autonomy, as it could be applied to other areas that have been annexed by China, such as Tibet and East Turkestan? After the establishment of the Hong Kong Special Administrative Region in 1997 (and the same applies to Macao in 1999), the Dalai Lama called for the same system to be applied to Tibet, with only defence and foreign policy remaining with the Chinese state, while all other powers would be left to the Tibetans with full internal autonomy. In fact, Hong Kong has retained considerable powers in foreign policy: it retains its membership of many international and regional institutions, it is allowed to conclude international agreements and even has its own currency, its economic order, tax and financial system, legal and judicial system based on the civil law modelled on the UK, civil and political freedoms, citizenship and competence for immigration. In short, a separate state order. This level of competence brings Hong Kong much closer to the status of an associated state than that of an autonomous region,

But the weakness of Hong Kong's autonomy lies in its institutional arrangement, which does not meet democratic standards: „The internal political system has a strong bias towards the chief executive, the head of government, who exercises strong control over legislation through vetoes, and also has a strong grip on legislative initiative itself. The head of government is appointed by the Chinese government and cannot be removed from office by Hong Kong's legislative body unless China itself agrees" (Ghai, 2000, 93).

On the other hand, the Head of Government cannot dissolve the Parliament. Parliament's weakness stems from its only partial democratic legitimacy. The majority of its members are appointed by narrow „functional constituencies" or special committees. These primarily reflect economic and business interests, which in turn want to keep China well-intentioned so as not to jeopardise the country as a business location. As a result, the Hong Kong government is neither able nor willing to rebel against the Chinese government, and even the more pro-autonomy members of parliament are unable to fully defend their interests vis-à-vis China.

Oskar Peterlini has identified the central weaknesses of this special position (Peterlini 2020, 124-125):

- Although the British-Chinese Joint Declaration of 1984 is binding under international law, the obligations arising from it cannot be enforced.

- The executive of the Special Administrative Region is appointed by Beijing, as are the top officials, on the proposal of the Hong Kong Head of Government.

- The Basic Law of Hong Kong is not part of the Chinese Constitution.

- There is no constitutional court in Hong Kong: „Ultimately, autonomy is decided by a political body, namely the central government" (Peterlini 2020).

- The special status is limited in time.

- The goals and interests of Hong Kong - at least the majority of its population - and those of the Chinese Communist Party diverge.

Authoritarian systems are in fundamental contradiction to autonomy, Peterlini concludes, because „constitutional and international guarantees and a democratic system are more important than the quantitative scope of autonomy" (Peterlini 2020,125).

The slogan „one country, two systems" could thus only be issued because of the lack of comprehensive democracy in Hong Kong, writes the autonomy expert Yash Ghai (Ghai 2000, 94). A genuinely democratic system in Hong Kong would not fit into „One Country", just as Taiwan does not want to voluntarily assimilate to Communist-ruled China. This contradiction stems from the very purpose of Hong Kong's autonomy, which is neither to protect an ethnic minority (98 percent of Hong Kong's population is Han Chinese), nor to introduce lasting autonomy with the right to determine Hong Kong's political status within China in free partnership. The basic purpose of this autonomy is rather to create a framework to keep Hong Kong functioning as a complementary economic zone to its economy for a transition period. Moreover, China uses Hong Kong as proof that two different legal systems can coexist in the same state, which should be taken as a constant invitation to join towards Taiwan. This is why official China immediately rejected the Dalai Lama's proposal to treat Tibet as well according to the „one country, two systems" principle. Tibet is already fully integrated into China's political and economic system and does not need a „transitional system", Beijing said.

Indeed, Hong Kong's status matches its official designation, namely a „Special Administrative Region" rather than a modern territorial autonomy. For a transitional period until 2047, the PRC allows a higher level of democratic rights and civil liberties, which, however, as in 2019 and 2020 clearly demonstrated by mass protests, will be gradually dismantled even before this kind of „autonomy" expires.

14

Doing justice to ethnic diversity: Autonomy in India

Members of the Karbi people in Diphu (Autonomous District Karbi Anglong, Assam, India)
Foto: Thomas Benedikter

India is the only state in South Asia to have some forms of modern territorial autonomy at the sub-state level, i.e. within the respective federated states. Art. 370 and 371 of the Indian Constitution provide for a special status for some territories or constituent states, namely for Jammu and Kashmir, Nagaland, Sikkim, Assam, Manipur and Arunachal Pradesh. The Indian federal system thus had some elements of asymmetry, because some of the now 28 states were given special rights. Some of these areas such as Arunachal Pradesh, Sikkim, Manipur, Mizoram, Meghalaya have subsequently advanced to federal states. The state of Jammu and Kashmir lost its special status in August 2019 and has been converted into a Union Territory. Such territories directly administered by the federal government with partial autonomy are defined as Union Territories (Art. 239 Constitution). Such a territory under more direct federal government (the chief governor is nominated by New Delhi) exists e.g. in Puducherry, the Andaman Islands, Chandigarh, Delhi itself, Ladakh (formerly part of the state of Jammu&Kashmir and Jammu and Kashmir (excluding Ladakh). Almost all truly autonomous districts of India are located in the Northeast.

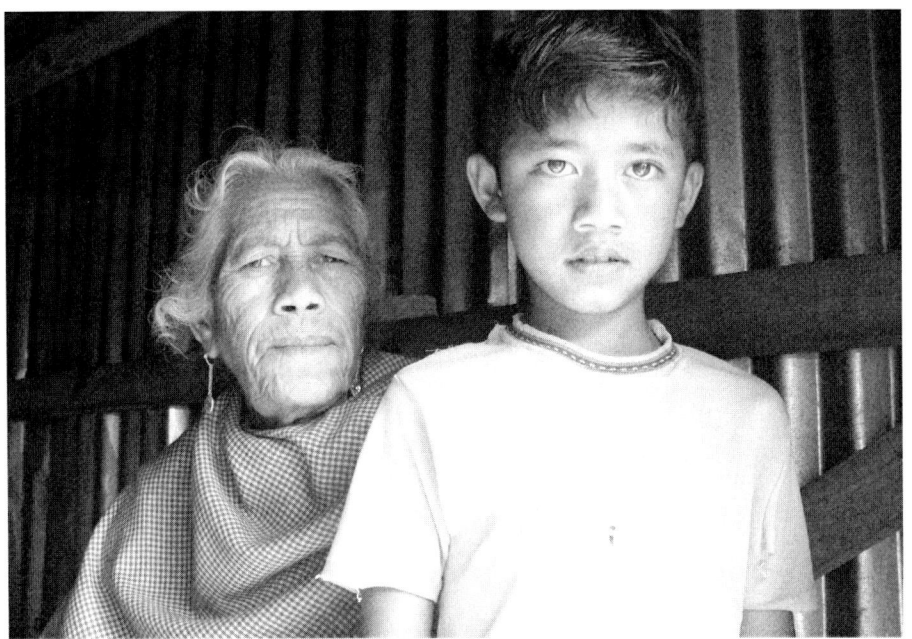

Members of the Khasi people in the Autonomous District of Jaintia, Meghalaya (India)
Foto: Thomas Benedikter

Territorial autonomy in India's constitution

Modern territorial autonomy, as it exists in 10 European states, has been introduced in India since the 1950s on the basis of the 6th Annex to the Constitution. This section allows the establishment of so-called „Autonomous District Councils" (ADC), especially in districts with a majority indigenous population. The main purpose of this provision is limited self-administration, which is intended primarily to ensure economic development and cultural self-administration. This is not a matter of ethnic reservations, but of mixed-population areas with democratically elected institutions, in which the recognised „tribal peoples" (scheduled tribes) as the titular ethnic group have guaranteed seats. Such district autonomy was established not only to protect minorities, but also to prevent ethnic conflicts and secessionist tendencies, especially in the troubled northeast of India (Assam state). 22 of the current 23 ADCs have been established in the north-eastern states of Assam, Meghalaya, Mizoram and Tripura, one in West Bengal (Gorkhaland). Only 10 of these autonomous districts are enshrined in the Indian Constitution (6th Annex), the others by state law.

India's constitution also contains various provisions to protect minorities. Article 26 of the constitution, for example, allows religious communities certain rights. Art. 30 recognises the right of ethnic minorities to their own educational institutions. Art. 371 protects the customary law, land rights and customs of indigenous peoples. Section 16 of the constitution protects certain rights of recognised castes, tribes without reference to an ancestral territory, i.e. within the framework of a kind of „cultural autonomy".

Source: en.wikipedia.org, adaptation by
Thomas Benedikter

Although there are 640 districts in India, roughly the size of a region of Italy with an average population of two million, there are no autonomous districts in the rest of the country. Unlike the autonomous districts, the other districts have no legislative powers. Territorial autonomy has thus remained the rare exception in India, although the country displays more ethnic and linguistic diversity than Europe. Today, numerous ethnic and social violent conflicts are affecting India. In several cases, the rather limited district autonomy has not been able to accommodate the desire for self-determination of smaller peoples.

In 1963, after years of uprisings and small-scale war, the Naga people of Assam were given their own federal state. A little later the new states of Mizoram, Tripura and Meghalaya were separated from Assam. The disputed area of Arunachal Pradesh, with its numerous indigenous peoples on the border with Tibet, was granted federal state status in 1987. Bodoland in Assam and Gorkhaland (Darjeeling) in West Bengal also vehemently demanded their own federal state, but have had to settle for territorial autonomy so far.

However, India's strategy of satisfying ethnic minorities and smaller peoples with this form of territorial autonomy remains rather contradictory. On the one hand, India's constitution emphasises equal rights for all ethnic groups and non-discrimination according to language, religion, caste, and therefore does not allow „ethnic autonomy" or North American-style reservations. But in order to pacify strong local conflicts, which are often carried out violently, this minimum level of territorial autonomy was created for ethnic groups that settle compactly in their ancestral territory. However, some minority peoples (titular ethnicities) who had imposed autonomous districts now felt tempted, in the context of majority democracy, to discriminate against internal ethnic minorities in the region or even to create a space for „ethnically exclusive political rule". Thus, in turn, institutional arrangements had to be put in place to maintain concordance democracy involving all groups. However, many indigenous peoples, especially those of the Adivasi natives in the states of Northern and Central India, have not yet reached this level of self-government either.

India's Autonomous District Councils

Autonomous District Council (ADC)	area (km²)	population (latest data)	capital city	part of federated state	year of constitution of autonomous entity
Bodoland	8.821	3.155.359	Kokrajhar	Assam	07.12.2003 27.1.2020 Reform
Dima Hasao (North Cachar Hills)	4.853	213.529	Haflong	Assam	17.11.1951 2.2.1970
Karbi Anglong	10.434	965.280	Diphu	Assam	17.11.1951 14.10.1976
Chakma ADC	686	45.307	Chawngte	Mizoram	1987
Lai ADC	1.870	75.477	Lawngtlai	Mizoram	1987
Mara ADC	1.445	55.000	Siaha	Mizoram	1987
Tripura Tribal Area ADC	7.132	679.720	Khumwng	Tripura	1987
Garo Hills	8.167	865.045	Tura	Meghalaya	22.02.1972 – 1979 separation
Jaintia Hills	3.819	295.692	Jowai	Meghalaya	22.02.1972
Khasi Hills	7.995	1.060.923	Shillong	Meghalaya	22.02.1972

Source: respective official websites of the Autonomous District Councils

Note: Section 6 (Schedule) of the Indian Constitution allows for the formation of autonomous districts to protect recognised minority peoples (scheduled tribes) at the sub-state level, which are roughly equivalent in size to regions in Europe. At present, all the existing autonomous districts are located in the Northeast of India (states of Assam, Meghalaya, Mizoram, Tripura, as well as in West Bengal). The Gorkhaland with capital Darjeeling of West Bengal geographically can also be counted as part of the Northeast. 10 of the 23 autonomous districts are enshrined in the Indian Constitution, 13 have been established at the state level, namely Chandel, Churachandpur, Sadar Hills, Senapati, Tamenglong, Ukhul (Manipur), Mising, Rabha Hasong, Sonowal Kachari, Thengal Kachari, Tiwa, and Deori (Assam) and Gorkhaland (West Bengal). These autonomous districts have hardly any legislative, but only administrative powers. The formerly autonomous mountain districts of Kargil and Leh in the state of Jammu and Kashmir have been converted into a separate "Union Territory" since August 2019.

Karbi Anglong: Persisting ethnic disputes despite autonomy

The Middle East of the state of Assam is home to a number of autochthonous ethnic groups, known in India as „tribals", without always carrying common features of tribal societies. They differ from the majority Assamese people in language, culture and history (Tibeto-Burmese or Austro-Asian groups), not necessarily in economic and social terms, as agriculture is the main source of income for the tribal indigenous people as for new immigrants as well. In the Karbi Anglong district, the Karbi form the relative majority, along with the Dimasa, Rengma, Tiwa, smaller groups and members of the majority Assamese population.

In the Autonomous District, which has been in existence since 1952, the Karbi language is recognised as the official language alongside Assami, but English dominates in the administration. In the sleepy district capital of Diphu, the district parliament meets once a month. Some of its members are elected (26), while others are nominated by the governor of Assam (4) to ensure that smaller minorities are represented. The state governor appointed by Delhi has a special power vis-à-vis India's district autonomies in general: not only does he appoint some of the members of the district parliaments, but he can refer back any district law or refer it to the president for approval. He can dissolve or suspend the district parliament and is fully responsible for public safety and order in the autonomous area.

The 12-member Executive Commission, a kind of district government, mainly manages some core areas of the regional economy of Karbi Anglong (agriculture, forestry, water, tourism, public services), but also has powers in the school system, culture and lower jurisdiction. However, as is often the case in India, autonomous politics at the district level is limited not only by the state, but also by finances. The Karbi Anglong Autonomous District is financed like other district autonomies from Delhi, but the money flows through Assam's state government in Guwahati. Given the low income level of its citizens, the district can hardly collect its own taxes, which makes it difficult for the government in Diphu to control the district's economic and social development significantly.

Karbi Anglong, like the autonomous district of Dima Hasao (North Cachar Hills) to the south, is a multi-ethnic district. This poses the permanent challenge of establishing political agreement among different ethnic groups. Karbi as an official language is only used to a limited extent, as the lingua franca is English. The smaller ethnic groups would not welcome a stronger role for the Karbi either. But even for them, this district autonomy offers too few opportunities for development. Following the pattern of similar fronts in Assam, Nagaland, Manipur and Tripura, radical groups have formed, which take armed action against the army and police and against migrants and settlers coming from outside.

A second line of conflict runs right through the district's society. For decades, Assam had forced the immigration of members of the majority population, while district autonomy did not provide the Karbi and other indigenous ethnic groups with sufficient means to control this migration. This is a problem that Karbi Anglong shares not only with other autonomous districts, but with the state of Assam itself, where radical liberation fronts like the ULFA have been militantly opposing immigration from West Bengal and the rest of India for many years.

In the neighbouring state of West Bengal, the ethnic Nepali in the Darjeeling district have been fighting for decades to extend their limited autonomy and to create their own state „Gorkhaland". In 2012 the new „Gorkhaland Territorial Administration" was constituted, replacing the old „Darjeeling Gorkha Hill Council" (1988-2012). However, the directly elected District Assembly has not been given real legislative sovereignty by the state of West Bengal.

The autonomous Bodoland

Kokrajhar, the capital of Bodoland (today officially: Bodoland Territorial Area District) does not give the impression of a state capital. Nothing indicates to the visitor that one of the few autonomous regions of India is governed from here. Only a few signs at the railway station and on public buildings indicate that Bodo is the co-official language of the country, in addition to English and the national language Assami. A language which, unlike most tribal languages of India, is also written and has a literary tradition. The Bodo language has been officially recognised in the Indian Constitution. As is often the case in India and especially in the multi-ethnic north-east of the country, the population is colourful. Not only Bodos who belong to the Tibeto-Burmese families live in Bodoland, but also Assami, Bengali, Nepali, Rajbongshi, Adivasi and a number of other recognised and non-recognised minorities.

The building of the Autonomous Regional Government, called the Executive Committee, is a more inconspicuous structure for an autonomous region of 3.1 million people. The legislative assembly of the Bodoland has a more representative seat. But Bodoland is also one of the poorest areas of Assam. It came into being as an autonomous region in 2003 as a result of a peace agreement between the state and the „Bodoland Liberation Tigers", the Bodoland Liberation Front, and was able to significantly increase its autonomy again in 2020.

The Bodos had already demanded self-government from the British colonial regime in 1929. In 1969, the „All Bodo Students' Union" ABSU was founded as the spearhead of a broad movement for political independence of the Bodoland. The ABSU fought for the preservation of the Bodo language and against the increasing immigration from other parts of India, especially from the densely populated West Bengal. Like other small peoples in India, the Bodos' demand for self-determination was ignored for decades. A turning point came for the Bodos in the 1980s, when a movement for autonomy or even secession emerged. The Bodoland Liberation Tigers (BLT) and the majority Christian National Democratic Front of Bodoland (NDFB) fought by force of arms for their own state along the lines of Nagaland and Mizoram. The dense jungle on the long border with Bhutan became a retreat area for countless attacks and attacks by the Bodo Liberation Tigers. But when Bhutan drove the Bodo fighters out, the Bodos came

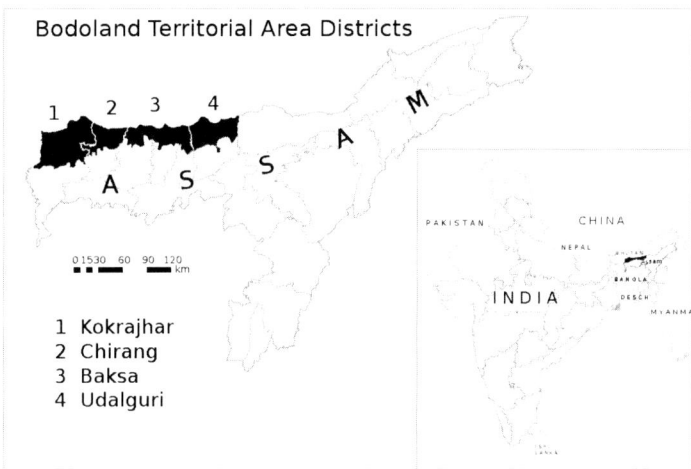

Bodoland Territorial Area Districts in Assam (India). Author: Furfur, Own work. Licence: CC BY-SA 3.0

under pressure and finally accepted a compromise solution, namely territorial autonomy within the state of Assam. Today, the ABSU still aspires to a separate state like Mizoram and Nagaland. Other Bodo political parties have reached a compromise with the state of Assam and the federal state to create a territorial autonomy.

With about two million people, the Bodos form the largest ethnic minority in the Assam lowlands, often referred to in India as „tribal society" (tribe). Under the Indian constitution, a distinction is made between „recognised tribes" (scheduled tribes) and non-recognised tribes (non-scheduled tribes). The word „Bod" means home. The Bodos had an influential kingdom until the 13th century. Once the Bodos had been the most powerful people in western Assam, but were gradually assimilated by the Assamese, who belong to the same ethnic family. The Bodo language has been written since the middle of the 19th century and has been used as a second language of instruction in the Bodoland schools since 1963. Bodo today is also officially used in the administration, in the media and in some Assamese universities. The Language Law of the State of Assam recognised Bodo as a co-official national language in 1985. According to the 2011 census, 30.5 percent of the population speak Bodo, followed by Assamese (23.7 percent) and Bengali (26.8 percent). The official languages may not be changed without Assam's consent, nor may the autonomous Bodoland unilaterally determine the languages of instruction in public schools.

On 7 December 2003, in Kokrajhar, thousands of Bodo fighters laid down their weapons in the presence of the Indian Deputy Prime Minister and the Assam Head of Government. The autonomous region was officially constituted as „Bodoland Territorial Area District" (8,821 km2, 2020: 3,155.000 inhabitants) according to the 6th Annex of the Indian Constitution, with the purpose of maintaining the economic, educational, linguistic, socio-cultural and ethnic identity of the Bodos and to promote the development of their autonomous region.

The Assembly Hall of the Bodoland Autonomous District in Kokrajhar. Foto: Thomas Benedikter

The central organ of autonomy is a directly elected state parliament with 40 directly elected members. 6 members are appointed by the Governor of Assam to represent the other ethnic communities. The regional assembly (Bodoland Territorial Council) elects a 14-member autonomous government and is responsible for economic development, education, land rights, language use, customs and ethnic identity, and infrastructure. The former head of the Bodo Liberation Tigers, Hagrama Mohilary, was appointed as the first head of the autonomous government. His party, the Bodoland Progressive Front, has ruled the autonomous region for three terms of office, also provides 11 members of the Assam Parliament and sits in the state cabinet. Mohilary and his party have been replaced in ruling Bodoland in the recent elections held in December 2020.

When the Indian federal government supported the creation of the new state of Telangana in 2013, which was split off from Andhra Pradesh in 2014, the agitation for a Bodoland state revived. There were strikes, rail and road blockades, government buildings went up in flames. After prolonged disputes, a new peace agreement was reached on 27 January 2020 between the Indian government, the government of Assam and the three most representative Bodo parties. This gave Bodoland a total of 40 legislative powers, almost all of which have already been transferred. Additional areas populated by Bodos were incorporated into the autonomous region, and some areas by majority not populated by Bodos were excluded. Also after this border adjustment of 2020 only a slight majority of the population of the Autonomous Region are ethnic Bodos. The 6th Annex of the Indian Constitution had to be amended to allow special regulations in this case, as Bodoland's District Council hat to ensure the representation of all ethnic groups of the autonomous territory.

Land rights are of paramount importance for a predominantly agricultural region like Bodoland. The Bodos had always tried to prevent the sale of „tribal land" to people who do not belong to recognised tribes. However, it was precisely this section of the population that had repeatedly complained about discrimination by the dominant Bodos. The Bodoland now no longer has jurisdiction over land transfer and inheritance law. Other Indian citizens who do not belong to recognised tribes can also acquire land.

Also of great importance is the development of the administration, which can organise the Bodoland autonomously. However, all ethnic groups must be granted access to administrative posts. The police force, which is under the responsibility of the state of Assam, does not remain under the authority of the Bodoland Territorial Council. In an economically rather backward region, particular attention will be paid to economic development and a fair share of infrastructure investments by the State of Assam. Here the Bodos have learned from the bad experiences of other autonomous regions of Assam. Today, the Bodoland enjoys a full say in the state's development planning and has secured a fair share of the investments co-financed by the Federal Government in Delhi. The new autonomy statute lays down a number of new development projects, such as the establishment of businesses and the construction of infrastructure, universities and research facilities. Bodoland has experienced an astonishing economic development since autonomy, but too much concentrated in the district's capital.

The Bodos have fought for decades for the recognition and protection of their language, comparable to the Basques in Spain. For the ABSU, language rights and education policy are the touchstone for the success of autonomy. It was not until 2020 that the ABSU was able to push through the establishment of a university in the state capital Kokrajhar, where Bodo also teaches. The quality of school teaching, language planning and development, autonomous school administration, teacher training: all this can now be managed by the autonomous Bodoland itself. There is now massive investment in education and research. Bodo had only been accepted as a language of instruction in schools since 1985. The school and higher education system needs more resources, which the new autonomy agreement of 2020 put more emphasis on by the student organisation.

On 27 January 2020, the representatives of the National Democratic Front of Bodoland (NDFB), the ABSU and representatives of the federal government in Delhi signed the new peace agreement. At the same time, 1,550 fighters of the various Bodo militias laid down their arms. The agreement includes the following main innovations:

- The Bodoland Assembly is increased from 40 to 60 members.
- A central university will be established in Barama.

- A factory in Bodoland will manufacture railway wagons.
- Indian Sports Authority centres will be established.
- A welfare authority will look after Bodos living outside Bodoland.
- A cancer clinic and training centre will be set up in Tamalpur.
- A new college for veterinary medicine is to be established.
- The federal government of India recognises the Bodo people as a „hill tribe".
- The government of Assam recognises the Bodo language in Devanagari script as the co-official official language of the state of Assam.

Overall, the new peace agreement provides the basis for self-governance, economic development and inter-ethnic relations in the Bodoland region. Concordance democracy remains a challenge, as the politically strongly united Bodos cannot govern alone in this multi-ethnic region. Compromises between the titular nation (Bodo) and the other minorities, between the recognised tribesmen (scheduled tribes) and the non-tribal population must be found continuously. The non-tribal population often feels disadvantaged, whereas the Bodo parties initially did not want to share power after the long struggles. So the peaceful coexistence of all ethnic groups with concordance democracy remains the Bodoland's biggest challenge. The region is considered the most advanced territorial autonomy of India. Nevertheless, the goal of creating a separate Bodoland state has not yet disappeared from the political agenda of the Bodo movements, even after the extension of autonomy in 2020. At the federal level, however, the creation of new, ethnically homogenous states in India is increasingly viewed critically.

Conclusion: reform impetus for more regional autonomy needed

The demand for regional autonomy is being voiced more and more loudly in India by various ethnic groups and regions, from the „tribal belt", the large central Indian strip from Madhya Pradesh to Orissa and its numerically significant Adivasi peoples such as the Santhal, Gondi, Ho and Bhili, to smaller groups such as the Karbi in Assam, the Rajbongshi in Cooch Bihar in Bengal, the Naga and Kuki in Manipur. But the formation of new states and autonomous districts is highly controversial in India. „Ethnic autonomy" is rejected above all by the Congress Party and the Left Parties in the name of national unity. On the other hand, ethnically conditioned conflicts, both between states and smaller ethnic groups and in connection with immigration from outside, are anything but resolved. In the north-east of India, it has become clear that the weak forms of „district autonomy" according to the 5th and 6th Annexes of the Indian Constitution are no longer sufficient to meet the demands for territorial self-government.

Umbrella organisations of indigenous peoples have also been created in central India, which are emphatically demanding more autonomy. Here, as in Nepal during the Maoist uprising, ethnic discrimination and social exclusion are threatening to intertwine, encouraging the Naxalite guerrilla organisations. On the one hand, previous forms of district autonomy have reached their limits in various cases (Gorkhaland, Karbi Anglong). On the other hand, India generally does not have a level of government between the states and the municipalities with legislative powers. The majority of India's states correspond to the large or medium-sized European states in terms of area and population. Thus, such a requirement not only arises from reasons of minority protection and ethnic conflicts, but also constitutes a fundamental deficit of Indian democracy. Around 50 of India's 640 districts - roughly comparable to the odd 300 regions of Europe - have a different majority from the language of the state to which they belong. It is not surprising that many of India's minority languages do not enjoy guaranteed rights and some are threatened with extinction.

India is not only a relatively centralised federal state with unusual powers for the Union government. This centralism is also repeated at the state level, while regional autonomy is completely underdeveloped. This is also the reason why regions (districts) usually demand their own federal state at once. Traditionally, India's political elite has put aside attempts at autonomy because they feared the centrifugal forces and have always fought secessionist tendencies resolutely with military force. Under the impression of the division of the subcontinent and the ethnic diversity of this state, „national unity" is a basic dogma. Now regional autonomy could pacify ethnic conflicts without calling state sovereignty into question. Today, it is not a matter of creating „ethnic reservations", but of modern territorial autonomies that combine consociational democratic self-government, territorial power sharing and the protection of minorities in the best possible way. The right to autonomy and its legal and political form within the constitution urgently need a reform push in India.

„Let's make the most of this autonomy!"

An interview with P.K Hazoari, former Chief Secretary of the Bodoland Territorial Council (Bodoland Territorial Area District, Assam, India)

Foto: Thomas Benedikter

Bodoland autonomy has been in force since 2003. What results so far?

Hazoari: Our autonomy has been functioning since 7 December 2003. of the BTC, the citizens of Bodoland are free to decide on the development of our country development of our country based on our local reality and the needs of our needs of our population. It has brought remarkable improvements in transport links, education, health facilities, drinking water supply, agriculture and a number of other areas agriculture and some other areas.

The Bodo people are the titular nation in the territory of the BTC, the autonomous Bodoland. What other ethnic groups or tribal peoples live in Bodoland and are equally recognised as scheduled tribes as the Bodos?

Hazoari: The other tribes residing in the BTC area are the Ravas, Garos, Hajongs, Modahi Kocharis. Except the Hajongs all the other communities are recognized as ST. The other ethnic communities that are not STs are Rajbongshis, Nath Yogis, and members of scheduled castes who are scattered in lower numbers all over the BTC area. There is also a larger proportion of members of the majority population of Assam and Bengal.

What importance does the status of STs have for the institutional order of the BTC and for the social and economic rights of the respective peoples? Is there any quota system applied in the civil service by the BTC on the basis of the ST status of the applicants?

Hazoari: With the exception of the Bodos, the other recognised ethnic groups do not have the numerical strength to be represented in the Bodoland Legislative Assembly. Therefore, according to the provisions of the 6th Schedule of the Constitution of India, 6 seats are reserved for the smaller indigenous communities in any case. 30 of the 46 seats are reserved for representatives of the recognised ethnic groups, 5 are elected in constituencies open to all voters, and 5 seats are reserved for constituencies of candidates who do not belong to the recognised ethnic groups. Thus, 40 members of the Bodoland Assembly are directly elected by the people, 6 representing the smaller tribal communities are directly nominated by the Assam government.

Bodo is recognised as the second official language alongside Assamese in Bodoland. Is Bodo therefore really on an equal footing with the state language? What languages are used in schools?

Hazoari: Bodo is the official language in Bodoland. Bodo, Assamese, Hindi and Bengali are used as languages of instruction in schools in our country. In addition, Santhali, Garo, Arabic, Urdu, Persian and other languages are also taught as language subjects in public schools. Rajbongshi is taught in some districts of Bodoland. There is no constitutional or state law provision in India to exclude any language as a language of instruction in the public school system.

Is there any provision in the Bodoland government for proportional representation of each ethnic group in the institutions?

Hazoari: No, in the 6th Schedule of the Constitution of India, on which our autonomy is based, there is no provision or guideline for the allocation of government seats according to the respective proportion of the population of Bodoland.

What happens if the autonomous Bodoland comes into conflict with the state of Assam in the exercise of its 40 powers? Do the laws of Bodoland prevail once they have been countersigned by the Governor of Assam?

Hazoari: To date, no contradictory situation or repugnancy has arisen in the field of legislation between the state of Assam and the BTC. There are specific provisions guiding the preparation and enactment of law in the Constitution. The law enacted by the State Legislature or Government cannot override the law enacted by the Government of India and the laws of the BTC legislature.

The purpose of territorial autonomy is not only the autonomous self-government of an area, but also the protection of the ethnic, indigenous minorities of the area, especially in the field of language policy, culture, media and school. Does Bodoland have sufficient powers for this purpose?

Hazoari: One cannot answer this with a blanket yes or no. To date, within the framework of the existing autonomy, the rights to regulate language use and education have proven to be sufficient. But the lack of funding for these programmes brings enormous obstacles to the development of Bodoland.

What is the general situation regarding the financing of the autonomy of the Bodoland BTC?

Hazoari: The BTC is not self-sufficient with respect to developing financial means to act as an agent of development. The funds received from the Government of India and the State of Assam are the only means of financing the development of the BTC area. They can be invested in the departments and transferred to the BTC for agriculture and forestry, transport and health care. The BTC has no power to impose taxes except on forest and land revenues. Therefore, the implementation of part of policies in education and language requires further means of funding.

The so-called Autonomous District Councils in India are usually funded by the federal government, with these funds being allocated through the respective constituent states. Does this work in the case of Bodoland and Assam and is this funding sufficient for the BTC?

Hazoari: The system of allocating funds through the respective state government works sufficiently well. However, channeling funds to the BTC through the State requires the positive participation of the Union, the State and the BTC. The flow of funds from the Union to the BTC makes a tedious journey as it takes at least 6 to 8 months if not more to reach the Council. It is noted that neither the Union, the State or the Council can be made solely responsible for the irregular flow of funds in a given process. Autonomy and its interpretation varies from area to area, community to community, country to country, and state to state.

How should the current constitutional provision on sub-state territorial autonomy under the 6th Schedule of the Constitution be improved to allow such areas as Bodoland a higher degree of self-governance?

Hazoari: It will be more practicable if the devolution of powers continues according to the experience gathered and the capacity entrusted to the Council of absorbing power and finance. The devolution of power from the Union to the State and from the State to the Council should be a natural process. With the passing of time as more experience is gathered, the scope of powers devolved from the Union to the States and from the States to the ADCs requires periodic review.

Does the BTC also have powers over local security and police?

Hazoari: No.

What representation rights do the Bodos enjoy in the Assam state parliament?

Hazoari: There is no specific legal provision in the Indian Constitution according the Bodo people special representation in the State Assembly. There are reserved Constituencies for the scheduled tribes (ST) in the Assam Assembly from which representatives of our population are elected to the Assam Assembly. At present there are 12 members of the Legislative Assembly of Assam and 3 Ministers in the Assam Cabinet from the Bodo community.

What are the main problems of Bodoland today?

Hazoari: That depends entirely on one's point of view. Seen through the eyes of a politician, the situation of Bodoland is different from the perspective of civil servants or ordinary citizens. In my personal opinion, the most important challenge for autonomous Bodoland is to maintain internal peace.

15

Autonomies in crisis: Nicaragua's Caribbean Coast and Indian Kashmir

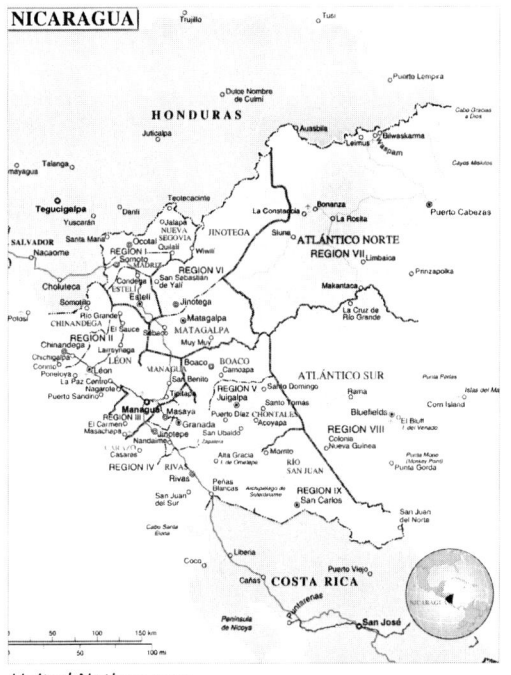

United Nations map

Two very different regions, one in Central America, the other in South Asia, were granted autonomy in very different constitutional forms decades ago. Today, both are in a deep crisis that threatens not only their proper functioning but also their very existence: the state of Jammu and Kashmir with its exceptional autonomy in the state of India and the two Caribbean regions of Nicaragua, to be seen on the map on Nicaragua's eastern part, once termed "Atlantico Sur" and "Atlantico Norte".

Nicaragua's autonomous Carribbean coastal regions

Nicaragua's Caribbean coastal regions are separated from the more densely populated western part of the country by mountains and dense rainforest. This region, formerly known as the Mosquito Coast, occupies more than half of the country's territory, but only 12 percent of its population. Three groups of people live in these two regions: firstly, the indigenous Miskito, Sumu and Rama peoples; secondly, the Garifuna, descendants of later immigrant Africans; and thirdly, the Spanish-speaking mestizos. While in the northern Caribbean region just over half of the inhabitants are indigenous, in the southern region a good 80 percent of the population are mestizos. The ethnic composition of the population of the Caribbean coast of Nicaragua has changed dramatically over the last 30 years. Thousands and thousands of mestizos have migrated from western Nicaragua, especially to the northern Caribbean coast, where the population has doubled to 480,874 (2015). The Caribbean Coast South region has a population of 385,000. Many immigrants have illegally appropriated land and refuse to comply with official eviction notices. Politically, too, the relationship between the ethnic groups has steadily deteriorated. This has led to growing tensions and, more recently, violence.

Land rights of indigenous peoples: a litmus test for territorial autonomy in Nicaragua

The issue of collective land ownership by indigenous peoples has been a problem in the history of relations between Nicaragua and its Caribbean coast since the annexation of this territory in 1894. In 1980, after the Sandinista revolution, this issue returned on the agenda and was one of the triggers for the military conflict between the revolutionary Sandinistas and the indigenous communities of the Caribbean coast. The FSLN (Frente Sandinista de Liberación Nacional) did not understand the fundamental importance of land rights for the indigenous peoples in the area. For the Miskito, Sumu and Rama, community ownership of the land is not only the basis for economic subsistence, but also crucial for culture, tradition and social cohesion, in short, their identity. The FSLN misunderstood this claim as an obstacle to the renewal of society in the sense of more social justice. The dialogue with indigenous organisations failed. Only after years of armed conflict, abused by the USA for the CIA-funded "contra" insurgence, did both sides agree to establish territorial autonomy. Autonomy for the Caribbean coast was enshrined in Nicaragua's constitution in 1987. Community ownership of the land of the indigenous peoples of the Caribbean coast has also been recognised in the Constitution (Article 89). In addition, the Statute of Autonomy enshrines the right to preserve language and culture, to traditional social and political forms of organisation and to their own local government.

But this territorial autonomy remained on paper until well after 2000, because the conservative governments ruling from 1990 to 2006 were unwilling to apply the Statute of Autonomy. It was not until 2003 that the State Law on the Common Land Ownership of Indigenous Peoples and Ethnic Communities of the Caribbean Coast was passed (Law 445). This law was not fully implemented either. Despite progress in demarcating indigenous land ownership - 31.6 percent of the total national territory - property rights are not respected in practice. So

- there is often a lack of land registration as a prerequisite for indigenous owners to assert their claim to ownership;
- this makes it difficult for the legitimate owners to remove illegal settlers from this land;
- there is a threat of expropriation of large areas of land by the state due to large-scale state projects, especially the planned Interoceanic Canal;
- the autonomous institutions are being undermined by a centralised policy of the state government. They are dominated by the representatives of new immigrants, who marginalise the indigenous people.

Against this background, the implementation of indigenous land rights has become the acid test for the success of the Caribbean Coast's territorial autonomy: does Nicaragua want to fulfil its legal obligations towards the indigenous peoples at all? Will the political representatives of the two autonomous regions manage to safeguard the legitimate rights of the indigenous peoples? Are the autonomous regions able to set limits on illegal infiltration from the rest of the country? If not, the autonomy of the Caribbean regions of Nicaragua would have lost its meaning.

The question of eviction of land by illegal settlers is a huge social challenge which the state would have to overcome in years of legal proceedings. But this does not happen, and so the potential for violence increases. The government calls for „cohabitation" of Mestizo settlers with indigenous communities. It is not seriously honouring its duty to end the settlers' illegal land occupations, but simply sticking to the status quo in order to „sit out" the indigenous demand. This leads to growing violent clashes between illegal settlers and indigenous people. The reason for this is that the FSLN does not want to jeopardise the sympathies of tens of thousands of such settlers and their political support. The illegal settlers are increasingly resorting to armed violence, which has already claimed hundreds of victims. Thus, for the indigenous communities, whether their collective land rights are enforced has simply become a matter of survival.

Moreover, since 2006, the FSLN in particular has been promoting a neoliberal model of tapping and exploiting the resources of the Caribbean Coast. The mega-project of the Interoceanic Canal, the „second Panama Canal", which would largely be dug through the southern Caribbean region, is of decisive importance in this context. The rights of the Rama and Creoles living there to refuse their consent are likely to be circumvented, their interests subordinated to those of foreign investors - whether from the USA, Mexico or China. Contrary to the original spirit and letter of autonomy, the state has not guaranteed the Caribbean Coast's autonomous decision-making power for its economic development. Although the FSLN, which has been in power again since 2006, has declared its external commitment to autonomy, it wants to exercise political control over the area in order to enforce its national development strategy. This can only lead to conflict if the autonomous political institutions want to protect collective land ownership, prevent massive environmental destruction and shape their own cultural, economic and ecological development.

The undermining of regional democracy

The directly elected regional assemblies of the two autonomous Caribbean regions have legislative sovereignty for a range of powers. Their 45 deputies come from all ethnic groups living there. The Assembly elects the autonomous government, the so-called „Regional Coordination". According to the statute, the state is obliged to support them in setting up a regional administration. Now, in the 34 years since the establishment of the Caribbean Autonomous Regions, real self-government has barely come to fruition, for three reasons (Gonzales 2015, 77):

1. Nicaragua's traditional centralism and the nationalism of its parties.
2. The non-functioning of the autonomous administration, which has excluded indigenous groups from decision-making processes.
3. The excessive power of Nicaragua's national parties, which have increasingly marginalised local political organisations and leaders.

In this context, the consensus-based decision-making processes of the indigenous peoples of the Caribbean coast have come into massive conflict with the Western model of party rule based on the majority principle. Autonomy and self-determination threaten to become hollow phrases in such a context if the state no longer complies with its constitutional mandate and legal obligations. Thus, both are at stake in the Caribbean regions: the political autonomy of the two areas and the implementation of land rights of the indigenous communities of the regions. Autonomy, land rights and cultural identity are to be defended against land occupations and alienation by the mestizos with the complicity of the state. If these violations continue, peaceful coexistence within a democratically governed autonomous region will no longer be able to function.

There are many examples in America, where it is precisely the deprivation of land ownership that has marked the beginning of the end for the Native Americans. Can territorial autonomy, established to protect the indigenous population, work if the state does not protect the territory from illegal immigration, land occupation and exploitation by foreign capital interests? Isn't autonomy being taken ad absurdum if the state floods the territory with members of the majority population and then the national parties in the autonomous region take power and push the indigenous people politically to the wall? The Caribbean Coast of Nicaragua thus becomes the acid test for the functioning of a territorial autonomy in such problematic situations.

State Law 445 established local and community administrations with tasks similar to those of European local governments. Their leaders are elected in local assemblies in accordance with customary procedures. The regional assemblies of the two autonomous regions must subsequently recognise and finance these local authorities. In 2014 and 2019, the FSLN has won about three quarters of the seats in the two regional assemblies and governs in both regions. Now, however, it is becoming increasingly common for local governments not to be recognised by the autonomous region if they are not party-politically on the same line.

Even democratic elections and the legitimisation of local governments are of no use if the regional government fails to recognize their public legitimacy as state institutions. This approach has led to great insecurity among the indigenous population and has undermined democratic processes. Only where FSLN-approved local administrators are elected can they count on the blessing from above and thus on the Autonomous Region's willingness to cooperate. Political representation is increasingly doubling, with only those representatives not elected by the people but legally recognised by the FSLN-controlled regional government able to make decisions.

Local elections, the very expression of autonomy and self-government, have thus become a battlefield of party interests. A policy that sows mistrust, frustration and a propensity for violence. This also has to do with the institutional design of the whole territorial autonomy in Nicaragua. Ethnic-territorial self-government has been sacrificed to the preserve in power of the offshoots of the state parties - above all the FSLN - which pursue their own interests, bring their own voters with them through forced immigration, and thus marginalise the ancestral population.

The FSLN has a centralist, authoritarian, now modernist vision of state and society. In this sense, indigenous self-government has to be subordinated to limited autonomy under the command of the same party. This puts Nicaragua on the same level as Indonesia, Bangladesh, Morocco and, interestingly, China. While numerous civil-society organisations are trying to rescue autonomy, the authoritarian leadership of the FSLN and the state under President Daniel Ortega is fundamentally questioning the autonomy of the Caribbean Coast.

Yet this chapter had begun in 1987 with the establishment of the Caribbean autonomies with many hopes. The armed conflict had been ended. The historically rooted mistrust between the population of the Caribbean Coast and the rest of Nicaragua had been resolved, and mutual recognition and respect were to be established. A territorial autonomy which was part of the general policy of recognising the multicultural character of the region and democracy in much of Latin America from 1992 onwards.

Until 1987, the idea of autonomy had to be enforced against the historical centralism of Nicaragua's political elites, and then right-wing governments were not interested in its implementation. Since 2006, the Caribbean region has been confronted with an increasingly authoritarian FSLN that tends to be neoliberal in its economic policy. All this has led to very unfavourable conditions for territorial autonomy, which is in deep crisis in both Caribbean regions of Nicaragua.

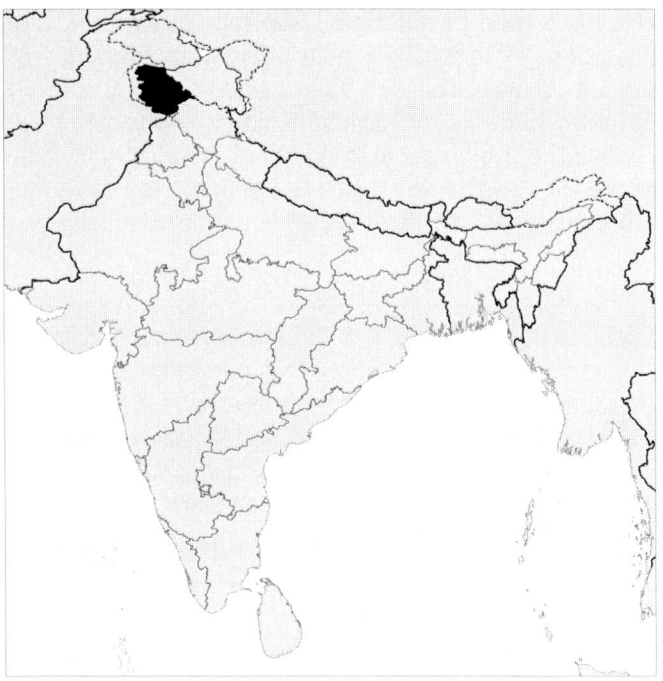

The new Union Territory of Jammu und Kashmir (since 2019)
Source: Wikipedia, author: TUBS, India location map

Indian Kashmir - Autonomy permanently lost?

On November 1, 2019, the Indian state of Jammu and Kashmir lost its special status in India's federal system, was split up and transformed into two union territories: the mainly Buddhist Ladakh in the north, the Kashmir valley and Jammu in the south. As such, these two new territories are directly governed by the federal government through governors appointed by Delhi, while the power of the elected parliament of the former state has been substantially reduced. Jammu and Kashmir had been granted its special status with the creation of the state of India in 1947 with an additional article in the Indian Constitution (Article 370), as a kind of substitute for the self-determination by referendum demanded by the Muslim Kashmiris, which had been promised by Pakistan and India to the UN, but ever since denied. This special status did not actually mean „territorial autonomy" in the sense outlined here, but corresponded to the status of a federal state with some special rights. Since only a few Indian states such as Sikkim, Nagaland and Mizoram have such special rights enshrined in the constitution, India cannot really be classified as an „asymmetrical federal state". India's federal state model is more comparable to that of Canada, which has only granted some special rights to its French-speaking province of Québec. Territorial autonomy in India exists only at the sub-state level. Nevertheless, in the case of Indian administered Kashmir, the term „autonomy" is often used.

On the basis of this Article 370 of the Indian Constitution - a „provisional provision" - all legislative powers have been transferred to the State of Jammu and Kashmir with the exception of foreign policy, defence and communications. A further Constitutional Article 35a, inserted in 1954, allowed the Parliament of that State to determine who is eligible to vote, to legally acquire land and to hold government offices as citizens of the State.

Since 1947, Pakistan and India have fought three wars over Kashmir, but everything has remained the same. Jammu and Kashmir's special status has been gradually eroded since 1953 without formally amending the Constitution. New Delhi's constant interference, the police's hard hand against any opposition and the curtailment of autonomy rights finally led to the Kashmiri uprising since the 1990s, with violence and counter-violence that continues to this day. After the bloody suppression of political and military resistance, India has driven the Kashmiri population of the Kashmir Valley into frustration and bitterness. The vast majority would probably support secession, but this remains a distant dream.

The Hindu nationalist majority in government under Prime Minister Narendra Modi did exactly the opposite. It was only a matter of time before these special rights of the state of Jammu and Kashmir were formally removed from the constitution. Law No. 34/2019, passed by the Indian House of Commons on 9 August 2019, not only abolished the special rights previously guaranteed by Article 370 of the Constitution. Jammu and Kashmir was also divided and degraded to a Union territory. The measure was justified by the continuing unrest in the region. It was imposed against fierce opposition from all parties in Kashmir, which will inevitably exacerbate tensions in the Kashmir Valley.

The former head of government of Jammu and Kashmir, Mehbooda Mufti of the People's Democratic Party (DPP), described 1 November 2019, when the abolition of Kashmir's special status came into force, as the „darkest day in Indian history". By lifting the special status, the Modi government fulfilled an old demand of the Hindu nationalist right. The latter never accepted the Islamisation of Kashmir that began in the 13th century and openly advocates forced immigration of Hindus into the Kashmir valley in order to change its population composition. This strategy amounts to the same strategy as that of China in Xinjiang and Tibet, Indonesia in West Papua, Morocco in the Western Sahara and Bangladesh in the Chittagong mountain regions.

The Kashmir conflict is a direct consequence of the collapse of the British colonial empire in South Asia and its division into two hostile states. At that time, the princely states had the right to choose between Muslim Pakistan and the secular state of India. Now, two-thirds of the population of the Princely State of Jammu and Kashmir was Muslim, but their prince, a Hindu Maharajah, chose India for reasons of retaining power. India seized the opportunity and occupied most of the former princely state, thus forestalling an invasion of Pakistan. India never fulfilled the UN's promise to the conflicting parties to hold an internationally supervised referendum on future status throughout the territory of the former princely state.

Indian soldiers in Kashmir. Foto: Thomas Benedikter

Historical Jammu and Kashmir has been divided since 1947, the demarcation line (Line of Control) is not an internationally recognised border, where gunfights and guerrilla actions occur time and again. Separatist groups have carried out attacks in Jammu and Kashmir for decades. Islamist groups also tried to use the Kashmir conflict for their own purposes. This led India to turn the state into a military occupation zone, where at times no less than 60,000 soldiers and paramilitaries were stationed. The peaceful political protests of the Kashmiri have been fruitless. Decades of bloody repression have led to enormous frustration and despair among the Muslim population. Seldom in the history after the World War II has there been such a blatant disregard for the right of self-determination of an entire people

However, the unification of three different parts of the country into a single federal state was unfavourable to a self-determination solution. First the completely Muslim Kashmir valley, then the predominantly Hindu Jammu and then Ladakh, a mountainous region in the north of the former state of Jammu and Kashmir that has been historically influenced by Tibetan Buddhism and is very sparsely populated. Ladakh itself had only been conquered by the Maharajah of Kashmir in the middle of the 19th century, but had remained part of the predominantly Muslim state even after the annexation to India. The western part of Ladakh (Kargil) is Muslim in character. Although Ladakh has enjoyed a certain autonomy as an „Autonomous Mountain District" since 2003, it has always felt somewhat discriminated against and alienated in Jammu and Kashmir. In contrast to the Muslim Kashmiri, the Buddhist Ladakhi had demanded the status of a Union Territory themselves, and thus the separation from Jammu and Kashmir. Relations with Delhi were free of conflict, in fact a guarantee for the preservation of the Buddhist character of this part of the country called Little Tibet. Ladakh lives from tourism and the stationing of large troops of the Indian army in this sensitive tri-border region between Pakistan, China and India, in addition to the barren mountain agriculture. Now, in 2019, the large territory has been transformed into a Union Territory directly governed by Delhi, which could have been done without abolishing the state of Jammu and Kashmir.

A Union Territory under Indian constitutional law does not meet the criteria of modern territorial autonomy, but is a hybrid between a member state and a territory directly subordinate to the central state. India's Union Territories are governed by a Lieutenant Governor appointed by Delhi, while the elected regional parliament has to be satisfied with consultation and hearing rights. Thus, the Council of Ministers of Jammu and Kashmir will be appointed by the centrally appointed Governor and not any more by the regional parliament. This removes an important element of regional democracy, which means that there is no longer any question of autonomy or statehood. The Governor can issue decrees that have the same status as laws passed by the regional parliament. Whereas in the past only small areas with an ethnic-geographical character were Union Territories such as the federal capital Delhi, the former French colony of Pondicherry, the Andaman Islands, an entire territorial state has now been degraded to such a territory.

Kashmir is thus being re-colonised to a certain extent: a good half of the 309 state laws have been eliminated and replaced by 106 laws of the central state. All independent commissions, such as the Human Rights Commission, have been dissolved. The Supreme Court of Jammu and Kashmir is now formally under the jurisdiction of the Supreme Court of India. Such a „coup d'état from above" against the will of the vast majority of the population can only be enforced by police-state means. In Kashmir, freedom of expression, freedom of assembly and the protection of individual human rights have been suspended for 30 years. More than in any other democratic state, the fundamental right to information has been seriously affected by the shutdown of the Internet and mobile phones. In Kashmir, thousands of political activists have been detained as a precautionary measure and no foreign journalists have been allowed in for many years. India, the world's largest democracy, is no more democratic and pro-minority in this part of the country than the People's Republic of China in East Turkestan and Tibet, or Indonesia in West Papua.

Today, Kashmir is a peaceful cemetery, secured by military occupation and police state surveillance. This massive disenfranchisement of the Kashmiri people will not only deepen the region's bitterness and alienation from the rest of India, but will also rekindle militant resistance. Democracy and free elections are no longer an option in Kashmir. While the Western democracies did indeed react in the case of the restriction of Hong Kong's autonomy since 2019, no significant international protest from the West was heard in the occupation and repression of Kashmir.

16

Between autonomy and independence: the Kurds in Iraq and Syria

The Kurdish inhabited area. Source: Perry Castaneda, Library Map Collection at the University of Austin, Texas. US CIA in 1992. Public Domain.

With at least 30 million, the Kurds are the largest people without their own state. Their settlement area was divided up among four states almost 100 years ago in violation of the right to self-determination. In all these states (Turkey, Iran, Iraq and Syria), the Kurds have experienced discrimination, oppression and persecution since the collapse of the Ottoman Empire, up to war, expulsion and genocide, as was the case in Saddam Hussein's Iraq, as is the case in Erdogan's Turkey today. Single attempts of Kurdish state foundations on the territory of Turkey and Iran failed after a few months or years. Today there is a constitutionally anchored territorial autonomy of the Kurds of Iraq and a de facto autonomy of the Kurds in Syria within the framework of the multinational „Federation of Northern Syria".

Independence postponed: The Kurdistan Region of Iraq

The persecution and oppression of the Kurds in the Middle East has its origins in the colonial period of the Ottomans and Europeans. After the collapse of the Ottoman Empire, the settlement areas of the Kurdish people were divided bet-

The Kurdistan Region of Iraq and disputed areas.

Source: Wikipedia.de, Author: TUBS, Spesh531

ween the victorious powers by the Treaty of Sèvres (1920), with the Kurds promised self-determination. However, as early as 1923 a new treaty, the Treaty of Lausanne, put a rapid end to this dream of the Kurds. The Kurds living in Kemalist Turkey lost any chance of self-determination, the Kurdish areas in Iraq came under British administration until Iraq's independence in 1932, and the Syrian Kurdish areas came under French administration.

Relations between Kurds and Arabs of Iraq, between Kurdish leaders and Iraqi rulers remained conflict-ridden throughout the 20th century. The new Iraqi state had a centralist orientation and, at the latest with the rise of the Arab Socialist Baath Party, there was no longer any talk of equal rights for the Kurdish people. With the interim constitution of 1970, the Baath Party had established a „democratic people's republic", de facto one-party rule, and from 1979 a dictatorship of Saddam Hussein's clan. His seizure of power in 1979 not only cemented the supremacy of the Iraqi Sunni, but also led straight to the systematic suppression of any kind of Kurdish autonomy up to the genocide during the so-called Anfal campaign. Only the invasion of the USA and its allies in 2003 put an end to three decades of reign of terror by the Baath Party and the Hussein regime.

In addition to the devastating consequences for the entire population, the second Gulf War in 2003 brought a deep political upheaval for Iraq: a new constitution of 2005 attempted to lay the foundations for a democratic and federal state in which all ethnic and religious communities could live together on an equal footing and in peace.

Iraq's current constitution of 2005 establishes the state as a federal and parliamentary republic, based on democracy and Islam. The Federal Government has its seat in Baghdad. The country is divided into federal regions and government districts. Currently Kurdistan is the only federal state in Iraq, which is usually referred to as the Autonomous Region of Kurdistan. However, the constitution allows the creation of additional states if existing governorates so request. The 2005 Constitution did not create a federal state with immediate effect, but held out the prospect of federal structure and outlined the way forward. The constitution grants the member states a high degree of autonomy, which is mainly attributed to the negotiating power of the Kurds in the process of constitutionalisation. The federal government has relatively few competences, while all remaining competences and thus most of the political power is in the hands of the Autonomous Region of Kurdistan. In the rest of the country, the central government plays a much stronger role.

The Kurds had already established an autonomous region in northern Iraq after the first Gulf War in 1991, after the Iraqi army had been decisively weakened and concentrated on crushing the Iraqi Shiite insurgency in the southeast of the country. Then Saddam Hussein's troops also attacked the Kurdish area, triggering a mass exodus. It was only thanks to the USA's imposition of a no-fly zone that the Kurdish Peshmerga were able to beat back the Iraqi army and enforce a ceasefire. The Kurds controlled most of the Kurdish populated areas, but not the territory of Kirkuk.

Soon afterwards, however, an internal war broke out in 1994 between the rival major Kurdish parties, the PUK of Jalal Talabani and the KDP of Massud Barzani, which lasted until 1998. After US mediation, the Kurdish territory was then divided into two zones of influence: the KDP ruled in the northwest, the PUK in the southeast. Only after the US invasion in 2003 and the final overthrow of the Hussein regime did these two forces form a joint government.

The Autonomous Region of Kurdistan experienced an astonishing economic upswing from 2005 onwards, as autonomy enabled the Kurds to use mainly the oil reserves themselves. Oil exports became the basis of a small economic miracle. The responsibilities of the Kurdish region also include defence and foreign policy as well as internal security. Actually, since 2005, Iraqi Kurdistan has been a state within a state rather than an autonomous region. On the other hand, the security and stability in post-war Iraq as a whole, which only recovered with difficulty from war and oppression, also benefited from this. A new crisis came in 2014 with the attacks of ISIS, which took control of a large part of northern Iraq with the megacity of Mosul and advanced to just outside Baghdad. It was only thanks to Kurdish support that the Iraqi army was able to push back this attack.

A constant bone of contention between Baghdad and Erbil, however, is the exploitation of oil reserves. More than 90 percent of the state revenues of Iraq and Iraqi Kurdistan come from oil revenues. According to the constitution, the oil industry is subject to the central state, but the Autonomous Region of Kurdistan does not only use the sources on its territory for its self-sufficiency. Rather, „Kurdish oil" is the main source of income for the region as a whole. Now Baghdad insists on the central management of the oil business in order to distribute its revenues equally among all parts of the country. This is one of the reasons why, following the independence referendum of the Autonomous Region of Kurdistan in October 2017, Iraq seized the opportunity to take back the oil-rich area of Kirkuk, which had been controlled by the Peshmerga until then.

A special feature of Kurdistan's autonomous status in Iraq is its army, which looks back on decades of tradition in the struggle for freedom. The Peshmerga (Kurdish for „those who look death in the eye") not only defended the Kurdish people's very existence during Saddam Hussein's aggressions and later the region's autonomy, but also successfully defended Iraq against attacks by the IS from 2014 onwards and finally, together with the Iraqi army, virtually eliminated it.

In June 2017 the Kurdish regional government decided to hold a referendum on the independence of the region. This step was declared illegal by the central government. The USA, allied with both Baghdad and Erbil, demanded a postponement of the referendum because a secession of Kurdistan would have weakened the entire state in a difficult phase of reconstruction. Iran and Turkey saw an independent Kurdistan as a natural threat to their national integrity. In the referendum held on 25 September 2017, with a voter turnout of about 70 percent over 90 percent of the citizens voted for independence. Immediately afterwards, the Iraqi central government, with the help of the army, regained control over previously Kurdish-controlled areas outside the established autonomous region, mainly in the province of Kirkuk. The Iraqi Constitutional Court declared the referendum unconstitutional on 20 November 2017. For most political forces and the population of Iraqi Kurdistan, the project of a separate state now remains postponed but not cancelled.

With the independence referendum of 2017, Barzani wanted to gain popularity and underpin his claim to leadership. But the KDP also wanted to distract attention from the rampant nepotism, waste and economic crisis in the Autonomous Region of Kurdistan. Moreover, Barzani wanted to weaken the old rival PUK and force the USA and Europe to show their colours and make a Kurdish state possible. But neither the EU nor the USA were willing to actively support Kurdish secession, to avoid complicating the situation in the Middle East. After all, Baghdad was supposed to use the referendum to negotiate over the areas claimed by the Kurds, such as Kirkuk. But it was precisely in this respect that the shot backfired. The conflict between the Kurdish regional government and the central government over the so-called „disputed territories" remains unresolved.

The establishment of a separate Kurdish state is not welcomed in the West, as it could endanger the fragile balance between the various states. The Kurds themselves are also divided. A unified and overarching "national movement" of the Kurds does not exist, despite their strong national consciousness. A broad network of Kurdish organisations is active abroad and fights with varying success for the rights of the Kurds in all four states. However, the most important Kurdish organisations form not one but two ideologically hostile movements, which

The entrance hall of the Parliament of the Autonomous Kurdistan in Erbil. Foto: Th. Benedikter

have not been united by the external threat. On the one hand, that of the „Social Union of Kurdistan" (KCK), to which the PKK-affiliated organisations also belong. On the other hand, the parties of the Autonomous Region Kurdistan-Iraq. The former, in its central orientation, is positioned against Turkey's policy, which has always been hostile to Kurds; the latter is allied with Ankara and institutionally linked to the state of Iraq. Massud Barzani, leader of the KDP, remained silent on the Turkish army's brutal crackdown on rebel Kurds in Turkish Kurdistan in 2015. The defensive struggle against the IS was waged by the Kurds in Syria and Iraq fought almost separately from each other, and in Sinjar in 2015 there was hardly any coordination between the various Kurdish units let alone an active cooperation and unity.

The situation is different with the Kurds in Iran: Tehran has long looked with suspicion at Erbil, although leading representatives of the KDP and PUK enjoyed political asylum in Iran for decades and cooperated with Iran during the Iran-Iraq war. Iran fears the „infection" of its own Kurds with nationalism across the border.

The Autonomous Region of Kurdistan in Iraq is the most advanced on the road to statehood. Iraq's Kurds also have the right to military self-defence, control their public finances and internal borders with the rest of the country, and maintain active foreign relations. The Kurds of Iraq form a separate polity in almost every respect - with the exception of religion. Due to their painful experiences under Arabic rule, they can also assert a moral claim to self-determination. For Arab Iraq, the departure of the Autonomous Region of Kurdistan would not change so much, although the complicated question of the areas populated by Kurds and partly claimed by the Autonomous Region of Kurdistan must first be resolved.

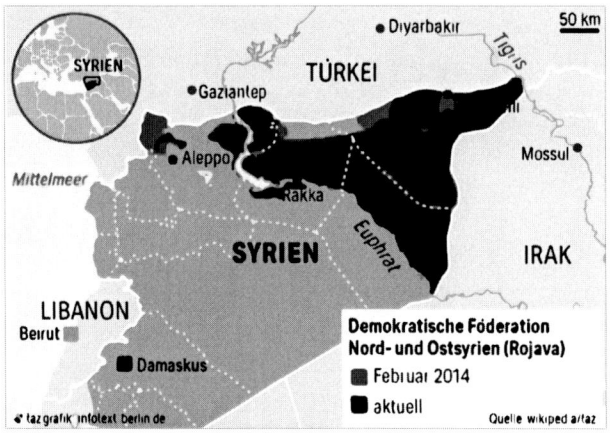

Source: wikipedia/taz; Infografik:infotext

The Kurds in Syria: autonomy in practice in Rojava

The war in Syria, which has been going on since 2011, has turned the political map of Syria upside down. The Kurds on the northern border with Turkey and on the eastern border with Iraq joining forces with other ethnic groups of the region have achieved de facto autonomy. In January 2014 representatives of all ethnic groups, declared the founding of the „Confederation of Northern Syria" with the three cantons of Afrin, Kobane and Cezire. This area, also called „Rojava" (Western Kurdistan), had to be defended first by the Kurdish self-defence forces against the Al-Nusra rebels in the west and the IS in the south, while the central government in Damascus did not intervene in order not to open another front. Northern Syria's autonomy thus arose out of necessity of self-defence in the middle of the Syrian civil war.

Before the war, the Kurds of Rojava made up about 8-10 percent of the total population of Syria. The first Kurdish organisation, Xoybun, had already emerged in 1927 in Qamishlo, the secret capital of the Kurdish region of Syria. In 1957, the Democratic Kurdistan Party (PDKS) was founded. But even then, Syria pursued an authoritarian and anti-minority policy against all non-Arab and non-Alevi groups. This became a system with the seizure of power by Hafez al-Assad, the father of today's dictator. As early as 1960, Syria committed the first massacres of the Kurdish civilian population. A sad climax of state violence against minorities occurred in 2004: 36 Kurds were killed by the Syrian police in the Qamishlo football stadium.

Since 1970, the Ba'ath regime has pursued a policy of systematic oppression and assimilation of the Kurds and other minorities. The Kurds, Assyrians, Turkmen and other ethnic groups were not recognised and had no right to education in their mother tongue or to political representation. Activists were arrested, tortured, killed and driven into exile. The Assad regime deliberately tried to turn Assyrian Christians against the Kurds. Similar to the neighbouring country of Iraq under Saddam Hussein, the state tried to change the population composition of the region: Kurds from the region were deprived of their citizenship and forcibly resettled in major cities, and Arabs from other parts of Syria were settled on the expropriated land of the Kurds. The Kurdish community resisted this persecution and discrimination by the Syrian regime. In the context of the rivalry between Syria and Turkey, the Assad regime had granted safe residence in Rojava in the 1980s and 1990s to the Kurdish Workers Party PKK and its leader Abdullah Ocalan. In return, the PKK abstained from any interference in internal affairs. Nevertheless, the PKK's ideology and policies and Ocalan's thinking had a lasting influence on the Kurdish autonomy movement in Syria.

The Kurds in the Syrian civil war

During the civil war, which broke out in 2011, the Kurds of Syria were courted by both sides. Initially, some Kurdish groups sympathised with the opposition, but in return demanded recognition of Kurdish identity and an autonomous or federal territorial unit in northern Syria. Because this did not happen, the Kurds decided not to take sides in the civil war and to go a third way, at the risk of being attacked by both the state and the Sunni opposition. However, a kind of standstill agreement was reached with the Assad regime. Led by the PYD (Democratic Union Party), the Kurds set up self-defence units and established a self-governing territory and new forms of social organisation. Already in 2011, the People's Defence Units YPG and Women's Defence Units YPJ were ready, recruiting fighters from all religious and ethnic groups in Rojava. In July 2012 these units were able to successfully hold the city of Kobane, located on the border to Turkey, after weeks of siege by the IS. There have been no serious clashes between the YPG/YPJ units and the Syrian army since the beginning of the war.

In 2012, the self-defence forces of northern Syria had to assert themselves against Sunni rebel militias in the west and against the IS in the south, which controlled a large area in Syria and Iraq, including the megacity of Mosul. In addition, Rojava went on to build autonomous institutions: schools, police, courts, cooperatives, agricultural enterprises. Rojava also had to receive and care for hundreds of thousands of refugees from the rest of Syria.

The Assad regime has not yet officially recognised the autonomous confederation of Northern Syria, which has been in existence since January 2014. The political representation of the region has so far been excluded from the peace talks in Geneva, even under pressure from Turkey. The proclamation of autonomy was a necessary step in order to subsequently enter into negotiations with Damascus. Autonomy initially led to a complete embargo on Rojava by Turkey and even a boycott by the Autonomous Region of Kurdistan-Iraq. The latter wanted control of the area itself, while Turkey feared that Rojava could become the PKK's new haven. After some time, the KDP ruling in Kurdistan-Iraq was able to commit itself to providing humanitarian support to Rojava and opening the borders.

The proclamation of the autonomous Federation of Northern Syria in 2014 was a milestone for the Kurdish minority: for the first time, Syria's Kurds were recognised in their identity and basic cultural rights. Under Assad, tens of thousands of Syrian Kurds had not even been recognised as citizens. Higher education had always been closed to the Kurds. Under the Assad regime, most Kurdish young people were excluded from any social advancement in the state apparatus.

In the Federation of Northern Syria, the rapprochement of different ethnic groups was also successful. A climate of mistrust had arisen as a result of decades of oppression of minorities, since it was mainly the new Arab settlers who were seen as colonisers. The Christian Assyrians had also suffered from the tensions. Reconciliation and understanding between the ethnic groups and between Christians and Muslims remains a major challenge for the politics and society of the autonomous Rojava.

The de facto autonomous Northern Syria today

Rojava-Northern Syria is a multi-ethnic and multi-religious society. This made the Kurds of Syria realise that they could under no circumstances rely on a nation-state model or even on Kurdish nationalism if the peaceful coexistence of all ethnic groups in an autonomous area was to be secured in the long term. Not only democracy and the protection of minorities were to form the basis of this new model of society in the Middle East, but also a secular state power and full equality for women. Kurds, Arabs, Assyrians, Turkmen, Chaldeans and other groups should be able to live together on an equal footing in an autonomous area of what will be a democratic Syria. This anti-nationalist attitude of the leaders of the Federation of Northern Syria actually created trust between the ethnic groups. Thousands of Arabs and Assyrians fought in the units of the Syrian Democratic Forces SDF and are now active in the autonomous police force. The leadership of the autonomous region promoted understanding between the groups in many forms.

The Kurds also received political, humanitarian, military and financial support from Northern Kurdistan (Turkey) during this period of civil war. Despite closed borders between Turkey and Syria, there is one between Turkish Kurdistan and Northern Syria-Rojava. During the siege of Kobane by the IS, the PKK sent fighters to Rojava. The first schools, universities and cultural institutions were established mainly thanks to the help from Northern Kurdistan. This cross-border cooperation had to make the nationalist Erdogan regime nervous.

In Kurdistan-Iraq, on the other hand, the KDP meets Rojava's largest party, the PYD, with mistrust, while the PUK in the parliament in Erbil pressed for more financial, political and military support for the Kurds of Syria. The KDP fears the extension of Turkish military interventions in northern Iraq and the autonomous region because of the PKK's retreat there. Tensions between the KDP and the PKK erupted in the conflict in the Sinjar mountains, where the PKK is training and equipping Yezidi militias after the experience of the IS attack on the Yezidi Sinjar. Iranian Kurds also came to Rojava to reinforce the YPG.

The situation first came to a head in early 2018 in the canton of Afrin in the west

Iraqi tank in the Museum of War of Süleimanya (Kurdistan). Foto: Thomas Benedikter

of the autonomous region of North Syria-Rojava. In February 2018, the Turkish army, supported by Syrian-Sunni Jihadist militia, invaded the canton and occupied the entire area in an act of international aggression. More than 200,000 Kurds were driven from their homeland, while Turkey, in a typical ethnic cleansing, tried to settle Syrian refugees in conquered territory. In 2019, the scenario was repeated further east: Turkey threatened to invade the confederation of Northern Syria in order to banish the „terror threat". Turkey and Russia agreed with their vassal Assad to establish a 30 kilometre wide „protection zone" along the Turkish-Syrian border, which would be jointly controlled. Again in blatant violation of international law, Turkish forces attacked North Syria's self-defence units on their territory. Today, a fragile cease-fire exists, under constant threat of new military aggression from Turkey (see the interview with Khaled Davrisch hereafter).

Which chances of a lasting recognition of Rojava's autonomy?

The crisis and civil war are still not over after 10 years. It brought threat, aggression, war, but also new opportunities for the Kurds. The Kurds were able to use the chaos in Syria to establish a new kind of self-government. In terms of democracy, secular state, equal rights for women, protection of minorities and freedom of religion, Rojava-Northern Syria has taken giant steps forward and offers an example for all of Syria and the Middle East. Internally, too, the peaceful coexistence of groups has been preserved and a consensus has been built for a new social project. Today it is at the same time a question of recognising the Kurds as an ethnic group with rights and entitlement to territorial autonomy, but also of ensuring democracy and justice in the area. The Kurds and other ethnic groups of Rojava are demanding the recognition of the autonomy of their region in a democratic and federal post-war Syria within the framework of a democratic constitutional state.

The chance of autonomy within Syria depends largely on international support for this political project. The UN has not supported the Autonomous Federation of Northern Syria except for some humanitarian aid during the five-month siege of Kobane. It was not until the end of 2014 that the threat from the IS jihadists was recognised in the US, Europe and Russia, when their cells carried terror into European cities. The liberation of Kobane and the successful suppression of the IS by the SDF units led to the broad recognition of the Syrian-Kurdish self-defence units. The military cooperation between the West (USA, France, United Kingdom) and the SDF as ground troops had proved its worth. After the victory over the IS, Northern Syria had to acknowledge that this did not automatically mean recognition as an autonomous subject. On the contrary: when Turkey attacked Afrin in 2018 and the north of Rojava in 2019, US president Trump announced that he would withdraw the small US force unit stationed in Rojava and abandon the Kurdish allies. Northern Syria now has permanent representations in the Czech Republic, Germany, Russia, France, the Netherlands, Denmark, Sweden and Norway, which amounts to a kind of „de facto recognition".

The existence of the de facto autonomous federation of Northern Syria-Rojava remains under threat today. The threat became particularly acute after the Trump administration threatened to withdraw US troops in 2018 and 2019. The Federation of Northern Syria was forced to immediately begin negotiations with Damascus. In doing so, the Kurds assumed that Syria's sovereignty would be preserved and that a democratic republic would be established, which would include northern Syria as an autonomous sub-region. The Kurdish offer provided for the following:

- The representatives of the Autonomous Administration are to become part of the National Assembly.

- The flag of the Autonomous Administration shall be hoisted together with the national flag of Syria.

- The Autonomous Administration shall be allowed to maintain its own diplomatic relations as long as they are in accordance with the interests of the Syrian nation state and the constitution.

- The Syrian Democratic Forces (SDF) are to be integrated into the Syrian National Army and form part of the border guard.

- Internal security forces are to be under the control of the regional assemblies in the autonomous region.

- In the Syrian regions of the autonomous administration, the Kurdish language is to be established as the language of education, while Arabic is to be retained as an official language.

- Faculties for history, culture, language, literature and other subjects are to be established, where teaching is to take place in the respective regional language.
- All natural resources are to be distributed „fairly and equally" throughout the country.

The Kurds of Syria see themselves as part of the regional multinational community and want to remain part of Syria as an autonomous territory. Kurdish self-organisation should be recognised by all states and cooperation between Kurdish communities across national borders should be allowed. The present self-defence units should be allowed to continue. Although the autonomous North Syria-Rojava is gaining more and more political legitimacy, the relationship with Damascus remains unclear. Only decisive pressure from the international community and above all from Russia, the main supporter of the Assad regime, can bring about lasting recognition of the claim to autonomy of the multi-ethnic community of northern Syria.

„We are basically fighting for the whole of Syria and all its people".

A conversation with Khaled Davrisch, representative of the Self-Government of Northern and Eastern Syria in Germany.

What is the current security situation in Rojava? Are there still attacks by IS? Are there violations of the ceasefire by Turkey or its allied jihadist federations?

Davrisch: We have to constantly fight terrorist attacks because there are active IS cells in different parts of our territory. Turkey's last invasion of northern and eastern Syria, especially in the area of Ras-el-Ain and Tal Abiadh, has exacerbated the danger of IS returning because it has given the IS cells new areas of retreat and operation. Turkish aggression continues at a low level. Turkey does not comply with the agreements reached with Russia and the USA and has ignored the UN's appeal to stop military operations due to the Covid-19 epidemic. However, the worst terror is suffered by the civilian population in the areas occupied by Turkey. There, Turkey is torturing people in the same style as IS did in the years before liberation. The US military presence continues on a reduced scale, as does cooperation with the SDF in the fight against terrorism.

What interests is Turkey pursuing in Syria and to what extent does the USA support this policy of Turkey as a NATO partner?

Davrisch: With its policy, Turkey is not only harming Syria, but also the entire greater Middle East region and Europe. This results in dangers of various kinds. As far as Syria is concerned, the Turkish occupation is pursuing the goal of permanently sabotaging a peaceful solution within Syria by supporting the Salafist militias and other mercenary groups. This policy of Turkey is carried out in violation of international law and humanitarian human rights, with an enormous amount of destruction and chaos. Turkey is pursuing concrete projects to partition Syria, be it as a territory or as a society. The US will only change its policy when it finally takes note of the dangers created by Turkey. These do not only concern Syria, but the whole world. Russia has also abandoned the Kurds of Syria.

Russia allowed the invasion and occupation of Afrin in spring 2018, which was agreed between Erdogan and Assad. As Assad's main supporter, what is Russia's position on a political rapprochement between Syria and Turkey?

Davrisch: We are witnessing a deep upheaval in Syria that started back in 2011, since the beginning of the civil war. The reality in Syria today is anything but stable. For almost 10 years, Syrians have been victims of the civil war and its effects. There can only be a solution if one starts from the needs of the civilian population. There are the most diverse interests at this stage. In any case, any attempt to go against a Syrian political force that has defeated terrorism and is building a democratic society from below would be a very serious mistake. It would be just as much of a mistake to involve Turkey in the peace efforts in Syria after all that Erdogan has done here. I hope that these mistakes will finally be recognised. In peace negotiations, the major powers must facilitate a solution within Syria and its political actors. Outside interference is not in Syria's interest.

After the repeated invasion of the autonomous region by Turkey, there is now a fundamental mistrust among the Kurds of northern Syria-Rojava towards the West, i.e. the NATO countries including Germany.

Davrisch: Germany, like the other NATO states, has continuously supported the Turkish governments with weapons. These states are engaging in blatant hypocrisy, as they themselves are involved in these aggressions against the Kurdish people. By supplying arms, the NATO countries make themselves accomplices in the Turkish war against the Kurds. With NATO weapons, thousands of villages and numerous old towns have been destroyed in Turkey, and with NATO weapons Turkey has invaded Syria. When NATO then talks about human rights, it is a mockery for us Kurds. The autonomous self-administration of northern Syria, on the other hand, is based only on the organisations of civil society, on the self-defence forces and the democratic parties. We hope, together with the democratic forces within the NATO countries, to end these forms of support for Erdogan and the Salafist militias and his aggression against us.

Under Erdogan's regime, Rojava-Northern Syria cannot be safe from further attacks by Turkey. Turkey is aiming for a buffer zone along the entire Turkish-Syrian border. Will the SDF and the Syrian army defend themselves against this together and also prepare for it together?

Davrisch: The SDF units are made up of young Kurds, Arabs, Christians and Assyrians and Turkmen, and they are responsible for the security of the population and the defence against attacks from outside. This basic principle of common defence is decisive for us and we put it into practice every day. But we are also open to cooperation to defend Syria's external borders and to continue to fight terrorism internally, but also to liberate Syria from foreign occupation.

Assad recently spoke of the need to liberate northern Syria from the „terrorist" forces of self-rule in Rojava after the „liberation" of Idlib. Do you fear a pincer grip of Turkey and the Assad regime against Rojava? Is there a coordinated strategy of Assad and Erdogan to act against Rojava-Northern Syria?

Davrisch: Assad is still counting on a military solution to get rid of any kind of resistance against his regime and to bring the entire national territory under his control. What surprises us Kurds is that he is far less aggressive and threatening towards Turkey than he is towards the Federation of Northern Syria and our autonomy project in Rojava. Yet Turkey occupies a considerable part of Syria. The Syrian and Turkish governments are secretly working together to bring down our autonomy project in Rojava. This is the poisoned fruit of the Astana Agreement, which Erdogan and Assad concluded under the auspices of Iran and Russia. On this basis, Turkey has been allowed to occupy Jarablus, El Bab, Afrin,

Serekanye, Tal Abiadh. The quid pro quo was that the Salafist militias withdraw from Aleppo, Damascus, Dar'a and Homs. Assad is threatening our autonomous authority with an invasion from Turkey: we should surrender unconditionally or they would allow Erdogan to launch a new invasion. This kind of blackmail is perceived by many observers today.

Are there any chances that the Assad regime will accept the Federation of Northern Syria as a negotiating partner and that serious negotiations will take place between Damascus and Northern Syria?

Davrisch: Assad is speculating on possible changes at the global and regional level and can currently count on the support of three sides to regain control of the entire territory of the state: Russia, Iran and Hezbollah. At present, he has no political solution to offer to the crisis. He will continue to run for the presidential elections and buy time for manoeuvres to bring down our autonomy project. But no one can any longer deny the new reality that has now emerged in Syria and especially in the northeast. Without the northeast, the entire crisis of the Syrian state will not be overcome in the interest of its people either.

What is Russia's position on negotiations on the recognition of the de facto autonomy of Northern Syria? Will Russia seek to initiate official negotiations between the Syrian government and the Federation of Northern Syria?

Davrisch: Russia has used the Syrian crisis to consolidate its presence in the Mediterranean, in concert with Iran, because both states have an interest in ousting the Americans from the entire Middle East. In order to assert its interests, Russia supports the so-called „Resistance Alliance", which includes Tehran, Baghdad, Damascus and Beirut. This also explains why Russia is trying everything to rehabilitate the Assad regime internationally while ignoring the entire opposition inside Syria. It is in this context that the Russian position towards our autonomy project should be understood. Because in all negotiations it becomes clear again and again: Russia subordinates everything to the overall goal of giving Assad control over the entire national territory again, if possible. This was demonstrated during the last invasion of northern Syria, when Assad's troops returned to our territory in collusion with Turkey. Apart from these machinations, we rely on dialogue to reach a solution inside Syria. We want to work with anyone who supports such a solution.

Does Russia actually support your demand for a certain degree of territorial autonomy, for admission as political representation of the Northeast of Syria in the constitutional committee and in the Geneva peace talks?

Davrisch: It is possible that territorial autonomy and a federal state are not a problem for Russia. Russia itself is a highly decentralised state with federal republics and autonomous units of various kinds. It is Turkey that thinks it cannot live with territorial autonomy on its borders. That is why it does not tolerate Kurdish representation in the peace talks on the future of Syria. Turkey fears that such representation will most likely have repercussions on its own policy towards the Kurds.

The official recognition of Kurdish autonomy presupposes that Syria renounces the previous model of a national unitary state in favour of a federal state, as happened in Iraq, for example, or at least allows special autonomy for your region. Is this conceivable with the Baath Party under Assad after this civil war?

Davrisch: The Syrian regime is currently not considering decentralisation of the state and is sticking to its centralist form of government. It simply does not recognise that the Kurdish question needs a special solution. The Arab Baath Party is a racist and chauvinist organisation that has set as its ultimate goal from the beginning the supremacy of the Arab nation to the detriment of all other nations. The Baath Party is convinced that the dominion of the Arab nation is geographically predetermined, stretching from the Toros Mountains in the east to the Atlantic Ocean in the west. From their point of view, non-Arab peoples in this space have no right to consider themselves as nations with equal rights. That is why all the Baath governments in Syria have repeatedly done their utmost to fight and uproot the Kurdish population, even to the point of cultural genocide. Assad is completely in the Baath tradition in this respect.

The Kurds in northern Syria envisage a far-reaching territorial autonomy under the sovereignty of Syria as a solution. A similar model already exists in Iraqi Kurdistan. In your view, how should Rojava's future autonomy be justified in terms of state and constitutional law?

Davrisch: In Syria, the president has all-encompassing power and authority, and with his decrees he usually overrides the parliament in the legislative process. The provincial governors are also all appointed by the president. The Minister of Local Government, according to Law 107 of 2011, organises the administration of the provinces and exercises supervision over the provincial councils. In a federal Syria, the powers of the provincial councils should be expanded and those of the central state limited. Only defence, foreign and financial policy should remain with the central state.

Should the Federation of Northern Syria be recognised as an autonomous territory, will the Kurds and other ethnic groups insist on responsibility for internal and external security? In other words, sovereignty over the police and self-defence forces?

Davrisch: The police forces, which are recruited locally, are responsible for maintaining internal security. The self-defence forces, and the SDF in particular, have the task of national defence, especially of the external borders. The SDF will keep their weapons and form the core of a new Syrian state army that will replace the current army. This future army must be completely non-partisan and not tied to any religious community or nationality. In that case, there will no longer be any need for the provinces to maintain their own armies.

TEV-DEM, that is the movement for a democratic society, a bottom-up movement for social and political self-government. How is this pillar of the organisation of the Federation of Northern Syria linked to the second pillar of formally elected institutions?

Davrisch: On 27 August 2018, TEV-DEM, the Movement for a Democratic Society, held a three-day congress. There it was decided that the creation and formation of the councils is the responsibility of the autonomous institutions, while the TEV-DEM is given the task of organising civil society and the trade union. All councils operating in the autonomous area will be directly elected. This applies to the municipalities, the provinces, the districts and the region as a whole.

In 10 European countries, there are autonomous regions, some of which have strongly developed autonomy, such as the Basque Country, Catalonia, Northern Ireland, some islands in Scandinavia. Are there territorial autonomies that represent a model for the Kurds of Rojava?

Davrisch: We try to learn from the experiences of others in contact and exchange. But we also know that among the existing autonomy models there is no ideal model that can be applied to our needs. Our reality is a very special one that does not exist anywhere else, and this also requires a very special solution.

What can the autonomous regions of Europe do for autonomous northern Syria at the political level?

Davrisch: Civil war and chaos have been taking place in Syria for a decade. It is only thanks to the autonomy movement in north-eastern Syria that a federal, democratic and secular project has been built here. We are not cultivating this vision for the whole of Syria in isolation, but are convinced that the future of the whole of Syria depends on it. We are basically fighting for the whole of Syria and all its people. We stand for the territorial integrity of Syria and for democracy. That is why we also recognise UN Decision No. 2254 on the situation in Syria. It goes without saying that any political achievement in this direction will benefit not only us but all Syrians. We are also putting pressure to bring about a political solution and hope that Europe and the whole world will support us in this.

17

The dream of autonomy: Turkish Kurdistan

Source: CIA, The World Factbook, author: çalak, CC-BY-SA 3.0

The division of the Kurdish territories between four states after the end of the Ottoman Empire and the establishment of the new Turkish Republic in 1923 was not accepted by the Kurds without resistance. Both a short-term state foundation and all uprisings of the Kurds in Turkey failed. In Kemalist Turkey, the Kurds have never been recognised as an ethnic group in their own right, let alone as a people, nor have any other national minority. Cyclical repression by the Turkish state led to the radicalisation of the Kurds and the establishment of underground movements. The coup d'état of 12 September 1980 triggered the foundation of the Kurdish Workers' Party PKK.

The aim of the PKK was to create an independent and socialist Kurdish republic. From 1984 onwards, the PKK launched a broad-based guerrilla war. However, a military solution had little chance from the outset, as Turkey has one of the largest and best-equipped armies in the world. As a NATO partner, it is also constantly being rearmed by Europe, Israel and the USA and has built up its own arms industry. In the 1990s, Turkey and the PKK signed three ceasefire agreements. But in 1999 the founder and undisputed leader of the PKK, Abdullah Ocalan, was captured with the help of the Israeli secret service and sentenced to life imprisonment in Turkey. Since then he has been in solitary confinement on the prison island of Imrali.

Öcalan`s proposals for a democratic solution to the Kurdish question

In addition to the PKK as a militarily organised part of the Kurdish resistance, a democratic movement for the rights of the Kurds also emerged 30 years ago. The „People's Labour Party" HEP was founded after the end of the Evren dictatorship on 7 June 1990. Its central demands included the constitutional recognition of the Kurds and protection as a minority according to international conventions. Despite constant repression by state authorities, HEP and its successor parties repeatedly managed to gain entry into the Turkish parliament. In the parliamentary elections of 7.6.2015, the "Democratic Party of the Peoples" HDP won 80 seats with 13.1 percent. In the parliamentary elections of 24.6.2018, the HDP won 11.7 percent of the vote and sent 67 MPs to Ankara, many of whom have since been sentenced to long prison terms. In addition, there are smaller left-wing and religious parties which also claim to represent the Kurdish population.

Since 1993, the PKK led by Abdullah Ocalan has expressed its willingness to find a peaceful solution to the Kurdish question through unilateral cease-fires and has made concrete proposals to that end. Also during his 1999 trial, Ocalan declared the PKK's willingness in principle to find a democratic peaceful solution to the Kurdish question within Turkey. That Kurds and Turks had lived together peacefully for centuries, said Ocalan, and could continue to do so in the future in a common state, while respecting collective fundamental rights. A separate Kurdish state in the region would not be conducive to this. Territorial autonomy or federalism were not ideal either, because Turkey's Kurds were widely dispersed. The only option was a deeper democratic solution within a union with Turkey. To this end, Turkey had to recognise the Kurdish language and culture, renounce military repression, allow all Kurdish political organisations and allow their participation in politics at all levels. Öcalan proposed the creation of a multinational Turkey, recognising cultural diversity and consistently developing democracy.

In 2004, Öcalan elaborated on his proposal concerning the legal status of the Kurds in Turkey. The democratic self-government of the Kurds should coexist with the public institutions and authorities of the Turkish state. The people should be given more rights for democratic self-government at lower governance levels. The Kurdish people would be permanently and directly involved in democratic self-government through People's Congresses and their elected representatives. Öcalan made it clear that this was not only a matter of safeguarding the rights of the ethnic groups, but also of a continuous democratisation of the mixed Kurdish-Turkish society.

This concept corresponds to a turning away from the idea of a Kurdish nation state in this region. The „confederal Kurdish entity" would not entail any revision of existing borders or attempts to establish a state. Rather, villages, municipalities and city councils should be largely self-governing in accordance with subsidiarity. This democratisation of society would require the constitutional recognition of the Kurdish identity and the fundamental rights of the Kurds and other minorities. Local and regional self-governing bodies should be allowed to cooperate across borders with the corresponding units in neighbouring states.

On the international level, Ocalan and the PKK have in mind a democratic transformation of the entire state system in the Middle East.

Following Benedict Anderson's definition of the nation as an imaginary community, Ocalan defined the nation as a „community of people sharing a state of mind" and the democratic nation as a „model of a nation that excludes oppression and exploitation". Thus, Öcalan's project of democratic modernisation strives for social emancipation in a broad sense, which includes gender equality, the fight against inequality and ecological sustainability. In Öcalan's conceptual world, democratic confederalism as an association of autonomous municipalities and communities is moving in the direction of a systems of people's direct council democracy, while the foundations of territorial autonomy - the transfer of legislative and executive powers to democratically elected representative bodies of an autonomous region - are not authoritative according to the Western model. Ocalan's theories continue to influence millions of Kurds and Kurdish women and have direct consequences in their political self-organisation and orientation, especially in Turkey and Syria.

What does this mean for Turkey?

Since 2005, „democratic autonomy" has become a core concept in the political discourse of the Kurds in Turkey. It refers to the relationship between the Kurds and Turks and includes the right to recognition and protection, while maintaining Turkish sovereignty over the Kurdish settlement areas. What is meant is a kind of „social contract" which allows for respectful coexistence under grassroots democratic conditions. The power of the central state is to be limited, based on the recognition of the Kurds' rights to cultural identity. The Kurdish language is thus to become the official language, the language of the public education system, the media and cultural life. This means a move away from the centralised nation state towards grassroots or council democracy with the greatest possible degree of self-government at lower levels.

This idea of Kurdish politicians and activists coincides with the concept of territorial autonomy, which in most cases is based on the ethnic-cultural specificity of a sub-area of a state. Democratic self-government, cooperation across borders and the preservation and free development of cultural communities in a multi-ethnic context are certainly guiding values for existing territorial autonomies all over the world. The basis for such autonomy is not only a functioning democratic constitutional state but also the extensive decentralisation of political decision-making power from the central state to the regions and municipalities. Today's highly centralised Turkish state needs such decentralisation in order to allow for more democracy at all. Decentralised democratic self-government is thus a challenge for Turkish democracy as a whole. In the imagination of the Kurdish forces, democratic autonomy should not be limited to areas with a Kurdish majority, but should also be introduced where Kurds form significant minorities through migration or historical development.

The application of this model to Turkey would not only require substantial constitutional changes, but also a profound revision of the state doctrine of what is still Kemalist Turkey. Turkey's multi-level system consists of municipalities, districts, provinces and the central state, although today the sub-state levels do not have any legislative rights or responsibilities.

Since October 2007, this proposal has been promoted in Turkey, mainly by the „Democratic Society Congress" (DTK), an umbrella organisation of numerous civil society organisations, political parties and trade unions. The DTK believes that ethnic and religious minorities should have guaranteed rights of representation at all levels and in all representative bodies. A total of 20-25 provinces with legislative sovereignty were to be created, while Ankara was to retain only the traditional central government functions. In many public debates, the DTK tried to flesh out Ocalan's ideas in detail and find broad consensus. This vibrant political life in Turkish Kurdistan until 2015 reflected the broad desire for freedom, democracy from below and self-government. One can imagine the Kurdish society of Southeast Turkey as a fermenting political laboratory, but without democratic freedoms, without autonomy, without protection of minorities. A society like that of Catalonia but without the slightest trace of recognised autonomy under the dark light of Turkish oppression.

Peace through territorial autonomy

Turkish Kurdistan is undoubtedly one of those large regions in the world where a minimum of modern territorial autonomy is most urgently needed. The DTK saw itself as an instrument to initiate such a reform by democratic and peaceful means. In 2007, „democratic autonomy" became the official orientation framework of the Kurdish movement, the broadly shared approach to a peaceful solution of the Kurdish question in Turkey. But in December 2009, the DTK was banned by the Constitutional Court. As a successor organisation, the BDP (Party for Peace and Democracy) emerged as the mouthpiece of the Kurdish democracy movement. In its demand for recognition of the Kurdish language and culture in the Turkish constitution, the BDP also referred to the European Charter of Local Self-Government of the Council of Europe, of which Turkey is paradoxically a member. At its party congress in September 2011, „democratic autonomy" was the generic term for the decentralisation of the Turkish state into 20-25 self-governing provinces with extensive autonomy. These demands have also been adopted by what is today the Kurds' most important political force, the HDP, which, however, left open the question of how many regions are to be introduced in Turkey. The HDP advocates regional autonomy above all to protect ethnic minorities.

In the last decade, the policy dominated by the AKP under R.T. Erdogan since 2007 has moved in the opposite direction, to the chagrin of millions of Kurds, namely towards the authoritarian, hyper-nationalistic state, which not only consistently denies minority rights, but systematically undermines the fundamental rights and political freedoms even enshrined in the Turkish constitution. Since

April 2009, thousands of Kurdish activists have been arrested, tried and sentenced on political grounds. The standard charges are „supporting terrorist groups" and the creation of Kurdish state-like institutions with the aim of sabotaging Turkey's national unity and territorial integrity.

As a result, in the summer of 2015, Kurdish grassroots communities in cities such as Diyarbakir, Sirnak, Cizre and Nusaybin declared themselves self-governing communities and attempted to defend them with simple weapons against police violence. The movement was crushed with the greatest brutality and massive use of Turkey's military machinery. A high number of victims and enormous destruction in the Kurdish old towns were to be mourned. In more than 100 cities and municipalities in south-eastern Turkey, elected Kurdish politicians were replaced by provisional administrators. The regime of the almighty President Erdogan literally crushed Kurdish resistance in the cities as well, after nearly 2000 Kurdish villages had been destroyed in the 1990s as huge parts of Turkish Kurdistan were attacked during the fight against the PKK. However, the struggle for democratic autonomy as an idea and concrete reform proposal lives on among millions of Kurds in Turkey and, despite all repression and persecution, will survive today's despotic and anti-minority regime.

For almost a century, the Kurdish people in Turkey have been oppressed in their fundamental rights, discriminated against in everyday life and subjected to war. Since 2015, the Erdogan government has been systematically fighting the Kurds in Turkey and outside the country. Autonomy and real democracy are currently only a dream for thousands of Kurdish activists, journalists and politicians, rather than a realisable project. This dream of democratic autonomy is alive and well among millions of Kurds in Turkey and, despite all the repression and persecution, will outlive today's despotic and anti-minority regime. Precisely territorial autonomy with regional democracy would be the decisive step towards a goal of paramount importance for both peoples: peace.

Autonomy for the Yezidi of Sinjar?

The mountainous region of Sinjar in northern Iraq gained sad fame in the summer of 2014, when troops of the Islamic State (IS) attacked the Kurds and Yezidi (also Yazidi) living here. Especially the Yezidi, with their ancient religion, which differs from Christianity and Islam, were targeted by the IS, which considered this minority as unbelievers and declared Yezidism to be a „pagan religion from pre-Islamic times". The city of Sinjar was taken, most of the villages in the mountains destroyed, and the inhabitants partly murdered, partly expelled. Women who could not flee were kidnapped and enslaved. A total of around 6,500 Yezidis were abducted, including 3,500 women and girls, 1,700 of whom are still in IS violence. Almost 1,300 people are considered to have been killed by the IS, 2,700 children became orphans. According to the assessment of a UN commission in June 2016, the IS committed genocide against the Yezidi. Through murder, rape, enslavement and starvation, the IS tried to exterminate the Yezidi population in the Sinjar. One of the many victims of the IS in the Sinjar, the Yezidi Nadia Murad was awarded the Nobel Peace Prize in December 2018.

A Yezidi militia, supported by YPG fighters from Syria and the PKK, was able to clear an escape route for 20,000 to 30,000 Yezidis in the summer of 2015. After a new major offensive in autumn 2015, the Peshmerga of the Autonomous Region of Kurdistan succeeded in liberating the district of Sinjar and driving out the IS in November 2015. On 3 August 2020, the President of the Autonomous Region of Kurdistan Barzani announced his intention to integrate the Sinjar district into his region. But do the Yezidis want to become part of Iraqi Kurdistan and what kind of self-government do they demand?

Sinjar: Home of the Yezidi

The city of Sinjar (Kurdish: Şhengal) is the capital of the district of the same name in the province of Ninava in northern Iraq, west of Mosul on the border with Syria and thus adjacent to the de facto autonomous confederation of northern Syria. The majority of the population is formed by the religious community of the Yezidi, who are ethnically and linguistically counted among the Kurds and speak Kurmanji. A further 400,000 Yezidis live in the Autonomous Region of Kurdistan-Iraq and abroad, mainly in Germany. The province of Ninava (Nineveh) is ethnically and religiously diverse overall. In addition to the Sunni Kurds and Kurdish-speaking Yezidis, Arabs, Turkmen, Chaldo-Assyrians, Kakai and Mandaeans also live here.

Iraq's current constitution does mention the Yezidi people, but does not define specific protection rights. As was the case for centuries in the Ottoman Empire, the Yezidi in Iraq have been persecuted and discriminated against in two ways: firstly as a Kurdish-speaking minority and secondly as non-Muslims. The Yezidis themselves founded a „Council of Yezidis" and self-defence units at the beginning of 2015 to defend the interests of the ethnic group in all matters. Although

Source: de.wikipedia.org, author: Ezidikhan, CC Attribution Share Alike 4.0 International

all parties in the Autonomous Region of Kurdistan, as well as the PYD of Northern Syria and the PKK, want to support the Yezidi people, there is no common goal or strategy. Masud Barzani, the former president of the Autonomous Region of Kurdistan, announced on 3 August 2015 that the region of Sinjar would become part of the Kurdish Autonomous Region. However, due to the now strong diaspora and the persecution of the Yezidis, especially in Iraq, a debate about the future of the religious community has arisen. According to Idan Barir (WIKIPEDIA), returning to their former settlement areas like Sinjar or Schaichān is no longer an option for most of the Yezidis who fled. The Yezidis' mistrust of the Arab population, some of whom collaborated with the IS organisation, is too great. In addition, the Yezidis did not consider themselves politically represented in the Autonomous Region of Kurdistan, and some even saw themselves as enemies. Many Yezidi are therefore looking for a future for their community outside Iraq. Others demand genuine protection and self-government as part of the Autonomous Region of Kurdistan.

Iraq is ethnically and religiously fragmented, and the rule of law and democracy are only slowly being established in the northwest of the country after the traumas of the Saddam Hussein dictatorship, the US invasions, the civil war and the IS reign of terror. The region of Sinjar is in a sensitive position between the autonomous Kurdish areas in Syria, Iraq and Turkey, where military action is repeatedly taken against PKK units. For the Yezidis there, not only the protection of minorities and self-government are on the agenda, but also existential security against new attacks.

Camp of Yezidi refugees from Sinjar in Sharya near Dohuk, Kurdistan-Iraq. Foto: Th. Benedikter

Autonomy as a permanent solution?

After multiple genocide crimes, the Yezidi of Sinjar demand not only improved protection from Iraq, but also the right to self-determination according to democratic principles within the national borders. Another genocide could lead to the complete destruction of one of the oldest religious communities in the Middle East. According to the post-war Iraq with its federal constitution of 2005, there are no protective provisions for the Yezidi. The status of the district of Sinjar is still unclear. The area could become a separate governorate of Iraq (province) or be incorporated into the existing Autonomous Region of Kurdistan. In theory, the population of the Sinjar has the right to decide on its own status within Iraq, according to Article 140 of the constitution. According to the Constitution, the citizens of this part of the Ninava province would have the right to proclaim by referendum their own province with a freely elected governor. This would be legitimate in the case of Sinjar, given its ethnic-religious characteristics and the persecution it has suffered. For linguistic, security and economic reasons, however, it would be more sensible and appropriate to integrate the Sinjar into the existing Autonomous Region of Kurdistan. Within this framework, the area could be given special status to meet the requirements of minority protection.

In the long term, it would appear that any Arab-Iraqi sovereignty over the area is not in line with the vital interests of the Yezidi, Kurds and other ethnic-religious minorities. In the long term, Iraqi Kurdistan will achieve independence, which was voted for by over 90 percent of the electorate in a free referendum on 25 September 2017. The future of the Yezidis lies in the union with the Kurds, to which they ethnolinguistically belong. The majority of the Yezidi of Iraq already live in the Autonomous Region of Kurdistan. Within the framework of Kurdistan,

Sinjar could be given autonomous status in order to do justice to the ethno-religious specificity of the area. Due to its own experience of decades of persecution and subsequent autonomy, Kurdistan has the political will to do so.

Such a two-tier territorial autonomy would not be absolutely new. It exists within the framework of federal states at sub-state level, e.g. the autonomous Bodoland in the state of Assam (India), the Aran valley of the Autonomous Community of Catalonia and the German-speaking Community of East Belgium, which is part of the region of Wallonia. The integration of an autonomous Sinjar into the Autonomous Region of Kurdistan would have to be anchored both in the Iraqi constitution and in the Autonomy Statute of Kurdistan, with clear demarcation of areas of legislative and administrative responsibilities, rights of representation in the Kurdistan Parliament, consociational democracy in the institutions of the new province, financing and demarcation of borders. Military security would also be better guaranteed by the jurisdiction of the Kurdish Peshmerga with the involvement of Yezidi units. The constitutional alternative of the Sinjar as Iraq's own federal unit - in addition to the three constituent states of Kurds, Sunnis and Shiites provided for or possible under the constitution - does not seem feasible, because the area is too small and economically too weak for this. Territorial autonomy as a part of Iraqi-Kurdistan offers great potential for a stable new order, for the protection of minorities and self-determination within a secure framework.

On 9 October 2020, the central government in Baghdad and the government of the Kurdistan Autonomous Region reached a preliminary agreement on the situation in the Sinjar, which is to be transformed from a mere district to a governorate in accordance with the Iraqi constitution. In an official and joint statement, many Yezidi organisations, parties and personalities welcomed the agreement, but a tripartite committee consisting only of representatives of Baghdad, Erbil and the Governorate of Nineveh without Yezidi leaders was not in the spirit of greater self-government. They also pointed out, however, that the Yezidi will only return to their territory if security and a stable political framework are guaranteed. To this end, the Yezidi self-defence militias should be integrated into the regular units of the Iraqi army. Yezidis would also have to be taken into account in the recruitment for the new local police force. With 2,500 members, this unit was far too small and should be increased to 9,000. The Yezidis and their representatives want to be involved in this political reorganisation, in the security structure and in reconstruction. After the 2014-15 IS raid, the Yezidis would have to be even better protected against threats: Turkey in the north, Shiite militias, underground IS fighters in the south. No hostility should emanate from Sinjar towards neighbouring countries, which in such case in turn would lead to military attacks on the Sinjar. The occupation of the most important administrative posts and the election of local representatives would have to be organised with the Yezidis. However, this agreement does not yet establish genuine territorial autonomy with a democratically elected regional parliament comparable to that of the Autonomous Region of Kurdistan.

Referendums on the political status of sub-state territories, 1994 - 2020

Nr.	Year	Concerned region or territory	Result
Referendums on the independence of a substate territory (to achieve sovereign statehood)			
1	1995	Québec (Canada)	Independence rejected
2	1997	Anjouan (Comoros)	Independence rejected
3	1998	Nevis (St. Kitts and Nevis)	Independence accepted, but turnout treshold not achieved
4	1998	Puerto Rico (USA) I	Independence rejected, yes to statehood within the USA
5	1999	Timor Leste (Indonesia)	Yes to independence
6	1999	Bermudas (United Kingdom)	Independence rejected
7	1999	Abkhazia (Georgia)	Yes to independence
8	2001	Somaliland (Somalia)	Yes to independence
9	2004-05	Netherlands Antilles (NL)	Independence rejected, different status
10	2005	Kurdistan (Iraq)	Yes to independence
11	2006	Montenegro (Serbia-Montenegro)	Yes to independence
12	2006	Southern Ossetia (Georgia)	Yes to independence
13	2006	Transnistria (Moldavia)	Yes to independence
14	2011	South Sudan (Sudan)	Yes to independence
15	2012	Puerto Rico (USA) II	Independence rejected, yes to statehood within the USA
16	2014	Luhansk (Ukraine)	Yes to independence
17	2014	Donezk (Ukraine)	Yes to independence
18	2014	Scotland (United Kingdom)	Independence rejected
19	2017	Kurdistan (Iraq)	Yes to independence
20	2017	Catalonia (Spain)	Yes to independence
21	2018	New Caledonia (France) I	Independence rejected
22	2019	Bougainville (Papua New Guinea)	Yes to independence
23	2020	New Caledonia (France) II	Independence rejected
Referendums on free association or annexation or incorporation in another state			
24	1994	Republika Srpska (Bosnia and Herzegowina)	Yes to incorporation into Serbia
25	2004	Cyprus	Reunification rejected
26	2006	Tokelau (New Zealand)	Yes to free association, but turnout treshold not achieved

27	2007	Tokelau (New Zealand)	Yes to free association, but turnout treshold not achieved
28	2014	Crimea (Ukraine)	Yes to incorporation into Russia
29	2017	Puerto Rico (USA) III	Yes to statehood within the USA
30	2020	Puerto Rico (USA) IV	Yes to statehood within the USA

Referendums on the constitution of a different political status under the sovereignty of an existing state (territorial autonomy or other legal status)

31	1994	Bonaire (Netherlands)	Yes to special status
32	1994	Sint Maarten (Netherlands)	Yes to special status
33	1994	Saba (Netherlands)	Yes to special status
34	1994	Sint Eustatius (Netherlands)	Yes to special status
35	1995	Bermudas (United Kingdom)	Yes to special status
36	1997	Scotland (United Kingdom)	Yes to autonomy
37	1997	Wales (United Kingdom)	Yea to autonomy
38	1998	Northern Ireland (UK)	Yes to autonomy
39	1998	Cordilleras (Philippines)	Yes to autonomy
40	1998	Northern Territory (Australia)	Yes to autonomy
41	1998	New Caledonia (France)	Yes to autonomy
42	2000	Mayotte (France)	Yes to département-entity
43	2002	Gibraltar (United Kingdom)	No to modification of relationship with UK
44	2003	Martinique (France)	Overseas département, against more autonomy
45	2003	Guadeloupe (France)	Unification département and region
46	2003	Saint Martin (France)	Separation from Guadeloupe, special collectivity COM
47	2003	Saint Barthelemy (France)	Separation from Guadeloupe, special collectivity COM
48	2005	Sint Eustatius (Netherlands)	Yes to special status
49	2005	Curaçao (Netherlands)	Yes to special status
50	2006	Gibraltar (United Kingdom)	No to modification of relationship with UK
51	2009	Mayotte (France)	Yes to département-entity
52	2009	Curaçao (Netherlands)	Yes to special status
53	2010	French Guyana (France)	Against more autonomy
54	2010	Martinique (France)	Yes to special status
55	2014	Sint Eustatius (Netherlands)	Yes to special status

56	2004	Bonaire (Netherlands)	Yes to special status
57	2004	Saba (Netherlands)	Yes to special status
58	2000	Sint Maarten (Netherlands)	Yes to special status
59	2003	Corsica (France)	Against modest degree of autonomy
60	2006	Bolivia I	Autonomy for Eastern lowlands
61	2008	Bolivia II	Autonomy for Eastern lowlands
62	2008	Greenland (Denmark)	Yes to extension of autonomy
63	2010	Guadéloupe (France)	No to extension of autonomy
64	2011	Wales (United Kingdom)	Yes to extension of autonomy
65	2013	Falkland Islands (United Kingdom)	Yes to self-administration
66	2017	Lombardy (Italy)	Yes to extension of powers
67	2017	Veneto (Italy)	Yes to extension of powers

Sources: Markku SUKSI (2016), *The Referendum as an Instrument for the Resolution of Territorial Disputes and for the Exercize of Self-Determination*, in: Peter Hilpold Hg. 2016), Autonomie und Selbstbestimmung in Europa und im internationalen Vergleich, Nomos, Baden-Baden, 84-111
WIKIPEDIA: https://en.wikipedia.org/wiki/Independence_referendum
IRAI: https://irai.quebec/wp-content/uploads/2017/09/IRAI_Rapports-experts-Catalogne_EN_final.pdf
WIKIPEDIA: respective entries on the concerned territories on www.wikipedia.fr; https://en.wikipedia.org; und www.wikipedia.de

Note: *The referendums in Republika Srpska (1994), in Abkhazia (1999), in Somaliland (2001), in Kurdistan-Iraq (2005 and 2017), in South Ossetia (2006), in Transnistria (2006), in Luhansk and Donetsk (2014), in Crimea (2014), in Catalonia (2017) have been held without a constitutional basis of the state of affiliation. They were held by self-declared de facto states (e.g. Somaliland, Transnistria, Abkhazia, Luhansk) or in constituent states or autonomous regions (Catalonia, Kurdistan-Iraq, Crimea) in disregard of the constitutional law still formally in force in these territories. Apart from the voting process itself, there is a gap between the rule of law and democratic legitimacy in these cases. Cases of unconstitutional secessions enforced by military force, human rights violations and expulsion (Crimea, Donetsk, Luhansk, Republika Srpska) in terms both of the democratic procedure and the constitutional legitimacy are not comparable with state reorganisation within failed states (Somaliland) or referendums based on regional law (Catalonia). However, they show the danger of violent reactions if democratic solutions are not brought about within the state. For this reason, they have been included in this list.*

18

When autonomy is no longer enough: Scotland and Catalonia

Like federal systems, autonomy systems are also subject to change. Some countries that once had autonomous status are now independent states, such as Southern Sudan, Eritrea, Kosovo, Abkhazia and South Ossetia. Still others have reformed their statute several times (Guna Yala, Greenland, Åland, South Tyrol, Bodoland). In the former cases, territorial autonomy proved insufficient to resolve the basic conflict between the autonomous community and the central state.

The autonomy rights of national minorities or peoples of these areas were not respected by the central state, as was the case with Kosovo in Serbia, Abkhazia and South Ossetia in independent Georgia. Existing autonomy was abolished, leading to resistance, expulsion and war (Eritrea under Ethiopia, Kurdistan in Iraq, Kosovo under Serbia). The formerly autonomous Netherlands Antilles opted for a different status vis-à-vis the Netherlands until 2010 after a long process of democratic decision-making. In New Caledonia (France) and Bougainville (Papua New Guinea), on the other hand, the agreement between the central state and the autonomous community establishing autonomy also provided for the holding of a referendum on independence within a set period.

Areas of existing states which are ethnically and culturally different from the majority population may undergo a process of national emancipation and opt democratically for statehood or another status. This is a process of conflict resolution which receives its strongest political legitimation through democratic referendums. The table on the previous pages 256-258 lists 67 referendums which from 1994 to 2020 have led to changes in the political status of a substate area or to become an independent souvereign country. Most of these processes have been carried out through peaceful and lawful procedures. As a rule, autonomous communities or regions with territorial autonomy cannot claim any right to self-determination. It depends on the political will and the constitutional system of a state whether, in the context of territorial autonomy, the autonomous community is also accorded the right to choose a different political status by democratic vote in the future. Here we look at the cases of Scotland and Catalonia, currently still autonomous regions, both aspiring to sovereignty.

Scotland on the road to independence: devolution as a phase of transition

Source: WIKIPEDIA, UK location map Nord-NordWest, author: TUBS

The Kingdom of Scotland was founded in 843 and united with the Kingdom of England in 1603 in a personal union. Scotland was a separate state until 1707. With the "Acts of Union" of 1707, the Kingdom of Scotland, which was already in personal union with England, was absorbed into the much larger and economically stronger Great Britain, thus losing the independence it had defended for centuries. It was the heavily indebted Scottish bourgeoisie, the nobility and the royal family who wanted to recover financially through this union. It was an elite project, because the Scottish people could not decide for themselves. A "union with less mutual affection" had never existed before, said the English poet Daniel Defoe, who was spying in Scotland on behalf of England at the time of the unification. Even after 1707, various Scottish institutions remained in existence, such as the Bank of Scotland and the Church of Scotland.

The call for greater political independence began to emerge in the 1920s. In 1928 the government in London appointed a separate minister for the affairs of Scotland. The Scottish National Party (SNP) was founded in 1934. The first devolution referendum did not take place until 1979, and although the majority of Scots voted to revive the Scottish Parliament, the low turnout prevented the vote from being valid. In the second devolution referendum in 1997, 74 percent of voters voted for devolution. A Scottish Parliament was thus re-elected in 1999, giving it legislative powers over a wide range of areas.

Only ten years later, the Scotland Act, the autonomy granted in 1998, was called into question. This had not happened for 300 years since the two kingdoms were united. In the course of applying the autonomy, the SNP succeeded in gaining more and more support from Scottish citizens. In 2011, the SNP won an absolute majority in the Edinburgh Parliament for the first time and ruled alone. The "first minister" Alex Salmond announced that he would strive for a referendum on Scotland's self-determination. Following an agreement between the British head of government Cameron and the Scottish government in 2013, the referendum was set for 18 September 2014. However, on that date, 55.3 percent of the Scottish voters, with a turnout of 84.59 percent, refused to break away from the United Kingdom.

Following the UK's BREXIT referendum on 23 June 2016, Scottish Prime Minister Nicola Sturgeon said it was unacceptable that Scotland had to leave the EU despite the fact that 62 percent of Scotland's electorate voted to remain in the EU. Sturgeon already announced a new independence referendum in October 2016. The Scottish Parliament agreed to this and instructed Sturgeon to negotiate with the government in London. Since then, support for Scotland's independence has continued to grow and in 2020 several polls showed a majority in favour of secession. Hundreds of thousands of Scots took to the streets time and again in Glasgow and Edinburgh for independence. In the 2019 general election, the SNP won a landslide victory with 48 of Scotland's 59 seats in parliament. Sturgeon saw this as confirmation of its mandate to call for a second independence referendum, which British Prime Minister Johnson categorically rejected on 14 January 2020. The question remains open.

What advantages does Scotland's leading political force see in independence? The Scottish independence movement wants political independence and rejects political paternalism by the British Parliament and Government ("Westminster"), which is dominated by the Englishmen. Instead of suffering decisions and laws made in London, Scotland would be governed solely by the freely elected members of the Scottish Parliament and Government, according to the SNP.

Independence is not an end in itself, the Scottish government emphasises in its White Paper on Independence of 2014, the overriding aim being to improve the living conditions of the people of Scotland. Only a government of its own could put the needs of the Scottish people first. The devolution since 1999 bore fruit, but in the areas remaining with the state, high costs and considerable disadvantages for the Scots have arisen. More prosperity, more social balance (fairness) and an economic development controlled by Scotland itself: these are the key values that the SNP sees safeguarded by independence. Moving the power of political decision-making from Westminster to Edinburgh means that Scotland's policies can be fully aligned with the values, aspirations and interests of the Scottish people and that a fairer society can be created. The period of neo-liberal counter-reform during the Thatcher era and subsequent Tory governments still angers millions of Scottish SNP voters today. Scotland is about a fundamental claim to self-determination by a historically evolved community which in many ways feels alienated from the majority in the UK.

The Scottish government formed by the SNP is aiming for four overarching goals with independence (cf. Scottish Government, Scotland's Future - Your Guide for an Independent Scotland, 2013):

1. A democratic Scotland

The Scottish Parliament has been responsible for health, education, justice, housing, agriculture and fisheries, transport policy, social welfare and a number of other areas since 1999. In an independent Scotland, the Parliament would be free to shape the tax system, social welfare with the pension system, immigration, foreign and defence policy. Forty-one of the 75 years since 1945, Scotland had been governed by British governments which had not achieved a majority in Scotland. On the contrary, the Tories, the dominant conservative party in England, lead a marginal existence in Scotland. Thus, the policy of the British government was mostly enforced against the Scottish MPs in Westminster. Scotland has so far been subject to a great deal of foreign political influence. The government cites the privatisation of the postal service, unfair social policies, cuts in public investment, excessive spending on Britain's nuclear weapons, and participation in the war in Iraq as examples. An independent Scotland could keep the taxes and duties of the Scots in the country and spend them on the welfare of its own people.

2. A more prosperous country

Even after devolution in 1999, the main economic policy decisions are still taken in London without a mandate from Scotland. The tax system, important areas of public expenditure, regulation of the business economy, competition policy and other key areas would be centrally controlled. While Scotland could have successfully tackled unemployment and encouraged investment, it was at the mercy of the United Kingdom.

The country is endowed with a wealth of natural resources, has an excellent reputation as an industrial location, world-class universities and research institutes, creative services, tourism and high quality food production. According to GDP per capita, an independent Scotland would rank 8th among the industrialised countries in the OECD. Even without North Sea oil, the Scottish economy would be at the same level of value added per capita as the UK as a whole. Scotland's oil and gas resources would even generate one fifth more economic output. On the other hand, as a part of the UK Scotland's growth rate for the years 1993-2013 has been lower than the rest of the UK.

The poverty rate in Scotland is far too high and life expectancy too low. According to the Scottish government, the Scandinavian countries should be used as a benchmark for the prosperity indicators, behind which Scotland is lagging. These neighbouring countries could decide for themselves thanks to independence. An independent Scotland could provide higher growth and a better quality of life for its citizens. All economic and fiscal policy decisions could be tailored to Scottish

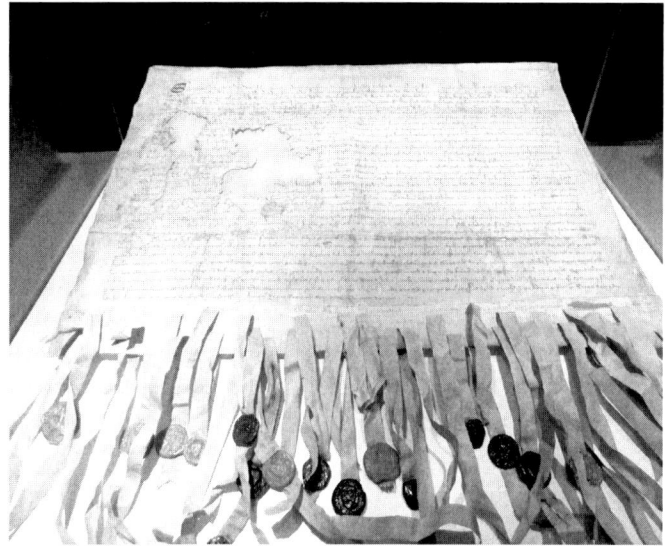

The „Declaration of Arbroath" on Scotland's independence of 1320.
Foto: Thomas Benedikter

needs. But if the pound sterling were to remain the currency, Scotland would still need to rely on the partnership with England on monetary policy.

3. A fairer society

As part of the United Kingdom, Scotland has a growing social inequality. Here the United Kingdom ranks 28th among the 34 OECD countries. Since 1975, inequality has increased more in the United Kingdom than in any other OECD country. This is the result of 40 years of British policy, not just the Thatcher government, the Scottish government states in its White Paper on independence in 2014. Social justice is not only essential for the quality of life of the socially disadvantaged, but also important for the economic success of a whole country. Thanks to autonomy, Scotland had been able to take countermeasures, but this would not have been enough to fight inequality. Independence enabled Scotland to create a more socially just society, to strengthen community spirit and shared responsibility, partly because a Scottish Parliament and Government reflected the political preferences expressed in Scotland itself.

4. More stable public finances

Scotland's public finances have played a central role in this. Scotland can afford to be financially independent as it has a healthier budget than the UK as a whole. Estimates for the years 1980-2012 show that Scottish taxpayers have paid more in taxes per capita than the national average. However, the share of public expenditure in GDP was lower in Scotland than in the UK as a whole. Building on more stable revenues, the Scottish Executive could abolish socially burdensome taxes and use tax relief to target business and the vulnerable. With its current autonomy, Scotland could only have 7 percent of its tax revenue at its direct disposal. Newly promised taxes would increase this share to 15 percent, but with independence it would be 100 percent. As part of the United Kingdom, Scotland is trapped in one of the most unjust development models in the Western world. Wealth, income and jobs are regionally concentrated in London and the southwest of England. The British economy is unstable with high national debt and this would be exacerbated by the Brexit.

The opportunities of independence

In the Scottish Executive's argumentation it is repeatedly emphasised that social and economic development is crucial to the independence issue. Among many other policy areas that an independent Scotland could shape itself, this area is a priority, while cultural differences with England play a secondary role. Public finances are also of the utmost importance. Self-determination in taxes and public spending is central to shaping economic development in Scotland's interests. The free health system for all is to be maintained in Scotland. The same applies to free access to higher education for all Scottish students, unlike the rest of the country. The pension system should be improved, as should social policy. On defence policy, the SNP argues that Scotland should remain in NATO, but British nuclear weapons should be removed immediately. With a smaller Scottish professional army, it should be possible to reduce military expenditure significantly.

The vast majority of Scotland's political representatives, and presumably the Scottish people too, are calling for independence in order to meet the long-term political aspirations of the Scottish people and to realise a different model of society. Scotland sees itself as closely related to the Scandinavian welfare state models. Devolution, i.e. territorial autonomy, has reached its limits in Scotland because autonomy cannot offer a comprehensive degree of political self-determination in all areas. This is compounded by the Scottish preference for EU membership, unlike the UK has definitely left. Scotland's advantage at this stage of history is that Britain recognises in principle the right of Scots to self-determination. A further referendum seems only a matter of time.

In a departure from the question raised here, "What can be achieved by autonomy?", the legitimate question in this and several other cases is: What can autonomy not achieve to provide? In Scotland, it is a matter of a fundamental claim to self-determination by a community that has grown historically and which feels alienated in many ways from the majority of the United Kingdom. Even Scotland's somewhat extended autonomy after the referendum of 18.9.2014 can no longer fulfil this claim. The United Kingdom's understanding of the state requires a permanent democratic legitimisation of "unification". Based on this principle, the Scottish people, as bearers of this right, are entitled to decide freely on their political status and will claim it again.

Catalonia and the limits of the "State of autonomous communities"

Source: Commons Wikimedia.org, CC BY-SA 3.0

The history of the Catalan nation goes back over 1000 years. In 1492 Catalonia was "forcedly married" to Castile. When Ferdinand of Aragon and Isabella of Castile, the "reyes catolicos", married, Castile and Aragon were united with Catalonia in personal union and in 1516, under Charles V, they were united to form the Kingdom of Spain. After the War of Spanish Succession in 1700-1713, Catalonia's political independence was completely lost. But as a cultural nation Catalonia remained alive.

In the course of 505 years of this "union by royal will" no one has ever asked the people of Catalonia in which state they would like to live. Despite struggles for freedom and much political and military resistance, the Catalans were kept in the Spanish state by Spanish monarchs or dictators. Catalonia finally gained autonomy in 1931 with a Statute (Statute of Núria) was approved by 99 percent of its population. But this autonomy, approved by the Cortes of Madrid on 9.11.1932, had a short life. It was suspended in 1934 and after the civil war the Franco regime abolished Catalonia's first autonomy in 1939.

With the 3rd Spanish Republic, Catalonia received a new Statute of Autonomy in 1979, which was accepted by 87 percent of the electorate in a referendum. In contrast to the Basque Country, the new Spanish Constitution of 1978 had also received a majority in Catalonia. The Catalans' claim to be recognised as a people with their own language, culture, history and traditions, and thus to be given the right to freely determine their political status, goes back centuries. However, the failed attempt to reform the 1979 Statute of Autonomy in 2005-2010 was directly decisive for the independence efforts of recent year. How could this happen?

From 2004 to 2005, the regional parliament of Catalonia (Generalitat) discussed intensively and deliberated until the reform statute was finally adopted on 30.9.2005 with 90 percent of the votes. The draft statute was approved by the Spanish Parliament at the end of March 2006 after a lengthy evaluation and some amendments. In June 2006, the Catalan electorate confirmed the new Statute with 73.9 percent YES votes and a 49 percent turnout. Only the centralist right of the Partido Popular openly opposed the new Statute. This extended the powers of the Autonomous Community, restricted the government's powers, extended Catalonia's fiscal sovereignty, strengthened the role of the Catalan language and recognised Catalonia as a nation in its own right, at least symbolically. In the Spanish constitution, the old concept of Catalonia as a mere "nationality", a kind of second-class nation, would have remained the same. The new Statute defined with extreme precision, in 58 articles, not only the individual competences, but all the sub-sectors of public activity in the Community. In order to prevent the permanent conflict with the central state before the Constitutional Court, the Statute introduced legal safeguards to provide legal certainty.

The Constitutional Court blocks Catalonia's new autonomy

For the Spanish right wing parties this all went too far. After the Statute of Autonomy was approved by the Parliament in Madrid with some amendments, the Partido Popular challenged no less than 114 of the 223 articles of the new Statute before the Constitutional Court. The Constitutional Court's decision was anything but easy. It was not until four years later, on 28 June 2010, that it decided to reject most of the genuine innovations of the reform statute. 15 essential provisions were rejected as totally or partially unconstitutional, with two particularly weighty objections. Firstly, Catalonia was denied the right to exclude any further access by the central state to exclusive competences. In other words, the Statute's approach of establishing exclusive, shared and executive administrative powers was rejected as such, thus striking at the very heart of Catalan territorial autonomy. This was not the task of an autonomy statute, the Constitutional Court ruled, but only of the constitution itself, with the Constitutional Court's interpretation being the only decisive one. The Statute's provisions on the powers of the Autonomous Community were simply considered not binding. Article 111, which defined the competences shared with the State, was also deleted in its entirety.

The second serious limitation was the need for a "binding interpretation" of 24 contested articles. The Constitutional Court ruling turned out to be a long list of binding interpretation criteria on numerous provisions of the Statute concerning competences, procedures and institutions. In short, the Statute as such was made subject to the respective position of the central government and the respective interpretation of the Constitution including the Catalan autonomy statute by the Constitutional Court. This largely undermined the concern of the autonomy reform to ensure greater clarity and autonomy. The substance of the autonomy was still left to Madrid's arbitrariness. For political Catalonia, the Constitutional Court's ruling was humiliating and unacceptable. On 10 July 2010, one million people took out to the streets in Barcelona to protest against the sentence.

The Constitutional Court's ruling - according to constitutional lawyer Xabier Arzoz (Arzoz 2019) - confirmed the symmetrical view of Spain's decentralisation, which has always been favoured by the central state, and thus autonomy to be established in the same way for all communities. The historical autonomous communities were thus denied the right to develop their autonomy themselves by means of statutes under the Spanish constitution. This abolished "statutory sovereignty", comparable to the constitutional sovereignty of the federal states in federal states. The only way to overcome this totally restrictive reading of the Constitution is to amend the Spanish Constitution. However, such an amendment is not only highly complicated as a procedure, but is also rejected by the major Spanish parties, thus almost impossible. Even if the autonomy reforms are approved by the Spanish Parliament, as in the case of Catalonia in 2006, the sword of Damocles of the Constitutional Court would still be hanging over them. Nationalist and centralist parties would always have the possibility to undermine more autonomy through this legal route.

Catalonia's first autonomy statute of 1932 Original cover of the Estatuto de Núria by Angel J. Navarro. Blogspot.com.es Public Domain

The democratic will of a region of 7.5 million inhabitants is rejected by a simple majority of an 8-member court, which is composed only of Spaniards.

Although the fundamental right and principle of territorial autonomy is enshrined in Spain's constitution, the distribution of powers is not. The regions receive their competences through special state laws ("organic autonomy laws") and other state laws. In 12 important areas, which the state unilaterally determines, the state can nevertheless encroach on autonomous competences. A Statute of Autonomy cannot bind the Spanish Parliament, according to the Constitutional Court in its ruling no. 31/2010, and it can even override the Statutes with simple State laws. As a result - according to Arzoz - the Statutes of Autonomy do not limit the state's rights of intervention. State laws, on the other hand, do restrict the communities. This undermines the very foundations of territorial autonomy. This was an appeal for Barcelona to react very strongly.

In Spain there is no clear division of responsibilities between the State and the Autonomous Communities. Conflicts of jurisdiction before the Constitutional Court have been accumulating for years. Between 1980 and 2014 there were 378 such judgments and 543 judgments concerning the attribution of competences. The power and influence of the Constitutional Court in Spain goes far beyond the usual extent in federal states. The political tensions between the State and the Communities, the ambiguity of the Constitution, the lack of direct involvement of the Communities in the formation of the State's political will, all of which lead to frequent conflicts before the Constitutional Court. The Constitutional Court has developed some interpretative schemes, but it has not set clear limits on the extension of the State's powers. In 2010, Catalonia has been denied to clearly define which powers are definitively and securely vested in the Autonomous Community. This opens the door to state interference in the autonomous competences. There are also no procedural steps that would allow the Autonomous Communities to have a say in state legislation in advance, as they are not represented as such at central level. Moreover, all constitutional judges are nominated by the Spanish State. The participation of the Autonomous Communities is undermined. The Statutes are not even immune to unilateral amendment by the State. The Autonomous Communities are not involved as such in constitutional amendments and do not have the right of veto if their power is curtailed.

The Constitutional Court's sentence No. 31/2010 marked a watershed in the development of the autonomous state of Spain. The failed reform of the Catalan Autonomy Statute in 2006 clearly showed the narrow limits of territorial autonomy in Spain. Catalonia did not want to be satisfied with only minor enhancements. The Catalan parties were formally pushed to self-determination if they wanted to achieve more substantial autonomy. While the advocates of independence had previously been in the minority in Catalan society, a broad movement for self-determination emerged in a few years from 2010 onwards.

Catalonia: a politically divided society

In the autumn of 2017, events in Catalonia came thick and fast: on 1 October, the independence referendum was held despite a ban by Madrid. With a turnout of 42.3 percent, over 90 percent of the Catalan voters voted for independence. The Spanish police obstructed the voters where they could, even with brutal force. On 27 October the President of the Autonomous Community, Carles Puigdemont, proclaimed the "Republic of Catalonia". Madrid reacted the same day by suspending Catalonia's autonomy. The Catalan leaders were charged with rebellion and misappropriation of public funds. Puigdemont evaded arrest by fleeing abroad. The Barcelona Parliament was dissolved and new elections were called. On 21 December 2017, the parties of the self-determination platform regained a narrow majority of seats in the Generalitat. In spring 2018 the central government lifted the forced administration, but the conflict with Madrid remained. For the ruling parties in the Generalitat, headed by President Quim Torra, autonomy remains a transitional phase towards independence.

In its history since 1492, Catalonia had never ceased to consider itself an independent cultural and linguistic community and to exercise sovereignty, at least on a cultural and social level. Even after the suppression of the 1714 uprising - since then the 11th of September has been Catalonia's national day of commemoration - Catalonia continued to have movements for political and cultural renaissance. The 2nd Republic of Spain started this self-determination movement

The Parliament of the Autonomous Community of Catalonia in Barcelona.

with the autonomy in 1932, which already collapsed in 1936 under the attack of Franco's troops. The traumatic experience of the Spanish Civil War and the 40-year dictatorship of General Franco is deeply rooted in the Catalans' historical consciousness. Together with the Basque Country, Catalonia was one of the main targets of repression by this regime and, both at home and abroad, one of the main sources of cultural and political resistance against Franco.

After the language bans were relaxed somewhat in the 1960s, the "Asamblea de Catalunya" was founded in 1971 to organise Catalan civil society independently with a view to a soon to be democratic Spain. After the restoration of democracy, secession and independence were initially out of the question. In 1978 the majority of Catalans voted in favour of the new Spanish Constitution, which granted the Autonomous Communities the right to autonomy. With the 1979 Statute of Autonomy, the Generalitat was re-established as the totality of the country's political institutions. 87 percent of Catalans in 1979 voted for the Statute of Autonomy. This also introduced official bilingualism and recognised Catalan as "lengua propia", but Catalonia did not enjoy such an extensive fiscal autonomy as the Basque Country and Navarre. During the first 25 years under the government of Jordi Pujol, with a healthy majority of liberal-conservative CiU, the Autonomous Community concentrated on the re-catalanisation of society. It was only in Pujol's "Programa 2000" that the concept of the "nation of Catalonia" reappeared, with which statehood and sovereignty was no longer excluded in the long term. The immediate objective was to reform the 1979

Statute, which proved to be increasingly inadequate. The Republican Left Party ERC, however, had been consistently advocating Catalonia's independence since the 1970s. As stated above, the vast majority of Catalonia's political forces were committed to reforming the Statute by 2006. Only the Constitutional Court ruling of June 2010, which annulled the essential pillar of the reform as unconstitutional, triggered the turn towards the option of self-determination.

In Catalonia this was perceived as national humiliation. This was exacerbated by the austerity measures of the Rajoy government, which severely affected Catalonia. The Catalan parties shifted to the line of "sovereignty", because it had become clear that within the Spanish constitution a more extensive autonomy and special position of Catalonia was not achievable. As Eduardo Ruiz Vieytez (cf. interview in chapter 5) explains, the other Autonomous Communities were keen to establish symmetry in order to level the autonomy of all regions at the lowest possible level. Moreover, the "historical" smaller nations of Catalonia and the Basque Country, which are striving for more self-rule, have no chance of bringing about a constitutional reform in the sense of more autonomy or even federalism, or even of introducing the right to decide freely on their sovereignty.

Because of its history, culture, language and political self-image, Catalonia still sees itself as a cultural nation, but defines itself not on the basis of ethnicity, but as a community of people living in Catalonia. In this sense, it is no different from the Spanish understanding of nation, which classifies all peoples and cultural communities living on Spanish territory as "nationalities" and only chisels the Spanish one into the constitution as an "indissoluble nation".

In Catalonia, the independence movement is not motivated by the rejection of the obligation to financial solidarity with poorer parts of Spain. It is a matter of the felt sense of belonging to an independent nation which, like other - even much smaller - European peoples, claims its own state. As in Scotland, Catalan independence advocates want a Catalonia embedded in the EU, even if some things about the EU do not fit. For its part, the EU has refrained strictly from intervening in the Madrid-Barcelona conflict.

With the reform of its statute, Catalonia not only wanted to establish its claim to recognition as a "nation". More important was the substantial expansion and safeguarding of autonomy as a distinct political sphere of self-rule. This aspiration was endorsed by 88.9 percent of the Catalan parliament and, in 2006, by 73.9 percent of the Catalan electorate. The Catalan parties had not derived any direct claim to secession from this. But the autonomy reform blocked by Madrid in 2010 has formally forced them to do so.

Today the Catalans insist on being allowed to decide for themselves on the status of their country. They first tried to do so in 2009 in self-organised referendums in 166 municipalities, then in a self-organized countrywide referendum in 2014, and finally in the referendum organised by the Generalitat on 1.10.2017. Nevertheless, the "right to decide" of the Catalans, i.e. a democratic popular vote on Catalonia's political status, claimed by almost all Catalan parties, is rejected by almost all Spanish parties. The Spanish constitution itself categorically excludes it. This political conflict can only be solved by a democratic process.

Autonomy as an intermediate phase towards statehood?

Territorial autonomy has, in most cases of its application from 1921 to 2020, led to lasting conflict resolution and prevented secessions. Even though constitutionally rarely provided for, peoples and ethnic communities with initially accepted autonomy do not give up their fundamental right to self-determination. In addition to various forms of autonomy, the democratic exercise of the right to self-determination is not only legitimate under international law, but has also led to conflict resolution. As listed above, there have been 67 referendums since 1994 on the political status of a sub-area of a sovereign state. In dozens of cases, the people concerned voted for independence, in some cases against it, in others even against autonomy. The most significant referendums were held in Scotland in 2014 and in Iraqi Kurdistan and Catalonia in 2017.

In all three cases, territorial autonomy has exhausted its historic task for a significant part of the population. In such cases, autonomy has not failed, but has been a transitional development phase for an emancipating nation. Catalonia, Scotland, Kurdistan: three historic nations, medium-sized peoples who, after a period of forced union with larger neighbours, are now seeking to regain statehood, as has happened in many cases with much smaller communities in the history of the 20th century. If international law often enshrines the right of peoples to self-determination, why should millions of Scots, Catalans and Kurds be denied it?

The Autonomous Region of Kurdistan is now already a state within a state, with over 90 percent of its inhabitants wanting their own state, which they should have been granted 100 years ago. It was also the absence of a state that left the Kurds of Iraq at the mercy of oppression and genocide until 1991. Neither the democratic legitimacy nor the legitimacy under international law of this claim is contested, only the lack of international support and the many outstanding practical problems between Iraq and Kurdistan prevent this step from being taken today.

In Catalonia too, the majority of the population wants the Catalan nation to be recognised. The claim of this grown European cultural nation to decide on the political status of its country itself is not only legitimate, but also a consequence of the refusal of the Spanish state, or more precisely of some constitutional judges, to grant it more autonomy. It is the reaction of the Catalans to a deeply rooted Spanish state nationalism that is working in secret. Such insistence on statehood - as in the Basque Country, Scotland and Flanders - is then often dismissed as "petty statehood" and particularism and its supporters as backward-looking nationalists. In the current discourse critical of nationalism, the striving for statehood is presented as irrational and anachronistic, and the defence of national integrity against all separatism as legitimate and future-oriented.

While these peoples without their own state are often denounced as "nationalists", the nationalism of the established nation states remains unquestioned and untouchable (Radatz 2019). This is an obvious perceptual disturbance. At the latest when a smaller people or a regional community makes the leap to statehood after all, the criticism falls silent: "Nobody today would dare to criticise Ireland, Latvia, Iceland, Norway, Slovenia, Slovakia, Croatia, Estonia etc. for their historical separatism" (Radatz 2019).

From this perspective, only the 195 UN member states that "made it" could be considered legitimate, while nations without a state are not nations but at best trouble provinces (Radatz 2019). While movements of peoples without their own state are often denounced as "nationalists", the nationalism of established nation-states remains unquestioned and untouchable (Radatz 2019). Does this mean that the Catalans and a number other medium-sized peoples without a state, such as the Uyghurs, Palestinians, Kashmiri, Kurds, Tibetans, Papuans, permanently assigned the lot of an "internal affair" of the existing states? The international legal order indeed seems to cement the exclusive club of existing states and even deny the fundamental right to self-determination in the face of obvious political fundamental right to self-determination.

In the 20th century worldwide and in Europe too, smaller states have gone through and completed a process of self-determination. Sometimes this step was preceded by the abolition or denial of territorial autonomy combined with violence and oppression by the central state. In the case of Catalonia it was the rejection of a higher quality of autonomy and internal self-determination. The national emancipation of the Catalans can no longer be absorbed by limited territorial autonomy, and Catalonia no longer wants to remain at the mercy of Spanish nationalism. Scotland, too, will in the next few years reclaim its right to decide. The democratic choice between internal self-determination (autonomy) and external self-determination (independence) must be opened in such cases. It is a task of international law and national constitutional law to meet this desire for emancipation of smaller nations and to regulate and establish the democratic and constitutional procedures for this together with the citizens directly affected.

19

Open domestic conflicts: Territorial autonomy as a viable option

As things stand today, since 1921 territorial autonomy has been established in at least 24 countries (including some areas in Ukraine, the Netherlands, Georgia, Nicaragua and Sudan, where territorial autonomies no longer exist), according to the criteria applied here. Several countries have several autonomous regions, such as Spain with 17 autonomous communities, India with 10 autonomous districts on sub-state level, Italy with 5 regions with special status, the United Kingdom with three autonomous „countries". Finland (Åland) has had a functioning territorial autonomy for 100 years and the latest addition to the territorial autonomies is the 2019 enlargement of the Bangsamoro autonomous region in the Philippines. In some countries the former autonomous status of individual parts of the country has shifted to another form of partial sovereignty, such as the Netherlands Antilles (overseas territory, associated state). Other regions have lost their autonomy through political events, such as the Crimea, formerly part of Ukraine. In addition, there are formerly autonomous regions such as Kosovo, Southern Sudan, Abkhazia, South Ossetia and soon Bougainville, whose citizens have decided to become an independent state by exercising their right to self-determination.

It is difficult to make comprehensive comparisons between the individual autonomy systems of these 60 autonomous regions, because the vast majority of regulations are tailored to the individual case with its specific features and embedded in a different constitutional legal system. In addition, these regions were created for different historical, political and cultural reasons. A comprehensive and empirically based evaluation of all autonomy systems in comparative analysis is still pending. However, partial comparisons are certainly possible. Like federalism, territorial autonomy is a precisely defined form of internal division of powers between the central state and one or more sub-areas of that state. The basic characteristics of territorial autonomy are the same in all parts of the world, which is why its regulation and effectiveness can be compared.

Are existing autonomy regulations transferable to other conflict situations, some of which are similar? Can territorial autonomy be applied as a solution to open conflicts between a state and one of its regions or national minorities living in compact form in their traditional territory? It is legitimate to develop hypotheses about this,

1. whether territorial autonomy is applicable in a specific political context;
2. which basic features such autonomy should have in a specific case in order to solve the open conflict;

3. which successful single elements of existing territorial autonomies could be transferred to the conflict in question.

Which procedures, institutions, regulations have proved successful in comparable cases and can be applied to the specific case? This should be examined more often, although the parties to the conflict - the central state and the region or minority or people concerned - are naturally not spared the task of negotiating the innumerable details of an autonomy solution appropriate to the individual case.

In many states there are currently tensions between the state government and regional communities, smaller peoples or national minorities. As WIKIPEDIA reports (List of ongoing armed conflicts), such conflicts are often carried out by force or military means. For example, the armed conflicts registered for 2019 and 2020 with more than 100 victims in Cameroon, southern Thailand, Azerbaijan, Ukraine, Turkey, Mali, India, the Democratic Republic of Congo and Angola are caused by ethnic tensions and secessionist movements. In such crisis regions, the political struggle for more rights for a sub-region often mixes with violent protests by radicalised insurgents, terrorist violence and militarily organised resistance against the state, which strikes back violently. Ethnically motivated violence still exists in Europe too, as in the case of the Donetsk Basin in eastern Ukraine, for example, which is also being fomented from outside.

These conflicts are often the result of systematic discrimination against entire ethnic groups and indigenous peoples. Some conflicts have their roots in the neo-colonial strategy of those states that have inherited the European colonial powers, such as in the case of Morocco, Indonesia, India, Cameroon and Chile, without respecting the right of self-determination of smaller peoples provided for by international law. Other conflicts are due to the highly centralised structure of the state, with a nationalist state doctrine which denies smaller peoples and ethnic minorities any recognition, protection and special rights. A classic example of such a policy for almost 100 years is Turkey.

In some of these smouldering hotbeds of conflict, territorial autonomy as a permanent solution to conflict is a concrete possibility. This is not merely a theoretical and academic consideration, but is based on the fact that one of the parties to the conflict demands genuine territorial autonomy or the state offers such autonomy as a substitute for secession. In a few cases, the state has established a functioning territorial autonomy for certain minority regions, but has refused to do so in similar cases (Indonesia, Philippines, France). In the following, eight such open conflicts between central states and individual sub-regions are addressed because

- territorial autonomy is already successfully applied in other parts of the State concerned;
- autonomy would at least be welcomed by the political representatives of both parties to the conflict;

- secession is out of the question because it would lead to increased inter-ethnic tension and violence in multi-ethnic regions;
- border changes could lead to international disruption with neighbouring states.

In all these cases, territorial autonomy naturally presupposes a democratic constitutional state. In dictatorships and authoritarian states, an autonomy arrangement could end violence, but democratic regional autonomy would by definition not be possible. China's policy in East Turkestan, for instance, takes autonomy ad absurdum, and its approach in Hong Kong proves that the principle of „one country, two systems" is more propaganda than reality. However, democracy at both state and regional level remains essential for genuine territorial autonomy. In addition to anchoring autonomy in the constitution, historical experience has shown that it would be very helpful to safeguard autonomy under international law, for example by involving a neighbouring state or an international organisation (EU, Council of Europe, AU, OAS, ASEAN, Arab League). Here are seven examples for such cases.

1. The Cordillera region (Philippines)

The Gran Cordillera is the longest mountain range in the Philippines, covering about one-sixth of the northern island of Luzon. The majority of the population is made up of the indigenous Igorot people („The People of the Mountain"), but the population is ethnically mixed. In addition, minorities like the Ifugao, Kalinga, Abra and others live in the area together with members of the Philippine majority population. In this densely wooded mountain area, the indigenous peoples formed a common front in 1984, the "Cordillera People's Alliance", which united 120 political forces and civil society organisations. The main aim of this movement is to establish an autonomous region following the example of the Bangsamoro Autonomous Region of Muslim Mindanao. To date, the central government in Luzon has not granted any real autonomy, but has only established the „administrative region of Cordillera" (19 422 km2 with a population of about 1,722.000). However, the Cordillera People's Alliance is seeking genuine territorial autonomy with legislative power through a regional assembly, with a Cordillera government and a „Cordillera Bodong administration". The Philippines is currently in the process of becoming a federal state, which could lead to the formation of a separate state on Luzon. However, since Luzon is clearly dominated by the Philippine majority popu-

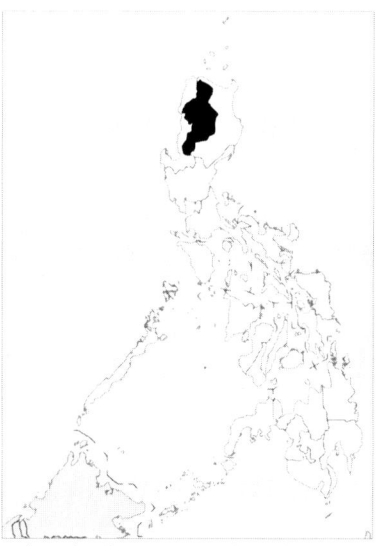

wikipedia.de, TUBS, Nord Nordwest

lation, which is mainly located along the coast, this would in turn run counter to the desire of the Igorot mountain peoples for genuine self-government in their inland areas. New conflicts are emerging.

2. West Papua (Indonesia)

The western part of the second largest island in the world, Papua New Guinea, is home to some 900 different indigenous peoples, mostly of Melanesian origin. West Papua has the world's highest ethnic diversity within a closed territory. Since 1848 the island had been dominated by various colonial powers (Great Britain, Germany and the Netherlands). When Indonesia won its independence against the Netherlands in 1949, it also claimed the western part of the island of New Guinea. However, the trust powers of the Netherlands and Australia prepared for the independence of West Papua and ceded this responsibility to the UN in 1962. Right after Indonesia used this interregnum to occupy the western part of the island in a coup d'état. On 1 May 1963, West Papua was annexed by Indonesia without granting the ancestral population the right of self-determination promised by the UN. In 1969, Indonesia held a „referendum" by 1,000 selected voters, all of whom voted for annexation. A farce that was even supported by the UN.

Today the indigenous peoples of West Papua are discriminated against in all areas of life, their rights are disregarded. Indonesia is not only interested in the exploitation of the mineral resources and the immense rainforest of West Papua, but wants to solve its problems with the overpopulation of Java with the resettlement programme „Transmigrasi". In this framework, about one million Javanese have already been resettled in West Papua, outnumbering the approximately 900,000 local inhabitants. Even after the suspension of the controversial Transmigrasi programme, Indonesian migrants continue to arrive on the island on their own initiative.

Source: wikipedia, user Vardion, author: Mandavi, CC-Licence 3.0

The Papua Independence Movement Organisasi Papua Merdeka (OPM), founded in 1964, fights for political self-determination, but any political and military resistance by the indigenous peoples of West Papua has since been bloody repressed and is almost ignored on the international stage. To date, more than 100,000 of the 700,000 Papuans have lost their lives through violence. In 2000, a new proclamation of independence for the Republic of West Papua was made, which was again not recognised by Indonesia. In return, the province was granted internal autonomy on 1 January 2001. In 2003, the province was divided between the two provinces of Papua Barat (West Papua) and Papua, with considerable protests from the local population. Under the special autonomy law of 2001, the indigenous people of West Papua should have been consulted. Indonesia's unilateral approach is perceived by the Papuans as a strategy of division and domination, and the autonomy proclaimed by the state is considered a farce by the indigenous peoples of West Papua.

Genuine territorial autonomy can also be considered a compromise solution for West Papua because Indonesia has already granted autonomy to its westernmost province, Aceh, in Sumatra, which is working. Territorial autonomy in West Papua requires not only the recognition of the fundamental rights of indigenous peoples, but also strict migration control and the involvement of an international organisation as the guarantor and protector of these peoples. Otherwise, the indigenous peoples of West Papua would be left defenceless against the 200 million people of Indonesia and their development needs even after the establishment of genuine autonomy.

3. The Anglophone Northwest of Cameroon (Ambazonia)

In Cameroon, in the centre of Africa, separatists and government security forces have been facing armed conflict since 2016, which has its roots in its colonial history, which gave the country two European languages. As a former colony of the German Empire, Cameroon was divided after the First World War by the League of Nations between Great Britain and France. Great Britain received a mandate for the north-western border region with Nigeria, France for the much larger remainder of the country's territory in the south and east. As expected, the two colonial powers left their cultural imprint on both mandates. In northwest Cameroon, English became the new official language and its legal and educational system was based on the British system. In the rest of the country, France shaped the social, legal and political norms and created a centralised state structure based on the French model. When the French-speaking part of Cameroon gained independence in 1960, the English-speaking part joined the newly founded republic after a referendum, on the condition that French and English would have equal rights within the framework of a federal republic. Thus, although Cameroon is still an officially bilingual nation (a state with two official European languages), the French-speaking main part has always marginalised English. Administration and higher education function only in French, and the federalism provided for by the Constitution has not been implemented.

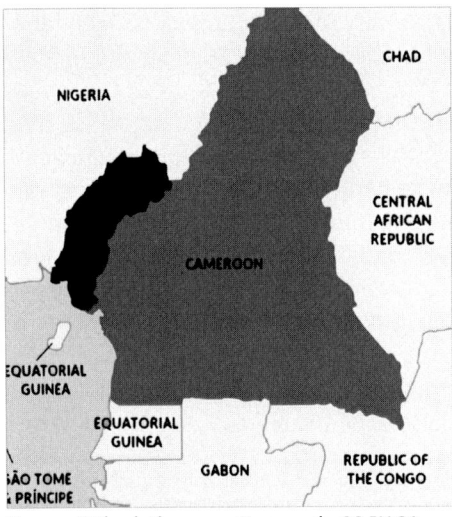

Source: Mikrobølgeovn - Own work, CC BY-SA 4.0, commons.wikimedia.org

After independence, the English-speaking provinces were initially given considerable powers of self-government. However, the federal system was abolished in 1972 after a rigged referendum against the will of the Anglophone population. The federation was replaced by the „United Republic of Cameroon", which divided the anglophone northwest Cameroon into two provinces. Paul Biya, President of Cameroon since 1982, placed increasing emphasis on the centralisation of the state. Since then, the anglophone northwest has been systematically discriminated against by the State with the exception of a small elite, which has caused dissatisfaction to grow.

The government has filled almost all key positions in the English-speaking provinces with Francophone people, especially in the judiciary, the police, hospitals and civil administrations. This also affects civil servants in the regional ministries of education. The Anglophone forces have been pushed out of politics, the region has been economically neglected by the state and francophonisation has been accelerated. This inevitably had to lead to indignation and resistance. The conflict finally escalated in 2016, when the president wanted to francophone not only the education system but also the legal system. In doing so, he undermined the constitutional principle that enshrines English as an official language with equal rights. The English-speaking lawyers started a peaceful protest in order to achieve a return to the federal system. First the teachers joined in, then large sections of the population. Since 2017, the government has been trying to quell the protests with violence and threw hundreds of opponents into prison. Since there were no concessions on the part of the state, the demand for independence became widespread.

In 2017, the separatists proclaimed their own republic called Ambazonia. Fighting between separatist groups and government forces has claimed more than 3000 lives since 2016. In the shadow of international attention, already almost 700,000 people fled from the troublesome northwest Cameroon. Territorial autonomy is also a good way of resolving this conflict because a federation of two unequal parts of the country has not worked, but the northwest of Cameroon can claim a special position due to its cultural characteristics and historical background.

4. Caracoles de Chiapas (Mexico)

On January 1, 1994, the Zapatista Liberation Front EZLN occupied part of the state of Chiapas in southern Mexico, where indigenous peoples - mainly Tzeltal, Tzotzil and Tojolabal - make up a high percentage of the population. The EZLN demanded cultural autonomy, land rights, democratic self-government, the withdrawal of Mexico's neoliberal economic policies, at least for these areas, and recognition of the indigenous peoples' distinctiveness. All these would also be essential reasons for the establishment of territorial autonomy. The Zapatista movement was a shining example of the militant struggle for the social, cultural and political rights of the indigenous peoples not only in Mexico, but throughout Central and South America. Mexico even recognises a number of rights of this kind in its constitution and has established reservations for some smaller indigenous peoples, but no real territorial autonomy at the sub-state level. As a result, none of the 31 states (plus Mexico City) has introduced modern territorial autonomy for single territories, although indigenous peoples make up 35 percent of the total population in Chiapas, 37 percent in neighbouring Quintana Roo and 53 percent in the state of Oaxaca.

On 9 August 2003, the so-called Caracoles (snails) were created in the territory controlled by the EZLN, five regional administrative centres where the „Juntas of Good Government" have their headquarters. These areas broke away from state control and established institutions of democratic self-government. This includes their own health care system, education system, cooperatives and networks for self-sufficiency. The Zapatistas declared the establishment of autonomy structures a strategic step to counter what they saw as ignorant official policies towards the indigenous population. Since 1995, 38 autonomous municipalities had already existed at the municipal level, which have now been grouped together in the five regions, the Caracoles. A separate legislation, e.g. to protect the tropical forests, was attempted. The Zapatista de facto autonomy has found imitators in several Mexican states.

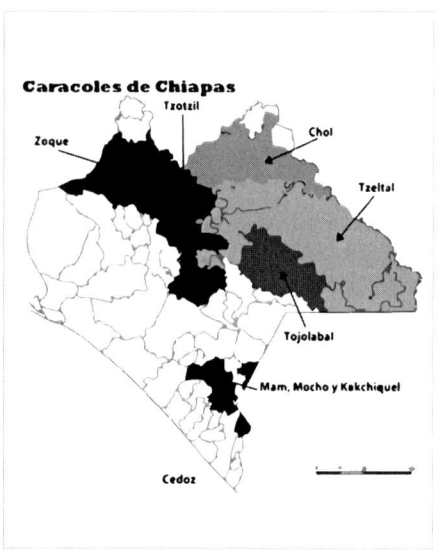

Source: en.wikipedia.org, author: Mirrormundo, CC Attribution Share Alike, 3.0

According to the EZLN, this self-declared autonomous region does not question Mexico's sovereignty and does not want to secede from Chiapas. Autonomy from the perspective of the EZLN means the self-determination of indigenous peoples in all areas of life, without forming their own state. However, the core of the self-declared autonomy remains the cultural uniqueness of the indigenous peoples, which had previously been far too little protected and promoted in the state of Chiapas. Neither the indigenous languages nor the common ownership of land, which forms the economic basis of the indigenous peoples, have been recognised. The EZLN wants to put an end to the centuries-old cultural and economic discrimination against the indigenous people and demands the official recognition of minority rights. Since this „Autonomous Zapatista Region" is only de facto, but not de jure, autonomous, it cannot be considered a functioning territorial autonomy. It is constitutionally recognised neither at state nor at member state level. Negotiations to establish such an autonomy arrangement under the Mexican Constitution could be started at any time.

5. Wallmapu (Chile)

The Mapuche indigenous people live in the central and southern regions of Chile and neighbouring Argentina. Their name means translated „people of the earth". Estimates of the number of Mapuche in Chile vary between 800,000 and 1.4 million, making them the largest ethnic minority in the country.

The Mapuche are divided into several groups that are native to different regions. They are divided into three main groups: the Picunche („people of the north"), the Pehuenche („people of the central-southern part of Chile") and the Huilliche („people of the south"). Their language is Mapudungun, which meanwhile is spoken by only 10 to 15 percent of the Mapuche. Their communities are not organised hierarchically, and Mapuche live in harmony with nature. However, social ties and kinship are very important. The proper name Mapuche also implies a close connection to the land as part of the collective identity of the people. On the one hand, it serves as a livelihood and on the other hand, it is respected and valued as the land of the ancestors.

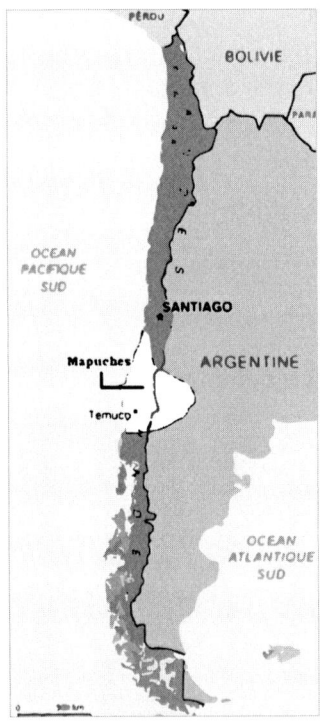

Source: Wikipedia.de, CIA-World Factbook, Chile political map

The Mapuche were able to assert themselves successfully against both the Incas and the Spanish. In the Treaty of Killin in 1641, Spain even recognised Mapuche territorial autonomy. Between 1879 and 1884, Chile, which had become independent, tried to subjugate and assimilate the Mapuche once and for all. In the process, tens of thousands of Mapuche were driven from their land or killed. Under the Pinochet dictatorship (1973 - 1990), the Mapuche land was exploited and expropriated on a large scale, and their indigenous inhabitants were forced back into comunidades (small reservations).

Today, the relationship between the Chilean state and the Mapuche is mainly burdened by the unresolved conflicts over land rights and resources. Mapuche communities protest against deforestation, dams or construction projects that endanger the environment and thus their livelihoods. Despite the International Labour Organisation (ILO) Convention 169, ratified by Chile, which states that indigenous consent must be obtained for any project, the situation of the indigenous people has not improved. The Chilean government classifies protests such as road blockades or land occupations as „terrorist threats". This makes it easier for the state to criminalise the protests.

Within the Chilean population, the Mapuche have the highest poverty rate today and belong to the part of society with the lowest level of education. In everyday life they are exposed to discrimination and prejudice, comparable to Sinti and Roma in Europe. Human rights violations against the Mapuche people are increasing significantly. For example, in the capital Temuco in the Auracanía region, police violence, violent house searches and death threats are part of everyday life for the Mapuche.

6. Pattani (Thailand)

In the three southernmost provinces of Thailand, Pattani, Songkhla and Yala (Satun), the majority of the population is made up of ethnic Malay, who differ from the Thais in culture, language and religion. In this region called „Pattani" there is a Muslim majority, while the state religion of Thailand is Theravada Buddhism. Pattani was a quasi-independent sultanate for centuries until it was incorporated into the Thai state in 1909. Economically, Pattani is backward compared to the north. At the same time, within Pattani there are significant income differences between Malay Muslims on the one hand and ethnic Thais and Thais of Chinese descent on the other. The 1.8 million Muslims in southern Thailand (4.6 percent of the total population) form an ethnically and religiously homogeneous and relatively well organised minority in Thailand.

As early as the 1960s, resistance to the centralist state and to Thai nationalism was already being voiced in Pattani. Only in 2004 did militant resistance groups appear on the scene (BRN, PULO, the Pattani United Liberation Organisation). As is often the case in such conflicts, the resistance escalated after the

Source: BpB, mr-kartographie, CC

bloody suppression of the initially peaceful protests of the population. Armed guerrilla units were formed with the aim of liberating the entire Pattani region from Thailand. The police and the army took brutal action against the separatists, which in turn earned them growing sympathy and support from the Malay civilian population. The whole Pattani region lost confidence in the Thai state. It was not until mid-2015 that peace talks were held between the government and six resistance groups that had formed a common front called MARA Patani (Majlis Syma Patani). However, this front did not last long. During the peace negotiations MARA Patani put the following central demands on the table:

- The creation of a political-administrative unit which would allow the people of Pattani far-reaching internal self-determination;
- The proceeds from the exploitation of resources and the local tax revenues of the area should be fairly distributed and invested for the benefit of the whole region;
- The identity of the Malay people should be strengthened, their language protected and declared a co-official language. The school system should be guided by fundamental Islamic values, while the rights of other religious communities should be protected.
- Public order and security should be maintained by a local or regional police force, not by the state army.

These demands obviously amount to the establishment of territorial autonomy. One problem, however, has arisen from the fact that the Malaysian liberation movements are internally divided and increasingly involved in criminal activities. In Thai public opinion, they are increasingly being equated with Muslim terror groups, although the root of the conflict lies in Thai nationalism. The neighbouring state of Malaysia, which declaredly has no direct interests in Pattani, offered itself as a mediator. However, the military and liberation movements could not agree on the establishment of „security zones". The BRN, the most important political force of the Malays of southern Thailand, had not even been included in the talks.

Territorial autonomy would obviously be the key to solving this long-running conflict. There are already three examples of functioning autonomy in the same geographic region: Aceh in Indonesia, Bangsamoro in Mindanao (Philippines) and New Caledonia, which belongs to France. In addition, the neighbouring state of Malaysia has offered to act as a protecting power and mediator, declaring that it has no interest in this ethnically related area. The Thai nationalist leadership is still not prepared to make such a concession.

7. Donetsk-Luhansk (Ukraine)

Since late summer 2014, a war fuelled by Russia has been raging in eastern Ukraine, with more than 10,000 dead by now. This conflict began in the days after the Maidan revolution in early 2014, when Russian special units were deployed in the autonomous region of Crimea, which belongs to Ukraine. In a referendum staged by Russian-speaking separatists in Crimea with Russian support, 96 percent of voters voted for Crimea as an „inseparable part of Russia". The Crimean peninsula and the city of Sevastopol were incorporated into the Russian Federation, and Crimean autonomy was ended. Neither the referendum nor the annexation of the Crimea is still internationally recognised today.

The beginning of the „revolution of dignity" on 21 November 2013 can be seen as the beginning of the Ukrainian crisis inasmuch as this uprising implicitly also represented a questioning of the Russian political system. The first small protests were triggered by the postponement of the signing of the Ukrainian Association Agreement with the EU. After the bloody break-up of a tent camp of pro-European students on Kiev's Independence Square, the protests expanded rapidly. The anti-oligarchic and pro-democratic mass movement culminated on 21 February 2014 in the victory over the kleptocratic regime of the then Ukrainian President Viktor Yanukovych and his flight from Kiev. Parliament subsequently removed the President from office and called new elections.

The war in eastern Ukraine began in spring 2014 with the violent occupation of government buildings in the Luhansk and Donetsk regions by armed pro-Russian groups, mostly financed, advised or led by Russian citizens. In April 2014, the so-called People's Republic of Donetsk was proclaimed in eastern Ukraine, followed by the so-called People's Republic of Luhansk. On 5 September 2014 a ceasefire brokered by the OSCE was agreed in Minsk (Belarus), which was only partially observed („Minsk I"). On 12 February 2015, a new agreement between Ukraine and Russia („Minsk II") was signed, brokered by Germany and France, with the aim of ending the fighting and achieving a sustainable ceasefire. At the heart of the agreement was, among other things, the negotiation of a so-called demarcation line and a buffer zone from which the warring parties were to withdraw all heavy weapons. An OSCE mission was assigned to monitor the agreements.

So far, these agreements have not led to an effective ceasefire or to the restoration of Kiev's control over the territories of the two „People's Republics" in eastern Ukraine.

Source: BpB, mr-kartographie, Licence CC BpB

One consequence of Minsk II was that the conflict in eastern Ukraine turned into a trench warfare, with only marginal shifts in territory. But the fighting continues to this day. Since 2014, more than 10,000 people have died in this war. At times, 3.4 million people were dependent on humanitarian aid and around 2.8 million people were forced to flee, of which 1.6 million are now living as internally displaced persons in Western Ukraine. The former coal and industrial area of the Donetsk Basin is in ruins.

Other examples of open internal conflicts between the central government on the one hand and a smaller people or national minority settling compactly in their ancestral territory on the other are found in Western Sahara (annexed by Morocco), Szeklerland (Transylvania, Romania) and the Kurdish area of Turkey. Territorial autonomy is also a concrete proposal for the solution of these conflicts. All three cases are dealt with in a separate section in this volume. Negotiations to resolve the conflict in this sense are particularly urgent in those six of the eleven cases mentioned here, where there is a threat of further violence from both sides and bloodshed.

Territorial autonomy can be described as a typical compromise solution in such self-determination conflicts: the region or ethnic community seeking autonomy renounces secession; the state renounces central political management and control of the territory, but not its sovereignty. Overall, it can be observed that the conflict resolution potential of autonomy is underestimated, while the danger that territorial autonomy could be the first step towards independence is overestimated. In such cases, international organisations could play an important role both in mediation and as guarantor powers of an agreed autonomy solution.

"Autonomy is beneficial for both, minorities and majorities."

An conversation with Loránt Vincze, President of the Federal Union of European Nationalities and Member of the European Parliament

Loránt Vincze (1977), journalist and politician of the Hungarians of Romania, has been elected to the European Parliament in May 2019 for the Democratic Union of the Hungarians of Romania (RMDSZ). He was a radio journalist in Neumarkt/Cluj/Temesvár and Bucharest for 16 years and then editor-in-chief of a Hungarian-language daily newspaper. International Secretary of RMDSZ since 2011 and President of the Federal Union of European Nationalities (FUEN-FUEV) since 2016. Vincze was one of the main initiators of the European Citizens' Initiative „Minority Safepack - One Million Signatures for European Diversity".

You are a member of the Hungarian minority of Romania. Currently there are only bleak prospects to achieve some territorial autonomy for the Szeklerland, as proposed by the Szekler National Council. Is there any chance that European institutions such as the EU and the Council of Europe will urge the Romanian state to take further steps in this direction?

Vincze: In Romania, actually, there is no serious intention of the Parliament to support such a law of autonomy for the Szeklerland. There have been five different autonomy proposals, all rejected. The most recent one has been rejected by the senate of Romania in April 2020, without any discussion.

Lobbying for autonomy looks fine, but what counts is always what we achieve on the ground. If you look at it from a structural point of view, we need more international support for both the territorial autonomy for one part of the Hungarian community and fundamental minority rights for all national minorities, which is the basis of our minority rights pyramid. If you don't have the basis, also the top arrangement of protection of minorities is not ensured which would be territorial autonomy and the right to decide on their cultural development. Without the basis you even cannot get the top of the pyramid. For the time being in

Romania we need to fight to implement and to preserve the existing legislative provisions regarding language rights and minority education it is difficult to imagine a real debate on an autonomy framework. You need a partner to be able to carry a dialogue. The Romanian majority or the political elite is not a partner for this purpose.

What's about the general minority rights of the Hungarians in Romania?

Vincze: When you look to Romania, out of about 1,2 million Hungarians half of them live in the Szeklerland. Territorial autonomy would be a good solution for them, but we have to keep in mind also a solution for the other 600.000 Hungarians outside that area where a territorial autonomy could not be established. Even minority rights are not easily applicable as only half of the Hungarian minority lives in municipalities with more than 20 percent minority presence, the rest in municipalities with less than 20 percent where minority members are not entitled to certain rights.

In that case there would exist three different degrees of minority protection in Romania?

Vincze: Throughout the history there has been a kind of administrative autonomy in Transylvania. Today the autonomy should be tailored to the respective pattern of settlement of the Hungarians: partly territorial as in South Tyrol, partly a collective minority rights scheme as for the Swedes of Finland for all Hungarians of Romania, and the third one is cultural autonomy as established in Hungary for very small communities of national minorities. There would be a whole system of autonomy of different kind tailored to the living conditions of the different Hungarian communities. We cannot focus only on the issue of Szeklerland's autonomy.

Could a general decentralization of the Romanian state be helpful? What's about the planned entities in accordance with European NUTS-II-regions?

Vincze: Yes, the general decentralization of the state could definitely be helpful to foster special requirements of self-government and to enable economic development. It's always about the right to run several powers in a delimited territorial unit. Romania is a highly centralized state, which is reluctant to transfer some more powers to local authorities. For us as Szeklers it would be useful to empower the counties of Covasna, Harghita and Mureș, and the municipalities as well. Then at least a higher degree of administrative autonomy could be achieved, without any ethnic feature and motivation. We are also struggling for such a kind of decentralization in Romania. In the past 100 years this area has been deprived from massive investments of the central government.

As for the NUTS-II-regions for the moment they call it "Economic Development Regions", designed to receive and manage the EU regional and structural funds. But such entities will neither have any legislative powers, nor will they be linked to the history, ethnicity and traditions of the territory. As Hungarians we claimed a reorganization of Romania in smaller regions respecting historical traditions and boundaries, that would enable a better absorption of EU funding in the whole state. The first reaction of Romanians was: we cannot do that, since this way an overwhelmingly Hungarian region would be created, and perhaps their next claim will be the secession from Romania. It is totally stupid to imagine that a region in the middle of Romania would become independent. But it is still good to get some nationalistic votes. This is still the same language as in the 1990ies, nothing has changed.

Besides Romania's Szeklerland in the EU some regions are striving to achieve autonomy, some others even claim the "right to decide" and independence as Scotland and Catalonia. What can be done, also by the FUEN, for those ethnic minorities in Europe which want to achieve some territorial autonomy?

Vincze: From a strategic perspective Catalonia is not helping our cause, as it has already got a very strong autonomy in many regards, but nevertheless it claims independence. This in turn fosters the anti-autonomy discourse of Romanian politicians: they consider territorial autonomy the anti-chamber of independence. If you want to prove the positive role of autonomy, the first step must be mutual recognition: the minority's integration in the society at large and the State's recognition of the minority and its rights. By that way the fear to lose the unity and integrity of the state can be overcome. From this fundamental recognition all other fundamental minority rights can be derived. For this purpose the international conventions and the positions of international organizations such as the Council of Europe and the EU are extremely important. The application of these conventions on national level must be seen as a conflict prevention. Not assimilate minorities, but respect their rights, that is the best way to keep the state united. That's what FUEN is advocating and fighting for.

On 30 October 2013 the Congress of Regions and Municipalities of the Council of Europe has adopted the Resolution 346 (linked to Resolution 361) about "Regions and Territories with special status in Europe. At letter it states: "The regional level of self-government remains an under-exploited structure for the political and economic development of European states and for responding to the legitimate demands of their citizens." Furthermore (letter c): "Special regional autonomy status can be an effective counterbalance to secessionist tendencies." Based on these assumptions the Congress of Regions and Municipalities has asked the Committee of Ministers to invite member states to make greater use of the special status model and to involve the Council of Europe's Parliamentary Assembly and Venice Commission. As far as you know, have these institutions taken further provision to push for the establishment of "special status" for some European regions?

Vincze: There are a number of very good resolutions in the Council of Europe and in the European Committee of the Regions. Even the European Parliament adopted two important decisions on minority rights in the pasty mandate, yet there are no legislative follow-ups to the valuable arguments presented. This remain only on paper, they are not translated into laws. I agree with the approach of the UN Special rapporteur on minority issues, Mr Fernand de Varennes when he constantly speaks about minority rights as human rights. Once such a recognition is codified in international documents, the path to proper legislative solutions, including autonomy would become more natural.

Many states, especially newly independent or newly democratic states with centralist structure, are very reluctant to establish any kind of autonomy. What could be done to reassure the political elite of such countries that autonomy does not pave the way to secession and independence claims of minorities?

Vincze: Indeed, some European nation states, such as Romania and Slovakia, where many minorities live, continuously reject the idea of self-government of regions, arguing that autonomy would be a kind of ethnic separatism. In France and in Greece the problems are even deeper, as there is even no recognition of national minorities, for example no recognition of the Turkish in Western Thrace, Greece. To speak about autonomy in France is still a provocation, the language groups are not even recognised. If we want to convince the political forces of the national majorities we need to underscore the benefits for the state and society at large. When the minority groups are well integrated in the state, this will be beneficial for all. Respecting language and cultures of minorities does not mean breaking up the state. Ethnic minorities should feel OK in their community, this sentiment can be achieved via a good legislative framework that accommodates them. Then they will have a positive and loyal attitude towards the state and potential conflicts can be prevented. This is also a geopolitical interest. If autonomy ensures the application of such rights, it will be a key for settling conflicts or potential conflicts between the state's majority and minorities.

According to art.4, (2) of the Treaty of the EU the European Union may not intervene in the internal political order of the member states. Thus, the EU shall not act on behalf of ethnic or national minorities proposing or claiming any kind of autonomy, even not local-administrative autonomy. Has the EU got any other political instrument to influence or urge all member states or one specific member state for establishing some regional self-government or autonomy?

Vincze: Indeed, the EU has no competence to interfere advocating territorial autonomy, there is no such provision in the EU-Treaty, but the EU can do it for minority rights. Look at the role of the EU when it comes to impose the rule of law in member states. In the current discussion about EU-budget conditionalities linked to the respect of rule of law, minority rights are also included. The EU should create and impose standards on human and civil rights including various kinds of social minority groups. This refers also to the rights of persons belonging to national minorities, and this could help us. This is also the main task of the European citizens' initiative termed Minority Safepack. We are convincing the EU to adopt some measures, to establish new tools and provide additional funding for this purpose.

What is the FUEN doing on European level to urge states to adopt autonomy solutions?

Vincze: Today we urge the EU to adopt measures and act to support minority cultures and languages. And on level of the Council of Europe you have got as main legal instrument the Framework Convention for the Protection of National Minorities and the European Charta of Regional and Minority Languages. Very good texts, but when it comes to the implementation, very soon we touch the limits because the states simply do not accept the interference and doesn't fear sanctions as there are no sanctions. In this context, fighting exclusively for autonomy is not efficient. So FUEN has in its charter autonomy as an ultimate goal, but this cannot be the only means and solution we are committed to. It has to be left to of each minority, depending on their goals and preferences: We need to see autonomy not as a universal therapy for all cases, but as a tool which has always to be tailored on the single case.

What do you think about the feasibility of cultural autonomy of ethnic minorities which in Eastern and South Eastern Europe is termed "national cultural autonomy". Such a form of personal autonomy is working in Hungary, Estonia and Serbia, with different degrees of efficiency and success. Is cultural autonomy an efficient means to ensure the rights of minorities'?

Vincze: National cultural autonomy can be included in the general legislative framework for the protection of minorities. Also in Romania the law on cultural autonomy, submitted to the Parliament in 2005, contained these elements, but never has been adopted. It provides the right to the community to administer its own education and culture, it contains no threats and it is not at all a revolution, nevertheless it was rejected by the majority. But when I look to the German community in Denmark or the Danish one in Germany they are happy with these rights. Also in Serbia it is working, although some elements are to be improved. The same in Hungary. In cultural autonomy generally much depends on the funding. In Hungary the amount of funding of entities of cultural autonomy is 6 times more than 10 years ago. Now they have more money to manage schools, theatres, media production etc. A very good framework. We support all these solutions as we want to help all our members in different context and situation.

When we look on the current application of territorial autonomy all over the world there are not more than about 60 cases, including all 17 Autonomous Communities of Spain and 10 Autonomous Districts in India. Why so far this concept of power sharing has been used only seldom to settle ethnic conflicts or state-region-conflicts?

Vincze: To settle such conflicts there have been various approaches, from federal states to the autonomous entities of Russia. In America you can find different solutions with ethnic reservations for indigenous peoples. There are other solutions as well, but the reason for this lack is mainly this one: if the state is ready to recognize an ethnic community as a group with collective rights or if the state considers only the individuals belonging to a minority, as in Romania. The Romanian constitution just recognises individual citizens, but not the group as such. So the Hungarians with 1,2 million members have the same rights as a few thousand Italians about whose existence nobody knows. The problems is to pass from individual rights to collective rights. If a state accepts the minority as a collectivity, the group as such is accepted as negotiating partner. Whenever a state refuses to recognize minorities as communities with their collective rights, neither cultural nor territorial autonomy is at stake.

In regions with ethnic communities striving for autonomy, often the local members of the national majority are a major obstacle to make further steps to autonomy. They are opposed to autonomy because afraid of losing advantages and positions. What can be done to convince the members of the majority community of a given territory to accept territorial autonomy?

Vincze: I have a strong personal idea, not necessarily identical with that of my organisation, the RMDSZ. The Romanian minority in such territories has to become partner to integration. This can be done providing internal power sharing in the autonomous government and consociational mechanisms in the legislative assembly as in South Tyrol. The Italians have their participation rights, and so they support that autonomy, preserve their positions and share political power. In Romania indeed, ethnic Romanians have most of the high ranking positions in public service and institutions, whereas Hungarians are underrepresented. There should be an equilibrium, but Romanians are afraid to loose positions - that are effectively privileges -, in an autonomous entity under stronger regional rule with less influence of the national government. It is not easy to make the Romanians a partner in fighting for autonomy.

In 1994, the FUEN submitted a draft convention on "Autonomy Rights of National Minorities and Ethnic Groups in Europe" to the Council of Europe (CoE). Also the European Parliament was addressed with this proposal, which, however, never was admitted to an official debate in none of these organizations. Has the FUEN ever reiterated this proposal? Has it ever resumed its lobbying for such a convention?

Vincze: The CoE parliamentary assembly adopted some years ago the Kalmár-report that includes the concept of collective rights and autonomy. But there has been no follow-up on state level. We can only ensure to keep it up on the agenda of the institutions and to speak about it. The decision is not coming around the corner. The Chamber of Regions of the EU and the Congress of Local and Regional Authorities of Europe CALRE of the CoE have the concept on their agenda, and several times they adopted recommendations and resolutions supporting autonomy and regional democracy. Autonomy can provide a good solution, beneficial not only for minority groups, but also for the internal minorities of autonomous territories. But the road to get a territorial autonomy established is long. The EU, the Council of Europe, the UN whatsoever, are not able to impose autonomy to anybody, this will be a decision of the affected state alone.

The Draft European Charter of Regional Democracy was initiated by the Council of Europe's Congress of Local and Regional Authorities in Europe (CALRE) in 1997. The original idea behind the Charter was to set out the key principles that should underlie effective regional democracy in Europe, covering areas such as financial autonomy and legislative powers. However, the Charter failed

to attract the support of a sufficient majority of Member States at the Ministerial Conferences in Helsinki in 2002 and Budapest in 2005, with disagreements emerging over whether the instrument should be legally binding. In order to restart the debate on the Charter, the CALRE has developed a new text, which responds to the objections raised by the Member States and also takes into account developments in the field of regional democracy over the past ten years. Has the new draft Charter ever been approved?

Vincze: The new text of the Draft European Charter of Regional Democracy was presented in 2008, however the Committee of Ministers could not give a favourable consideration to the document. In these circumstances, the CDLR recommended to the Ministers' Deputies that, particularly in the context of zero real growth budgeting, no further Council of Europe resources, which are available for the priority activity of promoting democracy at all levels, be used to pursue legally binding convention-based standards on regional democracy. Obviously some member states vetoed the adoption of the Charter and it is highly improbable that for such a draft there will ever be a unanimous decision in the Committee of the Ministers. This is sad for our engagement, but it is the reality we need to take into account when lobbying for this topic.

Today, the main reference document on autonomy is the Council of Europe Reference Framework for Regional Democracy, which was adopted in 2009, it is not a legally binding document, but is mainly based on the aforementioned draft European Charter. The authors recognize also that „this reference framework must be considered as a step in the right direction; nevertheless, the goal remains the adoption of a European Charter of Regional Democracy." Later, another recommendation concerning autonomy was adopted in 2016 under the coordination of Mr Lambertz.

The UN was engaged for mediation in the South Tyrol case, which was an international dispute between Italy and Austria. Can the UN do anything to promote autonomy solutionsgen, as in other cases of ethnic conflict?

Vincze: In principle, yes, but the road to achieving territorial autonomy is long. The EU, the Council of Europe and the UN cannot force a state to establish territorial autonomy. This remains solely the decision of the of the state concerned. Of course, the UN had decisive weight in the case of South Tyrol, but this was due to the special agreement between Italy and Austria of 1946. Then there was a decision by both parliaments in Vienna and Rome to ratify this agreement and to approve the Statute of Autonomy. Unfortunately, however, this case has remained an exception rather than the rule.

A binding right to autonomy?

In its Recommendation No. 346 of 30.10.2013 (www.coe.int/congress), the Congress of Local and Regional Authorities of the Council of Europe recommended regional autonomy status as an „effective counterweight to secessionist tendencies". In doing so, this body of representatives of regions and municipalities assumed that Europe had pioneered multi-level governance (local, intermediary, regional, national and supranational) and that peace and prosperity also depends on the prevention and resolution of conflicts. For this, „satisfactory models of decentralised democratic governance should be developed for regions with specific problems and identities." By this the Congress obviously meant territorial autonomy in the sense discussed here, as applied in 38 regions of Europe. Regional autonomy is an „underused structure" for economic development and the need for regional democracy. In its usual diplomatic tone, the Congress of Local and Regional Authorities asks the Committee of the Council of Europe, with the involvement of the Congress, the Parliamentary Assembly and the Venice Commission, to consider the special status model as a „realistic option for resolving pending conflicts" on regional territorial issues. Since 2013, however, no new region in Europe has been granted special autonomous status in this sense.

Also the Conference of European Regional Legislative Assemblies (CALRE) in its conference of Madeira held on 30.10.2001 raised these demands, which since then have been reiterated again and again:

- the recognition of regions with legislative powers by granting them a special status in the European treaties;
- the strengthening of parliamentarianism in Europe and the participation of regional parliaments in the cooperation between the European Parliament and national parliaments;
- a clear demarcation of the legislative powers conferred on the European and the national or sub-national levels;
- the recognition of the right of regions with legislative powers to appeal to the European Court of Justice in the event of conflicts concerning their powers;
- strengthening the Committee of the Regions by giving it the status of an institution, through an organisation better adapted to the differences between the various regional bodies, and by recognising the right of the Committee to appeal to the European Court of Justice (www.calrenet.eu).

The umbrella organisation of Europe's national minorities, FUEN (Federal Union of European Nationalities), went further than this body in 1994. The FUEN submitted to the Council of Europe a courageous draft for an international convention entitled „Autonomy Rights of European Nationalities". The draft is based on the indispensable human and international right of self-determination and the right of every state to preserve its territorial integrity. According to FUEN, the right to self-determination also includes a freely chosen autonomy with which peoples or ethnic groups can exercise their political, economic and social rights, social and economic problems within the given national borders.

An international convention should create the foundations for territorial autonomy as a legal umbrella for the basic civil, political and cultural rights of minorities without questioning the national borders of the state concerned (Art. 1,2). It is not the territory that would be decisive, but an ethnic group that differs from the majority population according to identifiable properties. Ethnic groups would have a right to recognition, because it should not be left to the discretion of a central state to recognise a minority constitutionally. Although the right to autonomy, according to the proposed draft convention, would be reserved for ethnic groups that form a majority in their home region, FUEN's draft convention also recognises the rights of groups that form a minority in that region (cf. Art.2).

This right is defined as „the right to a special status within a demarcated territory with autonomous legislative, executive, administrative and judicial powers to administrative and judicial powers for the regulation of internal affairs". The purpose of autonomy, according to the draft convention, would be „to provide all public opportunities which fall within the exclusive or predominant interest of a community in a given area and which can be administered by that community itself with its own means within its territory", including unimpeded access to the natural resources of the area concerned" (Art. 4 draft convention).

With such a convention under international law, territorial autonomy would have gained a clear legal-political profile, namely as a comprehensive set of rules and minimum requirements, while retaining flexibility in its concrete application. Thus, territorial autonomy would have emerged from the definitional arbitrariness in which nearly all forms of domestic decentralisation up to quasi-independence are contained. An international convention would be of utmost importance in order to define the standard of autonomy or even to determine model solutions. This could serve as a point of reference for both interested states and minority representatives in serious negotiations.

The draft convention of the FUEN was presented to all relevant institutions, but never reached the stage of an official debate. Today, 100 years after the introduction of the first modern territorial autonomy, there is still no obligation of any kind under international law for states to grant territorial autonomy. Yet such an obligation and the corresponding collective group right seems to be the commandment of the hour when many state-region-conflicts are to be settled. The proposal of 1994 provides an idea of how such an international convention could be designed and remains of undiminished relevance.

20

An interim balance sheet and outlook on the future of territorial autonomy

The considerations in this volume were aimed at taking stock of the experience with territorial autonomy to date. This form of vertical separation of powers between states and one or more sub-areas has been applied for 100 years in the Åland Islands, for 70 years in several other regions of Western Europe, and since the 1990s in Eastern Europe and other continents. In some regions the autonomous status has been reformed and extended several times, but in some others it has failed. In various open conflicts between states and regional communities, autonomy is on the negotiating table as a solution option.

A global overview of autonomy requires clarity about the content of this concept. According to our definition, a functioning constitutional state with a democratic political system is the basic prerequisite for the existence of „genuine" territorial autonomy. Today, in many non-free states there are „autonomous territories" at sub-state level with legislative and administrative powers, but without democratically elected representative bodies and decision-making procedures, without a constitutional state with an independent judiciary and full separation of powers. In the best case, a certain decentralisation of power can be said to exist, for example when party bosses in the capital transfer some decision-making power to party cadres in the region concerned. This kind of ruling is not equivalent to a modern territorial autonomy.

Modern autonomy differs from pre-modern forms of transferring power from the centre to the periphery precisely in this respect: a political system with all civil liberties and fundamental political rights and free and fair elections. There are no democratic islands against the background of an authoritarian state power that intervenes at any time at its discretion in the internal affairs of the region. Autonomy without democracy existed in some countries even before World War I, but autonomy in a modern, democratic, constitutional form only since 1921 (Åland). Autonomy in this sense existed in the 20th century in 25 states in more than 70 regions, whereas currently only 60 regions in 19 countries can call themselves a territorial autonomy in the stricter sense defined above, provided that all 17 autonomous communities of Spain are included in this circle. There are far more regions with legislative powers that correspond to this definition of territorial autonomy, but as parts of a „symmetrical regional state", while territorial autonomy usually concerns special cases, i.e. it is an exception in the state-wide pattern of vertical division of powers.

So what is the point of territorial autonomy?

From a legal point of view, territorial autonomy is a rather complex set of rules, based on constitutional or constitutional statutes, its own implementing norms, in some cases even international agreements (bilateral or multilateral). One can also mention the jurisdiction of the supreme or constitutional court in the event of conflicts between the state and the region concerned. In this respect, territorial autonomy is even more complex than some federal systems. Autonomy statutes, the basic laws of autonomy systems, are fleshed out with autonomous laws and regulations and their concrete application. What is the point of such autonomy regulations?

- For the protection of ethnic or linguistic minorities, small or indigenous peoples, territorial autonomy forms a legal-political framework in which this protection is organised and guaranteed by the citizens concerned themselves. Equal rights for languages, the education system, the media and all culturally relevant policy areas can be regulated within a regional framework by the people concerned in conjunction with the other ethnic or language groups living in the area. It constitutes an overriding objective enshrined in the respective statute of autonomy.

- In political terms, territorial autonomy, like federal systems, brings the exercise of power closer to the citizen. Particularly in smaller regions, the members of the regional parliament are still known personally. With less effort, the electorate can organise itself into regional parties and lists, appoint candidates and control the elected mandataries. The representatives directly elected by the population can legislate and decide on the main political issues of importance to the region, and national legislation is still considered the overarching framework at best. Regional media control the political elites much more closely, and regional courts decide in accordance with autonomously determined rules.

- Autonomy - as well as federalism and symmetrical regionalism - creates a space for citizen-oriented policies, quite apart from the main purpose of protecting minorities and balancing in multilingual, multi-ethnic regions. Autonomy should and must provide for regional democracy, because self-government takes shape with many different policy areas and areas of responsibility. In this territorial dimension, citizens can have a direct say in decision-making through forms of direct and deliberative democracy, which is often difficult to organise at state level.

- The history of territorial autonomy has also shown that genuine autonomy can only function in a constitutional state based on the rule of law. The relationship between the central state and the autonomous region remains conflictual in nature. Even with the finest division of responsibilities between the state and the region concerned, it has not been possible to prevent legal disputes entirely. Such conflicts between the levels must be dealt with before the Supreme Court. Again a phenomenon which territorial autonomy shares with member states in federal systems.

A robust territorial autonomy must, of course, be entrusted by the state with the widest possible range of responsibilities. History also clearly shows a tendency to constantly expand the core of autonomy, namely the nature and scope of the competences of the autonomous representative bodies. Whether this can be achieved, however, depends on the political power relations in the state and region. Where this does not succeed, as in Catalonia and Scotland, for example, secessionist tendencies are given a boost.

How will territorial autonomy become successful?

In these 100 years of modern territorial autonomy, a number of essential factors have emerged for the success of territorial autonomy, most notably the following:

1. A territory clearly defined by consensus between the State and the Region, possibly with legitimacy through democratic votes by the population of each sub-regional territory. The boundaries of the autonomous territory must in any case be accepted by both parties.
2. The entrenchment of territorial autonomy in the Constitution or in a special law of the State, which is not at the mercy of political conjunctions and majorities, but can only be modified by consensus between the central State and the autonomous region joint State-Region commissions are responsible for settling disputes prior to disputes, drawing up the rules of application and negotiating financing. Independent courts decide on conflicts of jurisdiction.
3. A minimum level and clearest possible demarcated number of responsibilities must be transferred from central government to the region. Constant disputes over the transfer of jurisdiction paralyse both sides, the State and the autonomous region. This level of competence must enable the Autonomous Region to shape its cultural, social and economic development in a substantial way. Mere administrative decentralisation is not autonomy.
4. Regional democracy in the autonomous region must be able to develop without central government influence. On the other hand, the electorate of the region must be free to send its representatives to the State Parliament in order to participate in the political decision-making process at State level. Territorial autonomies are not reservations of indigenous peoples. Political independence also means that the state has no right to appoint the region's political representatives (president of the executive or the legislature), which would be tantamount to a break in the autonomous democratic legitimacy of the region's citizens.
5. A success factor of modern autonomy is the political and legal equality of citizens legally resident in the region and the equal rights of all ethnic groups in the region. There must be no discrimination in fundamental rights, and minority protection must be provided in accordance with the Statute and

Constitution. Ethnic autonomy may sometimes be useful, even indispensable for the survival of indigenous peoples. But territorial autonomy must function for the benefit of all inhabitants and ethnic groups in a region. In this sense, autonomy regulations that allow for consociational democracy, rights of participation and inclusion of all linguistic-ethnic groups have proven their worth. This factor promotes peace, inter-ethnic harmony and shared responsibility.

6. Historical experience has shown another factor to be important: forms of autonomous control of immigration into an autonomous region, without prejudice to the fundamental right to free movement of persons under the rule of law and under the constitution, which in the EU also applies to the entire territory of the EU. In non-European countries in particular, it has been shown that central states, even if they are fundamentally willing to grant territorial autonomy, tend to increase their power and influence by changing the composition of their population. The examples of Nicaragua (Caribbean Coast), Bangladesh (Chittagong Hill Territories), Indonesia (West Papua), Morocco (Western Sahara), Bodoland (Assam, India), formerly also South Tyrol (Italy) and Corsica (France) bear witness to this, not to mention pseudo-autonomies such as Tibet and Xinjiang in the PR China. Long-term stability and internal peace depend on such controllability of migration by the autonomous region itself. This does not have to mean sealing off against immigration and assuming migration control, since such a right presupposes a kind of „regional citizenship" such as that which actually exists only on the Åland Islands. However, it is also possible to take precautions at the political level to ensure that the population composition does not change seriously to the detriment of the original population.

   Autonomous regions are not responsible for fundamental rights such as citizenship, freedom of movement, residence and employment, nor for the right to free movement of labour, capital, goods and services as laid down in the EU Treaties. Autonomous regions can lose control over their own development in the context of borderless markets, globalised financial flows and internationally regulated migration and asylum rights. This calls for regulatory competences in accordance with national and international law, which allow the autonomous regions to participate in migration and freedom of movement regulations.

7. Sound and stable financing of the autonomous entity which is commensurate with the scope and expenditure requirements of the delegated competences and allows the region to manage its own economic and social development. A minimum level of fiscal sovereignty is also important for the success of autonomy.

8. A final important success factor is the international responsibility for securing autonomy. If a self-determination conflict between the central state and a sub-state entity has a cross-border character (ethnic-cultural kinship with a minority or titular nation in neighbouring states), the inclusion of this „protecting power" can only be helpful for conflict and peace resolution.

The following can serve as examples: Hungary for the Hungarians in Szeklerland, Algeria for the Sahrawi in Western Sahara, Pakistan for Indian Kashmir, Malaysia for Pattani. The model for this is provided by those autonomous regions which have secured their autonomy on the basis of such an agreement, such as the Åland Islands with Sweden, South Tyrol with Austria and Northern Ireland with Ireland. Other states (Australia in Bougainville) or international organisations (the Islamic Conference in Bangsamoro) can also play a mediating and guarantor role: this used to be the League of Nations, then the UN, now the EU, the AU, ASEAN, the OAU, the Organisation of Islamic States.

Has territorial autonomy in these 100 years met expectations in most or all of the 60 cases of its application? Has it ensured peace, stability, protection of minorities and self-government? The overall picture - as described above - has several facets. Some historical territorial autonomies have failed, experienced uprisings and wars, and mostly have become independent states, such as Eritrea (former Ethiopia), Southern Sudan (former Sudan), Kosovo (former Serbia), Abkhazia and South Ossetia (former Georgia), Bougainville (independence from Papua New Guinea decided but not yet implemented). Other formerly autonomous regions have given up autonomy through secession and annexation (Crimea, formerly part of Ukraine) or have been given a different status in a democratic negotiation process, such as the Netherlands Antilles, which have become overseas communities or territories in free association with the Netherlands. On the other hand, a few territorial autonomies are in deep political crisis, such as the Caribbean Coast North and South of Nicaragua and Indian Kashmir.

On the other hand, there are autonomous regions that are seeking to enter a new phase in their history as part of a „national emancipation process". Based on the right of self-determination of the peoples, which does not expire even with the granting of territorial autonomy, and based on democratic majorities expressed in referendums, these regions are striving to break away from their state of affiliation and achieve full sovereignty. In recent history, this process has been observed in Catalonia, Scotland, Iraqi Kurdistan, New Caledonia and Bougainville. In Greenland, too, the Statute of Autonomy itself could make it happen. Like federal systems, territorial autonomies are not meant to last forever. As long as democracy and the rule of law are respected, this is also in line with international law.

In a „Dynamic Panel Data Analysis" Jean-Pierre Tranchant in 2016 checked the results of regional autonomy for the period 1950-2010 (Tranchant, Decentralization 2016). The core result is that territorial autonomy is a powerful device to reduce risks of ethnic conflict. The effect of autonomy is maximized when regional governments do enjoy substantial powers of self-rule and political decetraization is strong ensuring the participation of the internal minorities in governments. The magnitude of the estimated impact of autonomy on conflict risk is significant: „For instance, the combination of regional autonomy and wide-ranging decentralization reduces the incidence of civil wars by about 60-70 percent" (Tranchant, Decentralization 2016, 40).

Hence, in the vast majority of existing autonomous regions territorial autonomy has proved its worth and is hardly ever questioned by the population and protected ethnolinguistic communities. In most cases, intra-regional conflicts and tensions between state and region or ethnic communities have been resolved, violent conflicts have been shifted to the political terrain, minorities have been permanently protected. Discrimination against new internal minorities of those regions was not completely excluded and some territorial autonomies have waited a long time for the concrete implementation of their statute. But if today States fear the granting of territorial autonomy as a first step towards secession of this territory, this is unfounded. In the majority of the territorial autonomies functioning today, there are no significant aspirations for self-determination and secession. On the contrary: a functioning and far-reaching autonomy prevents a minority from seeing insurrection, secession or even armed resistance as the only chance for self-assertion.

What's about the future of territorial autonomy?

In this volume various facets of autonomy have been examined: successful models, autonomous regions in crisis, pseudo-autonomy, failed autonomy, minorities and smaller peoples seeking autonomy; but also national communities for which autonomy is no longer sufficient.

All in all, it can be said that despite many ethnically conditioned internal conflicts, territorial autonomy since 1921 has surprisingly rarely been used all over the world. The majority of functioning autonomous regions are still located in Europe. In some countries, the separation from hitherto autonomous regions from the state is on the agenda, in others, regional communities since many years are striving for territorial autonomy without success so far.

If we look at the high number of ethnically determined conflicts in Africa, for example, autonomy seems to be an almost uncharted territory. Despite its 100 languages and a large number of ethnic minorities, India has only 10 sub-state territorial autonomies. Due to its colonial history, the form of the ethnic reserve has been most widely used in America, while modern territorial autonomy has remained the exception. In mixed-populated areas such as the Caracoles in Chiapas and Wallmapu in Chile, territorial autonomy may well be considered, with the collective ownership of land by indigenous peoples being the most important. Autonomy remained the absolute exception even in the mostly centralistic nation states of the predominantly Arab MENA region (Middle East and North Africa). In South East Asia, autonomy has been successfully applied since the 1990s. Overall, it can be concluded that territorial autonomy has not yet been able to fully develop its conflict resolution potential. Autonomy is far from being introduced where it has long been aspired to by the vast majority of a region's population: this is also true for Europe, as the examples of Szeklerland (Romania) and Corsica (France) show.

Why is this so? In view of the large number of smaller peoples without their own state and ethno-linguistic minorities worldwide, it may surprise that today there are only about 60 genuine territorial autonomies. The potential for stabilisation and reconciliation in minority conflicts that territorial autonomy offers is not being realised. Also the number of federal states has been stagnating for years as in 2020 there were only 24 states with federal constitution worldwide. In many cases, the political elites of today's dominant nation states still see territorial autonomy, just like federalism, as a threat to „national unity". They fear that autonomy is the first step towards self-determination and that in the long run it will promote secessionist tendencies. In the light of the 100 years since the first territorial autonomy was introduced, this fear has no basis. The best recipe against this is domestic confidence-building and bilateral or international legal arrangements to preclude demands for self-determination as long as state obligations for autonomy are respected. Today, however, such reforms of international law are opposed by the widespread nationalist state doctrine.

Territorial autonomy must also not be overloaded with expectations. Ultimately, autonomy is not a panacea that can solve every kind of conflict. Even the application of the right to self-determination has provided a lasting solution to state-region conflicts in many cases. While autonomy offers globally relevant and applicable solutions, none of the existing territorial autonomies can claim to provide a universal answer to the complex problems and needs that exist in ethnically, linguistically or religiously diverse regions. Each of the autonomies functioning today has its own distinctive history and political background. Nevertheless, a clear pattern emerges from the experience to date, both in the process of establishing autonomy as well as in the design of the vertical division of powers. Again and again, the basic desire to establish a stable balance between the collective rights of national minorities and the sovereignty and unity of the central state is expressed.

However, territorial autonomy is not only an ideal solution for the protection of minorities, but also offers interesting opportunities in the 21st century with regard to the further development of democratic systems. It allows more subsidiarity, the solution of political problems at the level closest to the citizens concerned. On the one hand, local and regional communities have a higher problem-solving capacity, and on the other hand, the democratic legitimacy and chances of participation of those affected increase. The regional level is still woefully neglected in the multi-level system of the EU or even in large federal states. For example, out of 270 regions of the EU (NUTS-II) there are only 70 regions with legislative sovereignty. In India there are currently 640 sub-state level districts, of which at least 50 have an ethnic-linguistic majority that does not match the constituent state's main ethnic group. Nevertheless, there are only 10 districts with territorial autonomy in India, all in the Northeast. If more participation and closeness to the people are the quality and depth of a democracy, it is precisely the regional and municipal levels that need to be strengthened. Symmetrical regional autonomy and federal systems, and even territorial autonomy for particular sub-areas, besides minority protection do also provide for more democracy.

Keeping its first 100 years in mind, territorial autonomy must be seen as a process. Like the constitutions and EU treaties, statutes of autonomy are not intended to last forever, but are constantly being amended and developed in democratic and bilateral consensus (examples: Åland Islands, South Tyrol, Vojvodina, Catalonia, Greenland). A certain level of autonomy today does not prevent a higher degree of self-government tomorrow. Autonomy must keep pace with legal and political developments in the state as a whole, as well as with the social and economic dynamics within it. However, the ethnolinguistic groups in an autonomous region must pull together: if they work together on a joint project to extend autonomy, the state will also give in. If, on the other hand, internal conflict smoulders with the risk of further discrimination against non-dominant groups of that territory, central states will be reluctant to give these regional majorities more power.

If territorial autonomy even appears to be the first step towards secession of a region, central states will have strong reservations. Bilateral agreements with neighbouring states, on the other hand, are helpful in preventing border changes and ethnic conflicts with autonomy. Secession can be less justified if a smaller people or national minority claims a functioning autonomy and enjoys all essential minority rights.

Not only states are called upon to evaluate the wealth of experience of territorial autonomy and consider autonomy in various forms to protect their minorities. The community of states and the various regional organisations such as the Council of Europe, the AU, ASEAN and the OAS are also called upon to give greater consideration to territorial autonomy. An international agreement on the right to autonomy could define precisely under which circumstances peoples or ethnically determined regional communities have the right to internal and external self-determination and in which cases an internationally anchored territorial autonomy is the appropriate solution.

A broad trend in Europe could promote territorial autonomy, namely the decentralisation of state tasks and powers under the sign of subsidiarity throughout the entire national territory through the formation of regions with legislative sovereignty. The Council of Europe and its Congress of Local and Regional Authorities (CALRE), but also the Committee of the Regions of the EU and the Assembly of European Regions (AER), with more than 270 regions from 33 countries and 16 interregional organisations, regularly press for this form of „symmetrical decentralisation" in resolutions and draft conventions. Should European states wish to strengthen the regional level as such, territorial autonomy as a special regional status would have greater legitimacy and could serve as an illustrative example. In any case, the concept as such has a future.

References and further readings

Section 1 - What is territorial autonomy? A clarification

Benedikter, Thomas (2013), *Eine Typologie moderner Formen politischer Autonomie*, in: *Autonomie – Hoffnungsschimmer oder Illusion*? Aue-Stiftung, Snellman Helsinki

Benedikter, Thomas (ed., 2009), *Solving Ethnic Conflict through Self-Government*, EURAC

Benedikter, Thomas (2012), *Moderne Autonomiesysteme der Welt*, EURAC Bozen

Weller, Marc/Nobbs, Katherine (2012), *Asymmetric Autonomy and Settlement of Ethnic Conflicts*, Univ. of Pennsylvania Press

Finaud, Marc (2010), *Can Autonomy Fulfil the Right to Self-Determination?* Geneva Papers, Geneva Centre for Security Policy

Gagnon, Alain/Michael Keating (2013), *Political Autonomy and Divided Societies: Imagining Democratic Alternatives in Complex Setting*, Palgrave Macmillan

Gamper, Anna/Pan, Christoph (2008), *Volksgruppen und regionale Selbstverwaltung in Europa*, Baden-Baden

Ghai, Yash/Woodman, Stephanie (eds. 2013), *Practising Self-Government*, Cambridge University Press

Hannum, Hurst (1996), *Autonomy, Sovereignty and Self-determination - The Accommodation of Conflicting Rights*, Philadelphia 1996

Haller, Max (2015), *Ethnic Stratification and Economic Inequality around the World*, Ashgate

Hilpold, Peter (Hg. 2016), *Autonomie und Selbstbestimmung in Europa und im internationalen Vergleich,* NOMOS, Wien

Lapidoth, Ruth (1997), *Autonomy – Flexible solutions for ethnic conflicts*, Washington, 1997

Malloy, Tove/Palermo Francesco (eds. 2015), *Minority accommodation through territorial and non-territorial autonomy*, Oxford University Press

Malloy, Tove/Salat, Levente (2020), *Non-Territorial Autonomy and Decentralization – Ethnocultural Diversity Governance*, Routledge

Pan, Christoph/Pfeil, Beate S., (2006), *Minderheitenrechte in Europa, Handbuch der europäischen Volksgruppen*, Band 2, Springer-Verlag, Wien New York

Ryan, Stephen (1997), *Nationalism and Ethnic Conflict*, in: B. Little/H. Smith, Issues in World Politics, Macmillan, London

Salat, Levente/Constantin, Sergiu/Osipov, Alexander/Székely, István Gergö (2014), *Autonomy Arrangements around the World: A Collection of Well and Lesser Known Cases*, Cluj-Napoca

Suksi, Markku (2011), *Sub-State Governance through Territorial Autonomy: a Comparative Study in Constitutional Law of Powers, Procedures and Institutions,* Springer Verlag

Skurbaty, Zelim A. (ed. 2005), *Beyond a one-dimensional state: an emerging right to autonomy?* Leiden

Skurbaty, Zelim A. (2000), *As if peoples mattered*, Kluwer, The Hague/Boston/London

Tarr, Alan G./Robert Williams/Josef Marko, *Federalism, Subnational Constitutions and Minority Rights*, Praeger, Westport 2004

Toniatti, Roberto/Woelk, Jens (eds. 2017), *Regional Autonomy, Cultural Diversity and Differentiated Territorial Government*, Routledge

Weller, Marc/Wolff, Stefan (ed. 2005), *Autonomy, self-governance and conflict resolution*, Routledge

Section 3 - From Åland to Bangsamoro: a short story of autonomy

Benedikter, Thomas (2012), *The World's Modern Autonomy Systems*, EURAC

Benedikter, Thomas (1998), *Il dramma del Kosovo*, DATANEWS, Rom

Benedikter, Thomas (2015), *Territoriale Autonomie als Mittel des Minderheitenschutzes und der Konfliktlösung in Eu*ropa, GfbV-Dossier, http://www.gfbv.it/3dossier/eu-min/autonomy-de.html

Ghai, Yash/Woodman, Sophia (2013), *Practising Self-Government. A Comparative Study of Autonomous Regions*, Cambridge University Press.

Suksi, Markku (ed., 1998), *Autonomy – Implications and applications,* Kluwer Law International

Schneckener, Ulrich (2002), *Auswege aus dem Bürgerkrieg,* Suhrkamp

Section 4 - The first modern territorial autonomy: Åland

Ackrén, Maria (2011), *Successful Examples of Minority Governance – The Cases of the Åland Islands and South Tyrol*, Report from the Aland Islands Peace Institute, No.1/2011

Autonomous Government of Åland (2020): https://www.aland.ax/en

The Parliament of the Åland Islands: https://www.lagtinget.ax

Mäkinen, Eija (2005), *Åland und sein Sonderstatus.* In: Jahrbuch des Föderalismus. Nomos-Verlagsgesellschaft, Baden-Baden, S. 350–362.

Olausson, Pär (2002), *Autonomy and the European Island Regions,* Mid Sweden University&Abo Academy University, Östersund

Simolin, Susann (2018*), The aims of Åland and Finland regarding a new Act on the Autonomy of Åland - An analysis of three Parliamentary Committee reports (2010-2017),* in: Journal of Autonomy and Security Studies Vol. 2, Issue 1 (2018), 8-48, available online at: http://jass.ax/wpcontent/uploads/2018/06/JASS-Vol-2-I-Simolin.pdf

Spiliopoulou Akermark, Sia (2019), Åland Islands, at: http://www.world-autonomies.info/tas/aland/Documents/Aland_2019.pdf

Suksi Markku (2014), *Territorial Autonomy: The Åland Islands in comparison with other sub-state entities,* in: Zoltán Kántor, Autonomies in Europe: solutions and challenges, L'Harmattan, pp. 37-58

Section 5 - Rescuing a language through autonomy: the Basque Country

Arraiza, José-Maria (2015), *Making Home Rules for Mother Tongues. The Legal Implication of Linguistic Diversity in the Design of Autonomy Regimes.* Turku: Painosalama Oy

Britannica, Basque Language, https://www.britannica.com/topic/Basque-language

Elorza, Antonio (2017), *Alsace, South Tyrol, Basque Country: Denationalization and Identity,* in: Grote, Georg/Obermair, Hannes (Hg.), A Land on the Treshold – South Tyrolean Transformations 1915-2015, Peter Lang Verlag, 307-325

EUSTAT, VI Encuesta Sociolinguistica y Estadística de Población y Viviendas 2016

Galparsoro, Patxi Baztarrika (2019). *El Euskera: un caso de revitalización*. In: Javier Giralt Latorre/Franco Nagore Laín (eds.). La normalización social de las lenguas minoritarias: experiencias y procedimientos para la salvaguardia de un patrimonio immaterial, Collection Papers d'Avignon, Zaragoza

Gorter, Dirk/Zenotz/Etxange/Cenoz (2014), *Multilingualism and European Minority Languages: the case of the Basque*. In: Gorter/Zenotz/Cenoz (eds.), *Minority languages and multilingual education: Bridging the local and the global*, Berlin Springer Verlag, p. 278-301

Gobierno Vasco, Consejo Asesor del Euskera (2013), *ESEP 2013 – Plan de Acción para la*

Promoción del Euskera, Vitoria-Gasteiz

Gobierno Vasco, Viceconsejería Política Linguistica (2016), VI Encuesta sociolinguistica: https://www.euskadi.eus/contenidos/informacion/argitalpenak/es_6092/adjuntos/Resumen_VI_Encuesta_Socioling%C3%BC%C3%ADstica_EAE_%202016_1.pdf

Ruiz Vieytez, Eduardo (2019), *The Spanish Mosaic: an Asymmetrical Recognition of Minority Languages*, in: Integration and Exclusion. Linguistic Rights of National Minorities, International Conference, 27.11.2015, Vilnius, 77-94

Ruiz Vieytez, Eduardo (2013), *A New Political Status for the Basque Country?* In: Journal on Ethnopolitics and Minority Issues in Europe, ECMI, Vol.12, No 2, 2013, 79-105 http://www.ecmi.de/fileadmin/downloads/publications/JEMIE/2013/Ruiz.pdf

Tumler, Susanne (2004), *Zur sprachlichen und sprachpolitischen Situation im Baskenland*, Europa Ethnica 2004, S. 75-81

WIKIPEDIA, „The Basque Language" and „Autonomous Community of Basque Country"

Section 6 - Italy's rocky road to greater regional autonomy

Buscema, Luca (2019, *Unità nazionale, regionalismo differenziato e pluralismo dei valori*, in: Nazioni e Regioni n.14/2019, 7-28

Commissione parlamentare per le questioni parlamentari (2014), Audizione del prof. Oskar Peterlini, Autonomie differenziate per un Paese variegato, 26 giugno 2014.

Carboni, Giuliana Giuseppina (2020), *Il regionalismo identitario. Recenti tendenze dello Stato regionale in Spagna, Italia e Regno Unito*, CEDAM, Padova.

De Fazi, Simonetta/Benvignati Fabrizio (2019), *Instant Dossier "Autonomia differenziata"*, ACLI Dip. Studi e Ricerche, 1.7.2019

Groppi, Tania (2014), *Lo Stato regionale italiano nel XXI secolo tra globalizzazione e crisi economica*, federalismi.it, n.21/2014

Groppi, Tania (2007), *L'evoluzione della forma di Stato in Italia: uno stato regionale senz'anima?* in: www.federalismi.it n.4/2007

Louvin, Roberto (1997), *La Valle d'Aosta – Genesi, attualità e prospettive di un ordinamento autonomo*, Musumeci

Louvin, Roberto (2016), *Statica e dinamica nell'ordinamento di una micro-regione*, in: F. Palermo/S. Parolari (a cura di), Il futuro della specialità regionale, Napoli, Edizioni Scientifiche Italiane, 112-154

Poggi, Annamaria (2020), *Perché abbiamo bisogno delle Regioni*,federalismi.it n.5/2020

Pallante, Francesco (2019), *Nel merito del regionalismo differenziato: quali "ulteriori forme e condizioni particolari di autonomia" per Veneto, Lombardia ed Emilia Romagna?* Federalismi.it 6/2019

Peterlini, Oskar (2007), *Föderalistische Entwicklung und Verfassungsreform in Italien*, FÖDOK 27, Innsbruck 2007

Marcantoni, Mauro/Baldi, Macro (2013), *Regioni a geometria variabile. Quando, dove e perché il regionalismo funziona.* Saggine

Senato della Repubblica, Servizio Studi, Il regionalismo differenziato con particolare riferimento alle iniziative di Emilia Romagna, Lombardia e Veneto, n°1057305, http://www.senato.it/japp/bgt/showdoc/17/DOSSIER/1057305/index.html

Senato della Repubblica - Servizio Studi, Il regionalismo differenziato e gli accordi preliminari con le regioni Emilia-Romagna, Lombardia e Veneto, n°1067303, https://temi.camera.it/dossier/index.html/senato-della-repubblica-servizio-studi-br-regionalismodifferenziato-e-accordi-preliminari-regioni-emilia-romagna-lombardia-e-1.html

Section 7 - A much vaunted but incomplete autonomy: South Tyrol

Autonomie-Konvent Südtirol (2017), *Abschlussbericht des Konvents der 33, Vorschläge zur Überarbeitung des Autonomiestatuts*, http://www.konvent.bz.it und „So denkt Südtirol"

Benedikter, Thomas (2016), *Mehr Eigenständigkeit wagen. Südtirols Autonomie heute und morgen*, POLITiS, ARCA Lavis

Benedikter, Thomas (Hg. 2014), *Mit mehr Demokratie zu mehr Autonomie*. SBZ-POLITiS

Happacher, Esther/Obwexer Walter (2013), *40 Jahre Zweites Autonomiestatut. Südtirols Sonderautonomie im Kontext der europäischen Integration*. Facultas Wien

Happacher, Esther/Obwexer Walter (2015), Rechtsgutachten: Entwicklung und Veränderungen der Südtiroler Autonomie seit der Streitbeilegungserklärung 1992, Bozen/Innsbruck

Happacher Esther (2012), *Südtirols Autonomie in Europa,* Jan Sramke Verlag, Wien

Marko, Joseph/Palermo Francesco/Woelk Jens (2005), Die Verfassung der Südtiroler Autonomie, EURAC, Nomos

Marko, Joseph/Palermo Francesco/Woelk Jens (2008), T*olerance through Law, Self-Governance and Group Rights in South Tyrol,* M. Nijhoff, Leiden/Boston

Peterlini, Oskar (2012), *Südtirols Autonomie und die Verfassungsreformen Italiens. Vom Zentralstaat zu föderalen Ansätzen: die Auswirkungen und ungeschriebenen Änderungen im Südtiroler Autonomiestatut,* New Academic Press, Wien

Peterlini, Oskar (20168), *Die Verfassungsreform Italiens und ihre Auswirkungen auf Südtirol – Ein Thesenpapier,* 3.7.2018

Piffer, Paolo (a cura di 2018), *Verso il 3° Statuto: i contributi della Consulta*. URL: https://www.consiglio.provincia.tn.it/news/giornale-online/Pages/articolo.aspx?uid=179786

Schulte, Felix (2019), *Toward a Multi-Causal Model of Successful Conflict Regulation through Territorial Self-Government – Lessons from South Tyrol*, in: Österreichische Zeitschrift für Politikwissenschaft, vol. 47 (4), Universität Innsbruck

EURAC on South Tyrol's autonomy: https://www.autonomyexperience.org/

Autonomy or reservation? Ethnic autonomy versus territorial autonomy

Barsh, Russell (2000), *Der rechtliche und politische Status nordamerikanischer Indianer*, https://www.arbeitskreis-indianer.at/der-rechtliche-und-politische-status-nordamerikanischer-indianer/

Blazer, Mario (2010), *Indigenous Peoples and Autonomy. Insights for a Global Age*, University of British Columbia Press

Dahl/Tauli-Corpuz/Noningo/Limbu/Olsvig (2020), Building Autonomies, IWGIA

Frantz Klaus (1995), *Die Indianerreservationen in den USA,* Aspekte der territorialen Entwicklung und des sozio-ökonomischen Wandels, Steiner (2.Aufl.), Stuttgart

GTZ-Reader (2004), *Indigene Völker in Lateinamerika und Entwicklungszusammenarbeit,* in: http://www2.gtz.de/indigenas/deutsch/service/reader.html

Mattioli, Aram (2017), *Verlorene Welten. Eine Geschichte der Indianer Nordamerikas 1700-1910,* Klett-Cotta

Stroschein, Sherill (2014), *The Autonomous Structures of Native American reservations,* in: Salat, Levente/Constantin, Sergiu/Osipov, Alexander/Székely, István Gergö (2014), Autonomy Arrangements around the World: A Collection of Well and Lesser Known Cases, Cluj-Napoca University, 187-200

Wilkins, David/Heidi Kiiwetinepinesiik Stark (2017), *American Indian Politics and the*

American Political System, 4. Auflage, Roman&Littlefield, Lanham

WIKIPEDIA, Indianerpolitik, https://de.wikipedia.org/wiki/Indianerpolitik_der_Vereinigten_Staaten

WIKIPEDIA, Navajo Nation, https://de.wikipedia.org/wiki/Navajo_Nation_Reservation

The complete list of the reservations of the First Nations in the USA: https://de.wikipedia.org/wiki/Indianerreservat#Liste_der_US-Reservationen

Section 8 - Conflict solving through autonomy: Northern Ireland

Adams, Gerry (2004), *Hope and History. Making Peace in Ireland*. Brendon/Mount Eagle Publication

Anghey, Arthur (2005), *The Politics of Northern Ireland. Beyond the Belfast Agreement*, New York

Cox, Michael/Guelke Adrian/Stephan Fiona (eds. 2006), *A Farewell to Arms? Beyond the Good Friday Agreement,* Manchester

Dickson, Brice ((2005), *The Legal System of Northern Ireland,* 5th Edition, Belfast

Hain, Peter (2008), *Der Friedensprozess in Nordirland: ein Modell zur Konfliktlösung?* Blickpunkt Großbritannien, Friedrich Ebert Stiftung, London

Knoll, Christian-Ludwig (Hrsg., 2004), *Nordirland auf dem Weg ins 21. Jahrhundert,* Nordthor Verlag

Otto, Frank (2205), *Der Nordirlandkonflikt. Ursprung, Verlauf, Perspektiven.* C.H. Beck

Section 9 - Corsica on the way to autonomy

Fazi, André (2019), *La specialità nello statuto della Corsica: l'inizio di una nuova stagione*, in Presente e Futuro, n.29/2018, 29-40

Fazi, André (2014), *The multilevel politics of accommodation and the non-constitutional moment: Lessons from Corsica*, in: Constitutionalism and the politics of accommodation in multinational democracies, a cura di LLUCH Jaime, Basingstoke, Palgrave Macmillan, pp. 132-156

Fazi, André (2015), *Vers un nouveau statut pour la Corse? Pour comprendre les mutations actuelles du système politique insulaire*, «Pouvoirs locaux», Trim. N.103, IV/2014-2015, CIII, pp. 54-61

Fazi, André (2020), *How language becomes a political issue: Social change, collective movements and political competition in Corsica*, «Internat. Journal of the Sociology of Language», CCLXI, pp. 119-144.

Fazi André (2019), *La résistance de l'État unitaire, ou un nouveau défi pour le nationalisme corse*, https://www.researchgate.net/

Mastor, Wanda (2018), *Pour un Statut constitutionnel de la Corse*, Rapport à M. le President de l'Assemblée de Corse

Simeoni, Edmond (2019), *Corsica! Le secolari battaglie di un piccolo popolo per la libertà.* Curatore: Alessandro Michelucci. Il Cerchio

Section 10 - Transylvania's Hungarians struggle for autonomy: the Szeklerland

Bakk, Miklós (2009), *Romania and the Szeklerland* – Historical Claim and Modern Regionalism, in: Thomas Benedikter (Ed.), Solving Ethnic Conflict through Self-Government, EURAC Bozen.

Dabis, Attila (2017), *Misbeliefs about Autonomy. The Constitutionality of Szeklerland*, Corvinus University Budapest

Constantin, Sergiu (2004), *Linguistic Policy and national minorities in Romania*, in: Revista de Sociolinguistica; http://www.gencat.cat

Felip, Bela (2018), *Die Szekler suchen ihren Platz auf Rumäniens Landkarte,* NZZ, 15.5.2018

Hermanik, Klaus-Jürgen (2017), *Deutsche und Ungarn im südöstlichen Europa*. Identitäts- und Ethnomanagement, Böhlau Verlag

Kiss, Tamás et al. (ed., 2018) *Unequal Accommodation of Minority Rights: Hungarians in Transylvania*. Palgrave Macmillan

Rósza, Laura (2010), *Autonomie in Transsylvanien,* Vdm Verlag Dr. Müller

Salat, Levente (2010), *The Chances of Ethnic Autonomy in Romania between Theory and Practice*

Szekler National Council, The Manifest of the Grand Székely Assembly, www.sznt.org/en

Section 11 - The German-speaking community of East Belgium: the „happiest Belgians"

Lejeune, Carlo/Brüll, Christoph (2014), *Grenzerfahrungen: eine Geschichte der Deutschsprachigen Gemeinschaft Belgien*s, Bd. 5, Grenz-Echo Verlag, Eupen

Lambertz, Karl-Heinz/Entel, Stefan Alexander (2018), *Von Eupen nach Europa. Ein Plädoyer für eine föderale und regionale EU,* Media for Europe

Lambertz, Karl-Heinz (2012), *Sammelband einer Auswahl von Reden*. Regierung der Deutschsprachigen Gemeinschaft. www.lambertz.be

Parlament der Deutschsprachigen Gemeinschaft Belgiens (2016), Die Besonderheiten des belgischen Bundesstaatsmodells und ihre Auswirkungen auf die Rechtsstellung der Deutschsprachigen Gemeinschaft, Schriftenreihe Band 3

Parlament der Deutschsprachigen Gemeinschaft Belgiens (2016), Die Deutschsprachige Gemeinschaft und ihr Parlament, Eupen

Parlament der Deutschsprachigen Gemeinschaft Belgiens (2018), Mögliche Szenarien einer Staatsreform nach 2019, Schriftenreihe Band 9

Parlament der Deutschsprachigen Gemeinschaft Belgiens (2015), Die Rechtsstellung der Deutschsprachigen Gemeinschaft und der deutschen Sprache in Belgien, Schr. Band 5

Parlament der Deutschsprachigen Gemeinschaft Belgiens (2011), Grundsatzerklärung des Parlaments zur Positionierung der DG im Prozess der Staatsreform, 27.6.2011

Die offizielle Website der DG: www.dg.be

Section 12 – A state offers autonomy: Morocco and the Western Sahara

Benedikter, Thomas (2019), *Factors for the Success of Territorial Autonomy in Theory and Practice and Conclusions for the Case of the Sahara Region of Morocco,* New York

El Ouali, Abdelhamid (2008), *Democratic Self-determination and Western Sahara: How to bring an end to a long-standing conflict*, Faculty of Law University Hassan II, Casablanca

El Ouali, Abdelhamid (2008), *Saharan Conflict: Towards Territorial Autonomy as a Right to Democratic Self Determination,* London, Stacey International

Khakee, Anna (2011), *The Western Saharan autonomy proposal and political reform in Morocco*, in: NOREF Report, June 2011

Moroccan Government (2007), *Moroccan Initiative on Autonomy for the Sahara Region,* http://moroccoembassy.vn/FileUpload/Documents/S_2007_206-EN.pdf.

Zunes, Stephen/Mundy, Jacob (2010), *Western Sahara: War, Nationalism and Conflict Resolution*, New York, Syracuse University Press

Section 13 - Autonomy in name only: Xinjiang/East Turkestan and the autonomous entities of China

Delius, Ulrich (2007), *Chinas Uiguren ringen um Menschenrechte und Demokratie*, http://www.gfbv.it/3dossier/asia/uigur.html

Feldbacher, Rainer (2016), *Die Situation der Uiguren in Xinjiang*, auf: http://www.gfbv.it/3dossier/asia/uigur-feld.html

Ghai, Yash (2000), *Autonomy regimes, in China: coping with ethnic and economic diversity*, in: Ghai, Yash (ed.), *Autonomy and ethnicity: negotiating competing claims in multiethnic states*, Hongkong 2000

Ghai, Yash (2017), *Dilemmas of "genuine autonomy" for Tibet*, in: Toniatti Roberto/Woelk, Jens, Regional Autonomy, Cultural Diversity and Differentiated Territorial Government, Routledge, 67-90

Lobsang Sangay (2006), *China's National Autonomy Law and Tibet: a Paradox between Autonomy and Unity*, October 2006

Tibetan Parliamentary Policy Research Centre (2005), *Autonomy and the Tibetan Perspective*, New Delhi

Toniatti, Roberto/Woelk, Jens (eds. 2017), *Regional Autonomy, Cultural Diversity and Differentiated Territorial Government*, Routledge

Wang, Shuping (2004), *The People's Republic of China's Policy on Minorities and International Approaches to Ethnic Groups: a comparative study*, in: International Journal on Minority and Group Rights, vol. 11, 1-2/2004

World Uyghur Congress: www.uyghurcongress.org

Hong Kong: „One country – Two systems"?

Die Chinesisch-Britische Deklaration und Grundgesetz: http://www.info.gov.hk

Ghai, Yash (1998), *Autonomy with Chinese Characteristics: the Case of Hong Kong*, in: Pacifica Review, vol. 10, n.1/February 1998

WIKIPEDIA, Proteste Hong Kong, https://de.wikipedia.org/wiki/Proteste_in_Hongkong_2019/2020

Peterlini, Oskar (2020), *Hong Kong – Die Schwächen einer starken Autonomie. Gründe für ihre Krise – Aufbau und Vergleich mit Südtirols Rechtssystem*, in: EUROPA ETHNICA Nr.3/4 2020, 113-125

Benedikter, Thomas (2010), *Moderne Autonomiesysteme*, EURAC Bozen, S. 260-272

Section 14 - Doing justice to ethnic diversity: autonomy in India

Benedikter Thomas (2009), *Language policy and the rights of linguistic minorities in India*, LIT Verlag Berlin/Münster

Benedikter, Thomas (2009), *Territorial autonomy in India*, in: Toniatti/Woelk (ed.), Regional Autonomy, Cultural Diversity and Differentiated Territorial Governance, GlassHouseBook, Routledge 2017

Ganguly, Rajat (2012), *Autonomy and Ethnic Conflict in South and South-East Asia*, Routledge

Manchanda, Rita (ed., 2006), *The No Non-sense Guide to Minority Rights in South Asia*, South Asian Forum for Human Rights (SAFHR), New Delhi

Samaddar, Ranabir (ed., 2005), *The Politics of Autonomy – Indian Experiences*, Kolkata

Sukanta, Sarkar/Suman K. Chaudhury (2014), *Autonomous District Councils and Tribal Welfare*, Kalpaz Publications

Section 15 - Autonomy in crisis: Nicaragua's Caribbean Coast and Indian Kashmir

Arraiza, José-Maria (2014), Weaving Miskito and Mestizo Imagination: The Atlantic Coast of Nicaragua, in Salat, Levente/Constantin, Sergiu/Osipov, Alexander/Székely, István Gergö (2014), *Autonomy Arrangements around the World: A Collection of Well and Lesser Known Cases*, Cluj-Napoca University, 85-112

Benedikter, Thomas (2005), *Il groviglio del Kashmir,* Editori Fratelli Frilli, Genova

Gonzales Miguel (2016), *The Unmaking of Self-Determination: 25 Years of regional Autonomy in Nicaragua*. Bulletin of Latin America Research, vol. 33, no 3 (2016), 306-321

Gonzales Miguel (2015), *Indigenous Autonomy in Latin America: an Overview*, in: American and Caribbean Studies 10,1-2015

Informe del Gobierno de Nicaragua a la OEA. Diagnostico. Region Costa Caribe Norte. 13.12.2016, Estatuto de Autonomía de las Regiones de la Costa Caribe de Nicaragua

Section 16 - Between autonomy and independence: the Kurds in Iraq and in Syria

Gesellschaft für bedrohte Völker (2015), *Kurdistan brennt*, POGROM Nr. 291 - 6/2015

Ghadi, Sary (2016), *Kurdish Self-governance in Syria: Survival and Ambition*, Chatham House

Hennerbichler, Ferdinand (2018), *Zukunftsoptionen von Kurden in Eurasien*, Europa Ethnica 2018

Jongerden, Joost (2019), *Governing Kurdistan: Self-Administration in the Kurdistan Regional Government in Iraq and the Democratic Federation of Northern Syria*, in: Ethnopolitics, vol.18/1, 61-75

Knapp Michael/Ayboga Ercan/Flach Anja (2016), *Laboratorio Rojava*. Red Star Press, Roma

Küpeli, Ismail (2019), *Kampf um Rojava, Kampf um die Türkei,* assemblage, Münster

Schmidinger, Thomas, (2017), *Krieg und Revolution in Syrisch-Kurdistan*, Mandelbaum, Wien

Schmidinger, Thomas (2018), *Von Rojava zur Demokratischen Föderation Nordsyrien*, in EUROPA ETHNICA Nr.1-2-2018, 49-54

Sido, Kamal (2016), *Rojava – "Schutzzone" für religiöse und ethnische Minderheiten in Nordsyrien*, GfbV, www.gfbv.org

Yezidi autonomy in Sinjar?

Barir, Idan (18.09.2014), *Expert Analysis / The Yezidis: Traumatic Memory and Betrayal.* https://web.archive.org/web/20170510152415/https://english.tau.ac.il/impact/yezidis [10.05.2017].

Jesidische Persönlichkeiten, Parteien, Institutionen und soziale Organisationen, Stellungnahme zum „Sinjar Agreement" zwischen Bagdad und Erbil, 22. Oktober 2020; auf: www.gfbv.it

Staatssekretariat für Migration (2020), Focus Irak. Bern

Kizilhan, Jan Ilhan (2015), *Strategiepapier über die regionale Autonomie Sindschar (Sengal)*, GfbV, http://www.gfbv.it/3dossier/kurdi/ezid.html

Wikipedia: https://de.wikipedia.org/wiki/Sindschar

Section 17 - The dream of autonomy: Turkish-Kurdistan

Hennerbichler, Ferdinand (2018), *Zukunftsoptionen von Kurden in Eurasien*, Europa Ethnica

Oeter, Stefan (2015), *Die Kurden zwischen Diskriminierung, Autonomie und Selbstbestimmung*, EUROPA ETHNICA 1/2 2015, 82-94

Olgun, Akbuluk/Elcin Aktoprak (eds, 2019), *Minority Self-Government in Europe and in the Middle East*, Studies in International Minority and Group Rights, Brill-Nijhoff

Öcalan, Abdullah (2019), *Jenseits von Staat, Macht und Gewalt*, Mandelbaum Verlag

Strohmeier Martin/Yalcin-Heckmann Lale (2016), *Die Kurden. Geschichte, Politik, Kultur*, C.H. Beck

Section 18 - When autonomy is no longer enough: Scotland and Catalonia

Arzoz, Xavier (2009), *Das Autonomiestatut für Katalonien von 2006 als erneuter Vorstoß für die Entwicklung des spanischen Autonomiestaats*, in: Zeitschrift für Öffentliches Recht und Völkerrecht, Nr. 69/2009, 155-193

Arzoz, Xavier (2019), *Extents and Limits of Devolution in Spain*, in: European Public Law 25, no.1 (2019): 83-104

Belser, Eva Maria et al. (2015), *States falling apart? Secessionist and Autonomy Movements in Europe.* Publications of the Institute of federalism, Fribourg, Stämpfli Verlag, Bern

Benedikter, Thomas (2017), *Selbstbestimmungsrecht und Volksabstimmungen. Erfahrungen in Europa und Italien, Perspektiven für Südtirol.* POLITiS-Dossier 13/2017

Cederman, Lars-Erik/Simon Hug/Andreas Schädel und Julian Wucherpfennig (2015), *Territorial Autonomy in the Shadow of Future Conflicts: too Little, too Late?* In: American Political Science Review 109.2, 354-370

Devine, T.M. (2015), *Independence or Union? Scotland's Past and Scotland's Present*, Penguin Books

Eser, Patrick (2013), *Fragmentierte Nation – Globalisierte Region? Der baskische und katalanische Nationalismus im Kontext von Globalisierung und europäischer Integration*, transcript Verlag Bielefeld

Himsworth, Chris (2013), *The autonomy of devolved Scotland*, in: Ghai, Yash/Woodman, Stephanie (eds. 2013), *Practising Self-Government,* Cambridge University Press, 349-382

Oliver Araujo, Joan (2014, director), *El futuro territorial del Estado Español. Centralización, autonomía, federalismo, confederación o secesión?* Tirant lo Blanch, Valencia

Radatz, Hans-Ingo (2020), *„Nation ohne Staat" oder „Unruheprovinz"? – Spanien, Katalonien und die Nationalismuskritik*, EUROPA ETHNICA, 1/2 - 2020, S. 67-78

Ruiz Vieytez, Eduardo (2019), *Territorial Autonomy and Minorities in Spain: Catalonia and the Basque Country;* in Olgun Akbulut/Elcin Aktoprak, Minority Self-Government in Europe and in the Middle East, Brill Nijhoff 2019

Salmond, Alex (2013), *Scotland as a good global citizen*, The Brookings Institute

Scottish Government (2013), *Scotland's Future.* Your Guide to an independent Scotland, www.scotreferendum.com

Section 19 - Open domestic conflicts: territorial autonomy as a solution

Benedikter, Thomas (2003), *Krieg im Himalaya – Hintergründe des Maoistenaufstandes in Nepal*, LIT

Gustav Blomberg (2015), *The Åland Example Applied – A case Study of the Autonomous Region Muslim Mindanao.* Report from the Åland Islands Peace Institute, Nr.2/2015

Europarat (2003), *Positive experiences of autonomous regions as a source of inspiration for conflict resolution in Europe* (rapporteur: Andi Gross), DOC 9824, 3. Juni 2003,

Gagnon, Alain/Keating, Michael (2012), *Political Autonomy in Divided Societies. Imagining Democratic Societies in Complex Settings,* Palgrave Macmillan

GfbV Südtirol (2013), *Der Mapuche-Konflikt. Entstehung und Status Quo,* http://www.gfbv.it/3dossier/ind-voelker/mapu1-de.html

Schneckener, Ulrich (2002), *Auswege aus dem Bürgerkrieg*, Edition Suhrkamp, Frankfurt

Stefan Wolff (2010), *Resolving Territorial Self-Determination Disputes. A Comparative Review of Contemporary Practice.* www.stefanwolff.com

A binding right to territorial autonomy?
Congress of Municipalities and Regions of the Council of Europe, Resolution n. 346 of the 30.10.2013 on: „Regions and Territories with Special Status in Europe", https://search.coe.int/congress

Section 20 - An interim balance sheet and outlook: the future of territorial autonomy
Benedikter, Thomas (2009), *Die Qualität von Autonomiesystemen im Vergleich,* in Europa Ethnica, 1-2/2009, Braumüller, 64-73

Gesellschaft für bedrohte Völker (2011), *Autonomie – Überlebenschance für „kleinere Völker",* POGROM Nr. 267 /4/2011)

Golüke, Ulrich (2001), *Making use of the future: scenario creation as a new framework for mediation of regional autonomy conflicts*, CAP working papers, München

Meinert, Sascha (2001)(Centrum für angewandte Politikforschung der Bertelsmann Stiftung), *Zwischen staatlicher Integrität und gesellschaftlicher Vielfalt: Regionale Autonomie als Lösungskonzept für multinationale Staaten*, CAP working papers, München

Roach, Steven (2004) *Minority Rights and an Emergent International Right to Autonomy: A Historical and Normative Assessment*, in: International Journal on Minority and Group Rights 11, p.411-432

Meloni, Francesco (Hg.), *Regionalisation Trends in European Countries 2007 -2015*. Congress of Local and Regional Authorities of the Council of Europe, June 2016

Schulte, Felix (2018), *The More, the Better? Assessing the Scope of Regional Autonomy,* International Journal of Minority and Group Rights, 84-111

Jean-Pierre Tranchant (2016), Decentralization, Regional Autonomy and Ethnic Civil Wars: a Dynamic Panel Data Analysis, Institute of Development Studies, Univ. Sussex

Institutions and Non-Governmental Organizations
Autonomie-Portal der EURAC Bozen: www.world-autonomies.info
EURAC zur Südtirol-Autonomie: https://www.autonomyexperience.org/
Gesellschaft für bedrohte Völker: www.gfbv.de
Gesellschaft für bedrohte Völker Südtirol: www.gfbv.it
Akademisches Netzwerk zur Territorialautonomie: www.academicautonomynetwork.com
Bundeszentrale für politische Bildung: www.bpb.de
Minority Rights Group International: https://minorityrights.org
International Working Group for Indigenous Affairs: www.iwgia.org
Online-Zeitung NATIONALIA (Ciemen, Barcelona): www.nationalia.cat
Federal Union of European Nationalities FUEN: www.fuen.org
European Center for Minority Issues: www.ecmi.de
International Crisis Group: www.crisisgroup.org
Unrepresented Peoples Organisation UNPO: www.unpo.org
Europarat: www.coe.int/congress
Åland Islands Peace Institute: www.peace.ax

The author

Dr. Thomas Benedikter (1957), economist and political scientist, publicist, today executive director of South Tyrol's Center for Political Studies and Civic Education POLITiS. Professional activity in the South Tyrolean provincial administration, vocational colleges, in empirical social and economic research focused on current issues of South Tyrol's society, politics and economy. Professional activity for human rights organisations (e.g. 1992-1998 head of the South

Foto: Hanna Battisti

Tyrolean section of the Society for Threatened Peoples), for civic education and participatory democracy projects. Co-operation with various research institutes in South Tyrol and beyond. Projects on comparative autonomy research with EURAC Bozen and about two years of research and project activities in Latin America, the Balkans (Kosovo, Bosnia-Herzegovina) and South Asia (Kashmir, Nepal, North East India). A series of publications on ethnic conflicts, minority rights and autonomy in various regions of the world, including „The World's Modern Autonomy Systems" (EURAC - ATHESIA 2010).

The co-editor

POLITiS (South Tyrol's Center for Political Studies and Civic Education)

A vibrant democracy needs critically thinking citizens who are committed to the common good and who want to have a say in politics and participate in shaping it. This is one of the reasons why the Greek name politis = citizen has been chosen for this new educational and research institution. Participation requires the necessary background knowledge, collective reflection and public discussion. Dealing with power relations and developing critical confrontation with political issues of any kind enables the citizens to qualified political commitment. POLITiS, as an independent civil society organisation committed to the common good, which is primarily intended to provide assistance to non-dominant groups in our society. POLITiS elaborates political studies mostly on South Tyrolean issues, provides civic education and consultancy to non-dominant groups and movements in our society:

- Research on current issues affecting South Tyrolean society in the fields of social, economic and political sciences,
- Publications, public events, policy consultancy for citizens' initiatives and politically active Individuals and organisations,
- a wide range of civic education activities for different target groups.

www.politis.it

Thomas Benedikter
100 Jahre moderne Territorialautonomie – Autonomie weltweit
Hintergründe, Einschätzungen und Gespräche
100 Jahre nach Gründung der ersten modernen Territorialautonomie, die Åland Inseln in Finnland 1921/22, fragt der Band: Wo war Autonomie erfolgreich, wo ist sie gescheitert, wo ist sie in Krise, wo wird sie angestrebt? In welchen Fällen könnte Autonomie offene Konflikte zwischen Staaten, Minderheiten und regionalen Gemeinschaften lösen? Das Buch präsentiert Hintergründe und Einschätzungen zu Erfahrungen und zur Anwendbarkeit von Territorialautonomie, ergänzt um Gespräche mit herausragenden Persönlichkeiten aus Politik und Wissenschaft und einem Vorwort von Oskar Peterlini.
Autonomie und Politik / Autonomy and Politics, Bd. 1, 2021, 314 S., 29,90 €, br., ISBN 978-3-643-25012-4

Thomas Benedikter
Language Policy and Linguistic Minorities in India
An appraisal of the linguistic rights of minorities in India
India not only is concerned with inevitable multilingualism, but also with the rights of many millions of speakers of minority languages. As the political and cultural context privileges some major languages, linguistic minorities often feel discriminated against by the current language policy of the Union and the States. They experience on a daily basis that their mother tongues are deemed worthless dialects that have little utility in modern life. Many such languages have definitively disappeared, and several more are on the brink of extinction. Is this the inevitable price to be paid for economic modernization, cultural homogenisation and the multilingual fabric of India's society at large?
This book is an effort to map India's linguistic minorities and to assess the language policy towards these communities. The author, a senior researcher of the EURAC (South Tyrol, Italy), assuming linguistic rights as a component of fundamental human rights, codified in a number of international covenants and in the Indian Constitution, provides an appraisal of the extent to which language rights are respected in India's multilingual reality, which takes into consideration the experiences of minority language protection in other regions.
Asien: Forschung und Wissenschaft, vol. 3, 2009, 232 pp., 29,90 €, br., ISBN 978-3-643-10231-7

Andrzej Marcin Suszycki
Nationalism in Contemporary Europe
Concept, Boundaries and Forms
Region – Nation – Europa, vol. 85, 2021, ca. 280 pp., ca. 34,90 €, br., ISBN-CH 978-3-643-91102-5

Bert Preiss
Conflict at the Interface
Local Community Divisions and Hegemonic Forces in Northern Ireland
More than two decades after the Northern Ireland peace agreement, conflict still flares between deprived Protestant/Unionist/Loyalist and Catholic/Nationalist/Republican working-class interface communities, who remain divided by numerous 'peace walls'. In light of Brexit, the Irish border issue and the power-sharing impasse progress in local peacebuilding has stalled. This might even jeopardise the overall peace process. Within this context, this book explores, largely empirically, the nature and causes of conflict at the interface. An attempt is also made to provide an outlook on peace in Northern Ireland and to highlight potential lessons for other conflict-ridden, divided societies.
Internationale Politik, vol. 34, 2019, 450 pp., 39,90 €, br., ISBN-CH 978-3-643-91191-9

Theodor H. Winkler
Living in an Unruly World
The Challenges We Face
In his new book, Winkler looks at the transition from an US-led to a multipolar world. With a time horizon of 2100, he identifies the megatrends that will shape the century – demography, migration, climate change, the technological revolution –, looks at the leaders and strategies of the key players, notably the US, China, and Russia, and identifies the areas of potential conflict as well as the implications of the decay of the multilateral system and of the growing fragmentation of national politics. The author makes concrete proposals how to cope with the challenges we face. A must for everyone interested in politics.
Außenplitik – Diplomatie – Sicherheit@Ausenplitik – Diplomatie – Sicherheit, vol. 7, 2019, 252 pp., 34,90 €, br., ISBN-CH 978-3-643-91176-6

Theodor H. Winkler
The Dark Side of Globalization
And How to Cope with It
Außenplitik – Diplomatie – Sicherheit@Ausenplitik – Diplomatie – Sicherheit, vol. 3, 2018, 222 pp., 39,90 €, br., ISBN-CH 978-3-643-80265-1

Theodor H. Winkler
The Box was Happy that I was Thinking Outside of It
Memoirs
Außenplitik – Diplomatie – Sicherheit@Ausenplitik – Diplomatie – Sicherheit, vol. 2, 2018, 300 pp., 39,90 €, br., ISBN-CH 978-3-643-80264-4

LIT Verlag Berlin – Münster – Wien – Zürich – London
Auslieferung Deutschland / Österreich / Schweiz: siehe Impressumsseite